East of Samarinda

East of Samarinda
Carl Jacobi

Edited by
Carl Jacobi
and
R. Dixon Smith

Bowling Green State University Popular Press
Bowling Green, Ohio 43403

Acknowledgements

"Crocodile" copyright © 1934 by Street & Smith Publications, Inc., for *Complete Stories*, April 30, 1934.

"Letter of Dismissal" copyright © 1934 by Street & Smith Publications, Inc., for *Top-Notch*, October, 1934.

"Sumpitan" copyright © 1935 by Street & Smith Publications, Inc., for *Top-Notch*, October, 1935.

"Death On Tin Can" copyright © 1937 by Street & Smith Publications, Inc., for *The Skipper*, December, 1937.

"East of Samarinda" copyright © 1937 by Street & Smith Publications, Inc., for *The Skipper*, July, 1937.

"The Jade Scarlotti" copyright © 1948 by Short Stories, Inc., for *Short Stories*, July 10, 1948.

"Death's Outpost" copyright © 1939 by Better Publications, Inc., for *Thrilling Mystery*, May, 1939.

"Leopard Tracks" copyright © 1938 by Short Stories, Inc., for *Short Stories*, July 10, 1938.

"Deceit Post" copyright © 1935 by Street & Smith Publications, Inc., for *Complete Stories*, February 18, 1935.

"Jungle Wires" copyright © 1934 by Street & Smith Publications, Inc., for *Complete Stories*, September 24, 1934.

"Holt Sails the 'San Hing'" copyright © 1938 by Short Stories, Inc., for *Short Stories*, January 25, 1938.

"Quarry" copyright © 1935 by Popular Publications, Inc., for *Dime Adventure Magazine*, December, 1935.

"Trial by Jungle" copyright © 1939 by Standard Magazines, Inc., for *Thrilling Adventures*, September, 1939.

"Hamadryad Chair" copyright © 1941 by Fictioneers, Inc., for *10 Story Mystery Magazine*, February, 1942.

"A Film in the Bush" copyright © 1937 by Street & Smith Publications, Inc., for *Doc Savage*, September, 1937.

"Redemption Trail" copyright © 1941 by Standard Magazines, Inc., for *Thrilling Adventures*, October, 1941.

"Black Passage" copyright © 1936 by Metropolitan Magazines, Inc., for *Thrilling Adventures*, May, 1936.

"Spider Wires" (as by Jackson Cole) copyright © 1936 by Metropolitan Magazines, Inc., for *Thrilling Adventures*, January, 1937.

"Tiger Island" copyright © 1937 by Metropolitan Magazines, Inc., for *Thrilling Adventures*, May, 1937.

"Dead Man's River" copyright © 1936 by Metropolitan Magazines, Inc., for *Thrilling Adventures*, January, 1937.

"Submarine I-26" copyright © 1944 by Street & Smith Publications, Inc., for *Doc Savage*, March, 1944.

It's a lonely place, this jungle, filled with the unknown dangers of flora and fauna and the known dangers of intruders—other men.

—Captain J.W. Renburg, Royal
Netherlands Indies Army, Commandant
of the Long Nawang garrison,
Onderafdeeling of Apo Kayan

CONTENTS

Preface

Carl Jacobi

Quite a few years ago when plane travel and plane mail delivery in the Far East were not as available as today, I learned of an outpost in the deep jungle interior of Dutch Borneo. For some time I had been searching for a locale, a setting for a series of adventure stories, one that was remote, colorful and pregnant with danger where a group of characters might find themselves pitted against the forces of nature as well as other men.

My letter of inquiry went first to San Francisco, then to Hongkong, then to Singapore. From there it went by coastwise freighter to Bandjermasin in Borneo. Here I had routed the letter up the Mahakam River to a vaguely designated unexplored area called Apo Kayan. But the Mahakam was not navigable that season, so my letter went around to the east coast to a place called Tandjong-Selor. Here it waited six weeks and finally went up the Kayan River by military transport. It was sealed in a soldered-shut tin to prevent the excessive humidity from blurring the ink. The final lap was overland by native runner.

My letter reached its destination, a garrison of forty men called Long Nawang, and my reply came from the Captain Commandant in the Royal Netherlands Indies Army, who as luck would have it wrote English as well as Dutch.

The reply opened whole new vistas in what I had always regarded as my detailed and accurate research. Correspondence! Of course men living on the spot could supply a wealth of information the most up-to-date travel journal or guidebook could not equal.

I wrote another, this one to Ambunti, 230 miles up the Sepik River in the heart of the headhunting country, Northeast New Guinea. Here a lonely District Officer and his assistant watched over a kingdom of stone-age savages.

Again I hit the jackpot. The assistant was a personable young man who was only too pleased to post me on his surroundings: the muddy reed-entangled crocodile-infested river, the steaming heat, the electrical storm that came out of nowhere each night. He told me of the

1

Sangumenke, a secret death society among the natives, and he told me of the flora and fauna I could have learned nowhere else.

I wrote more letters, to ship captains, harbor masters, traders and trading stations, American vice-consuls, conservators of forests, anywhere I thought I might be able to obtain background information not available on the printed page. In most cases I received replies, some long and detailed from men who, cut off from western civilization, were glad to engage in pen-and-ink companionship so lacking in their lives.

But I didn't limit myself to correspondence between individuals or even foreign offices. Now maps have always held a fascination for me. One day while studying a wall map of the South Seas my eye was caught by a tiny pinpoint of land designated as Tiger Island. So sighting the germ of a story I wrote the Rand McNally Company for information. They replied rather uncertainly that Tiger Island was in the Longan archipelago and referred me to the Pacific Islands books. They also referred me to the U.S. Navy Hydrographic Department. The Navy said they had no knowledge of a Longan archipelago and in turn referred me to the British War Office and the British Ordnance Survey in Southampton. It was astounding how little was known of sea lanes at that time. From these multiple sources I gathered that an island named Tiger had been wrongly identified by a German sea captain who was off his course and that the island he called Tiger was probably one named Wuvulu. Now even then there were restrictions on pearl diving. Pearl fisheries were under government control. If Tiger Island were in the original reported position, pearl diving there was under British jurisdiction; if in the secondary position, it was under Dutch control. Using this variance of authority as a basis for a plot, I wrote a story with that name as a title. Years later I was to learn that the American movie actor William Holden had leased an estate on Wuvulu.

On another occasion a speech in the House of Commons was reported in brief by the London *Times*. I wrote for a copy of that speech. It described the deplorable condition of a government-subsidized narrow-gauge railroad that led into the North Borneo interior through savage-infested country inland from Sandakan.

A number of my stories were laid aboard ships in the Java, Arafura, and Sulu seas. Such ships of large or small tonnage were of varied types. Some had well decks, some had cabins amidships under the bridge house and the chart house was abaft the wheel house on the bridge. At that time shipping companies were not averse to adding additional revenue from their freight carriers by equipping them with accommodations for ten or twenty passengers. To advertise the bargain rates even the most obscure trading companies would furnish on request cross-section drawings or blueprints, showing the location of travelers' quarters. Thus I was able to obtain complete layouts of freighters whose ports of call were Singapore, Batavia, Kuala Lumpur or Palembang. To write these sea stories it was also necessary to know the principles of navigation, to lay out a course with the correct latitude and longitude. Also it was necessary to know the wireless jargon of radio operators who kept these ships apprised of storm warnings and other messages.

Sooner or later my off-the-trail correspondence was bound to result in some (shall I say?) strange friendships. Perhaps the strangest was with a man named St. Ives. Colin St. Ives was in his middle thirties when I first wrote him at the Raffles Hotel in Singapore. Even then his reputation had preceded him. He had trekked across most of Asia, from the Khyber to Outer Mongolia. He had wandered through the Hindu Kush, searching for artifacts from the legendary lost regiment of Alexander the Great. His forte seemed to be running down old wives' tales and half truths that had the lure of forgotten treasures.

At first his letters were casual, unassuming and traditional. But as more correspondence passed between us his restraint vanished and he began to describe in detail some of the most incredible adventures ever to come out of the Eastern Circle.

It was my original intention to include these letters in a special bibliographical section of this book, *East of Samarinda*. A final letter from St. Ives, however, ended that. St. Ives wrote me that he had been offered a considerable sum by the one-time publisher of Richard Halliburton, Peter Fleming and Carveth Wells to bring into print the correspondence he had written me. St. Ives said he had no illusions as to his writing ability, but the publisher had assured him that that was of secondary importance. As usual St. Ives was broke, so he had accepted the offer.

It meant that the time I had spent editing this correspondence would be "love's labor lost." It meant that the subtitles I had fixed on the letters would never see the light of day. Let me list some of those subtitles:

June 23rd. Crossing the impenetrable crocodile-infested N'Glyan swamp to find an albino native girl ruling a tribe of Kenyah Dyaks, and her offer to St. Ives to join forces and become "King of the River."

July 10th. The affair of the mad Sultana and St. Ives' entrance into the pink palace of Tenggarong, sixty miles up the Mahakam River, and his "removal" from the palace strong room of thirty priceless emeralds.

August 15th. St. Ives plays "main po," an Oriental game of chance, in the Casino of a Hundred Dancing Girls in Singapore with the stakes three images of Oceanic Jade, while six Casino Sikh guards watch with drawn pistols.

September 4th. St. Ives meets a beautiful Eurasian girl (he enclosed a photo) whom he calls Tondelayo, presumably after the famous stage character in *White Cargo*, and who becomes his partner in crime.

October 12th. St. Ives follows the trail of Alexander Selkirk, the prototype of Robinson Crusoe, to the island of Juan Fernandez where he was marooned, forming the basis of the castaway story. On the island he finds a buried treasure of untold value. But the treasure is under the jurisdiction of the government which owns the island, and he is unable to claim or remove it.

November 6th. St. Ives and Tondelayo, presenting themselves as Prince Hussein and wife Alepo, exchange fifty bogus bonds on the city of Saigon, exchange them for 200,000 francs drawn on the Bank of France. They voluntarily reveal their part in the hoax in "consideration" of the confession of an important Indo-China government official and his agreement to leave the country. St. Ives returns to the gaming tables of the Casino of a Hundred Dancing Girls and loses all of his gains in the deal, playing Chemin de Fer.

Six weeks later, on December 12th, the *Shanghai Gazette* carried the tragic news. The Ming Toi, a Chinese junk, foundered in a storm that swept the Java Sea. Listed on the insurance manifest of those "lost at sea" was my friend Colin St. Ives and Tondelayo Smith.

Minneapolis, Minnesota

March, 1989

Introduction
Open Hell Without Quarter

R. Dixon Smith

Sandakan, Samarinda, Bandjermasin, Tandjong-Selor, Bulungan,
Long Iram. The Apo Kayan district of Dutch East Borneo, swarming
with savage Dyak head-hunters. The winding, silt-heavy Mahakam River,
its yellow-muddy waters teeming with man-eating crocodiles. The
brooding jungle looms dark, wet, and forbidding, its floor thick with
decay, massive Seraya and Palapak trees, and razor-edged rip grass. The
low-throated growl of a leopard crouched in readiness; the hooded menace
of a fourteen-foot hamadryad, the dreaded king cobra. Nipa-thatch Dyak
huts, festooned with ghastly, shrunken human heads. Finally, the Royal
Netherlands Indies garrison at Long Nawang, the most remote military
outpost in the interior. Nothing but monotony, solitude, and loneliness;
jungle, heat, and rain; fever, sudden death, and constant danger. White
sahibs and tuans versus jabbering Kenyah Dyaks; Lugers and Webleys
against deadly Sumpitan blowpipes, parangs, and Malay krises. Whiskey
and sweat and blood: the sullen smell of high adventure. A steamy world
of hypocrisy, deceit, greed, murder, and retribution. Welcome to Borneo.

Carl Jacobi's fame rests almost exclusively on his haunting tales
of the supernatural and the macabre. He was, after all, one of the chief
contributors to *Weird Tales*, and also appeared in such pulp magazines
of the bizarre and uncanny as *Thrilling Mystery, Startling Stories,
Thrilling Wonder Stories, Planet Stories*, and *Strange Stories*. Why, then,
is the present collection culled from the pages of such pulps as *Thrilling
Adventures, Complete Stories, Top-Notch, Short Stories, The Skipper,
Doc Savage*, and *Dime Adventure Magazine*? Because Carl Jacobi was
also one of the pulp era's most durable practitioners of adventure fiction.
Surprising as it must seem, one of every three yarns he has ever spun
is straight adventure.

Unlike such fellow fictioneers as E. Hoffmann Price and Hugh B.
Cave, however, Jacobi has spent virtually his entire life in his native
state of Minnesota. His feet never touched the soil of Borneo, New Guinea,
or the islands of the South Seas, the settings for most of his action thrillers.
This in itself is not unusual. Edgar Rice Burroughs wrote an entire
series of John Carter adventures without once ever having visited Mars;

while German novelist Karl May produced dozens of stories set in America's wild west, similarly without benefit of first-hand experience. How, then, did Jacobi acquire the background knowledge necessary to give his adventure tales the ring of authenticity? Out of his mind? He didn't travel, but his imagination did? Yes, in part, but supplemented by meticulous research.

Shy and introverted since childhood, young Jacobi read adventure yarns voraciously—Frank Merriwell, Tom Swift, the Boy Allies, the Submarine Boys, the Rover Boys, and a great number of the scientific romances of Jules Verne—and dreamed of visiting faraway lands. The irresistible lure of the unknown soon claimed him. Fueling his fantasies were the wilds of Dutch East Borneo, which, to any midwestern American teenager, seemed impossibly exotic. In due course he grew up, as all boys must, and enrolled at the University of Minnesota in 1927, where he began to haunt the library stacks, devouring everything he could lay his hands upon which dealt with the Far East. Two things had by this time become unshakable parts of his makeup: the desire to write for pulp magazines, which he had discovered in high school; and a strong leaning toward the strange and wondrous, already evident in his juvenilia, both horror and adventure.

A biographer considers himself fortunate indeed if his subject's files are even moderately intact; in Jacobi's case, his card catalogue contains not only entries for each of the volumes he consulted at the University, but also his evaluations of each. Among them we find *Decade in Borneo* ("Written by wife of man who started Sandakan and British North Borneo Co. Most of it old stuff. One chapter, however, at the end gives a complete description of Sandakan."); *Twenty Years in Borneo* ("Little information about the interior."); *In Borneo Jungles* ("There is a brief and none-too-good description of Samarinda."); *Through Central Borneo* ("In two volumes. All about Dutch Borneo. Good books filled with lots of information though not much about wild animals usable in a pulp story. Rivers, tribes and natives described in detail. The Mahakam."); *The Home-Life of Borneo Head-Hunters* ("Although not as accurate as Lumholtz's two books, this volume is filled with detail. The first part spends pages over the construction of the native houses, etc."); *Field Book of a Jungle Wallah* ("Narrative of a naturalist. Mostly concerned with insects and small wildlife."); *Head-Hunters: Black, White, and Brown* ("Starting with Thursday Island and islands of the Torres Straits, this book then touches Sarawak and British New Guinea. Much of it has to do with the customs of the people. Rather good."); *North Borneo* ("No good. Simply the memorial story of a British officer who lost his life in the development of North Borneo. Absolutely of no value as a research book."); and *Where the Strange Trails Go Down* ("Lurid description of the evil quarters of Sandakan, Samarinda, opium farms, evil streets, filth, etc. Description of the palace of the Sultan of Kotei on the Mahakam. From this book Hugh B. Cave got his idea for 'Hamadryad.' Excellent source book.'').

Jacobi would use this geographic, ethnic, tribal, and wildlife lore to good effect during the next several decades. In addition, he augmented his fund of knowledge by corresponding with the commanding officers in charge of the military outposts at Long Nawang, Borneo, and Ambunti, New Guinea, as well as by exchanging letters with such organizations as the British Admiralty Hydrographic Department and the Ordnance Survey at Southampton, England. But as Carl has discussed the nature and results of such correspondence in his own preface, I should merely like to mention that readers wishing to peruse these fascinating documents may find several of them reproduced in facsimile in my biography, *Lost in the Rentharpian Hills: Spanning the Decades with Carl Jacobi* (Bowling Green State University Popular Press, 1985).

By the mid-Thirties, Jacobi's by-line was becoming as well known among devotees of the adventure pulps as it had already become to the faithful followers of *Weird Tales*. Here, then, are twenty-one of his finest exercises in pulse-pounding action: fourteen of them set in Dutch East Borneo, his favorite locale; two each in British North Borneo and New Guinea; and, for good measure, two in the South Seas and one off the coast of the Unfederated Malay States.

Red foam flecks the Mahakam in "Crocodile," wherein a murder is avenged in as unexpected a manner as any to be found in its author's horror stories. Such a grisly tale is not so very far removed from Jacobi's weird fiction after all, as evidenced by the following extract:

Then one of the logs floating silently twenty feet away leaped into sudden life. It whipped around, revealing black eyes and the gaping jaws of death.... The water boiled in a mad whirlpool. Air bubbles and miniature waves churned the surface. A sound, hollow and grating, came from somewhere below. Seconds passed and a ribbon of scarlet appeared.

"Letter of Dismissal" finds three supposed cartographers fomenting an uprising of Dyak head-hunters in order to loot a diamond mine. Struggling against deadly odds to prevent the slaughter all along the upper Mahakam is a young Royal Netherlands Indies officer who already faces the humiliation and disgrace of dismissal for insubordination. (Jacobi later reworked this tale into a science-fiction yarn, "Assignment on Venus," which ran in the Fall, 1943, issue of *Planet Stories*.)

The threat of murderous raids by fierce Kenyah Dyaks throughout all Apo Kayan is chronicled in "Sumpitan." In an electrifying conclusion, a young Long Nawang lieutenant prepares to battle a native chieftain in a firelit clearing jammed with Dyak warriors. The only escape is death, for each is armed with a Sumpitan blowpipe and three palm-rib darts. Drums throb. The duel begins.

In "East of Samarinda," a young surveyor who expects to plot the course of the Mahakam with a contact from the Pacific Geographic Company learns that the man, who had been using an assumed name, has been murdered, and that there is no such outfit as the Pacific Geographic. What is the sinister significance of the jade ring carved in the likeness of three cobras entwined in an interlocking circle? The hero of this novelette finds out, as he plunges headlong into a morass of intrigue, secret societies, and international espionage.

Discover why the packing case supposedly containing a big-game hunter's rubber-tree seedlings contains no air holes, and who killed whom to obtain "The Jade Scarlotti," a fabulous bas-relief fashioned from a solid block of oceanic jade, in one of the most briskly paced tales its author has ever produced.

A supposed surveyor for a rubber company and two self-styled gold prospectors cross paths at Joe Klay's Trading Post in Menda Laong. One of them is willing to commit murder to acquire missing motion-picture footage worth a fortune, in "Deceit Post."

"Jungle Wires" tells of two telegraph operators stationed at a relay outpost far up the Mahakam. One of them is selling rifles to the natives, and the situation threatens to lead to an uprising of thousands of heavily armed, bloodthirsty Dyaks. Jacobi's description of the Dutch East Borneo Telegraph Company Station No. 5 is quite detailed:

They were lonely holes, these telegraph relay outposts. Twelve of them, at evenly spaced intervals, stretched across the Borneo jungle from Bandjermasin to Bulungan. Two operators were stationed at each. It was their duty to prevent the Dyaks from tearing down the wires and insulators and to keep the Dutch government informed of native conditions and the all-too-frequent head-hunting outbreaks.

It is worth noting, however, that there was no Dutch East Borneo Telegraph Company Station No. 5, for the simple reason that there never existed any such company. It was entirely a product of Jacobi's vivid imagination.

A relentless manhunt up the Mahakam and through the Apo Kayan jungle figures in "Quarry," a tale of ambush and treachery which jolts to a nerve-shattering climax. (This is another yarn that Jacobi later converted into science fantasy, as "Canal," which appeared in the Spring, 1944, issue of *Startling Stories*.)

A young ethnologist treks up the Mahakam and into the Apo Kayan interior in search of a lost gold deposit near the headwaters of the Merasi in the lower Mueller range, in "Trial by Jungle." But his mission has been compromised from the beginning, for the two white renegades he hires as guides plan to murder him once he reaches his destination.

In "A Film in the Bush," a Pacific Cinema Corporation travelogue shot in the Apo Kayan's forbidden head-hunting territory reveals the location of a rich platinum deposit—as well as details of a brutal murder. "Spider Wires" concerns the strange fate of a fugitive murderer, hiding out upriver near the Dutch East Borneo Telegraph Company Station No. 5, who schemes to rob a Kenyah Dyak totem post of its five sacred emeralds—a sacrilege that would lead to open, bloody revolt all along the Mahakam. Authorship of this yarn was attributed to Jackson Cole, a house name the Thrilling publication chain customarily employed whenever more than one story by the same author appeared in the same issue. That issue of *Thrilling Adventures* also ran, under Jacobi's own by-line, "Dead Man's River," which tells of a man falsely accused of murder, the real killer, and a fortune in rare orchids awaiting one of them at the other end of the Mahakam.

Set during the Japanese occupation of Borneo in the Second World War, "Submarine I-26" chronicles a daring escape to freedom by the thirty men of the Royal Netherlands Indies Army stationed at Long Nawang. Adding a dash of spice are a commandeered enemy sub, a mysterious cryptogram, and an imminent Japanese attack on Port Darwin.

Here are two tales of British North Borneo: "Leopard Tracks," a novelette which exposes a diamond-smuggling operation in the rubber-rich Sepitang jungle, tabu territory inhabited by savage, head-hunting Muruts; and "Redemption Trail," which dramatizes the bitter plight of another innocent victim of blind justice. Fleeing from a false murder charge, he is tracked through Saputan head-hunting country by an officer whose life he once saved. In an inspired set-piece, the long, arduous pursuit culminates in a perilous encounter high atop a bamboo cat-walk stretching across a yawning chasm.

Here also are two yarns set in the South Seas: the theft of a valuable cache of pearls during a pearl-diving raid leads to "Death On Tin Can"; while a frantic fight on the ocean floor, sixteen fathoms down, puts an end to pearl poaching in Dutch waters off "Tiger Island."

Then there is "Holt Sails the 'San Hing'," which concerns no less important a matter than a rajah's smuggled riches and mutiny, en route to Palembang, off the coast of the Unfederated Malay States; or "Black Passage," a novelette about gun running, contraband diamonds, and high-seas piracy off the steaming jungle coast of Dutch New Guinea, aboard a quarantine ship manned by a cutthroat crew of treacherous Lascars and Straits Chinese.

Moving into the more familiar territory of the weird-menace yarn, stop off at "Death's Outpost"—Ambunti, 230 miles up the Sepik River and the most isolated police garrison in the New Guinea interior. Terrorizing its residents are the Sangumenke, a murderous, head-hunting cult said to have developed a process whereby they can graft the head of a crocodile onto a decapitated human body and still maintain life. Or seat yourself, it you dare, in the "Hamadryad Chair" awaiting you at a forlorn rubber plantation back in the Apo Kayan district of Dutch East Borneo, and learn of the horrifying native superstition that "anyone who sits in it will have his arm changed to a hamadryad, and his soul will thereafter become the soul of a snake." But is it mere superstition? It would appear to be all-too-terrifyingly true: "The right arm rest of the chair was alive! A writhing, twisting serpent was there—a deadly hamadryad!" Curiously enough, Jacobi originally wrote this story as a straight adventure yarn, under the title "The Palapak Chair," and only later revised and retitled it, injecting the terror angle—a fortunate transformation, for it produces the shudders one expects from Carl Jacobi.

Such shudders are not confined, as it should by now be quite clear, to his weird and terror tales alone. His adventure fiction bears many touches which are highly reminiscent of his work in the macabre. The horrors that lurk at every turn, the shadowy figures that materialize out of the gloom (be they in a hostile jungle or in a small town in Carver County, Minnesota), and the things dark and sinister that lie at the very heart of existence—all permeate his entire output.

In the Thirties and Forties, the period during which the stories in this collection were written, adventure fiction by such authors as Rafael Sabatini and P.C. Wren crowded the book stalls, while motion pictures such as *Lives of a Bengal Lancer*, *The Charge of the Light Brigade*, *Beau Geste*, *Gunga Din*, and *The Four Feathers* enjoyed similar popularity. Carl Jacobi's adventure yarns resemble these films, but in miniature, their shorter length producing a smaller sweep. In cinematic terms, their kinship is to the short subject rather than the feature presentation. More than anything else, they are reminiscent of those old Saturday matinee serials whose hairbreadth escapes, cliffhanger endings, and unexpected plot twists thrilled millions of moviegoers for decades. (It is difficult to imagine "East of Samarinda" being filmed, for instance, without envisioning someone like Kane Richmond or Herman Brix in the lead.)

Somewhere along the way, however, the romance of high adventure fell victim to changing tastes during the past couple of decades. But more recently, the genre has begun to exhibit new life, at least in the cinema, as evidenced by the mass appeal of such pictures as *Raiders of the Lost Ark*, *Indiana Jones and the Temple of Doom*, *Romancing the Stone*, and *The Jewel of the Nile*. Might we not look forward to a similar rekindling of interest in adventure fiction as well?

Until comparatively recently, most pulp enthusiasts have tended to specialize in such genres as detection and mystery, horror and the supernatural, science fiction, and perhaps an occasional railroad, war, or western. Seldom, therefore, have we seen straight adventure reprinted from the pages of the pulps. (Notable exceptions do, of course, exist—among them the work of Edgar Rice Burroughs, Robert E. Howard, and Talbot Mundy.) Lately, however, interest in, and demand for, adventure yarns from the pulp era—a staple of that once-thriving industry—has become more vocal. Even publishers are beginning to take notice. One of them is Bowling Green State University Popular Press, thanks to whom we now have a major collection of some of the most skillful action yarns produced by a versatile and veteran pulp fictioneer.

Exotic locales and powerful drama, packed with excitement, danger, suspense, violence, brutality, courage, and thrills. Mix these classic elements together, package them in a striking facsimile edition of their original pulp-magazine appearances, and you have a direct route to some of the most spellbinding high adventure ever to summon you to lands unknown. Carl Jacobi wrote over four dozen action-adventure thrillers that helped to define the genre. His stories play to please. They entertain. As a fan recently observed, "He was outdoing Spielberg and Indiana Jones years ago."

The "wrong" story told to the "right" person.

By Carl Jacobi

CROCODILE

SQUATTING before his tent, McNair heard the sounds from the shadows beyond the fire at the same moment that the Dyaks did: the thump of a discarded pole and the soft swish as a sampan nosed into the ooze of the river shore.

In silence he got to his feet, loosened the revolver in his coat pocket, kicked another piece of wood onto the dying flames. Visitors, white or native, were an occasion this far up the Mahakam in Borneo.

A moment later the reeds parted and a heavy, hulking white man strode into the clearing. His hat was gone, his clothes hung in tat-

ters, and there was a fresh scar across his left cheek.

"Gaynor," he said huskily. "Steve Gaynor. Come down from the Taban territory. Been on that blasted river six days. Can you give me a drink and somethin' to eat? I'm starved."

The man had been through hell, that was apparent. Six days alone in a sampan under a Borneo sun isn't any picnic.

"Come into the tent," he said. "I'll see if I can fix you up."

He led the way under the mosquito flap, lighted a carbide lamp and placed it on the folding table. Then he produced a whisky bottle.

"You look as though you were done up," he said. "Help yourself to some of this. I'll have something more substantial for you soon."

The stranger nodded and lost no time in complying. He reached for the whisky, fastened his lips around the neck and drank until he was gasping. McNair called to a Dyak standing outside the doorway, gave an order rapidly in Malay. "And hurry," he said. "The white sahib is hungry."

"Yes, tuan."

Then McNair moved over to an opposite chair, sank into it and crossed his legs slowly.

"Quinine?"

Gaynor shook his head. "No. I've been living on the stuff. How far to the coast?"

"About four days."

"Better than I thought. I figured five. Must've passed the last village in the dark. Either that or I was sleepin'."

A moment later the newcomer was wolfing a bowl of steaming rice. For a long time neither man spoke again. McNair got a pipe out of his coat pocket and packed it while he watched the man eat.

In the glare of the lamp Gaynor was not a lovely sight. His face was unshaven, stained with sweat and dirt, and livid in some places with insect bites. The eyes were deep-set, close together, and the mouth was a thin-lipped sullen line.

STEADILY Gaynor ate, until the dish before him was empty. Then he looked up abruptly and wiped his mouth.

"Seen you somewheres before," he said. "Used to be up in British North, didn't you, working for the Company? Surveyor or somethin'? What doin' down here?"

A frown crept across McNair's bronzed face as he struck a match and moved it back and forth over his pipe.

"I'm still surveying," he replied as cordially as he could. "For a railroad. The Dutch are planning to run a narrow gauge through here in a couple of years. And you?"

"Me?" Gaynor snorted, and reached for the whisky. "Don't know me, eh? Well you would if you stayed in civilization long enough. Collecting's my racket—wild animals. Catch 'em alive, haul 'em back to the coast and sell 'em to an agent in Singapore. Ever hear of the Sintang python?"

"I don't believe so." McNair puffed slowly and shook his head.

"I caught that. Biggest snake ever come out of Borneo. Lost three natives getting the thing in a cage." He leaned back heavily, drew a dirty package out of his torn shirt and lighted a cigarette. "But it's too dangerous," he continued, "and there's not enough returns any more. I'm changin' my line to somethin' more profitable—rocks!"

McNair glanced across the table curiously. "You mean geology——"

"I mean jewels—especially emeralds. Got interested in 'em only a week ago. Easy to get, easy to hide through the customs, and big money.

"To-day's the fifteenth, ain't it?" he went on, helping himself to another drink. "That means near six weeks I been in this blasted jungle. Left Samarinda July 1st, coming up the Mahakam with twelve natives and a complete outfit. Went as far as I could navigate and crossed over into Taban country. Got a tiger and a black leopard, then had to leave everything and come back alone. Barely made it, too."

"Dyak trouble?" the surveyor

asked. "There's been quite a lot of it lately."

"Dyaks and everything else." Gaynor hiccuped. A deep flush had entered his cheeks, and it was clear that if the man drank any more he would be intoxicated. He leaned back now, studied the glowing tip of his cigarette before he spoke. Then he said:

"It's quite a story, stranger. Maybe you wouldn't be interested. Or even if you were, maybe, since you're workin' for the government —maybe you have a habit of passing things you hear along to the police."

McNair shrugged. "I'm surveying for a railroad," he said coldly. "My relations with the government go no further. Suit yourself."

FOR a moment Gaynor sat in deliberate silence, staring hard across the table. His small eyes inspected McNair critically. His mouth opened revealing yellow teeth, and closed again. Then he slapped both hands flat on the table and grinned.

"All started with a green-livered kid I met in Samarinda," he began. "Bloke called himself Fielding. That was his first name. He never did tell me the rest. Funny guy, wore glasses and always had some kind of a charm hangin' around his neck—miniature horseshoe. He came up to me at the river jetty just as I was startin' upcountry.

"'You're Steve Gaynor,' he says, in a soft voice. 'Aren't you?'

"'Sure,' I says. 'What about it, Baby-face?'

"'Steve Gaynor, the famous collector of wild animals? I want to go with you.'

"Just like that, he said it, as if I was takin' a pleasure cruise. A kid, mind you, all dressed spick-and-span

in that hole. Then he argued and talked blue murder for half an hour. Well, it's a funny thing. Seems he was fresh to Borneo, just come in on the boat an hour before, and he wanted to get used to his surroundings real quick. Had a date to meet some one there in Samarinda in a month or so, and he'd come early just so he could show that person he was an experienced white man in the tropics. You know, book stuff.

"The idea was, near as I could figure it out, I should let him string along in one of the sampans and give him a chance to help cage whatever I was after. Well, at first I just booted him out of the way. Me, Steve Gaynor, takin' a milk-drinkin' softy along. Not so's you could notice it. Then, the first thing I knew, I was lookin' into a fistful of money.

"'I'm willing to pay,' the kid says. 'This ought to be sufficient to cover the additional expense and trouble for my presence.'

"Cover it? Stranger, for the right amount of money I'd paddle the rajah to Sandakan and back and kiss his feet every five minutes of the way. I took one look at that handful of bills, and I said: 'O. K., kid. Stow your stuff and get in.'"

Gaynor stirred restlessly, shot a quick glance over his shoulder at the triangle of blackness beyond the tent flap, then turned back satisfied.

"We made it fast to Laong Pinoh, the first village. Then the natives slowed me down for three days while they waited for some damn tabu of theirs to pass over. Fielding was a pretty good man to have along at that. Talked a lot of nonsense most of the time about the beauty of a parakeet's plumage and the verdure along the shore. And he kept makin' notes in a little book that was always open before him.

"But he was a good worker and, strange enough, a good shot. That sorta surprised me. On the night of the fourth day we found a cobra in our camp. I was nearest the thing, and before I knew it, it was ready to spring. The kid was cool as a cucumber when he pulls out a fancy pistol and blows off the snake's head.

WHEN I left Samarinda it was my original intention to go up the Mahakam as far as the Kutei, then follow that for a ways. But when I reached the fork all I had to show for my work was a black leopard, a couple of baby orangs, and a monkey. I left these at a native village to be picked up on my return, and decided to stick to the Mahakam if I had to go clean to Bulungan.

"Finally we got into Taban territory. No health resort there either, if you know what I mean. The Dyaks along the river are quiet and sullen, and it's easy to see white men ain't welcome.

"But I know what I'm doin', and one day in a village almost at the narrows the natives gives us the information I'd been hopin' for—man-eatin' tiger. It was a big fellow. Seems he'd killed five men of the village includin' the witch doctor, and the rat-faced chief was scared out of his wits. He offered anything to the man who could kill the pest.

"If it had been anything else, I might have hesitated. I get hunches sometimes, and I had one then that everything wouldn't turn out so well. Foolish, too, because if you look at it right I had the best luck in my life. Anyway, there's always an open market for tiger. So I started makin' preparations.

"Then the kid busts in. The crazy fool wanted to know if I would give him my permission to hunt for the tiger on his own hook. Said I could go one way and he'd go another, and may the best man win. Well, I had his money, and it didn't make any difference to me if he got his head chewed off. I just laughed and told him to go to it.

"I wouldn't let him have any of my Dyaks, of course. He got his natives from the village, and we started off, me followin' the beast's most recent trail and the kid plungin' into the jungle at random.

"For a week I stalked and baited that blasted tiger. For a week I worked my head off. I didn't get a glimpse of it. Finally, swearing mad, I trekked back to the village.

"Well, sir, the minute I entered the village I got the surprise of my life. There's a big cage right in front of the long house and a bunch of jabberin' natives standin' around it. I'll be blowed if in that cage isn't the biggest striper I ever saw or heard of.

"The kid, he just sorta laughs and begins tellin' me over and over how he caught it. All excited he was; so was the chief of the village. At first it didn't make much difference to me. This was my expedition, and anything caught during it was mine. The kid understood that before we started. Then the old chief announces he is going to keep his promise and pay Fielding for his services in ridding the district of a great danger. He goes through a long ceremony that night with the Dyaks dancin' like mad and the new witch doctor screamin' at the top of his voice. Drums poundin' everywhere. Finally, at the end of it all, he hands the kid something that glitters green in the firelight.

"'Keep it, tuan,' he says. 'It has been in my house for many, many seasons, given to me by my father, and to him, by his father. I know not from where it came.'

"Fielding looks sort of dumb for a moment. He stands there like he'd just woke up from a pipe dream. Then he walks over to me, holds out his hand slowlike and says: 'Look. It's a real emerald.' "

Gaynor's fingers were trembling now as he lifted the whisky bottle and drained the last of the contents.

"Well," he said, lighting another cigarette. "It was an emerald all right. I don't know much about stones, but it's easy to see this one's worth a small fortune. The kid thanked the chief, made arrangements to have the tiger kept for us in the village, and the next morning we continued upriver.

FOR a while I kept my mouth closed and didn't say nothing. Then we hit slower current and there wasn't much poling to do. I had a talk and started claimin' my rights. I told Fielding flat that when we got back to Samarinda we'd sell the stone and divide it fifty-fifty. That was fair enough, considerin' it was my expedition and I was directin' everything.

"But he just looked at me in that quiet way of his and said: 'No. I caught the tiger. That's yours; but the emerald is mine. It was given to me and I mean to keep it. I paid you to take me along.'

"Of course I saw right off there was no use arguin'. So I sat back in the boat and kept quiet and watched the dirty river flow by. The kid was silent too. But he thought I was only in a sulk and I'd get over it in a while. The crazy fool didn't know Steve Gaynor. I ain't been done in yet, and no baby-faced kid was goin' to start it.

While I sat there, the old think box was workin' hard, tryin' to figure out a plan to get that emerald. It's a hard problem, but after a couple of hours I had it.

"You see, I couldn't just put a slug in the kid and take the stone. That wouldn't work because my Dyaks were coast Dyaks, and they'd be sure to report the matter soon's we got back in Samarinda. I had trouble with Dutch law once, and I know how fast it works. And I couldn't start a fight and take the emerald by force. Fielding wore that pistol in an open holster at his belt, and I'd seen before how quick he could use it. So I just waited my time.

"We camped that night at the narrows. The water was almost stagnant here and smelled strong. Lot of smooth shiny places along the shore told the story to any one that recognized the signs—crocodiles. The place was alive with 'em, and they was part of the plan. I'd been in that district before.

"All the time we was sittin' around the fire, talkin' and eatin', I was goin' over my plans, makin' sure there wouldn't be a single slip. Then after the kid had gone to sleep I got things ready.

"I sneaked down to the river with a big piece of fresh meat. I searched along the shore until I found a fifteen-foot length of bamboo, sharpened this at both ends, jammed the meat on one end and poked the other deep into the mud. The whole thing was hidden in the reeds so that even the natives wouldn't see it unless they were lookin' for it. Get the idea? That pole was slanted out over the river on a forty-five degree angle. The meat was hangin' there just over the water, just out of the crocs' reach. Before I had finished I knew the smell had reached 'em. I could hear 'em slitherin' and splashin', openin' and closin' their jaws. Then I took a long piece of rope and stretched it on the ground between two stakes just at the river's edge, hiding it as well as I could in the long grass.

"Well, it was simple. It worked like clockwork. Next morning, when the kid wakes up he complains of a feeling of dryness about his face and forehead. That's part of my doings too. The day before I'd sprinkled some carbonate of lime on the sweatband of his helmet. It absorbs the natural moisture of the skin. I was figuring down to the smallest details, see, and I didn't want anything to prevent this from working.

"Naturally, the kid goes down to the river to wash his face, and he does just what I'd expected. He trips over the rope and falls head first into the water. There's a deep drop there, right at the bank. And as I said, the river was swarming with crocs—hundreds of 'em. With that smell of fresh meat hangin' over their heads all night, they were all crazy mad.

"The kid falls in, tries to swim back, and the next minute it happens. One of those big logs floatin' out in the center whips around and comes in like an express train. The kid screams and goes under.

"Course I pretended to the Dyaks I was excited and all that, and I did a lot of unnecessary shootin'. But in a few seconds a big splotch of red came to the surface, and we knew it was all over.

"I walked back to the camp, lookin' sad as I could and began to get my stuff together. For a while the Dyaks stood around quietlike, watchin' me. But gradually they began to get excited and started mumblin' and jabberin' amongst themselves. Finally their leader came up to me and said they'd rather not move on for a while.

AND that, stranger, was part of my plan, too. You see, when a croc kills anybody, these Dyaks have a crazy superstition that they must kill every crocodile in the vicinity and rip it open until they come to the one whose belly shows it's the man-eater. Otherwise the dead man can never go to heaven.

"Fielding was white, but that didn't make any difference. He'd made friends with the Dyaks coming upriver, treated them like equals, and now that he was dead they wanted to protect his soul by having a croc hunt right away.

"Well, sir, we hung around that spot for two days, and by that time we'd killed nine of the things. Big fellows, some of them. I began to get a little nervous, thought maybe my luck had turned. But the tenth proved to be the killer. The Dyaks let out a howl when they found the stuff in its belly. A watch, a belt buckle, part of a ring, and a few other articles, includin' the emerald. Clever, eh? The kid out of the way by an unavoidable accident, which even to a Dutch official was fool proof, and I had the stone.

"Then I got excited and made my first mistake—not a big one, you understand. I'm not the kind that makes big mistakes. But just the same this one let me into a lot of trouble. I gave one of the Dyaks the watch, and another what was left of the ring, and I instructed all of them that if they were asked any questions back in Samarinda about the disappearance of Fielding, they should simply tell the truth: that he had been killed by an accident.

The emerald I didn't think to hide, but slid it openly into my pocket.

"The minute they saw the stone they wanted that, too. I said before that ever since we'd come into this district those natives had grown sullen and hard to handle. Now they began to get meaner than ever. I whipped one within an inch of his life to settle the matter.

I GUESS I started what followed by letting two of them have it with my revolver. Usually that's the only way: show them right from the beginning who's master. But they were aroused now, and in a minute there was a fight for fair. Those dirty heathens came at me with knives. I shot one in the stomach and another in the arm, and then it was give and take with my huntin' knife slashin' like mad. Well, it looked mighty black there for a while. I got this slice on my left cheek and a nasty jab in my leg above the knee. But gradually I worked my way backward out of the clearing and into the jungle. Then I turned and ran for it, ran like hell.

"Stranger, it wasn't easy. Takes brains to get out of a mess like that when you figure you're up against natives that know every trick there is. I doubled in my tracks two or three times, but even so they stuck right on my trail. The devils had blowpipes, and every time I broke into the open I'd hear a yell and see one of those poison darts go whizzing by my head.

"But I wasn't running blind. I was makin' a big circle that'd take me back to the river right in front of the camp. When I finally reached it I just had time to jump in one of the sampans, cut the others loose and pole like mad across to the other shore. I made it."

Gaynor hiccuped and twisted in his chair as he suddenly came to a pause. He reached unsteadily for the bottle, felt that it was empty and flung it to a far corner of the tent.

"I made it," he repeated a moment later. "The emerald is right here on my person. It goes back with me to Samarinda, but it won't be sold till I reach S'pore where it'll bring a tidy sum with no questions asked. Enough to last me a long while, enough to stake me so I can get more of the things. Smooth, eh? Ain't one man in a thousand would've thought of a plan like that."

For a moment McNair sat in silence. His pipe had gone out. His lips were clenched motionless over the stem. A faint gleam had entered his eyes. The lids had narrowed slowly. At the base of his throat a nerve had suddenly appeared, twitching to the pulsations of his heart. He rose to his feet slowly.

"You bunk here," he said, pointing. "If you want anything, call one of the Dyaks. I'm going out for a bit of air."

Gaynor nodded, started to unbutton his shirt, then he leaned forward, drawing an ugly revolver.

"I said the emerald was on my person," he snarled. "Don't let that give you any funny ideas you can get it while I sleep."

McNair shook his head. "Don't worry," he replied. "I won't disturb you. I don't steal—blood stones."

He pushed aside the mosquito flap and went out, pacing by the sleeping natives to the black mound in the center of the clearing that had once been the fire. Mechanically his boot stirred the ashes until a few remaining coals gleamed up at him.

Half an hour passed and McNair did not move. He stood there, head bent forward, shoulders slightly sagging, eyes staring blankly into the deep shadows of the surrounding jungle.

Slowly a tremor swept through the surveyor. He turned and looked over his shoulder at the tent. For an instant he stared, listening. Then, very quietly, he strode across the clearing, pushed his way through the reeds and headed for the river.

MORNING came and Steve Gaynor was a changed man. His talkativeness had disappeared with the wearing-away of the whisky. He ate the breakfast McNair had served him in stony silence. If he remembered anything of the night before and the story he had told, he did not mention it.

"I'm leavin' right away," he said finally, the meal finished. "I'll be takin' some of your supplies and a Dyak too, if it's all the same to you. Sick of breaking my back on that damn pole."

McNair nodded and stood up. "I'll give you food and water, of course," he said. "And I guess I can spare a native to manage your sampan. But before you go I want you to come down the river a ways. There's a spot there I've selected to span with a bridge, when and if the government ever gets around to building this railroad."

Gaynor was moving toward the tent door. "What do I care about a bridge?" he said. "I got to get going. It's a long drag to Samarinda."

There was a queer tightening of the surveyor's lips as he stepped quickly to Gaynor's side and grasped the man's arm.

"You said last night you were interested in jewels?" he began significantly.

"Well——"

"Well, I found something in that river no one seems to have suspected was there before—not jewels, not emeralds, but something equally interesting."

Gaynor's eyes opened slowly. He got a cigarette out of his pocket, lighted it with a match scratched on his thumb-nail.

"Meanin' just what?" he queried.

"Meaning gold. Not a lot. A man would have to work for it. But it's there, washed down from the mountains. And if enough were panned regularly, there'd be quite a fortune for whoever wanted it. Now, are you interested in that site for a bridge?"

"Why do you tell me this?" he asked.

"Why? Perhaps because I'm lonely. It's two months since I've talked to any one but a native. Perhaps I'm looking for a partner. There's plenty there for both of us."

Gaynor stood still, thinking. Gold, was it? Good luck was coming in buckets these days. If McNair was right—well, it wouldn't be hard to get rid of him and work the claim himself. He nodded slowly.

"Let's have a look."

McNair picked up a shallow tin dish, stepped out of the tent and led the way in the direction of the river. Down through the tall reeds and rip grass he went with Gaynor, smiling and expectant, a few steps behind. Reaching the shore, the surveyor turned right, following the water's edge. He walked slowly and deliberately. His helmet was pulled far forward, hiding his face in shadow.

FOR a quarter of an hour they fought their way through the undergrowth. Gaynor began to lag behind and halted several times to scrape leeches from his legs and arms. But at length the two white men emerged into a wide, open space where the bank ran into the river in a tiny peninsula of sand.

McNair drew up abruptly and pointed. "The bridge will go across here," he said. "Two hundred and ninety-five foot spread. There'll be four wells filled with concrete for foundation with probably a center pier in the middle of the river. It's the best place——"

"Damn the bridge!" snapped Gaynor. "Where's the gold?"

For a moment McNair made no reply. He turned away slowly and stood frowning at the river. His eyes were sunken and bloodshot, betraying a sleepless night. His fists were clenched. Out there before him swirled the Mahakam, yellow and muddy, giving off a faint haze in the morning sun. A few low-floating logs mottled its surface. Beyond, stretched the jungle.

"I'm not so sure but what I've changed my mind, Gaynor," McNair said then. "Maybe I don't need a partner. Maybe there isn't any gold here at all. Maybe——"

"No go——" Gaynor stiffened, then took a step forward. "Tryin' to crawl out of it, eh?" he said. "Tryin' to pull the wool over my eyes. Well, it won't work. Damn you, give me that pan and I'll have a look myself."

He snatched the tin dish from the surveyor's hands, turned and strode toward the river. Moved straight forward down the little peninsula. It wasn't all sand, that arm jutting out into the water. The far end, made more fertile by the alluvial drift from the river, was a thick mass of moss plants and heavy rip grass.

"Wait!" called McNair. "I'm warning you. Don't go any farther. There isn't any gold here and——"

But Gaynor, paying no attention, continued his advance. Three feet, five feet, and he was deep in the rank vegetation. Then suddenly his boot crashed into something hidden in the undergrowth. Had he looked down he would have seen a length of twisted rattan rope stretched taut between two stakes. But Gaynor had no time to look. He flung his arms wildly forward, sought to regain his balance, and fell with a heavy splash into the river.

On the shore McNair stood like a man in a dream, watching the drama on the stage of his making. His eyes were cold, his lips a hard line.

For a fleeting second nothing happened. Gaynor came to the surface sputtering, attempted to draw himself back to shore. Then one of the logs floating silently twenty feet away leaped into sudden life. It whipped around, revealing black eyes and the gaping jaws of death.

Gaynor screamed but once, then he was pulled under. The water boiled in a mad whirlpool. Air bubbles and miniature waves churned the surface. A sound, hollow and grating, came from somewhere below. Seconds passed and a ribbon of scarlet appeared.

McNair, standing on the bank, watched it widen, swirl gently, and give way to a yellow-brown flow of silt. A sob broke from his lips.

"It was coming to you, Gaynor," he said huskily. "The kid you murdered back there didn't lie when he told you he was going to meet some one in Samarinda in a month. He was going to meet me. Fielding— Fielding McNair—my son!"

There's Dynamite Wrapped In Parchment When a Man Is Tempted!

Letter of DISMISSAL

By CARL JACOBI

"You're slippery, all right," Mueller said, "but I'm putting you out of my way right now!"

I WAS NEAR nightfall when Lieutenant Henston reached the mouth of the Boh River. Six days from the Long Nawang garrison through Dutch Borneo's most dangerous head-hunting region had been passed without trouble. Ahead was the Mahakam, an almost-unbroken route to the coast.

But Henston, as he strode down the swamp trail toward the nameless Dyak village that lay a quarter of a mile inland, showed no signs of relief. Coming into the Mahakam completed but the first stage of his hazardous journey. Anything could happen before he reached military headquarters at

21

Long Iram. And when that time came, it meant for him only disgrace and humiliation.

The trail widened abruptly into a small clearing with a double row of nipa-thatch huts. Henston halted, found himself staring at the village in perplexity. The place was deserted.

Right hand dropping to his holstered army pistol, he paused there a long moment, eyes narrowed, every sense alert. Slowly he paced forward, An instant later he stopped dead in his tracks and shouted a surprised welcome: "Mueller! What the devil are you doing here?"

Three white men, dressed in dirty whites and canvas mosquito boots, appeared in the doorway of a near hut. They stood there gaping, quickly descended the ladder, and advanced to the lieutenant's side.

"Hodge, Strouts," continued Henston in a dazed voice. "Well, I must say the Globe Map Co. hasn't got very far. It's three weeks since you were at the garrison. Where are the natives?"

Mueller, a heavy, florid-faced man with a bull neck and huge jowls, extended his hand.

"We've been expecting you, lieutenant," he said. "Knew you'd stop off here on your way downriver. Didn't think you'd be alone, though."

"I left my Dyaks at the old landing," Henston replied briefly. "Kenyahs and Punans don't mix, you know. But what's wrong here?"

"Nothing wrong. The natives moved out on us yesterday; that's all. Some big celebration. Come over by the longhouse. I'll tell you about it."

Ten minutes later the four men were squatted around a fire in the center of the village.

They weren't a lovely trio, these Globe Co. men. Mueller was their leader. Hodge was a swarthy man with black, kinky hair. And Strouts, deformed slightly, with one shoulder sagging lower than the other and a hand that hung stiff and unnatural, wore a cartridge belt bandolier-fashion across his shirt.

Cartographers, they called themselves—map makers. Employed by a Dutch-American outfit with headquarters in Batavia, they claimed to be making a detailed chart of the upper Mahakam and its drainage country.

"How come you've moved so slow?" Henston asked quietly. "And what made you say you knew I was coming?"

Hodge crammed a chew of plug tobacco into his mouth and grinned. "We know a lot of things," he replied, hooking his hands around his knees. "For example, that you're traveling to military headquarters with a letter from the commandant at Long Nawang; that one part of that letter asks for reënforcements at the garrison because sickness has laid up so many of the men; and that the other part demands your dismissal from the post because of insubordination. Insubordination—refusing to obey orders. Right, isn't it?"

Henston stiffened.

IT WAS the truth, however, and not exaggerated. Batu Danum, the district witch doctor near Long Nawang, was behind it all. That skulking Dyak with his rat face and evil pig eyes was wanted at the garrison for attempted murder and for inciting several mutinies. Henston had been ordered to find him and shoot him in the leg. It was a white man's old trick to lower a native's standing with his tribe when he became dangerous.

Somehow when the lieutenant had the Dyak in range, his finger had refused to press the trigger. Shooting in a skirmish was one thing, but firing a cold-blooded shot that was intended to maim didn't seem civilized. Henston's conscience had rebelled.

He had gone back to the commandant and in bitter words told him point-blank what he thought of the idea. Even while he was speaking, Batu Danum had sneaked inside the stockade and severely wounded two garrison men with blowpipe darts. It made a nasty mess.

A moment dragged by while the three men sat in silence. Mueller tossed another piece of wood on the flames and stirred the fire with his boot. Presently he got up, strode toward one of the huts, and returned carrying a canvas duffle bag and a magnifying glass. He unbuckled the flap and drew forth a small leather sack, fastened at one end with a draw string. This he opened, permitting five tiny objects to drop into his hand. He shoved his hand forward into the brighter light of the fire.

"Take a look at these," he said thickly.

Henston edged closer, squinted through the glass, saw five diamonds glittering there in the heavy palm. They were cut and polished. The largest weighed about five carats, the smallest two. One of them, the lieutenant noticed, was slightly bluish in color.

With a pudgy forefinger Mueller rolled them back and forth.

"Not large," he said. "But if a man had enough of them he could take it easy for a long time. I plan on doing just that. I plan on getting more, and I know where. I'm asking you, Henston, why not let the post and the government go to blazes and join in? You're getting a rotten deal, anyway."

The lieutenant stared across the fire, shifted uneasily. "You mean," he said slowly, "you want me to disregard my letter to Long Iram and tag along with you? But I thought the Globe Map Co.——"

"We're not map makers, Henston. That was just a story we cooked up when your commandant at Long Nawang got too nosey and started asking questions. And we ain't geologists, either. But it don't take an expert to work a diamond mine.

"Last year in the midst of the monsoon I was up here, and I found a lode of the things—a real strike. The only trouble was the mine was native property near a big Dyak Village. It was all I could do to get these five and skin out with my head on my shoulders. I went back to Bandjermasin, had the stones cut and appraised, and tried to figure out how I could get more.

"The plan I doped out is simple. I go back to the village, see? I hide near its outskirts until one of the natives comes through the bush alone. I jump him from behind, run a knife through him before he knows what's happened, and I beat it. But before I go I make the whole thing look like the work of Punan Dyaks from the villages up north.

"That ain't hard. I know my woodcraft, and I know how these different tribes do things. Little while later the Dyaks find the native's dead body. Now, I ask you, what's the first thing they do?"

Henston's lips were slowly tightening as he reached for a cigarette. "Anybody could see the answer to that," he replied. "The village immediately declares war on the other tribe, on the Punans. They start a head-hunting expedition to get revenge and——"

"Exactly! And while they're gone on this head-hunting expedition, what do we do? We slip in, work that mine fast, and get out with a haul of stones before they return."

The speaker paused to tilt a canteen to his mouth. He passed the water to Strouts and wiped his mouth.

"Now, then, how about it, Henston? You've as good as lost your stripes already. You're carrying a letter asking for your own dismissal. String along with us, and we'll treat you right. We need another man. We'll give you, say, a sixth of all we get. What's the answer?"

For a moment the lieutenant stared

at the white smoke trailing from his
cigarette.

"Just where is this mine, near what
village? And when do you figure on
putting your plan into operation?"
Mueller laughed. "It's in operation
now," he answered. "The dead native
was found last night. That's why
there are no Dyaks here. They all lit
out for the big war dance some place
downriver. Even took the women and
kids with 'em. And the mine is just
a day's travel south, near Batukelan
village."

Like a slack wire jerked taut, Henston jumped rigid. His jaw sagged;
his eyes opened wide.

"Good heaven!" he cried. "Do you
realize what you've done? Batukelan
village is the headquarters for almost
all the Kenyah Dyaks in the district.
The natives there hate the Punans more
than anything in the world. It means
an open outbreak all along the upper
Mahakam."

"Does it?" inquired Mueller calmly.
"So much the better. We'll have more
time then to work the mine."

"But—but the whole country will be
an inferno when that raid gets under
way. Every village will join in. And
the Dyaks won't rest until they've
slaughtered everything in their path.
Long Nawang will be wiped out."

Mueller yawned deliberately and
stood up. He swept his boots through
the fire, scattering the coals before him.
"Think it over," he said. "Sleep on it
and give us your answer in the morning.
If you come along, remember I said
we'd give you a sixth. If you don't
—— But I think you will."

FLAT on his back Henston lay in
one of the native huts of the village,
staring into a pit of blackness. Outside,
in the gloom just beneath the door,
Hodge sat with his back to the bamboo-
entrance ladder, a rifle across his knee.

For a long time Henston had realized
he was a prisoner.

It wasn't difficult to analyze the mo-
tives of the three pseudo map makers.
Should he be permitted to continue
downriver to Long Iram and deliver
his letter, it would mean a fatal
interruption of Mueller's plan. The
commandant at Lang Nawang had
asked for reënforcements. Those
reënforcements, coming up the Mahakam, would be sure to stop off at
Batukelan village and sight the illegal
operation of the mine. They would
realize that the three white men were
behind the native outbreak, and arrest
would follow.

Henston strained his ears, listened.
He heard nothing. Yet not far to the
south he knew the night was alive with
the pounding of countless drums. Infuriated Kenyahs would be gathering
from every river village. The lieutenant
had not been away from the coast long
—five months at the garrison and a
short trip up the Barito a year ago. He
was still green.

But he had lived long enough in the
interior to know the procedure of those
Kenyahs only too well. They would
dance and drink *tuak*—native rum. For
three nights and three days they would
work themselves into a frenzy, wailing
over the tragedy that had come to them,
planning revenge against their enemies,
the Punans, whom they thought responsible for the crime. And on the
night of the fourth day they would
embark in their prahus on a mission of
murder.

Once in Punan territory, the Kenyahs
would be madmen, thirsting only for
human heads. Long Nawang with its
flimsy stockade and its men weakened
by beriberi and fever would be helpless.

The lieutenant moved across to the
door and looked down into the shadows.
There was no escaping at this point.

And yet why escape? He had nothing to lose. Mueller had not been wrong

in predicting what would happen when he—Henston—reached Long Iram.

His hand reached in his pocket, drew forth a long Manila envelope. In the dim light of a pocket flash Henston looked down upon the writing, upon the seal-of-the-queen in the lower right-hand corner. His lips twisted bitterly. The words of the commandant at Long Nawang when he had given him that letter and ordered him downriver still rang in his ears:

"This is a government watch post, lieutenant; not a summer hotel. We need men. We have no use for rotters who question and refuse to obey orders."

Henston extinguished the flash and returned the letter to his pocket. For ten minutes he sat there in the darkness. Then slowly he rose to his feet and reached for his hunting knife. Whatever happened, he was still a soldier.

Cautiously he groped to the rear wall of the hut, pried the knife in the reeds and began to move the blade back and forth. At the end of a short time he had an opening large enough to admit his body. He listened. Very quietly he squirmed through to the outside and slid down one of the supporting piles to the ground. Then he darted across the open space and entered the jungle.

In a wide circle he fought his way through the inky undergrowth back to the swamp trail and the river. The three Dyak boatmen were there near the beached sampan. Henston hesitated. He must go on alone; that was certain. To continue with Punan boatmen in present conditions would only hamper him. He drew forth a small notebook, scribbled a few lines on one of the pages and handed the note, folded, to the Dyak leader.

"Lukut," he said, "I take the sampan myself. You go on foot back to Long Nawang and deliver this message to the tuan commandant. You will travel fast,

stopping only when you need sleep. Do you understand, Lukut?"

The Dyak rose to his feet and nodded quickly. "Yes, tuan. We go."

A moment later the three melted into the gloom. Henston stepped into the sampan, seized the pole, and thrust the clumsy craft out into the black river.

IT WAS NOON of the next day before he sighted Batukelan village. A bamboo mast was propped up at the end of the native wharf, and it bore an ancient, dried Punan head suspended upside down from a length of rattan. That head was a signal of war.

All night as he had feverishly poled the sampan down the winding river he had heard drums pounding in the distance, had heard them answered by more drums from points farther back in the jungle. And once his keen ears had caught the rhythmic slap of paddles approaching from behind. He had had barely time then to drive the sampan inshore among the reeds and hide until the prahu slipped by.

Docking at the wharf without challenge, Henston advanced into the village. He found the place a hive of excitement. Hundreds of Kenyahs in full war regalia with feathered headdresses and shields jammed the clearing around the long-house. The confusion was so great that his arrival was not noticed until he had paced well into the village. Then a howl went up, and ugly faces peered at him with looks of menace.

Straight to a short, thickset figure seated in the background that he recognized as the village chief, Henston strode. Reaching the native's side, he stopped short, raised one hand above him and said in Malay:

"I come from the white tuan's post, Long Nawang in Apo Kayan. You know of where I speak?"

The chief's pin-point eyes were sullen with distrust as he nodded slowly.

"The God of the white tuans has told me you are planning to lead your tribe into war, to take the heads of your brothers, the Punans; that you will leave upriver in many prahus before two more nights have passed. This is so?" Again the Dyak nodded, disdaining to answer.

"You are very unwise. The Punans know nothing of the warrior found dead. He was killed by one of three white men who desires to enter the village when you have gone and steal the stones-that-glitter from your mine."

"Lies!" The chief leaped to his feet, his rat face contorted into a mask of hate. "It was Punans who killed our warrior. White men do not take the head of a man they have killed, nor leave behind a knife with a Punan-carved handle. Lies, I say."

"I do not lie," Henston said firmly. "The evil white man took the head to trick you, and he left behind the knife for the same reason. I have proof. In a short time those three white men will come here. Even now they are on their way and——"

A hoarse laugh sounded behind the lieutenant, jangling through the silence. Henston whirled and stared, jaw agape. Five feet away, swaying on the balls of his feet, hands hooked on his belt, stood Mueller. The pseudo map maker was leering like a gibbon. Behind him, satisfaction showing on their hard faces, lounged Hodge and Strouts. So it was the outlaws' boat that had passed him in the night! Henston's right hand slid toward the holster at his side.

His grin rapidly changing to a sneer, Mueller ripped an automatic from his shirt and strode forward. "I wouldn't advise you to try it, Henston," he said. "You wouldn't live long. Thought you'd trick us, hey? Thought you'd barge in here, spoil all our work and then do a nice act of snitching when you reach Long Iram. Just remember two can play at that game."

As from far off the lieutenant saw three natives jump to the chief's command, felt them pinion his arms to his sides. Then a sharp blow crashed down upon his head from behind. A burst of colored lights swirled in his vision, and he slumped downward unconscious.

HENSTON came to with a dull nausea in his middle and a vague feeling that hours had passed. He was lying at one end of a huge room that seemed to stretch ahead endlessly under the nipa-thatch roof. Along the side walls were mounted spears, blowpipes, grass mats and brilliant feathers. Light came through slits in the ceiling.

The lieutenant nodded slowly as his vision cleared. It was the interior of the long-house, the community structure peculiar to some villages in Borneo, housing many families. For a second time in a few hours he was a prisoner.

Outside in the clearing there was only noise and confusion as the Dyaks made ready for their second night of preparation. The drums had started again, booming ceaselessly through the hot air. Above the din sounded the droning chant of the village witch doctor.

Henston bit his lips. His first move had been blocked. His explanation to the chief had not been believed. Mueller and his three followers in some way had established themselves here before. Their word was trusted.

Once again, hardly knowing why, Henston drew out his official letter to Long Iram, scowled down upon it.

He stood up, walked slowly from one end of the long room to the other, looking about him on all sides. Abruptly he stopped, and his gaze centered on a hideous thing perched on a bamboo rafter in the ceiling.

It was a mask, a witchcraft mask used by Dyaks in funeral ceremonies and feasts where the power of the spirits was invoked. Once on the head of a writhing, dancing native, it became in their superstitious eyes much more than a piece of dried, painted skin, buffalo horns, and long hair grass. It became a jungle god malignant with power.

For several seconds Henston stared at the thing. Then he shuddered involuntarily, sat down and lighted a cigarette. The situation was bad. There didn't seem to be the slightest loophole.

His cigarette burned itself out, and mechanically he moved to light another. But halfway the match dropped, and a sudden glitter darted into his eyes. He got up, lurched across to the center of the room again, examined the gruesome mask from all sides. Reflectively his fingers drummed his belt buckle. Then, with a low exclamation, he turned and paced across to the door.

A Dyak sentinel stood motionless just below. Henston bent down, seized a gourd from the floor and flung it at the native's feet.

"Tell your chief to come here instantly," he snapped. "Tell him to come or the village will be consumed by fire. Now, do you hear? The tuan besar orders it."

For an instant the Dyak stared foolishly. Then, impressed by the white man's quiet manner and the daring words, he motioned to another native to take his place and hurried off. After that, time dragged by. Henston waited impatiently.

It was a long while before he sighted the procession moving toward him, the chief in the lead, guarded by two warriors, followed by his wives. Face alive with curiosity, but asking no questions, the chief stalked into the long-house and glared in sullen resentment at the lieutenant.

"You have said all I have told you were lies," Henston began tersely. "You have chosen to accept the words of other white men rather than mine. So be it! Now I will give you a prophecy.

"To-night the God of the white tuans speaks. He will send a message into your midst. That message will be in sticks. Do you understand? Branches, pieces of the Palapak tree, the tree which is sacred, and in the hollow trunk of which you bury your dead. For each stick you must wait one more day before starting your raid against the Punans. Two sticks, two days. Three sticks, three days. That is all. I have spoken."

The chief drew himself up proudly. He turned without a word and stepped out of the long-house. And a moment later Henston realized just what impression his words had made. Two Dyaks entered, threw him to the floor and bound his wrists and ankles. Yet when they had completed their work the lieutenant smiled.

WITH NIGHTFALL the village became a place of madness. The drums pounded louder, faster. A huge fire in the center of the clearing probed its light through the open doorway and far into the long-house where Henston lay. Around that fire the Dyaks yelled and danced in a slow, never-ending circle.

Alone in the shadows, the lieutenant worked steadily at his bonds. His knife and revolver had been taken, and he was forced to rely on the flexibility of his wrists and fingers. But the natives had done a hurried job with the fastenings, and he had been straining at them for hours. Presently the knots slipped, the lashings fell, and he stood up.

He massaged the circulation back into his veins and fell to work quickly. With the aid of a long Dyak spear, he dislodged the witchcraft mask from its place on the rafters and caught it in his hand. Then he moved to the rear door and peered out. Back turned to him, a guard stood there like an ebony statue. Beyond was semiblackness, fifty feet of open space and the jungle.

A single powerful blow from the spear dropped the guard without a sound. Henston slid noiselessly to the ground, captured the guard's knife and sped forward. He was halfway to the safety of the bush before he was discovered. A young Dyak stopped short and uttered a surprised cry.

Before the native could give an alarm, the lieutenant was upon him. He seized him by the throat, spun him around, and forced him to the ground. Then, while the Dyak gasped and struggled, Henston slowly tightened the pressure of his hands. For two minutes they fought silently. The grip finally told. The native moaned and fell backward. Henston, retrieving the witchcraft mask, passed safely into the underbrush.

He circled to the river. At the wharf he stared out upon twenty large prahus, craft which had carried distant Kenyahs, brought by the drums. Moving with the utmost caution, Henston selected a small dugout for himself. At the stern of this with a length of rattan he fastened one of the prahus. Then silently he paddled out into the river.

Through the blackness for twenty minutes Henston kept the two boats moving at a furious pace. This time he headed upstream in the opposite direction from his destination at Long Iram.

And now the lieutenant did a strange thing. Making sure the two boats would not drift off, he pushed his way through the growth with the aid of his pocket flash. And presently he found what he was looking for—a small Palapak tree, held in awe by some Dyaks because of their practice of burying their dead in the hollow trunk. He reached upward, seized several lower branches and broke them off. Next he ripped free a ten-foot piece of stout vine. On the ground he groped back and forth until he found several lengths of dried root.

At the shore again he propped the grinning mask in the exact center of the prahu and fastened one of the longer branches perpendicular to the prow. With flying fingers he peeled off the leaves from the vine and stretched it like a clothesline from branch to mask. At six-inch intervals along the vine he hung a series of twelve sticks, branches from the Palapak tree.

"Twelve sticks, twelve days," he said aloud. "I wonder if it will work."

As a final procedure he mounted the broken roots along the prahu's gunwales and ignited them. The Dyak boat was now a lurid thing, the flaming torches giving off a weird light that spread far over the water.

He braced himself in the ooze of the shore and shoved the prahu far out into the river. For a moment it floated idly. Then it swung into the current and began to drift downstream.

In a few minutes the lieutenant, lunging on the paddle of his own dugout, had passed it. The prahu became a diffused ghostlike radiance far behind. Henston kept well into the reeds of the opposite bank when he slipped past Batukelan village. But presently he was safely around a bend, paddling into the darkness.

MORNING found him miles southeastward with his face and arms bleeding from insect bites. He turned inshore at an open space, secured the dugout, and plunged into the bush in search of game.

Henston realized now the value of carrying more than one firearm. The small automatic he always kept concealed under his shirt came into play, and within an hour he returned to the glade with a mouse deer. He prepared the meat, cooked it, and ate.

At intervals he paused to listen. The drums had long since dwindled into the distance. There was no sign of pursuit. And yet his whole escape seemed too easy. He told himself Mueller would never accept the situation as it now stood. There was too much at stake. As for his piece of theatricals last night, Henston could only wonder.

He knew the Dyaks must have sighted the flaming prahu drifting downriver. And he knew that it, together with the prophecy he had made to the chief, would have a startling effect. Twelve sticks of the Palapak tree! Would that mask apparently gliding out of nowhere be sufficient to dampen their frenzy and cause the much-wanted delay?

The meal finished, he lay down and rested for a quarter of an hour. Then, not daring to waste any more time, he climbed into the dugout and headed downriver again.

And then, a little after noon, Henston, sweeping his hand idly to his pocket for a cigarette, made a discovery. His letter was gone. He dropped the paddle and searched his clothes frantically. Automatic, compass, cigarettes—all were there in their usual places, but of the letter there was no sign.

Scowling, he sat there, the dugout adrift, trying to guide his mind backward into the memory of his past actions. He had had the letter at his last camping place, remembered touching it when he reached for matches to start the fire. Since then he had not moved from his position in the canoe. It must be back in the clearing where he had cooked the mouse deer.

For a moment he hesitated. The part of the message pertaining to reënforcements for the garrison could be given orally, of course, and meant little in the light of his recent discoveries. But that section regarding himself and his past record at Long Nawang was different. If he failed to deliver that letter, sooner or later he would be accused of throwing it away. It would mean another case of funk, of mental cowardice, of insubordination. His face hardened. With a thrust of the paddle he whirled

the dugout about and began to retrace his course.

The Mahakam and the forbidding green shores faded slowly out of his vision now. He paddled with his thoughts. Once again he passed the two villages on the east shore. And then, as familiar landmarks near his camp rose up before him, Henston began to realize what he was doing. It was selfishness that had driven him this far back trail. He was returning for a grim sort of personal satisfaction. Deliberately taking chances when the stakes were far higher than himself or his own feelings.

But the camp site was just ahead. It would be mad to turn about now that he had come this far. He beached the dugout and hurried through the reeds.

Carefully, moving in a wide circle, the lieutenant began a systematic search over every inch of the glade. Positive remembrance was with him that he had had the letter subsequent to his shooting of the mouse deer. Then a fern writhed gently in the hot breeze, and he gave a cry of satisfaction. The official envelope lay where it had fallen in a clump of long rip grass.

He strode forward and bent down, hand extended. Halfway he stopped, rigid. Slowly he rose and turned.

AT THE EDGE of the glade beyond the last fringe of reeds a man was approaching. He was tall and hulking with a florid face and huge jowls. He wore a dirty suit of whites. In his right hand, leveled before him, gleamed a revolver.

Henston stiffened. "Mueller!" he said in a low voice.

Ten feet away the man stopped. He shoved his helmet far back on his head, wiped the sweat from his neck and sneered.

"Well, Henston," he said, "you're a damn slippery one. Mighty clever all right, floatin' that boat into the village with the mask and all the rest of it. Twelve sticks from the Palapak tree, hey? A day's delay for each stick. It would give you plenty of time to reach Long Iram and jam up things in general. Henston, that was a smooth idea."

Motionless, the lieutenant made no reply.

"The Dyaks took it at face value, too," continued Mueller. "They've delayed their head-hunting raid until the new moon, and they think you disappeared from their village through the power of the white men's God. You're not as green as I thought, Henston. But you're not goin' to Long Iram. I had another look at that mine while the natives were in the midst of their celebration. It's rich—a fortune for the taking. I want those stones. I'm goin' to get them. And I'm putting the last obstacle out of my way right now."

Henston's face was a block of granite. He stood erect, feet braced far apart. His eyes had narrowed to thin crescents.

Then Mueller belched profanity and swung into action. His right hand jerked at the revolver.

Even as Henston saw the tightening of the muscles on the outlaw's wrist, he threw himself low and lunged forward in a flying tackle. His outstretched hands caught Mueller by the ankles. His head struck him hard in the calf. The two men crashed to the ground.

They rolled over. Back and forth, with the powdery ashes from the fire billowing over them, they struggled. Mueller, gasping, panted a steady stream of curses.

"You snivelin' yellow-bellied puppy!" he snarled. "I'll——"

With a roar of triumph the renegade thrust out his right hand and gripped the revolver he had dropped when he went down. He shoved up on one elbow, swung the gun, and fired point-blank.

Henston felt a searing pain shoot through his left side. For an instant his eyes blurred to the thunder of the report and the stifling fog of powder smoke.

Then blind anger seized him. He shot out both hands, twisted that gun arm with all his strength, forced the weapon free. Unmindful of a brutal kick into his spine, he doubled his arm and ground an infuriated fist into Mueller's jaw. Again and again he struck while a roar pounded in his temple and a mounting heaviness pressed down upon him. And at length Mueller sagged limp and fell back unconscious.

SIX DAYS later a dugout bearing two haggard men turned midstream and slipped to a mooring beside the double jetty at Long Iram, Dutch military headquarters on the Mahakam. The face of the younger of those men, as he threw down his paddle and climbed out, was white and drawn. The shirt and upper part of his duck trousers were stiff and blackened with blood. The other man lay helpless in the bottom of the dugout. His hands and feet were tightly bound with rattan.

Henston helped his prisoner onto the jetty, untied his feet, and with drawn revolver marched him across the fifty feet of open space and through the stockade door. A crowd of young officers and Dutch colonial troopers gathered to meet him. Questions followed curious glances in a steady stream.

Henston smiled wanly, singled out one of the men and delivered Mueller over to him. "Put him in the guardhouse," he said shortly. "And see that he doesn't escape."

Then he paced across the inclosure and entered the little office of the major in charge. For a moment he stood there swaying, half supporting himself against the flat-topped desk. A moment later he saluted and began a short, graphic description of all that had occurred. At intervals he paused to stare down upon the long Manila envelope clutched in his hand.

"Long Nawang needs help, sir," he concluded. "There were six cases of beriberi at the post when I left and as many cases of dysentery and fever. The Kenyahs at Batukelan village will begin their raid at the new moon—five days. It means a general outbreak, extending far into Punan territory. But if troops are rushed downriver it can be prevented."

The major in command at Long Iram was a huge angular man with open eyes, a clipped mustache, and an immaculate suit of whites. He had been in Java and the Celebes, and there were six years behind him in the colonial service of Holland's queen. Now as he sat there on the straight-backed chair, hands opening and closing around the edge of the desk, his face was an expressionless mask.

"Good work, lieutenant!" he said. "That trick of yours to delay the raid was worthy of a man of far more experience. As for Mueller, we've suspected him for a long time. Information came through only to-day that he's wanted for murder under another name in Makassar and for a lot of other crimes in every port south of Sandakan. The men will go upriver in an hour."

Henston nodded. Then he drew himself up slowly and handed across his letter. His eyes were staring blankly at the farther wall. "And now, sir," he said huskily, "I'm ready for my disranking."

The major shot a keen glance upward as he reached across for the envelope. Quietly, without a word, he slit open the flap and drew out the single sheet of paper inside. He read the message slowly, while a clock on the wall ticked off the passing seconds.

"Lieutenant," he said abruptly, looking up, "how long have you been at Long Nawang?"

"Five months, sir."

"And during those five months you have had but few occasions to be intimate with the garrison's commandant. You have, let us say, known him only from a distance?"

Again Henston nodded, this time a frown of puzzlement crossing his brow.

The major leaned back and selected a white cheroot from a bamboo humidor on the desk. An almost imperceptible glitter had entered his eyes as he struck a match and puffed slowly.

"Let us drop military formality for just a moment, lieutenant. Borneo is a country by itself, and sometimes matters come up which require their own peculiar kind of handling. It so happens that your commandant at Long Nawang is a very shrewd person. Lieutenant, take a look at this letter."

Slowly Henston picked up the white paper from the desk and began to read. For a moment his eyes fell upon only detailed matters, conditions at the garrison, the request for reënforcements. Then he saw a single paragraph at the bottom containing his name.

"—and am sending this letter by a Lieutenant Henston, a newcomer to Long Nawang, as you know, whom I understand has been away from Bandjermasin only a short time. The boy had the usual case of nerves brought about by the damnable solitude and constant danger here at the post, and I am using the usual method of curing it. Let him rest over at Long Iram for a month. Then send him back. He has the makings."

And across the flat-topped desk the major stroked the corners of his clipped mustache, puffed on his cheroot, and smiled.

SUMPITAN

by Carl Jacobi

Hollistan was sneeringly triumphant. "Behold the ogre in person."

IT WAS the thirtieth day into the interior, and the military transport had passed the halfway point, the abandoned *kampong* of Pelaban. Captain Van Rudin, squatting in the first of the three *prahus,* trained his gaze beyond the Dyak paddlers into the glaring river ahead. They should be sighting Renburg's dugout any moment now.

Van Rudin's spirits had been dropping steadily since he left the coast. Another grueling month and he would be back at Long Nawang, that most isolated of outposts, where for two years he must serve as commanding officer over a varied assortment of white and native troopers.

Mail would be delivered once every four months—if rain, fever, river tribes, or a thousand other obstacles did not prevent succeeding transports from passing. And monotony, loneliness would be the order of the day.

Van Rudin sighed, twisted his

32

cramped legs and glanced over his shoulder. In the *prahu* following, a few rods behind, a second white man sat high on an improvised stern thwart, a long tubular shaft across his knees. His dark, angular face was turned toward the passing shore.

Queer person, Boyer. Junior lieutenant, new to Borneo and the Royal Netherlands Indies army, he had changed after his first real day into the jungle. He had lost his smile and become strangely quiet. In Tandjong-Selor the country had fascinated him. He had bought *parangs, krisses,* weavings, native gimcrackery of all kinds, including a Sumpitan blowpipe and a basket of darts.

It was the blowpipe he held now, had held most of the wearisome trek upriver. Van Rudin frowned as he slid a cheroot between his lips and watched. Unaware of the scrutiny, Boyer sat motionless, staring out over the water.

Abruptly a floating log came into view. Boyer stiffened. With a quick movement he brought the blowpipe to his lips, puffed out his cheeks, and squinted down the shaft. A sharp *thwack* sounded as his breath expelled the dart outward. A thin shadow slipped through the air, struck the log with a dull thud.

The log drifted quietly a moment, then became a thing of sluggish life. Gaping jaws appeared lazily above the water. A twenty-foot saurian body stirred up a circle of ripples. Then like a miniature U-boat, it sank below the surface.

Van Rudin turned back, let smoke drift up from his lips. Shooting at crocodiles with a rifle or revolver would have been dangerous and foolhardy, but even with a blowpipe the act went deeper than just casual pastime. Undoubtedly something was troubling Boyer. The many petty fears perhaps, instilled by the jungle, had found in him a victim, and the lieutenant was trying hard to conceal his feelings.

But where was Renburg? According to custom, the retiring Long Nawang officer was to have met his successor officially at Pelaban village. There they were to have spent a night together, before parting. Yet at Pelaban the transport had found only a line of deserted huts, a weed-choked rice paddy.

Far ahead, where the winding Kayan River made a sharp turn to the east, a single, brownish blot appeared, midway between the thick shores.

Van Rudin relaxed as he saw it, shouted an order to his six Dyaks. "Pull," he said in Malay. "Full speed ahead."

The *prahu* leaped forward. Behind, in the second boat, Lieutenant Boyer, hearing the order, repeated it to his own rowers. Paddles of the three craft churned water.

THE BROWNISH BLOT grew nearer. Van Rudin slipped his binoculars from the case at his belt, placed them to his eyes and looked long and intently. For a moment his bronzed face was expressionless. Then his eyes shut to crescents, and his lips changed to a grim line.

"Boyer," he called over his shoulder, "there's something wrong. That's Renburg's dugout, but there are no paddlers, and it's drifting. Watch yourself."

He cased the glasses, drew out his heavy service revolver. Barely three hundred yards separated them from the oncoming dugout now, but the sun glinting on the water made it hard to see.

And then, five minutes later, Van Rudin stared overside into the captive canoe and felt his hands grow suddenly cold. He choked, swallowed hard.

Sprawled full length under the *kajang* thatch cabin lay the familiar figure of Captain Renburg. His nailed, linen-topped shoes were stuck curiously upward, one over the other. His solar topee, puggree cloth ripped to shreds, half covered his round, bland face. Protruding from the abdomen was a black-handled knife.

Vaguely Van Rudin was aware of the second *prahu* thumping alongside, of Boyer's startled exclamation, of the jabbering Dyaks. Something hot and dry gathered in the captain's throat. Fighting for control, he spoke quietly: "Lieutenant, lash the dugout to your boat and head for the right bank. Move fast. This may be an ambush."

The boats turned midstream. At the east shore, Van Rudin leaped out onto a bar of sand, cast a quick, penetrating glance at the jungle wall. No foreign sound broke the silence. Lowering his revolver, he silently knelt over the dead officer and drew the knife from the body.

"What do you make of it, sir?" Boyer asked, stepping forward.

Van Rudin turned the knife over and over in his hands. "A Kenyah *parang*," he said softly, without looking up. "Or rather, the *parang* of one particular Kenyah. The dugout has been drifting a long way."

He stood silent a moment, gnawing his lips. "Renburg," he continued, "was murdered by Naga Kai. The paddlers fled at the first sign of danger. Naga Kai is chief of the Kenyah village nearest the Long Nawang garrison. I'm afraid this means trouble."

"But"—Boyer was opening and closing his fists—"but I don't understand. How——"

"These marks," Van Rudin said, pointing to the knife handle. "It's Kenyah carving. The wavering line represents a python, which is Naga Kai's private symbol. I happen to have seen this knife before—four years ago."

"Four——"

"When I was at Long Nawang as junior officer. It's Naga Kai's without a doubt. Ever since the garrison was elected in his district, he's hated it, sworn to kill every white man stationed there."

Boyer forced his eyes back to the contorted form in the dugout. "Why," he asked slowly, "didn't he take the head?"

In the shade of his sun helmet, Van Rudin's eyes glittered coldly. "Naga Kai was too clever for that," he replied. "Head-hunting—white head-hunting—is pretty much an open and shut case, you know. Naga Kai thought he wouldn't be traced this way. But he wasn't clever enough to think any one would recognize his knife."

AN HOUR LATER the two white men, grim and quiet now, climbed into their loaded *prahus,* and the transport moved upriver again. Behind, on a higher knoll, away from the river shore, a low mound and a wooden cross marked the point where tragedy had brought its spell of gloom.

And twenty-nine uneventful days after that the transport swung to a mooring at the garrison jetty of Long Nawang. Van Rudin flipped a mechanical salute to the flag, hanging like a limp dishcloth over the blockhouse, paced into the stockade. He was met by the senior lieutenant in temporary command, whose name was Hollistan. Hollistan, a thin-lipped, swarthy man, clicked his heels together, acknowledged the introduction to Boyer and began to talk aimlessly while Van Rudin gave the post a perfunctory inspection.

Inspection over, the three men went into the officers' bungalow. The senior lieutenant slumped wearily into a fan-backed chair.

"Two more transports, and it's my turn to leave." he said thickly. "Eighteen months I've been in this damned hole. Oh. I know you served here once before, Van Rudin, but it was different

Deserting? No, a man didn't run away from Long Nawang—and lived.

then. The Mahakam was more navigable, and things happened. Now the natives sleep and——"

Van Rudin placed his hand flat on the *nibong* table. "You've had no trouble with Naga Kai?" he demanded abruptly.

Hollistan took a cigarette from a pocket case, lighted it and shook his head. "Not a bit. Why?"

"Because"—the words came slowly —"that miserable rat murdered your former superior officer on his way downriver."

The cold explanation fell like a bombshell. Hollistan jerked back in his chair, paled, gripped the table edge. "Renburg—murdered!" he whispered. "And by Naga! Are you sure?"

Van Rudin nodded. "Positive. I have his knife, and that's all the evidence I need. Renburg's Dyak paddlers were probably killed, too, before they could return to Long Nawang and report the attack."

"But only a few days—— Lord, it doesn't seem possible."

"Naga Kai must be brought in, given a trial," Van Rudin continued. "If we prove him guilty, the death penalty must be invoked. Bringing him in will be a one-man job. I'm assigning it to Lieutenant Boyer here. Think you can do it, Boyer?"

Boyer placed his finger tips together. He looked at the captain, then at Hollistan. "I'll try," he said shortly.

"It's got to be done at once," Van

Rudin went on. "Otherwise there'd be open hell here before the next monsoon. From what I remember of Naga Kai, this is the spark he's been waiting for."

NEXT MORNING Lieutenant Boyer left Long Nawang for the downriver *kampong*. Clad in soft leather mosquito boots, with a holstered revolver at his belt, he poled slowly out into the stream. For six hours the post waited. Then, late in the afternoon, Boyer returned—alone.

Captain Van Rudin met him on the bungalow veranda, wiped the sweat from his neck and scowled. Sultry heat was not aiding his temperament at that moment.

"Well?" he demanded.

Boyer made no reply for an instant. He seemed searching for words.

"Naga Kai," said Van Rudin sarcastically. "You were sent to bring him here, unless you've forgotten. Where is he?"

"I don't know, sir. I——"

"Did you go to the *kampong*? Damn it, man, talk!"

"No, sir, I didn't exactly. I went as far as the village outskirts. I waited there in the reeds a long time. Then two Dyaks saw me, warned me to get out. There was some kind of a ceremony going on. I believe it's impossible to even see Naga Kai at the present time."

Van Rudin stared, then clenched his

fists. What did Bandjermasin headquarters mean, sending a numskull kid to the garrison? Ceremony in the village. Of course there'd be a ceremony. A big celebration probably, in honor of the fact that one of the hated white *tuans* was no more.

But that shouldn't have prevented Boyer from entering the *kampong* as a white soldier should enter, and demanding the chief's presence at Long Nawang. Even this far inland, Dutch law was respected, and the reply at the worst could only have been a refusal. Boyer was a cowardly fool!

Van Rudin said as much and marched angrily into the bungalow. Half an hour later, tilted back in a wicker chair, he looked out the window with a troubled frown. Before him, in the compound, Boyer stood under a glaring sun, a long shaft to his mouth. At intervals he blew through it, aiming toward the stockade wall.

Van Rudin swore and curled his lip. What could you do with a man who thought more of target practice with a Sumpitan blowpipe than anything else?

Five diplomatic days were permitted to pass in the hope that Naga Kai would forget the first, bungled attempt. Then the job went to Hollistan. And exactly five hours after leaving the post Hollistan returned, all smiles, all swagger, prodding his prisoner into the bungalow before him.

He stopped over the threshold, nodded at Boyer three feet away. "Behold the ogre in person," he sneered. "Better hide, soldier; you might get hurt."

Boyer flushed, said nothing. The trial began immediately with a photograph of Captain Renburg exhibited and the fatal *parang* offered in evidence. Dyak-fashion, Naga Kai proudly, stoically admitted the knife to be his property.

There was much talk in Malay. Dutch law was translated and explained, the rule of a life for a life stressed.

In the end Van Rudin pronounced the inevitable death sentence and, following military routine, set the execution for a week hence.

Naga Kai was led away to an inner room, and Boyer and Hollistan, an unspoken barrier between them, strolled out onto the veranda. There the senior lieutenant picked up a rifle from the table and began to polish the barrel with an oily rag. Leaning lightly against the veranda rail, he stared out into the hot air that shimmered over the compound.

"After all," he said presently, "after all, Boyer, this isn't a summer hotel, you know. You can't deliberately funk a piece of work and then forget about it. It's bad for the other men and——"

Boyer whirled, eyes hardening. "What do you mean?" he demanded.

"The trip to the *kampong*," Hollistan went on easily, a slight smile on his lips. "Practically nothing but a routine job. If you'd had any nerve you wouldn't have come back here empty-handed. I——"

With set lips Boyer strode forward, seized Hollistan by the shoulder, jerked him around.

"Stow that," he said, staring deliberately into the other's face. "When I want your opinions, I'll ask for them."

Hollistan answered the gaze a brief instant. Then with a snarl, his hands came up, struck out, a sweeping cut to the face. Boyer hesitated, surprised, answered with two blows to the chest. It was give and take in rapid succession, but it ended abruptly. The senior lieutenant sucked in his breath, doubled back his right arm and sent a heavy fist smashing forward. Boyer coughed, swayed dizzily, slid to the floor.

"Try that again," Hollistan snarled, "and you'll wish you hadn't."

AFTER THAT, although he seemed to have forgotten the incident, Boyer stayed by himself, appearing with Van

Rudin, Hollistan and the medical officer only at mess. He did his routine work silently and thoroughly.

The platoon of men under his direct command obeyed his orders to the letter, not only because of his crisp manner in giving them, but because they liked him, appreciated his quiet familiarity when they were at ease. But in his free time Boyer stood before the stockade wall, apparently oblivious to the mounting heat, blowing darts into the weathered piles.

Tension settled over the post. Van Rudin knew, and the men knew, that executing a kapala as popular as Naga Kai would not proceed without trouble. The tension increased until the day before the scheduled execution. Then suddenly, explosively, it reached a head.

Hollistan disappeared!

At first, Van Rudin, when the information was brought to him, thought an accident of some sort must have occurred. The senior lieutenant had gone out into the jungle with a high-powered express rifle and a double-barreled 450. He was after tiger. But tiger, plentiful as they were that season, were not responsible for his disappearance.

At dusk, two warriors from Naga Kai's village appeared at the stockade gate and gave their ultimatum. The white tuan who called himself Holishtan, by the grace of various gods, was now a prisoner in their kampong. Release Naga Kai and Tuan Holish-tan would be released. Kill Naga Kai, and the head of Tuan Holish-tan would be mounted on a bamboo pole. The two warriors departed.

Van Rudin drank too much that night and spent the still hours pacing the veranda. The whole affair, which should have been handled in a simple thrust-for-thrust manner, had now enlarged to a nasty problem.

It went a good deal farther than the two men involved. Release of Naga Kai would be a death ticket for the post, would erase every vestige of sahib prestige it held over the Dyaks. It had taken long, arduous years and much bloodshed to raise Long Nawang to its present standing of overlord of the Apo Kayan onderafdeeling. Did the life of one officer balance or overbalance that history?

For six hours Van Rudin lived a life of misery. He thought of Hollistan waiting, a prisoner in the kampong. He thought of Renburg and the exactness with which he had always upheld Dutch military law. He thought of the official report which eventually must be sent to Bandjermasin. It would not be a pretty document, that report.

In the end Van Rudin made his decision. The execution would proceed!

Yet he realized only too well what it meant to Hollistan. They might besiege the kampong, deploy through the reeds with machine guns, mow the Dyaks down—it would not save the life of the senior lieutenant. He would be taken deep into the jungle, thrust to his neck in poisonous marsh water and left a victim of the leeches.

VAN RUDIN, however, was unprepared for Boyer's reaction, when, rather coldly, the captain acquainted him with what was to happen. Boyer studied the end of his cigarette a moment, dropped it into an ash tray and said:

"If you don't mind, sir, I'm not in favor with your plans. It might be well to release Naga Kai, and then——"

"Release him!"

"Exactly, sir. Now I have an idea which——"

"Lieutenant"—Van Rudin's eyes narrowed to dangerous slits—"I happen to be in command here. Unless things have changed while I was away, the second lieutenant of the garrison does not advise his superior officer."

"But——"

"That is all, lieutenant. There are four machine guns mounted on the wall of the mess room. See that they are cleaned, oiled, and in firing condition."

Execution was scheduled for dawn. With full formality, Naga Kai was to face a firing squad of five coast-Dyak rifles. The coast Dyaks, having no love for their Kenyah brothers, would be indifferent. But the event was never destined to take place.

Next morning Van Rudin found himself faced by an excited orderly. Following the orderly down the corridor, the commanding officer stopped abruptly, burst into a stream of profanity.

The door to Naga Kai's prison chamber stood open. Its interior was empty. Beyond, at the farther window, stout bamboo bars, hacked in two, showed the method and way of escape. Once outside the bungalow, Naga Kai had only to cross the compound, slip past a drowsing sentry and scale the stockade walls.

Yet—and Van Rudin frowned slowly as the thought rushed to him—Naga Kai had no knife! All his possessions, save his bark loin cloth, had been con-

Then Boyer found an opening. His fist met Naga Kai's jaw in full swing.

fiscated before he was locked in the room. Was it possible a native had entered the post and aided the escape? Or even worse, but with less reason, had one of the men played treachery? Van Rudin tried the impossible immediately. He sent a Dyak soldier to the village with a bluffing demand that Hollistan be released at once or the "thunder sticks" of the post would blow the *kampong* to pieces. There was in his mind a vague hope that freedom of the chief would appease the natives and be considered fair exchange for the senior lieutenant.

Four hours later the Dyak staggered back, a hideous *parang* wound in his side. In the language of the Kenyahs, the answer was a decisive negative.

With the passing time, Van Rudin's rage passed. He stood on the veranda, staring out into the green jungle. He realized that the relentless march of events must be climaxed in one thing only—war. He must attack the village —even though such an attack might lead to an uprising throughout all Apo Kayan. He must kill Naga Kai, return Long Nawang to its proper and necessary prestige and try to save Hollistan. Heavily he gave orders for preparation. They would go downriver at dawn.

Feeling strangely alone and depressed, the captain went to his own room. He drank half a glass of Makassar rum, spent the next hour writing a detailed report of all that had happened. Later, if all went well, that report could be changed—supplemented.

THE HOURS dragged by. It was still early when Van Rudin undressed and stretched out on the bed. Outside the window he heard the occasional murmur of voices: Dyak soldiers discussing the situation in excited Malay.

Then quiet settled over the post, and Van Rudin's eyes drooped in sleep. The last sound that drifted to him was a peculiar hollow, hissing sound, repeated at regular intervals. Boyer, the crazy idiot, was practicing with his blowpipe again!

But at three o'clock, by the radium dial on the table, Van Rudin woke abruptly. He pushed aside the mosquito netting, groped to his feet. For an instant he stood there, listening. Then, dressing quickly, he seized his revolver and moved toward the room's latticed door.

Outside, in the corridor, footsteps padded slowly, moving toward the main room of the bungalow. They slowed as they came abreast of Van Rudin's room. Restrained breathing pulsed through the air. The footsteps passed on, continued in a slow diminuendo.

Van Rudin slipped his door open and followed. Reaching the center room, he was just in time to see a shadowy figure step out onto the veranda. The figure stopped, looked around cautiously.

Van Rudin stared at the gloom-outlined face and bit his lips to suppress an exclamation. What possible reason could Lieutenant Boyer have for skulking about in the dark, fully dressed, at this hour? Why was he moving off the veranda across the compound in the opposite direction from the stockade gate?

Making no sound, Van Rudin followed. A chill wind blew under a starlit sky. Somewhere far off a knocking-on-the-ice bird voiced its queer call. Then, abruptly, the far wall of the stockade loomed in the darkness. Boyer lifted himself upward, balanced a moment on the top, and disappeared. There was no sign of notice from the sentry posted at the gate. Without hesitation, Van Rudin braced his legs against the wooden supports, climbed, and dropped lightly on the other side after the lieutenant.

Forty feet ahead now, Boyer was circling the post, heading for the trail that led to the river jetty. Reaching the shore, he quickly unlashed the moorings of a small dugout, leaped in and paddled out into the river. Behind the bole of a Palapak tree, Van Rudin stared with puzzled eyes.

Deserting? But no, a man didn't run away from Long Nawang. He might curse the ill fortune that had brought him to the garrison, but he stayed on, knowing well that an attempt to reach the coast alone would be futile.

For five long minutes Van Rudin stood there. Then he stepped into a second dugout, freed it and deliberately continued his pursuit.

For an hour he paddled swiftly down the black river. But not until that hour had passed did he realize what it all meant. Then he stiffened, sat bolt upright, swallowed hard. Boyer was heading for Naga Kai's *kampong*.

Another hour, and ahead of him he saw the dugout lose itself in the deeper shadows of the inky shore. A moment later it thumped against the village log landing. Van Rudin steered his own canoe to the bank a hundred feet away, secured it to an overhanging branch and pushed into the bush.

THE VILLAGE lay back from the river, up on higher ground. As he fought his way toward it, a crimson glare rose up in the patches of sky visible through the trees. The glare increased. A drum began to beat.

Van Rudin penetrated a last fringe of trees and dropped abruptly in a clump of *lallang* grass!

The wide-open space before him was a blaze of illumination. The huge long-house-on-stilts and smaller *nipa* huts were outlined by three huge fires. Excited Dyaks jammed the clearing, milled about two central figures. Van Rudin stared at those two figures and left his jaw drop slowly. They were Boyer and Naga Kai!

Even as the captain mechanically slipped his service revolver from its side

holster and wormed a few inches closer, a hush dropped over the village. Then the drum began to beat again, louder, faster. More fuel was thrown on the three fires. Boyer, Naga Kai spoke to each other, nodded, began to walk slowly apart.

With counted steps they paced. At

Junior Lieutenant Boyer, of the Royal Netherlands Indies army.

opposite ends of the village they turned, faced each other. Each held a long, tubular shaft. The surrounding Dyaks pressed forward in a huddled half circle.

Van Rudin, watching it all, found it hard to believe his eyes. He was fairly well-acquainted with most Dyak ceremonies; yet this—— He gripped the revolver tighter, then lowered it. Something told him intervention would be one of the unwisest things he had ever done.

A Dyak warrior, paced forward, handed three palm-rib darts to the junior lieutenant, three to Naga Kai. Two more drums joined in now, following the same rhythm, throbbing through the night.

Suddenly Van Rudin felt a thrill run up his spine. Those shafts Boyer and Naga Kai held were blowpipes—Sumpitan blowpipes. And the queer, fixed stare in their eyes could mean one thing only—a duel. A duel between a white *tuan* and a native *kapala!* It wasn't possible!

But it was possible. Boyer and Naga Kai inserted darts in their weapons. The chief's face was an expressionless mask. Boyer, tense and pale, gripped the blowpipe with an experienced hand.

Then it began. Sumpitans jerked upward. The drums lapsed into silence. There was only the hiss and crackle of the fires.

For an instant Naga Kai crouched motionless, balancing himself on one bent knee. Then he slipped the blowpipe to his lips, took quick aim and expelled his dart outward. With a sharp *thwack* it rushed a messenger of death straight toward the junior lieutenant. Boyer ducked his head to the fraction of a second.

It was the white man's turn now. While his opponent raced to reload, he shot quickly, handling the pipe with the deftness of one long accustomed to its touch. Naga Kai was forced to throw himself face downward to escape the streaking dart.

Once again they fired, each avoiding the projectiles by the smallest margin.

Again they poised motionless, staring at each other, watching every move. Naga Kai edged slightly to the side, farther into the shadows. Swift as light the eight-foot tube leaped to his lips; he blew!

And Boyer leaped—like a cat. In mid-air, as he heaved his body out of danger, he swung the Sumpitan upward. There was a grim smile on his lips and a confident ease in his movement. He fired the last dart.

Forty feet away Naga Kai sought vainly to throw himself out of its path. But the shadows into which he had moved served a disadvantage now, confusing his sight. Something brown and quivering thudded into his shoulder. A hoarse cry came to his lips, a cry of defeat more than pain. Stumbling, he fell.

BOYER threw his blowpipe to the ground, raised one hand high above his head and paced forward into the brighter light of the fires.

"The bargain," he said evenly, "I have won. *Tuan* Hollistan is to be released. Now, at once."

Open-mouthed mutterings were rising from the Dyaks. Back in the shadows Naga Kai staggered to his feet. A stream of blood ran down his naked chest. He wrenched the dart from his shoulder.

"*Tuan* Hollistan," Boyer repeated. "Bring him here as you promised."

Three steps Naga Kai came on, swaying slightly from side to side. Without warning his right hand suddenly jerked down to the tufted scabbard in his loin cloth, came up with a heavy *parang*.

The *kapala* charged. Knife before him, he leaped at Boyer. The lieutenant's left arm jumped upward in protection. His right hand shot out, clutched the chief's oncoming wrist.

They clinched. Face twisted in fury, Naga Kai whipped his knife hand free and clawed for the lieutenant's throat. Back and forth they surged, the onlooking Dyaks howling in excitement, yet making no move toward interference.

Twice Naga Kai sent that hooked knife at Boyer's neck. Twice the lieutenant countered with an upthrust of his guard arm and a quick side step. Then Boyer found an opening. He drew his fist backward and launched out with a trip-hammer blow. It met Naga Kai's jaw in full career. The *kapala's* head snapped backward. He sank to his knees, toppled over and lay still.

Boyer stood over him a moment, rubbing his knuckles. He waited, as if expecting a renewal of the attack. Then, breathing hard, he drew out his revolver and leveled it at the gaping Dyaks before him.

"Bring Hollistan here," he said in Malay. "And move fast!"

IN the officers' bungalow at Long Nawang next morning, Van Rudin faced his two lieutenants across the mess table. For a quarter of an hour the commanding officer had been studying Boyer closely. Both he and Hollistan were strangely quiet.

"I don't quite see," Van Rudin said at length, "why you didn't go to the *kampong* the first trip instead of making it necessary for me to send Hollistan. It would have been far easier and——"

Boyer ran his finger across the table edge. The lids of his eyes closed, opened again. "I wasn't really myself then, I guess," he said slowly. "The jungle, the country, must have gotten me. And when I saw that ceremony in the village, found out that a funeral was being held for one of Naga Kai's wives who had died—well I——"

"When you found what?"

Boyer smiled sheepishly. "One of Naga Kai's wives," he repeated. "She'd died that day, and I was told no white man could enter the *kampong* at the time. When Hollistan went five days later, it was all over, I suppose. Then, after Hollistan was captured, it oc-

curred to me a duel with Naga Kai would be the only way to free him. Naga Kai was anxious to win back the respect of his tribe. The darts weren't poisoned, of course. But he didn't play fair and——"

Van Rudin wasn't listening. A single thought whirled in his brain. Funeral in the village—death of one of the chief's wives—— Good Lord, and he had ridiculed Boyer. No wonder the junior lieutenant had failed the first trip to the *kampong*. No wonder he had come back empty-handed. The funeral taboo—— There wasn't a white man from here to Samarinda—who knew—who would dare to even go near a Kenyah village at a time like that. It meant suicide.

Gravely the commanding officer opened a humidor and selected a cheroot. The affair was settled. Naga Kai from now on would be a *kapala* without a tribe, an outcast spurned by his people.

Five minutes before, another item had troubled the captain. Who had given Naga Kai the knife which had enabled him to saw his way free from his prison chamber?

But as far as Van Rudin was concerned, that question would remain unasked. Military discipline, he told himself with a slight smile, had its limits.

By
Carl Jacobi

It was hard to escape

Death On Tin Can

—as these crooks found out!

HARMON awoke abruptly as the clock on the bungalow wall struck twelve. Rigid, he lay motionless on the cot, listening. There was no sound save the wind moaning through the palms and the distant throb of the breakers on the island's lower shore.

He slid to his feet, reached for the automatic under his pillow and moved quietly to the door. Before him, the veranda and the clearing beyond lay silent and empty in the moonlight.

Something was wrong. He knew it, felt it with every nerve of his body.

He opened the screen door, paced barefoot down the gravel path to the edge of the cliff that marked the open end of the clearing. Tall and lean, he stood there, gazing down upon the silvery beach.

No lights showed in the bamboo shack below him. There was only the roar of the surf.

Yet since late afternoon, when the *Fortuna* had steamed away after discharging three passengers on the island, he had been uneasy. The three passengers—Catlett, Wicks and Singleton—had appeared genial enough. But beneath their veneer of pleasantry a sinister undertone had been apparent.

"Are you the resident?" Catlett had asked as he stepped off the jetty. And when Harmon had replied that he was merely the acting assistant in the chief magistrate's absence, the man had smiled blandly and proceeded to explain.

He and his companions were survey men for the South Pacific Cable Co. They had come here to Niuafou to look over the island as a possible site for a relay station for a new cable line to connect Sidney with Samoa and points west. They had a letter from the commissioner-governor in Suva, requesting every courtesy be extended them.

"But this is Tin Can Island," Harmon had objected. "There won't be another ship for six months."

"Don't worry about that," Catlett had replied. "A company boat from Suva will pick us up day after to-morrow."

And an hour later the *Fortuna,* with a farewell blast, had put out to sea.

IN the moonlight now, a grim smile twisted Harmon's lips. Tin Can Island! The name, which had almost superseded the native one, came from an odd array of facts. Six months of the year, during the southwest trades, the monthly inter-island steamer managed to scrape its way through the reefs, into the little

lagoon. But during the remaining six months, landing was impossible. The steamer stood off in deep water then, dropped mail in a sealed can, while two natives swam out and pushed it to shore.

With the resident laid up with fever in Apia and with the copra plantation temporarily closed down, Harmon had been the lone white man on the island. The arrival of the three cable men changed everything.

His suspicions had been aroused when, just at sundown, he had seen the trio saunter down to the lagoon and examine his diving gear.

That diving gear, plus the piles of pure white shell and the little dory drawn up on the sand, spoke volumes. It told any one who could read the signs that Harmon had found a paying proposition beneath the blue water of the lagoon. Pearls! For a year he had been working an almost virgin bed.

Suddenly Harmon tensed. A twig snapped loudly somewhere in the wall of undergrowth at his side. He whirled, lifted the revolver.

Twenty feet away a fern frond at the edge of the clearing moved significantly. And in the stillness, stealthy footsteps sounded. Eyes hard, Harmon moved forward cautiously.

He had almost reached the jungle wall when it happened. A rush of feet came from behind, and in a flash he realized he had been tricked.

He spun about to meet a heavy figure charging upon him. The revolver was knocked from his hand. A hard fist thudded into his jaw. Frantically he fought back, brought his long arms into play. He closed in, pumped his fists in and out.

But only for a moment. Something hard and heavy cracked down on his skull. A burst of flame and colored lights swirled in his vision. In a pit of blackness he felt himself falling——

WHEN he opened his eyes he was lying on the cot in his bungalow. The carbide lamp suspended from the ceiling had been lit and, by the table, slumped back in a chair, sat Catlett.

Harmon's head ached savagely. Dried blood had caked on his face. He eased himself up on one shoulder, saw that his wrists and ankles were securely bound.

Catlett slid a cheroot between thin lips and nodded quietly.

"Take it easy, Mr. Harmon," he said.

Harmon glanced across the room at the clock, saw that an hour had passed since he had been knocked out. Bitterness at his lack of caution engulfed him.

"What's the idea?" he demanded.

"The idea"—Catlett's button eyes glinted with triumph—"is quite simple. Temporarily you are our prisoner. Later, after you agree to a few demands, you will have your freedom."

The man got up, helped himself to a whisky bottle and a glass on a shelf and returned to his chair.

"I suppose you know by now," he said, "that we have nothing to do with a cable company. Our business is pearls, the same as your own."

He poured himself a peg of whisky and sipped it slowly.

"Unfortunately, as you know, most good fisheries have been taken over. They are either government or company-contract restricted. A virgin bed such as you evidently have been working here on Niuafou is difficult to find."

Harmon's fists clenched. "What makes you so sure there is a virgin bed?"

Catlett smiled. "Because, Mr. Harmon, a month or so ago you sent to Pago Pago for a new air hose for your diving suit. Now consider. Why would a man send to the American colony in Samoa for something it would be quicker and far easier for him to obtain in Suva? Because he is an American and wishes to use home prod-

ucts? Ah, no, I reason. Because he has found something he is anxious others in these waters will know nothing about." He tapped the ash from his cheroot. "You follow me?"

The sardonic suavity of the speech cut into Harmon like a knife. "And what do you plan to do," he said bitterly, "poach?"

For answer, Catlett opened the drawer of the table and took out a small tin box. "Poaching infers leased fisheries. The lagoon here is open to any one who cares to work it.

"We are taking off your hands the pearls you have already gathered," Catletl went on, pointing to the box. "You are selling them to us for fifty dollars. I have the money and a bill of sale. You will sign it, please."

"Fifty dollars!" Harmon cried. "You're crazy! Those pearls are worth at least——"

"I know perfectly well what they are worth. Nevertheless, you are selling them to me at that price."

Catlett got up and advanced to the cot with a paper and a fountain pen.

Deliberately Harmon studied him. Catlett was small, almost feminine in stature. His hands were soft and smooth, with tapering fingers. But in spite of the casual smile, there lurked in those dark eyes a gleam of savage cruelty.

"Are you going to sign?"

"I don't think I will." Harmon's lean face set defiantly.

The little man's smile vanished as his lips quivered with slow-mounting rage. He slid a revolver from his pocket, fingered it lightly, suddenly leveled it at the prone man and fired point-blank.

The shot was deafening in the room. The slug, as it tore through the flesh of Harmon's left arm, sent a stab of agony through his body.

"You will sign, Mr. Harmon," Catlett said, his suavity returning. "If you do not——"

FURTHER resistance was foolhardy. Silently, lips tight with pain, Harmon took the pen and scrawled his name at the bottom of the paper. Then, utterly done in, he fell back. With a nod, Catlett folded the sheet, placed it in his pocket and paced out on the veranda.

A moment later the screen door banged and he returned with his two companions: Wicks was a heavy-set, florid-faced man with a diagonal scar running across his left cheek. Singleton, stiff in carriage, yet loose-mouthed, had all the earmarks of a cashiered British naval officer.

"All set?" Wicks asked.

Catlett nodded. "Everything is ready," he said. "You, Singleton, will leave at once for the native village on the other side of the island. You will recruit as many natives as you can. If they have canoes, see that they bring those.

"Wicks, your job is to take care of our foolish friend here, Mr. Harmon. Wash and bandage his wound and——"

"What for?" Wicks, an ugly grin on his face, strode forward and planted a kick in Harmon's side. "Stick a knife in his gizzard, that's my way."

"I said you will bandage his wound," Catlett snapped. "There will be no murder for the present. Later, if it is necessary, it will be done in a complete and thorough manner."

The voices and the light faded for Harmon after that. He fought to remain conscious until he felt the searing pain as Wicks poured iodine on his arm. Then for a second he slumped back into oblivion.

HE awoke with the late morning sun in his eyes. For an instant he lay there, all the events of the night before vague in his memory like a wild dream. The ropes that had bound him lay on the floor, and the bungalow was empty.

Weakly he stumbled to his feet, groped across the room to the cabinet in the far corner. As he had expected, the two rifles and pistol he kept there were gone. Gone, too, was his hunting knife and even the native spear which had been mounted on the wall.

Harmon swayed, inhaled deeply to force the dizziness from his head. Then he went out and made his way haltingly down the path to the cliff edge.

His eyes blinked as he surveyed the scene below him.

The space in front of the beach shack, which Harmon had told the cable men they could take over during their stay on the island, was ablaze with activity. Fully twenty natives squatted on the sand, opening and casting aside shells. Another group was carrying shell from the edge of the lagoon to the shack. And out on the lagoon he could see Wicks and Singleton in his dory. At intervals a brown head appeared on the water, and a pair of arms emptied a dripping reed basket into the boat.

Harmon's nails dug into his palms. Catlett was putting his plans into action, "raiding" the lagoon. And in doing so he was destroying all Harmon's hopes for the future. Harmon had employed no native help in his diving. He had preferred to dive alone with only Natoa, his houseboy, to handle the pump and lines of his scaphander. In that way he could select shell of mature growth without spoiling the potential value of the bed.

Heavily he turned, went back to the bungalow. In the kitchen he made a breakfast, forced himself to eat. His wounded left arm felt sore and numb, but it was well bandaged, and he did not touch it. The meal over, he changed painfully from pajamas to duck trousers and shirt, and went out once more.

FIVE minutes later he stood before Catlett in front of the beach shack.

The dark man smiled an oily smile. "Been waitin' for you to come around," he said. "You start workin' right away."

"Catlett," Harmon said quietly, "you've got the upper hand now. But in a month the regular mail packet will come and——"

Catlett laughed. "I know all about the mail packet," he sneered. "It can't land. It stands off beyond the reefs and waits for a couple of swimmers to take away or bring out the mail. There won't be any outgoing mail.

"Get into that dugout," he snapped. "Take two native divers and see that they bring up plenty of shell. Move, damn you!"

As he moved slowly down the beach, Harmon singled out a brown figure before him, and he received one more shock. Natoa, his houseboy, was among those carrying shell to the shack. Promised rewards no doubt had blinded his sense of loyalty.

For six hours Harmon sat in the blistering dugout while alternate sets of divers went down to bring up shell. The sun was low in the west when Catlett signaled to halt work. On shore he strode up to Harmon, surveyed him sardonically.

"I see you know how to obey orders, Mr. Harmon. From now on you will spend each night in your bungalow as usual. But native guards will be posted to see that you do not leave. We, of course, will take over the resident's house."

Harmon nodded. "How about the resident's pets?" he said.

"His pets?"

"Exactly. The resident has quite a number of them: a yellow-bellied parakeet, a monkey, some pigeons, and a couple of tame flamingos. They have to be fed and——"

Catlett ripped out an oath. "Do you expect me to be nursemaid for a bunch of animals?" Then his eyes narrowed, and his voice quieted abruptly. "They will be fed," he said. "When the steamer comes there must be no suspicion of anything wrong."

THREE hours later Harmon sat on his bungalow veranda, surrounded by night darkness. A native guard squatted on the step just outside the door. Another, he knew, lurked not far from the entrance in the rear.

"Boxed up like a squirrel in a cage," he muttered. "And there'll be six more months of it."

Faintly, on the wind, he could hear loud voices and the discordant jangle of the phonograph in the resident's house. Catlett and his companions evidently had discovered the resident's liquor store and were making the most of it.

Bitterly Harmon sucked his pipe. There didn't seem to see a single way out. Moving under a carefully arranged plan, the three fake cable men had thought of everything.

Harmon pulled the pipe from his lips, sat rigid. He thought a moment, then forced a yawn, got up and went inside. The native guard turned sleepily, leaned back against the step.

In the main room Harmon waited ten minutes by his watch; then he extinguished the lights and threw himself heavily on the cot. The springs squeaked.

But an instant later he had slid soundlessly to his feet and was striding across the dark room to the window on the far wall. Here he drew a knife from his pocket and waited, listening. Only the distant sounds of the surf broke the stillness. Carefully he lifted the knife, began cutting away the mosquito screening.

The job done, he squirmed through, darted across the open space and entered the jungle without being seen.

Moving in a wide circle, he headed through the underbrush toward the house of the resident. Twice, at intervals, he stopped to peer into the thick gloom behind. But there was no sign of pursuit.

His clothing was torn, and his body was wet with sweat when he finally reached his goal. Emerging from the jungle into the clearing that surrounded the resident's quarters, he stared at the house, ablaze with lights, and considered.

Catlett, in his efficient cunning, had doubtless posted guards here, too. But no one would expect his entering from the fenced-in garden to the rear.

Hugging the wall of growth, he crept around the side of the house, then darted forward to the white picket fence and vaulted over it. Two shadows on stilts leaped to startled life.

"Steady!" Harmon whispered, calling out to the two flamingos. "Steady!"

The aroma of hibiscus filled his nostrils. He edged around the neatly plotted flower beds, closed in on the house. A pigeon cooed softly. Another flapped its wings.

And then suddenly he froze in his tracks. Whirling, he saw a familiar figure before him. An upraised revolver glinted in the half light.

"Mr. Harmon," Catlett said thickly, "you are most unwise. I have warned you not to leave your bungalow." The man had been drinking, yet through the intervening gloom Harmon felt those gimlet eyes boring into him.

"If you persist in making a nuisance of yourself, I shall be forced to hand you over to my companion, Wicks. He has his own idea of handling prisoners. Now, damn you, get out!"

For thirty seconds Harmon poised there on the balls of his feet. One leap, one jump forward, and he could smash that revolver from those womanish hands and——

But the dark man's sibilant voice arrested that thought even as it came.

"I wouldn't try it, Mr. Harmon. If you will turn your head you will see

there are two native guards directly behind you, armed with knives."

Harmon let his shoulders sag in defeat. Without a word he strode past Catlett, climbed over the little fence and headed back toward his bungalow.

THE next two days were days of grueling labor. With his revolver always within quick reach, Catlett directed the work from the shade of the beach shack. Systematically the native divers moved across the floor of the lagoon, bringing up shell. And the raiding was bringing results. Pearl after pearl was added to those in the tin box. But with each day the future of the bed was being destroyed.

On the third day, one of Singleton's divers brought something to the surface that opened Catlett's eyes in a wide stare of greed.

"Take a look at this, matey," Singleton said. "The queen of 'em all, says I."

It was a pearl, but what a pearl. The size of a small marble, with a steely-black lustrous sheen—fully fifty pearl grains.

Catlett snatched at the crystal, rolled it back and forth in his palm and pursed his lips in a low whistle.

"Ten thousand dollars or I'll be keel-hauled," Singleton said. "Don't forget —we split even."

Catlett nodded. He crossed over to Harmon.

"To-morrow," he said, "you go down in that diving suit of yours. You go down where Singleton found this pearl, and you see if you can bring up more just like it."

THAT night Harmon smoked his pipe and went over the situation in his brain. Yet, try as he would, he always arrived at the same unescapable facts. Legally speaking, as far as the lagoon went, Catlett and the others could not be prevented from fishing. They had a signed bill of sale to substantiate their claim. Even granting that the authorities could be convinced that half the pearls had been stolen, it was doubtful if they would be much concerned. It took nothing short of a murder to arouse a police official in these waters. It was late when Harmon finally sat down before the table. He took out two sheets of paper, thought a moment, then began to write. Ten minutes later he was staring down at duplicate copies of the following message:

If you would be interested in a black pearl large and even more perfect than the one you found this afternoon, come to my bungalow when you can, alone. My only price is a guarantee that my life will be spared when you leave the island.

Smiling grimly, he signed his name to both copies, addressed one to Mr. Wicks, the other to Singleton, Esquire. Then he went out on the veranda and called to the native guard.

"Here," he said, drawing a silver watch from his pocket. "Deliver this to Him-fella-fat, and this to Him-fellah-big-thin. No talk to either, and the watch is yours. Chop chap."

The guard grinned, nodded, and was off like a deer. Harmon lowered himself into a chair.

Wicks arrived first, mildly suspicious, casting furtive glances behind him.

"Well?" he said. "Talk up. What's the story?"

"The story," Harmon replied, "is sweet and simple. Briefly, I know where there's a black pearl that'll make the one you found to-day look like a button shell. In the lagoon. I opened the shell a year ago, but I didn't take it. Preferred to let it grow."

A tension of avarice gripped Wicks. He licked his lips slowly.

"Where in the lagoon?" he demanded.

"That," replied Harmon, "is my secret. And I intend to keep it until I'm assured I won't leave here in a box. I want you to help me. If you tell the others, the deal's off."

"Sure," Wicks said. "You lead me to the pearl and I'll break the guy that touches you."

Harmon nodded. "To-morrow, when I dive," he said, "I'll want Natoa to handle my lines. Meanwhile, please see that the resident's pets are fed and taken care of."

After Wicks had gone, Harmon slumped deeper in his chair. The only item that might mar his plans now was the time element. He prayed that Wicks would return to the resident's house without being seen by Singleton.

A long time passed before Singleton appeared. He came up the veranda steps unsteadily, glared at Harmon and leaned back against the railing.

Without preamble, Harmon told the same story he had told Wicks; offered the same proposition.

Singleton listened in silence. An almost imperceptible gleam entered his eyes as he rubbed his jaw slowly. Then he said:

"You're on. But remember, no tricks —or I'll plug you sure."

Harmon was smiling quietly as he went to bed that night.

NEXT morning he went over the valves of his scaphander, tested the air hose and made ready to dive. He singled out Natoa, ordered him to get into the dory and pushed out into the lagoon.

Flustered at first, aware of his desertion, the native houseboy helped Harmon silently into his diving suit, stood ready to lock the helmet in place.

"Natoa," Harmon said, "I don't know what Catlett has promised you in payment for your work. Much colored cloth, probably, and many knives. But listen to me. I will give you twice everything he promised. Do you understand—twice! Now, when I go down, I want you to continue working the pump no matter how long I stay below."

Natoa nodded. The helmet was fastened on, and Harmon went down in a stream of bubbles. His left arm was still stiff and numb, but Catlett's bullet had inflicted only a flesh wound, and he knew there would be no harm in using it. On the bottom he waited a moment until his body accustomed itself to the great pressure. Then, slowly, his triple-length air line trailing after him, he moved forward toward the west shore of the lagoon.

Through the marine growth he plodded slowly, through schools of tropic fish. The sea floor began to rise, and he knew he had calculated his direction correctly. The floor would continue smooth and unbroken to the sand beach. And if he moved the right distance, between him and the shore shack would be a narrow pinnacle of rock. Above and below, Harmon knew every inch of the lagoon.

Presently the shadow of the rock loomed up in the water before him. He pushed his way around it, mounted higher. The water changed from pea-green to blue.

And then his helmet broke clear into the dazzling sunshine. He bent down, unfastened his shoe weights and dragged himself to the beach.

Clumsily he seized a clamp on the side of the helmet and released it. The helmet free, he worked himself out of the rubber suit. Only the fact that the scaphandler was the one-man variety of new and light construction made possible his removing it alone.

He peered around the rock. Catlett, Wicks and Singleton were all sprawled in the shade of the beach shack across the lagoon, opening shell. Out in the dory, a metallic *clank, clank* sounded as Natoa rhythmically worked the air pump.

Harmon leaped across the beach and into the jungle. He was on a narrow, swampy promontory now, and the going was hard. Yet, once in the under-

brush, he threw caution to the winds, sped back toward his bungalow. It seemed an eternity before he reached it.

Inside, he seized paper and pencil and wrote a third note. Folding it, he ran out and raced across the upland trail to the deserted house of the resident.

Once again he climbed the picket fence and entered the garden. Once again he poked his way through the flower beds, while the two flamingos gazed at him disdainfully, and the pigeons flapped their wings and cooed.

LESS than thirty minutes elapsed before Harmon returned to the rock on the shore. The three white men were still unaware of his absence. He gave a low whistle, and the native houseboy rowed quickly to the beach. With Natoa's aid, Harmon raced into his scaphander.

He had the rubber suit on and was reaching for the copper helmet when a shout went up across the lagoon.

"Game's up," Harmon said quietly. "We've been missed!"

A moment later the three men came striding down the sand. Rounding the rock slam, Catlett stopped short.

"What are you doing here?" he snarled. "You are supposed to be diving."

"I took a walk down below," Harmon jeered, "and I guess I got lost."

Catlett's gimlet eyes narrowed with suspicion as, glancing at the dory, he saw it contained no shell.

"Get to work," he snapped. "And when you land, land across the lagoon, where we can see you."

"O. K." Harmon motioned to Natoa and climbed back into the dory.

FOR the rest of the day Harmon worked perfunctorily. When, at sundown, he headed for shore, his lips were set tight in anticipation of what was to come.

Even as the dory grated on the beach,

Wicks grasped the painter and whispered:

"Get it?"

Harmon nodded. "At my bungalow in ten minutes," he said. He climbed out of the boat and headed up the cliff. In the house he drank a cup of coffee, munched some tinned meat, then went out on the veranda and proceeded to wait.

Wicks came up the steps, ripped open the screen door and thrust out one beefy hand.

"Hand it across," he snapped.

Slowly Harmon lit his pipe. "I'm sorry," he said. "Your partner in crime beat you to the post."

"My partner—— You mean Catlett?"

"I mean Singleton." Harmon lied glibly. "My native talked, and he got the pearl. He was here only a moment ago."

For a long moment Wicks stood there, face revealing a slow change of emotions. Fists clenched, he took a step forward.

"Why, you yellow-bellied——"

Harmon crossed his legs. "Don't say it," he advised. "If you want that pearl, I suggest you see Singleton. Maybe he'll sell it to you."

With a snarl, Wicks turned, kicked open the screen door and rushed away into the darkness.

"Number One," Harmon muttered to himself. "I wonder if Number Two will get there before——" He shook his head. That was too much to expect.

But Number Two, in the person of Singleton, did come. He entered the veranda and asked point-blank for the pearl.

Harmon feigned a look of resignation. "Catlett's got it," he said. "He took it from me at the point of a gun."

Singleton received this news as though he had almost expected it. His reaction, however, came to Harmon as a complete surprise.

"Listen," he said, "I don't like this bird, Catlett, any more than you do. He's too damned bossy. Suppose you and I team together and work things out on our own."

For a long moment Harmon pretended to consider this. "What's your proposition?" he asked at length.

"Simply this: you and I sneak into the resident's house. We tell Catlett and Wicks who's boss, get the pearl, and then work the lagoon here on our lonesome. Afterward we split fifty-fifty."

Harmon rose from his chair slowly. "It's a go," he said.

THE two men went out the door and headed across the upland trail. As Harmon strode along, his lips pressed tight. He knew well enough Singleton could not be trusted. He knew the man would stop at nothing to attain his end, and that very shortly the situation he had prepared would come to a head.

What Harmon didn't know was that he had ignited a powder box with a triple fuse.

A single light was burning in the resident's house when they reached the clearing.

"You stay here," Singleton said. "I'll go in first."

Fists clenched, Harmon watched Singleton move onto the veranda and disappear into the house. The door banged, and there was silence for a long moment. Abruptly loud voices sounded. An instant later, stabbing the stillness, came the roar of a revolver shot.

With a lurch, Harmon broke into a run, raced up the steps. On the sill of the inner door, he stood staring, galvanized by what he saw.

At the far side of the room Singleton stood, feet braced wide, Catlett's revolver in his hand. Before him sat Wicks and Catlett. A trickle of blood was running down Catlett's forehead.

"Hand it across," Singleton said. "I

know you've got it, and I mean to have it."

"He's lying!" Wicks shouted. "He has the pearl himself, and he's trying to make us believe he hasn't."

Catlett took out a handkerchief, wiped the blood from his face.

"Put down that gun, you fool!" he grated. "I don't know what you're talking about."

And then, without warning, Catlett acted. He dropped the handkerchief, bent down as if to pick it up, and hurled himself forward. His outflung arms coiled around Singleton's legs. With a jerk of his right hand he seized the pistol, brought the butt down on Singleton's head. Quick as a spider he kicked the unconscious man aside and leaped erect, swiveling the gun to aim before him.

"You!" he snarled at Harmon. "You did this! You——"

Wicks rose slowly to his feet. His piglike eyes bored into Catlett. "Maybe you *have* got the pearl," he said. "Maybe Singleton told the truth. You damned little pussyfoot!"

"Stand back!" Catlett cried. "If you move an inch I'll drill you!"

But Wicks kicked back his chair and began to move forward. Two steps he advanced toward the bore of the revolver.

"Back!" Catlett screamed. He retreated a step, then suddenly fired.

There was a roar, a blinding flash and a scream of pain. Like a poled ox, Wicks threw up his hands and crashed headlong.

AS the gun roared, Harmon came out of his trance. There were no odds now. It was himself against Catlett. He lunged forward.

Halfway across the room the dark man's gun thundered again, and Harmon felt the slug rip into the calf of his leg. Unmindful of the searing pain,

he closed in, slammed his right fist outward.

A third time Catlett fired. The flame blazed into Harmon's face, but the bullet went wild. Then they were down, rolling over and over on the floor.

Small though he was, there was a tiger's strength in Catlett's arms as he clawed for Harmon's throat. A lashed-up knee jammed brutally into Harmon's stomach, sent a wave of nausea surging through him. They traded blow for blow.

And then, eellike, the dark man suddenly writhed sidewise, streaked his hand under his shirt and brought forth a long-bladed knife. He snapped his hand upward and rushed in.

But Harmon had fought knives before. He ducked to the split second, and with every ounce of strength he possessed, catapulted his right fist upward.

The fist met jaw like a mallet. Breath hissed from Catlett's lips. With a moan he staggered and dropped unconscious.

IT was the morning of the next day, and Harmon sat on the veranda of the resident's house, quietly smoking his pipe. In the chair opposite, arms and legs bound, Catlett glowered and mouthed a steady stream of profanity. Beyond, on the cot, Singleton lay, conscious, but still too weak to move.

"You can crow now," Catlett snarled. "But it won't be for long. We'll be here six months; don't forget that. When the steamer comes, I'll swear *you* killed Wicks and——"

Harmon moved to the railing and peered down the upland trail.

"You're wrong, Catlett," he said. "If you'll look, you'll see we have visitors already."

Five minutes later, six uniformed seamen led by a young British officer in immaculate whites entered the veranda.

The officer glanced about him and saluted stiffly.

"You're report was received, sir," he said. "I hope we came in time."

Harmon shook hands and smiled quietly.

"In time," he said. "But no doubt your arrival puzzles Catlett, here. You see, Catlett, Niuafou is Tin Can Island, all right, cut off six months of the year. But there are other means of communication. Those pets of the resident's you were kind enough to feed—a yellow-bellied parakeet, two flamingos, some pigeons——

"Only the pigeons were important, Catlett. Carrier pigeons. The resident keeps them here for just such an emergency. I had only to get into the garden, dispatch a pigeon back to its home in Apia, where the message was wirelessed to the *Queensland*. The *Queensland*, in case you don't know, is the district's British patrol boat."

"But——" Catlett's jaw was slowly sagging.

"How did the patrol boat land? It didn't, Catlett. Natoa, my houseboy, took care of that. He arranged with those natives left in the village on the other side of the island to meet the boat with outrigger canoes.

"You're under arrest for the murder of Singleton. And—oh, yes, one thing more, Catlett. My pearls, please, if you don't mind!"

A novelette
of stalking
death and
mystery in
Borneo.

By CARL JACOBI

*Surveying rivers in head-hunters country
is easy—if you don't lose your head!*

East Of Samarinda

CHAPTER I.

AN ODD PROPOSAL.

THE Samarinda water front that night, with the rain and the black, evil-smelling streets of the native quarter, was a good setting for trouble. Trouble seemed to lie in wait for Carson the moment he passed through the little Dutch immigration office.

He scowled, kept his right hand close to the automatic in the pocket of his pongee coat. As he strode along, heading for the hotel in the European sector, his gray eyes scanned each gloom-shrouded doorway cautiously.

So this was Borneo, eh? Well, he didn't think much of it. And he didn't think much of the Dutch officials, either. They had been polite, apologetic, anything but informative.

"Cornelius Van Helst? We are sorry, *mynheer,* but we do not know the man. The Pacific Geographic Co.? No, we do not know that, either. We have never heard of such a company in Samarinda."

And yet Van Helst had written Carson in Palembang that he would be on hand to meet him when he arrived. According to his letter, speed was imperative, and if Carson was interested in making a survey of the Mahakam River, he must leave Sumatra at once.

Carson *was* interested. River surveys were right up his alley. Only three weeks before, he had returned from a successful mapping tour of Sumatra's remote Battik country.

A tall man, Carson. Even under the pongee coat his muscles bulged generously. The puggree cloth, rolled up on his sun helmet, was worn and yellowed from long exposure to a tropic sun. His face, colored a deep bronze by the same sun, was lean and firm with a square jaw.

Ahead, a Chinese sign loomed up over a lighted doorway. As Carson approached he heard the wail of a reed flute, voices in a medley of tongues.

Abruptly those voices broke off. Two pistollike cracks resounded. A scream rent the air. A moment later, a brown figure hurtled through the doorway and fell writhing to the cobblestones. After it strode a hulking white man, clad in dirty ducks.

The white man lurched forward, brought a whip lashing down upon the native's body. "You dirty, double-crossing heathen!" he snarled. "I'll teach you to——"

The whip came up again. But before it had descended halfway, something stopped it. Carson planted himself between the white man and the fallen Malay, seized the whip wrist in a grip of iron.

"One moment. The fellow's had enough. If you hit him again, you'll kill him."

The white man wrenched his hand free, stared back through bleary eyes. "Who the devil are you?" he snarled.

"Never mind who I am." With one arm Carson bent down, lifted the cringing native to his feet. "You'd better go back in there and work some of that temper off."

Rage crimsoned the face of the man with the whip. His eyes closed to slits. Once again he jerked back his arm, brought the thong streaking downward.

CAUGHT off guard, Carson winced as the whip coiled about a shoulder. For an instant he stood there, lips slowly tightening. Then his right fist doubled, connected hard with the other's jaw. He brought his left around in a sweeping haymaker.

They went down, rolled over and over on the cobblestones.

As he fought, Carson realized grimly that his opponent had overcome his first surprise and waited an opening to use either the knife whose haft projected from his belt, or the revolver holstered under an armpit. Back and forth they struggled, clawing for each other's throat.

Carson's fears were a prediction. The knife came free, lashed up at his throat. And then it ended—suddenly.

In a last, frantic thrust the man opened his guard. Carson delivered a well-placed blow behind an ear and rose to his feet.

"There," he said. "I didn't come here for trouble, but you asked for it."

Carson stooped, retrieved his helmet, wiped the mud from his face.

"You saved my life, *tuan.*"

The native had groped forward and stood now gazing with expressionless eyes. Short, but powerfully built, his speech was slow and halting, suggesting the upriver *kampongs* of the deep interior.

Carson nodded. "What's your name?"

"Me Datumudi. Him fellah, *Tuan* Girard."

Girard, eh? Carson stared down at the unconscious man and shrugged. He turned again to the native.

"You're a Kenyah, Datumudi," he guessed. "You came here to the coast to find employment as a guide. Right?"

"Yes, *tuan.* And this man——"

"Come to the hotel in the white quarter to-morrow," Carson said. "I may have work for you."

Datumudi nodded, bowed shortly and moved off into the darkness. Carson hitched his trousers and smiled. It was quite a reception party that had welcomed him to the fair city. All that was lacking was a band. Yeah, that and maybe a kris in the back.

And then, about to move on, Carson stopped rigid. His keen eyes had caught a glittery something on the cobblestones by the unconscious man's side. He picked it up, stared down upon it.

It was a ring, a jade ring. The seal was square, and carved upon it was the likeness of three fang-protruding cobras entwined in an interlocking circle.

IN his room in the little Dutch hotel in Samarinda's European quarter Carson lay on the bed, examining the ring in the glare of the bracketed wall lamp. The wind billowed the window curtains inward, brought to his nostrils the warm odor of the jungle.

It was an odd ring. The cobras had been carved into the jade with rare artistry. But the setting was a cheap alloy, made to resemble platinum.

He was still lying there quietly when shoes scraped along the outside corridor, and a knock sounded on the door. Quickly, the ring was in a pocket.

"Come in," Carson said.

The door opened, and a man entered. He was young, with dark eyes that were clear and friendly. He closed the door and nodded.

"I heard you asking questions downstairs. You want to know something about Cornelius Van Helst?"

Carson bounded to his feet and surveyed the stranger curiously.

"My name's Barret, Peter Barret," the man said, "Van Helst was murdered yesterday afternoon in his bungalow."

For an instant, Carson said nothing. Then he strode forward, stared hard into Barret's eyes.

"Murdered! Good Lord, why?"

"I can't tell you why. I only know that Samarinda is a dynamite box at the present time. Would you mind telling me what your relations were with Van Helst?"

Carson hesitated. Something about the man before him was conducive of confidence.

"I don't mind," he answered. "I was in Palembang when Van Helst wrote me. Sumatra. He claimed to represent an outfit known as Pacific Geographic. I was to receive two thousand guilders for making a survey of the Mahakam River."

Barret smiled a grim smile, lowered himself into a chair. "You've been duped," he said abruptly. "There is no such company as Pacific Geographic. Strictly speaking, there was no such man as Van Helst. His real name was Ludwig Blueker.

"Blueker," Barret continued, "simply wanted a man who was experienced in leading an expedition into the bush. He could have found a man here easily enough, but he preferred to entice someone who hadn't an inkling of what was in the wind. He planned to have you lead him up the Mahakam before any of the others."

Carson raised his eyes slowly. "What others?"

FOR answer, Barret rose to his feet, paced to the door and locked it. Returning to the chair, he sighed heavily. "I suppose I'll have to start at the beginning. All right, listen closely.

"Two years ago my father, Wilson Barret, went into the Borneo interior, searching for a certain valley in the Mueller range. Dad hoped to find there a deposit of an ore known as coronium. Coronium is so-called because it was discovered spectroscopically in the corona of the sun. It has always been thought there was none on this earth.

"My father was an inventor. For six years, he had been developing a new kind of antiaircraft gun, which he planned to present to the United States government for coast protection. Information leaked out, and repeated attempts to steal the plans were made."

Barret's voice grew suddenly husky. "In January of this year, those attempts were partially successful. My father was killed, his drawings and models taken. You perhaps read of it in the press."

"I believe I did," Carson said. There was a glitter in his eyes now—a glitter of interest.

"Well," Barret went on, "to make a long story short, none of those drawings were of the slightest value. The coronium metal was missing, you see. The metal plays an important part in the construction of the gun's breech, and without it the weapon cannot be made.

"Father's trip was garbed in secrecy," Barret continued. "And I was away at school when he returned. Before I got back he had been killed, the house blown up, every inch of the ruins searched.

"But one set of plans—the perfect ones—were never taken. Dad had feared such an attack for months. He sent them to me with instructions to place them in a bank vault for safekeeping. He also sent a map of the Apo Kayan district, marking the place of the coronium deposit."

Barret stood up. "I don't know why I tell you all this," he said. "But I have that map and if I can find that metal, I believe I can construct the gun. There are tremendous forces fighting against me, however. The peace of all Europe definitely rests here in Samarinda."

His words died off. A look of determination shot into his eyes.

"Would you be interested in accompanying me upriver?"

CHAPTER II.
POWER OF THE RING.

CARSON stared. The proposal, coming as it did, out of a clear sky, staggered him. Here was a man, an utter stranger showing his hand without hesitancy, yet asking no questions as to who or what he was. The whole story carried a breath of mystery and adventure which Carson was quick to feel.

"This man, Van Helst," he said slowly, "he represented one of the powers fighting against you?"

Barret nodded. "Yes, and I believe he was killed because some one thought he knew more than he did."

Carson wet his lips. He tried one more question: "If you knew this pack of wolves was on your trail, why haven't you——"

"Gone upriver at once?" Barret shook his head. "That wouldn't work. I've been watched since I left home. When I go, it must be through a ruse that will give me a start."

For an instant longer, Carson hesitated. Then he stretched forth his hand.

"I'm your man," he said.

Five minutes later, the two men

parted, Barret going to his room farther down the corridor after promising to continue the discussion over the breakfast table the following day. Carson sank back on the bed and frowned thoughtfully.

Was he playing the fool? He had accepted a stranger's offer without the slightest guarantee of truth or remuneration. Well—— He sat up as footsteps sounded along the outer hall.

The door to his room vibrated as a heavy fist pounded against it. A voice demanded:

"Open up!"

Carson strode across to the door, twisted the key and pulled it open. Three men, clad in the uniform of the Dutch Colonial police, stood there. The foremost had a Lueger automatic leveled before him.

"Mynheer Peter Barret?"

Carson thought fast. A mistake had been made, of course. But something prompted him to nod in assent.

"Mynheer Peter Barret, I arrest you for the murder of Ludwig Blueker. Will you come quietly?"

"Blueker!" cried Carson. "But I thought——"

"Exactly. You thought by returning to this hotel and letting yourself be seen on the veranda you would cast aside suspicion. Unfortunately for you, you were seen and recognized. Your wrists, mynheer."

Before Carson realized what was happening, his hands were seized and steel handcuffs snapped about them. A moment later, flanked by a guard on either side, he found himself pushed downstairs and out into the street.

The procession turned a corner, entered a low, whitewashed building. Behind a desk a large, florid-faced man sat in a chair that seemed too small for his bulk.

Carson was jerked forward. A volley of rapid Dutch was exchanged. After which the man behind the desk said sternly:

"*Mynheer*, murderers are not tolerated in this port. We know nothing of Ludwig Blueker save that he was an orchidologist, a flower-hunter who came here from Java. But we will know more presently. Until your trial you will be imprisoned, according to our Colonial law."

Hands gripped Carson, propelled him through a connecting door and into a dark hallway. Crossing an open court, they entered a second building. An iron door creaked open, and Carson found himself in a black cell.

HE groped across to the cot protruding from the wall, lowered himself upon it, while his eyes accustomed themselves to the gloom.

A hard thought struck him. Suppose Barret were not all he claimed to be? Suppose the story he had told had been a clever lie, a scheme to shift the blame on himself?

In the narrow corridor beyond the grilled door, steps sounded as a guard paced back and forth. Carson sat quiet for half an hour. At the end of that time he paced impulsively to the door, hammered his fists against it.

The guard, a Malay, garbed in cast-off Dutch army uniform, approached quickly.

"Listen," Carson said, "there's been a mistake. Call your *kapitan* at once."

The guard stared dumbly.

"Don't be a fool!" Carson snapped. "I'm not asking you to let me out. I only want to see the officer in charge, and——" In muttered frustration, he jammed his hands into his pockets, felt something hard and round, and pulled it out. He thought a moment, then held it up for the guard to see.

"Bring the *kapitan* here, and this ring is yours," he said quietly.

A change swept over the Malay. He gaped at the jade seal, raised his right hand to his temple.

"Forgive me, *tuan*. I did not know. Cobras coil three."

He stood rigid, as if waiting a reply. "Cobras coil three," he repeated. Then, casting a cautious glance over a shoulder, he fitted a key into the door and swung it open.

A moment later, Carson was following him down the corridor. Twenty feet forward, the guard suddenly turned into a side passageway. Before another door he stopped, inched it open and peered out.

"There is no one in sight, *tuan*," he said hoarsely. "Cobras coil three." He dropped one hand to a side holster, pulled out a service automatic and gave it to the American.

A trap? Carson hesitated only an instant. He stretched out his hand, offering the ring as he had promised, but he touched only empty space. The guard was gone, moving back down the passageway.

Carson slipped out, groped his way across the open court until a wall loomed up before him. No sound came from either side. He braced, lifted himself up and over.

An instant later he stood on the cobblestone street, free but a fugitive.

FOR five years, Carson had been a resident of Malaysia. Surveys, hunting expeditions had led him from Singapore to Darwin, from the China Sea to New Guinea.

Now as he moved stealthily forward in the darkness, Carson knew he needed to find a spot where he could think the situation out.

At the first intersection, he got his bearings. He moved into a darker street, headed for the native quarter.

Ten minutes later, Carson sat at a table in an alcove on the upper landing of Liang Po's. A bead curtain hid him from sight of the noisy room below.

Carson pulled a pack of cards from a pocket, began to lay them idly on the table. As he played, he gave his brain full rein to work out the growing puzzle.

The ring, first of all. Certainly there were three snakes on the seal, but what had the Malay guard meant when he had said, "Cobras coil three"? And why had he, at the sight of it, effected Carson's escape?

Carson placed a black jack on a red queen and frowned. He got out his pipe, began to pack it slowly. Suddenly, he jerked to attention.

In the main room below, three figures entered the street door. The foremost, a tall man with deep-set eyes, stood out in sharp contrast, for he wore a loose-fitting suit of black. But it was the other two that had drawn Carson's gaze.

One of these was undoubtedly Girard, the man he had knocked out. The other was dressed in the voluminous dress sometimes worn by Christianized native girls.

But she wasn't a native girl. The hood slipped down as Girard pushed her into the room, and Carson caught a glimpse of golden hair gleaming in the lamplight. A moment later, the three were moving up the staircase to the second landing.

A white woman here, obviously against her will. What did it mean?

CARSON knocked the tobacco from his pipe and clenched his fists thoughtfully. He pushed aside the curtain and stepped out on the landing.

Six alcoves opened on the gallery. One of them was closed off with a door. It was into the room with the door that Girard, the man in black, and the girl had gone.

Carson moved forward until a murmur of voices came to his ears. Girard was talking:

"You just sit quiet, sister. It's that brother of yours we want. As soon as

he finds you're gone, he'll follow along pronto."

A rich contralto voice stifled a sob. "Why can't you let us alone? Haven't you done enough by killing our father?"

There was a short pause, and then a third, silky voice broke in:

"Perhaps it will not be necessary to wait for Señor Barret. Perhaps the señorita will tell us what we want to know."

A short feminine cry rang out as a chair scraped inside the room. Carson had heard all he needed. He loosened the automatic in his pocket, pushed open the door and walked in.

Like a startled cat, the man in black whirled in his chair.

"Fool!" he cried. "This room is private. Get out!"

Carson stood there, surveying the group. Girard, he saw with relief, did not recognize him. He kicked back a chair and lowered himself into it deliberately.

"Cobras coil three," he said.

CHAPTER III.
MURDER TRAP!

IT was clumsily done, without prologue or preamble, but Carson was speaking his thoughts as they came. Whether or not the strange phrase, spoken by the guard, would have any effect here, he didn't know.

But far back in his brain something told Carson it would. He let his right hand fall upon the table, revealing the jade ring.

For a moment, there was no response. Then the man in black leaned forward. "Señor Varne?" he asked, in a surprised voice. "I am Gomez. I did not know you were in Samarinda. I—— You are Varne, aren't you?"

Carson nodded and relaxed slightly. "Plans were changed," he said. "And now—who is the girl?"

Gomez smiled. "That is some of my

own work, señor," he said. "The girl is Madeline Barret, sister of Peter Barret. It is very simple. Soon we will have the map."

Stiff in his chair, Carson studied the man. He looked at the girl, noted her violet eyes, tightened now by fear.

"Do you not think I moved wisely, señor?" Gomez asked.

Carson took the plunge full stride.

"No," he said, banging a fist down on the table. "You have blundered. I have been instructed to let the Barrets go unharmed for the present. Fool, a map can be easily forged! The girl must be released."

The eyes of the man in black arched upward. "Released, señor? What do you mean?"

"Listen," Carson snapped recklessly, "I have a plan that will change everything. Liang Po, owner of this dive, has the details. We'll go down now, and I'll show you."

Carson stood up, as if his words had settled all questions. Gomez hesitated, then nodded, puzzled, and led the way out the door.

Downstairs in the main room they halted near the street entrance.

"Get Liang Po," Carson said to Gomez. "Tell him I am here."

Now was the instant Carson was waiting for. He moved to the girl's side, as Gomez threaded his way through the throng, whispered:

"Ready?"

Her eyes flashed, and a tense nod was her answer. Carson wheeled. "The door!" he yelled. "Run for it!"

With a single movement, he jerked free Girard's grip on the girl's wrist, swung his fist and sent the man reeling back. In a flash, Madeline Barret was spinning for the street entrance. A ringing hush clamped down on the room.

And then with a roar they were at him. Girard jerked a knife from his shirt, whiplashed it into space. Two tables overturned with a crash. A slant-

eyed Malay dived for Carson's legs. Yanking the automatic from his pocket, Carson pumped two shots into the crowd and ran for the door.

He was cut off before he reached it. Girard closed in, threw himself on the American, clawing for his throat.

But Carson had a trick remaining. He let himself go limp for a split second; then, without warning, he jerked Girard's hands from his neck and slammed the man back to the wall with four trip-hammer blows to the solar plexus.

Whirling, he was just in time to meet the black figure of Gomez hurtling upon him. His fist met the man's jaw in full swing. Gomez spat blood and dropped to the floor.

It was all or nothing then. Carson leveled his automatic at the carbide lamp suspended from the ceiling. A roar, a splintering of glass, and darkness swooped upon him.

Then he was ripping open the door, taking the steps to the street level four at a time.

On the cobblestones, a shadow detached itself from the gloom of the building wall. Madeline Barret's hand came out to touch his arm.

Silently, Carson forced her forward at a loping run. Behind, the door banged open; excited figures rushed into the street.

They ran on, man and girl, weaving to escape the slugs that caromed off the pavement on either side.

NOT until they were four streets away did Carson permit the girl to slacken pace. Then, at a fast stride, he led the way into the European district. Within sight of the hotel, he drew up, surveyed her quietly.

"My name's Carson," he said, a bit coldly. "I met your brother earlier in the evening. He told me something of what was up."

She nodded. "I know. You have

my profound thanks, Mr. Carson. I was in a bad fix back there. But I can thank you better when you accompany us upriver."

Carson shook his head slowly. "I'm not so sure I'm going," he replied. "How about this man, Van Helst? Did you know your brother is wanted for his murder?"

Her lips fell open; a flush mounted to her cheeks. "Peter!" she cried. "But that's impossible!"

"Not so impossible but that I had to break out of jail," Carson said. "The police arrested me under your brother's name by mistake."

She stared, then came forward and brought her face close to his own.

"Peter is innocent," she said huskily. "Please believe that. We need your help, Mr. Carson. You can't let us down now."

There was sincere appeal in her eyes, and Carson, looking into them, was mildly irritated to feel an electric glow course down his spine.

"O. K.," he said, at length, "I'll string along. But we've got to move fast. Have you made any transport arrangements?"

"Yes. Sin Fu has agreed to rent us his gasoline launch. We take that as far as Long Iram."

"And from there?"

"From there by proa with native rowers."

Carson nodded. "Good enough," he said. "We'll try and slip out before anything is suspected. Get your brother and meet me at the river jetty in half an hour."

She gripped his hand and moved off toward the hotel. Carson watched her slim figure until it was swallowed in the gloom. Then he turned and headed once again for the water front.

His goal was the abandoned copra warehouse near the immigration office where he had stored his equipment.

Carson moved warily, hugging the building shadows, regarding each native passerby with narrowed eyes. Twice, he stood still and turned his head, listening. The way behind was deserted, cloaked in a steady mist of drizzling rain.

A scowl crossed Carson's lips. Try as he would, he could not throw off the feeling that he was being followed.

He moved on, at a faster pace, turned again at the next intersection. But he saw no one, and at length he came to the copra warehouse. His hand was reaching for the latch, when a voice addressed him from behind.

"Tuan."

CARSON whirled. Then he relaxed, and a wave of relief swept over him. The figure that had come like a ghost out of the gloom was Datumudi, the Kenyah Dyak whose life he had saved from the renegade, Girard.

"You were following me?" he asked the native.

"Yes, tuan. I was not sure it was you, and I wanted to speak with you alone."

Carson nodded. He opened the warehouse door, motioned the Dyak inside. "What is it?" he asked.

"Tuan, after you put to sleep the man who calls himself Girard, I returned and followed him. You told me you would have work for me in the morning. Will that work have anything to do with a Tuan Barret?"

Carson's eyes snapped. "Barret?" he repeated. "What do you know about him?"

"Only this, tuan." The Dyak lowered his voice. "I overheard Girard speak to others. By questioning, he learned that tuan and Mem Barret planned to go upriver in Sin Fu's bang-bang boat.

"Girard and another tuan boarded Sin Fu's boat. When they came away, they said something I did not understand. They said it would make 'a big noise.'"

Carson frowned. "'A big noise,'" he

repeated slowly. "And what under the sun might that mean?"

A flash of understanding probed his brain, and he whirled to the door. He yelled an order to the Dyak to follow and raced down the black street.

As he sped through the darkness, Carson prayed that there would yet be time, that the Barrets had not yet left the hotel.

The water front opened up before him. Quickly, he singled out Sin Fu's gasoline launch, a weather-racked affair with the usual dragon prow, moored to the wharf end.

He advanced cautiously, let himself down on the little deck. The cabin door yawned open, revealing a framed square of ominous blackness.

Carson went down the companion ladder, found a rag in a dish of oil at the bottom step and lighted it. Then he began a systematic search.

At the end of five minutes he had found nothing, and a cold fear began to mount within in. Then his eyes caught something black and square under a rattan table.

It was not the usual time-controlled infernal machine. But once set off, its effect would have been the same. A cord connected the chair's back-rest and waited the slightest movement to trip a switch.

The switch separated a coil, a battery spark and a metal container packed with pyroxylin—guncotton.

Smiling grimly, Carson carried the thing up on deck and flung it overside. He lighted his pipe, hugged the cabin's shadow and proceeded to wait. In two minutes, Datumudi came.

"Go below," Carson ordered. "You're to act as guide. We'll pay you well."

Double footsteps sounded on the jetty. Peter Barret helped his sister aboard.

"We saw no one," Madeline said softly. "Is everything ready?"

Carson nodded. "Everything. I'll cast off."

CHAPTER IV.

DRUMS OF DEATH!

THE sun was a ball of brass in a cloudless sky. Between thick shores of poisonous green, the launch chugged its way slowly up the yellow river.

Under the faded midships awning Madeline sat in a wicker chair, staring absently at the long, floating logs—crocodiles—that drifted by. Peter Barret leaned against the rail. At the tiller, Datumudi was a motionless image.

Carson was not idle. On the aft deck, he was cleaning and oiling the launch's taffrail weapon, a Hotchkiss machine gun of ancient vintage. Two days had passed since they had left Samarinda.

The night of the first day they had stopped at Tenggarong, the palace residence of the Sultan of Kotei. There they had taken on more supplies and learned of the conditions that lay ahead.

One thing worried Carson: As long as they kept to the launch they were safe enough. With its stern gun, the craft could well resist all attacks. But drought had had its effect here in Borneo as in other countries.

Two days more, and they would reach Long Iram, Dutch military headquarters on the Mahakam. From that point on, the river would no longer be navigable to anything but native dugout canoes.

They moored at Long Iram at nightfall. Royal Netherlands Indies army officers came down to the post jetty and bade the party welcome.

Later, the *commandant* had the *kapala* of the neighboring *kampong* brought to the post and completed arrangement for the hiring of five proas and paddlers.

Then, loaded with equipment, the five proas headed out into the current, and the journey was resumed.

Carson, back propped against the *kajang*—cabin shelter—stared across at Peter Barret and sucked his pipe thoughtfully.

"Barret," he said, at length, "I've thrown in with you, and so far I haven't asked many questions. But the story you told me back in Samarinda was pretty vague. I'd like to know what this is all about."

A short frown crossed Barret's forehead. "I thought I'd told you everything," he said.

"You say you're heading for Apo Kayan," Carson said. "That's a pretty big district. Just how detailed is your map?"

FOR answer, Barret drew off one canvas-topped shoe, inserted a pocketknife under the leather heel and extracted a slip of yellow paper.

"The map," he said, "is pretty rough. But it shows the location of the coronium deposit in a valley known as the Valley of the Third Star. Somewhere halfway between the Mahakam headwaters and the Kayan River."

Carson nodded. He saw that the diagram listed such objects as a needle-shaped rock and a broken tree as landmarks. The coronium deposit was marked by a large "C," and near it a wavering arrow pointed to the secret entrance to the valley.

"How about the chaps that are following us?" Carson demanded. "Have you any idea who they are?"

"No." Barret shook his head. "I only know that any European or Asiatic power would risk all to obtain the secret of that gun."

For a long time after that, Carson kept to himself. He watched the yellow river narrow, the dense banks press close. Proboscis monkeys came out of nowhere to gibber at them. Argus pheasants sounded their harsh cry and scuttled off into the *lallang* grass. Above, the mounting heat pressed down relentlessly.

At intervals, Carson uncased his binoculars and carefully scanned the waterway to the rear. He saw nothing.

Yet somewhere along the miles behind, he knew they were being followed.

And then one day the guide, Datumudi, dipped his paddle and sent the leading proa turning toward shore.

"*Tuan*," he said, "we have reached the headwaters. Now we must walk."

The Dyak boatmen shouldered packs and changed their rôles to carriers. With Carson and Datumudi in the lead, they struck off into the jungle, south by east, heading for the headwaters of the Kayan River.

Though there was no boundary mark to tell them, they had now reached the outskirts of that district designated on the Dutch maps as the *onderafdeeling* of Apo Kayan.

Barret had said that his father, Wilson Barret, by following the Kayan, had reached Tandjong Selor on the east coast. The Valley of the Third Star must be close at hand.

Nightfall found them far inland, in the foothills of the low Mueller range, vague as to their exact position. Tents were set up in a little glade. Worn to exhaustion by their grueling overland trek, the Barrets retired early.

But Carson did not sleep. He lay awake for hours, brooding with his thoughts, listening to the *tok-tok-tok* of a distant Skipping-on-the-Ice bird. One item, impossible, unbelievable, hung before his eyes like an optic scar.

Before going to his tent, Peter Barret had sat for a time by the fire, quietly smoking a Burma cheroot. And by the light of the flames the watch chain on his shirt front had been revealed for a fleeting instant. Attached to that chain as a charm was something Carson had not seen before.

It was a ring with a square jade seal upon which three cobras were carved in an interlocking circle!

WHEN Carson finally dozed, it was with the sensation that he had been asleep only a moment before he sat up rigid. Through the hot night a low sound pulsed, hollow and muffled. A deep vibration, it was, rising over the tops of the *taphangs*, steadily growing nearer, louder. Carson listened, a scowl on his lips.

But it was Datumudi who, advancing to the front of his tent, voiced the warning.

"Drums, *tuan*," he said. "The river Punans are sounding their drums."

The sound was throbbing through the jungle now. As Carson paced out toward the dying fire he saw that the Dyak carriers were erect, staring at each other uneasily. An instant later the Barrets emerged from their tents. There was a drawn look in Madeline's eyes.

"What is it?" she said. "Is something wrong?"

Carson's face was grim. "I'm afraid there is," he said. "The river tribes are on the warpath, following us."

"Following——" Peter Barret's lips set tight. "You mean—head-hunters?"

"I'm not sure," Carson said, "but my guess is Gomez and Girard are playing to form. They realize we have a start. So they've managed to enlist the Punans. There's no more treacherous tribe in the country——"

His words died off. In the silence, the drums thundered louder.

"We've got to run for it!" Carson yelled. "Break camp!"

They gathered their equipment and raced into the jungle. There was no trail-breaking now. Headlong, they plunged into a world of blackness.

Vines and creepers tore at their clothing, drew blood on their arms. The very air seemed thick, moist, pregnant with danger. Behind, like a litany of doom, the drums grew nearer.

Then it happened. A sharp *thwack* sounded behind them. One of the Dyak carriers screamed, tore a short-feathered dart from his throat.

THREE brown men, their faces hideous with paint, lunged from the undergrass, parangs upraised. Carson swiveled, triggered the automatic twice.

A knife whizzed through the air, cut past him so close it brushed his clothing. Then the carriers swarmed in on the two remaining attackers, dispatched them quickly.

"Scouting party!" Carson yelled. "Come on."

They stumbled forward faster. A hundred yards forward and abruptly the jungle began to thin. Rocks, jagged boulders appeared on either side.

They penetrated a last fringe of forest and came upon a welcome sight. A nature-formed wall rose before them, extended like a jagged parapet across a broad open space. Back of it, a perpendicular cliff reared upward.

They took positions behind it. Carson singled out Datumudi, gazed a moment into the faithful Dyak's face.

"Take two carriers," he ordered, "and drift back along that cliff. See if you can find a passageway through it."

The guide nodded and disappeared like a shadow. Carson turned, peered over the rock wall. He saw nothing. But the throbbing of drums continued on all sides.

And then Carson made his decision. He had been traveling blind long enough. It was time for a show-down. He wheeled, faced Peter Barret.

"In five minutes," he said tensely, "anything can happen. Before it does, I want to know the truth. I want to know just how you figure in this." His forefinger stabbed out, to point accusingly at Barret's ring.

Barret paled. He opened his lips, snapped them shut again.

"Talk up!"

"I—I suppose I might as well tell you," Barret nodded. "For months that ring has plagued me. I'm—I'm sick of it."

Carson said nothing, waiting for him

to continue. He watched Barret's hands fold into each other, tremble spasmodically.

"It all goes back a long time," the husky voice began slowly. "It—it began when I was in school. As an undergraduate, I attended a secret political meeting with several other students. Before I knew what I was doing, I had signed papers and pledged myself to absolute secrecy.

"I thought it only a lark at the time, but later I learned my membership was a death-binding thing." Barret hesitated, faltered.

"The society, you see, was really a branch of an international spy ring. It was a huge organization, with arms reaching out into every important city in the world, with its roots somewhere in Asia. Each member wore one of these rings. The society made a business of stealing governmental secrets and selling them to the highest bidder."

Barret wiped a bead of perspiration from his forehead. "When information of my father's antiaircraft gun leaked out, I was informed that I must steal the plans and models. Naturally, I refused. I was sentenced to death and had to flee for my life. They've been after me ever since."

In the darkness, Carson studied the younger man for a long moment. "And Girard and Gomez?"

"Members of the society, but only lesser fry. The real heads, I believe, are in Singapore. But one thing I know for certain: If Girard and Gomez can be caught, they carry sufficient information on their persons to permit the attack of the entire organization——"

His voice broke off. From the jungle below wild yells suddenly burst forth. Brown figures emerged from the underbrush, raced out upon the rock floor.

Carson's automatic spat fire. Peter Barret turned quickly, thrust his rifle through a crevice and jerked the trigger.

CHAPTER V.

DATUMUDI REPAYS A DEBT.

IT was open hell without quarter.

A spear swooped over the wall, caught a Dyak carrier in the abdomen. Blowpipes discharged a hail of poisonous darts. Natives multiplied in the open space.

At Carson's side Madeline Barret worked her revolver, taking careful aim before each shot. And the defense was bringing results.

As the withering fire from behind the wall brought down Punan after Punan, the natives began to fall back. The attack stopped. Silence clamped down upon them.

"Not so good," Carson said. "The devils are up to something. They'll stay out there and try to smoke us out by trickery. We can't hold off forever."

Running steps sounded behind them.

"*Tuan*"—Datumudi's voice was heavy with disappointment—"I could find no passageway. It is all solid cliff, up which not even an ape could climb."

Fists tight, Carson peered over the protecting rock. The drums had stopped. He swung about.

"We can't stay here," he said. "There *must* be a rear way out, parallel with that cliff then, if not through it. There's *got* to be a way!"

He hesitated an instant longer, then snapped a low order and led the way back cautiously, a step at a time. Without interruption, they reached the cliff wall.

"Watch your step," Carson directed. "We'll hug the cliff as far as we can, then head into the bush. Maybe we can double our tracks and lose 'em."

Rocks, loose shale impeded their way. Behind, the silence became more impressive, like the calm presaging a storm. They advanced a hundred yards, and still there was no sign of pursuit. Heavy patches of vines mottled the cliff, but the rock wall continued smooth and unscalable.

And then Carson stopped. A larger patch of growth stood out in the gloom beside him. Sweeping through the tendril matting came a strong draft of air. The American whipped out a flashlight and sent a white ray probing inward.

A narrow defile was revealed by the beam. Split asunder by some ancient geologic upheaval, the cliff walls reared high on either side. Far ahead, the passage seemed to widen.

"Quick! Inside!" Carson snapped. He didn't know how far the cut ran back, but it seemed more than just a cave. He waited for the others to pass through the opening, followed, and carefully arranged the vines behind him.

And then Barret, who had been standing rigid a few feet in advance, sucked in his breath sharply. With a low cry, he grasped the flashlight from Carson's hands, ran forward,

"We've done it!" he cried. "We've reached our goal! This is the secret passage my father took to enter the Valley of the Third Star. See, here are his markings."

BARRET pointed a shaking hand. In the glare of the flashlight a rough arrow was visible, scratched before them on the rock slab. Beneath it were the initials, *W. B.* Wilson Barret.

Carson examined the stone, and nodded as he pocketed his gun. "It looks as though you were right," he agreed. A gleam of triumph entered his eyes. So far, so good. For the moment they were safe, but——

He took the flash again, studied the cliff above him. A moment later, he was fighting his way up the escarpment, digging his toes in small holes.

Twenty feet up, Carson motioned the others back and advanced to a jagged boulder, balanced there on a projecting ridge.

Carson braced and threw his weight against it. With a roar, the rock thundered downward. Carson rejoined the others and looked back with satisfaction.

The entrance was blocked. Squarely in the center the boulder prevented all passage.

They moved on cautiously. As Carson had suspected, the defile was short, gradually widening into the valley beyond. The powerful flash bored ahead, a gleaming white funnel. A hundred yards into the valley proper, and Carson stopped again, listening.

Water tinkled somewhere close at hand. At a brief command, Datumudi moved off into the darkness, to return a moment later with the report that a fresh-water spring lay just ahead.

Exhausted, they made camp in a low depression in the rock floor. Scattered boulders gave fair protection against attack.

"I'll stand first watch," Carson told Barret. "You can divide the rest of the night among yourself, Datumudi and the carriers."

But the night passed without further interruption. Morning, and they woke to a new world. Small and symmetrical, the valley stretched before them in the sunlight, the cliff walls rising sheer on either side.

A few stunted seraya trees grew in clumps here and there. Other than that the desolation was complete.

Breakfast over, Barret pried the leather heel from his shoe and drew forth his map.

"Pretty vague," Carson mused, as he studied it. He squinted up at a broken tree, drew an imaginary line with his eye across the valley. "The compass shows the valley to lie almost due east and west," he said. "Judging from that I should say the deposit lay somewhere over there."

Madeline Barret nodded. "We're not sure," she said. "But dad probably hid all traces of his discovery. It may take us some time to find it."

HALF an hour later, the carriers left behind in camp, Carson, Peter and Madeline Barret swung west and cut across to an outcropping patch that lay near the valley's center.

For two hours, they moved along the valley floor, examining the rock strata. At the end of that time Barret stood up, a puzzled look in his eyes.

"I'm certain this is the spot shown on the map," he said. "The signs of the deposit are all around—those reddish-brown streaks in the sedimentary strata between the igneous overcap. Coronium, you know, is found in limestone vugs, crystallized by ground-water drippings. And yet there is no trace of my father's minings."

All afternoon, while the blazing Borneo sun beat down upon them, they continued their work. Nightfall found them returning, empty-handed, to the camp at the spring.

The carriers had killed a small, wild boar. They ate in silence, depressed by their thoughts.

Seated cross-legged by the fire, Carson smoked his pipe quietly and went over again in detail each marking of Barret's map. Abruptly he lurched to his feet, rigid in every muscle.

"Stay where you are," he ordered. "I thought I heard something out there."

He paced forward into the darkness, moved noiselessly back toward the outcropping patch where their search had centered earlier in the day. At the edge of the rocky mass he halted, pulse quickening.

The rattle of a dislodged stone broke the stillness. Ahead, a vague form outlined itself momentarily in the gloom.

Carson's automatic slid clear of its holster. A step at a time, he groped his way, following the sound. Abreast of the cliff wall, he halted again.

Once more he heard the sound, the grating of booted feet, moving away cautiously, climbing.

And then the moon penetrated the cloud mass above, and Carson found himself staring upward. Thirty feet above, a projecting ledge was outlined against the night sky. Upon it stood a man, gazing down at him.

"*Buenos noches, señor.* Were you looking for some one?"

A cold chill gripped Carson. "Gomez!" he breathed.

Above him, the man laughed. "Of course, it is Gomez. Gomez and Girard. Did you think you had beaten us so easily, my friend?" He laughed again as beside him a second form, Girard, materialized out of the blackness.

"*Si, señor,* there is more than one entrance to the valley. The one behind us for instance, which the Dyaks were kind enough to show us after a little persuasion. Careful, señor! It will do you no good to shoot! You would be blown to bits before you could press the trigger."

CARSON'S lips opened, clamped shut again without reply. He shot a glance to either side, looking for some object of protection.

And above him, as the moon passed behind a cloud, that taunting laugh came again. Gomez switched on a powerful electric torch.

"Blown to bits, do you understand? The valley floor is mined with dynamite, from a point opposite that where you stand to within thirty feet of your camp. We—Girard and I—worked fast the last hour while you sat about your fire.

"But listen carefully, Señor Carson. We are still desirous of obtaining that map. Without it we will find the ore, but *with* it we can save ourselves much time and labor. Deliver that map to us in the hands of Señorita Barret in ten minutes, and we will let you and your party return to the coast. Ten minutes, do you understand?" The flash was cut off.

Carson turned slowly, brain in a whirl. His staring eyes stabbed the blackness around him. And then as hopes died within him, a shadow detached itself from the gloom, moved forward to grip his arm.

"Courage, *tuan*. There is yet a way. Run for the camp!"

Blankly, Carson stared into Datumudi's face.

"Go, *tuan*. It is not I, but the gods who have spoken."

Like a ghost, the native turned without further word, bent low, and darted toward the cliff wall. A bulky something was clutched in his hands.

Carson stood in his tracks one instant. Then, with one wild leap, he threw himself forward. He dashed madly down the valley, plunged across the uneven rock surface.

Peter Barret and his sister jumped to their feet as he raced into camp.

With a single movement Carson seized the girl, hurled her back, away from the fire. His voice barked, "Behind that rock slab, as fast as you can!"

And then it happened!

Back on the cliff wall, a blinding column of flame belched upward; a thunderous roar shook the earth.

Carson, thrown violently backward, had a fleeting glimpse of two sprawling bodies catapulted high into the air. Then a cloud of dirt, rock fragments rained about him, hid his vision.

Seconds later, when the last mad echo had trembled into silence, he picked himself up, stared down at the girl. She was sitting upright, unharmed, looking about her with bewildered eyes.

Slowly Carson turned, paced down the valley to where a lazy cloud of smoke billowed into the still air. Up above him in the returned moonlight, a huge, jagged hole blackened the cliff wall where the projecting ledge had been. Of the two men, Gomez and Girard, there was no sign.

A dark figure rose to its feet then, and limped toward him. Datumudi was gripping one arm from which blood ran freely.

"It is finished, *tuan*," he said. "The evil *sahibs* are no more."

Carson nodded slowly. "You changed their dynamite charge, Datumudi," he said. "You moved it so—— But I still don't understand——"

The Dyak shook his head. "I but returned to *Tuan* Girard the white sticks he so carelessly left behind, *tuan*. It was the will of the gods."

DAWN was slowly replacing the night's darkness. As they sat around the camp fire, Peter Barret, eyes bright, nodded to Carson and leveled a finger at the two articles that lay on the ground before them. One was a lump of reddish-brown slag. The other was a torn and powder-burned knapsack.

"Coronium," Barrett said. "The explosion broke through an entire vein."

His body relaxed, and a note of relief entered his voice. "And the knapsack is even more important," he said. "It belonged to Gomez, and it contains papers sufficiently incriminating to convict and destroy the whole spy organization he represented."

Carson puffed at his pipe. He looked down at the ore fragments, then across at Madeline Barret.

"You know," he said, "I'm rather glad I came along."

And Datumudi dug his toes into the dirt and grinned.

THE JADE SCARLOTTI

By CARL JACOBI

ENDERSON came aboard at Samarinda thirty minutes before the *Sela Luang* was about to get under way: an enormous man with a huge head, gray hair and a gray-black mustache, carefully clipped. I knew of course that he had signed on for passage as ordinary seaman, but that was a paradox in itself, for he was neither ordinary nor a seaman, although he looked as if he could do the work of any two fo'c's'le hands.

The Old Man came down from the ridge to welcome him personally. And then the two of them stood at the rail and watched the loading of Henderson's gear, the principal item of which was a large-sized packing case, tarp-covered and protected at the corners with slabs of rubber.

There was some argument at first as to where the packing case should be stowed. In the end it went down into the Number One hold, while Henderson took his rifles, his motion-picture camera, and his duffel bag to his cabin.

The *Sela Luang* weighed anchor, and I went up to my radio shack abaft the chart-house. So that was the great Henderson, I said to myself. Well, he looked the part. He looked big game hunter, every inch of him, and I could well believe that this was the man who, with his arm swollen like a balloon from a Hamadryad bite, had marched across miles of swamp and jungle until sheer driving will carried him to medical aid.

In the radio shack the smell of the *Sela Luang* was a little better, but not much. She was a lousy old tub. She needed paint and a good fumigating, and why anyone should deliberately take passage on her was more than I could see.

Later that morning the Old Man called me to his cabin and introduced me.

"There's been a little mix-up about Mr. Henderson's private cargo," the captain said. "That packing case you saw come aboard contains some rubber seedlings for experimental planting. It was supposed to hold— well, never mind. The point is, Mr. Henderson wants the case transferred to another ship before we reach port. The seedlings are—er—perishable, y'know, and they've got to reach S'pore in growing condition."

"What ship?" I said slowly. There was something funny here.

"The *Java Queen*," put in Henderson. "Do you know where she is at the present time?"

"Not exactly," I said. "I took a weather log from her operator a little while ago, but I don't remember her position. But the *Java Queen* isn't a freighter. She's a Dutch steamer and——"

"I know—I know," said Captain Fenner. "Captain Van Horn is a personal friend of mine. Try to raise her again, Sparks, and tell her to stand by for a message from me. Mr. Henderson is acting for a rubber-planter acquaintance of his and is anxious to have this matter taken care of."

Both men maintained a stiff silence until I left the cabin. Back in the radio shack I sent out a call for the *Java Queen*, but her operator wasn't on the air then, and I got nothing but a QRM interference signal from a copra freighter off Palembang. I leaned back in the swivel chair and lit my pipe. If Henderson's packing case contained seedling rubber plants, how come it was such an airtight affair? And how come a man as experienced as he in arranging cargo transportation would permit a mix-up?

Up on the far wall a couple of cockroaches were racing each other toward the door. I was watching them and laying mental odds on the bigger one when a heavy step sounded and Henderson entered. He had exchanged his sun helmet for a silk cap, and the new headgear made his skull look even larger. He sat down, slid a whitish cheroot between his lips and smiled what apparently was meant to be an engaging smile.

"Have you contacted the *Java Queen* yet?" he asked.

"Not yet." Something about the big man grated on me, and my answer was terse.

"Suppose it's only a matter of time until you do," he said. "All right, Sparks, I want you to send a personal message for me. Give me a piece of paper, and I'll write it down."

I laid my pipe in an ashtray and shook my head. "This isn't a liner, you know. Sorry, I can only take messages from the captain."

The line of his lips pulled back a little from his teeth, and a faint glitter entered his eyes.

"Of course," he said. "Ask the captain, if you wish. I wouldn't think of breaking regulations."

CAPTAIN FENNER was on the bridge, shooting the sun, when I came up to him a moment later. The sextant wasn't necessary, of course, but he had a habit of using it when time hung heavy on his hands. He listened to me and hesitated a moment.

"All right," he said at length, "send his message." Then he added, "Keep a copy of it. For the log y'know."

As I reentered the radio shack I saw that

Henderson had helped himself to my desk pad and was busy scribbling with a new type fountain pen. Finished, he tore off the sheet and handed it to me.

"Let me know if there's a reply," he said, stepping out with his long stride.

I looked at the message. It was addressed to A. W. Cavenaugh, 16 Kalang Dock Road, Singapore, and read:

RUBBER SEEDLINGS ON WAY. PROBABLY ARRIVE S'PORE BY JAVA QUEEN. TAKE ALL PRECAUTIONS. HENDERSON.

After that the big-game hunter kept more or less to himself, and I saw him only from a distance. He spent hours standing at the rail and watching the sea. He made a picture there in his loose-fitting corduroy bush coat and whipcord breeches with his massive frame at graceful ease like the tawny cats he had spent his life in tracking. Only once did he make any contact with other members of the crew, but that was a rather unpleasant contact. Just before dusk he sighted a streamer of smoke far off to starboard and, apparently deciding to investigate, started to climb to the bridge. He was met at the top of the ladder by the Second, Mr. Jarvis, whose watch it was. Jarvis simply stood there, effectually blocking Henderson's way.

"Passengers not allowed here," he said in his quiet manner.

"But I'm not a passenger," argued Henderson.

"I don't give a damn who you are," snapped Jarvis. "You can't come on the bridge."

Henderson stood there a long moment; then he shrugged and went back down the ladder. He turned and gazed an instant in my direction, and I saw his eyes. They were narrowed slightly, and they were dry and brittle looking with unplumbed depths.

Blinding heat centered down upon the *Sela Luang*. The sun was a shimmering brass disc in a cloudless sky, and the sea swept by us in long heaving swells, so bright and glittery it hurt the eye to look. It was hot even for the fo'c'sle crew, a mixture of lascars and Straits Chinese, and at intervals one of them would sluice down several of his companions with sea-water.

Meanwhile, a resistor in the haywire transmitter had opened up, and I spe sweating hours, trying to find it. Fina however, I got it in working order, rais the *Java Queen*, and sent Captain Fenne message. It stipulated a meet between t two ships at high noon on the twelfth latitude three degrees, twelve minutes Sou longitude 109 degrees, twenty-seven minu East. Captain Fenner stood looking over r shoulder while I tapped the key:

. . . INVOLVING A MATTER OF MUTU INTEREST AND THE TRANSFER OF A SMA AMOUNT OF CARGO TO YOUR SHIP. ALL I CONVENIENCES WILL BE TAKEN CARE (AND THE DEAL MADE WORTH YOUR WHIL TRUST ME.

The Dutch ship's okay came after a lor wait.

I didn't doubt for a moment but that tl Old Man and the skipper of the *Java Quee* had cooked up some deal between then selves. Captain Fenner was known up an down the islands as a man who would n hesitate to turn an extra dollar, honest (otherwise. But I fell to wondering wh. rubber seedlings had to do with it. Or wer they rubber seedlings? After all, I had on Henderson's and Captain Fenner's wor for it.

NOON day mess over, I exchanged little conversation via the key with Limey operator of a coastwise hooker u Penang way. Then I left the radio shac and sauntered casually below. Using only pocket flash for light, I made my way dowr into the Number One hold.

Presently I caught sight of Henderson' packing case. It stood in a corner and wa still tarp-covered, with no air holes visible I walked around it, sniffing. There was nc smell of fresh earth or growing things. I went back to the scuttle and took down a small crowbar from a hook. Then I started to pry open the cover.

It was hard, slow work, and I was getting no place fast. But abruptly a voice behind me spoke:

"My rubber seedlings seem to interest you, Sparks."

Henderson stood there, leaning against a hogshead. He was smiling, but in spite of the smile his face was utterly devoid of emoon. I dropped the crowbar and shoved my ands into my pockets.

"Maybe I'm wrong," I said, "but I've always been told that growing plants need a certain amount of oxygen. What kind of seedlings have you got here, petrified?"

He licked his lips slowly. He started to talk, then changed his mind and regarded me in silence for a long moment. "I had hoped I wouldn't have to go into this," he said at length. "Well, come along to my cabin and maybe I can explain."

Henderson's quarters were next to Jarvis', below the bridgehouse. Inside, he carefully closed the door, rumaged in his duffel bag and came out with a box of cheroots. He offered me one, lit one himself and drew in the smoke with a sigh of satisfaction.

"You're a smart man, Sparks," he said. "I can see that, and I can see that if I try to tell you half a story, you'll start thinking all sorts of things." He opened his wallet and handed me a rather worn photograph.

It was a picture of a smallish man in his middle forties, slightly bald with rather lonely eyes. He looked English, but he might have been anything.

"That's Stewart," Henderson said, "Dave Stewart. He doesn't look like so much, does he? You wouldn't think he had the nerve of three men and endurance to match. But he had." The big-game hunter leaned back in his chair, crossed his legs and stared out the open port. His thinnish lips were pressed loosely about the cheroot, but the muscles of his jaw and the way he held his hands gave the impression that he was tense and uncertain how to begin.

"Stewart was my companion-in-trade for more than fifteen years. When it came to hunting, he could follow a spoor long after most Dyaks or Malays had given up, and he handled a .60-110 express rifle like a wizard. He was a genius at organization work too, and this business of big game requires plenty of that. Besides the native carriers to be hired, the sampans or prahus to be obtained, and the food and supplies to be purchased and packed, the job necessitated a lot of skill in palavering with tribal kapalas and local chiefs, getting passage permission across their territory. Some of these natives of the interior were stubborn and troublesome, and I always left all that to Stewart. He handled it like a diplomat.

"During the war years, of course, we had to stop operations entirely. But three months ago we got a contract from the Zoological Gardens at Batavia to supply them with some leopards, both spotted and black, a good-sized female orang-utan and any number of bird specimens.

"We started at Samarinda, East Borneo, planned to go up the Mahakam River by easy stages, making side trips up the many tributary streams; then at the headwaters cross the Apo Kayan district to the Kayan River, and so to Tandjonp Selor and the coast. A difficult trip and a long one, but we were both anxious to get into the harness again.

"Stewart wangled a launch from a Chinese trader, and that carried us as far as Long Iram. There we spent three weeks organizing our party. Meanwhile, I had already captured two fine orangs and sent them downriver to be picked up later. After that we just coasted along and enjoyed ourselves and let the natives do the work. It was fine country, if you like jungle, which I do. The Mangroves and the Palapaks crowded close to the river's edge, and the sun was like gold slanting through the morning mist. And nights we sat around our fire and smoked, with everything peaceful and quiet and only the water rustling through the rip grass and reeds.

"I remember it was one of those nights far upriver that Stewart told me his real reason for wanting to hunt in that district. Seems that his son had served with the Aussies during the war and had taken part in the Borneo invasion. Stewart had never said much about his boy until then, but I knew he had been killed on the island, killed in some vague way not directly connected with the Japanese.

"But that night in the flickering campfire-light Stewart seemed anxious to confide in someone.

"He told a queer story. Like the Japs, the Australians, you know, made little attempt to penetrate inland. A few reconnaissance parties, however, did go incountry, and one of them, officered by Stewart's son, pushed on almost to the headwaters; that is to say about a day's paddling beyond where we were camped that night. It was their original intention to relieve a Dutch outpost that had been cut off by the Japs, but they learned that the post had been abandoned months before.

"The rains set in earlier than they had expected, and Stewart's party decided to lay over for a time in one of the larger villages that flanked the river. And there they saw the jade Scarlotti."

Henderson paused to relight his cheroot and glance across at me. I said nothing, waiting for him to continue.

"Remember, I'm telling you all these details because I'm convinced you're the kind of a man who wouldn't be satisfied with anything but a complete story. Now then, you've got to go back twenty or twenty-five years to the time Luigi Scarlotti first came into international fame. He was an artist of the first water: painter, designer, sculptor, an Italian by birth, though he lived in Boston. Scarlotti's paintings sold for a fabulous amount, and he was compared to most of the masters. All at once he sickened of his artificial life, converted all his possessions into cash and disappeared. For a while all kinds of wild tales circulated about his disappearance. He was seen in India, in Bangkok. He was reported dead a dozen times. The last anyone definitely heard of him he had boarded a Chinese trader, heading down the Malay coast.

"Stewart's son, of course, was too young to remember this, but he supplemented education for age. The boy had studied to be an architect before entering the service, and he had taken several courses in art appreciation. What he saw there in that upriver tribal village stunned him with its importance.

"It was a bas-relief carved from a solid block of pure Oceanic jade, and it was unquestionably Scarlotti work. The design showed the heads and foreparts of two adult leopards locked in a death struggle. Stewart's son asked questions, learned that a lone white man had stumbled out of the jungle years before, almost dying of fever. The Dyaks had nursed him back to health, and he had stayed on, living native fashion, glorying in his primitive surroundings. He had spent his life there, apparently without desire for civilization contacts. Here then was the answer to a two-decade mystery. But aside from that Stewart's son realized that he had made a great find in the jade carving, one which considering the jade alone was worth a fortune.

"But when he attempted to carry the thing away with him, he ran into trouble. To the Dyaks, it seems, Scarlotti had been more or less of a magician, and the evil gods of bad crops and plague were imprisoned in the carving. Remove it from its place of supplication, and those gods would be free to vent their wrath unhampered. Stewart's son was young and a bit devil-may-care, and his good sense at the time probably was blinded by what seemed to him an exciting adventure. At any rate, he attempted to take the Scarlotti by force and lost his life ingloriously. That was the story Stewart told me that night over the fire."

HENDERSON dropped the stub of his cheroot in an ashtray and got to his feet slowly. He strode across the cabin to a locker and took out a bottle of Irish whiskey. He filled two glasses, handed me one and slumped back in his chair.

"Next day," he continued, "we headed upriver again as if nothing had happened. But I began to watch Stewart, and I knew what was on his mind. He began to study the jungle-lined shores, and from time to time he wrote in a little pocket notebook. At high noon he suddenly ordered the Dyak boatman inshore.

"At first I could see no sign whatever of a village there. Then the river mist cleared a bit, and a bamboo ladder showed leading up a low cliff.

"Well, it was the place all right. I recognized it from Stewart's description. The longhouse was built in the shape of a rough ellipse, and a curious wide-eaved nipa-thatch hut at the far side of the village housed the jade Scarlotti.

"Stewart then utilized his diplomatic powers to the utmost. He told the kapala we were great hunters and asked his aid in securing native beaters. When the kapala was indifferent, he described the big feast that had been held in a kampong farther downriver as a result of our activities. Before he had finished, he had the entire village in a state of excited expectation for the coming hunt.

"Two days later we marched inland at the head of a company that included every ablebodied native. But, of course, Stewart wasn't interested in game. He made a great to-do of studying trails, then announced that he d I would go ahead and signal when we d sighted our quarry.

"You guessed it. What we really did was cle back to the village. The place was all t deserted, and Stewart had no difficulty in wing those that were left. With the aid of r boatmen we then proceeded to drag om its stone mounting in the hut the jade ock, carry it to the river shore, and float it two *prahus* lashed together.

"Not until then did I have opportunity to amine the thing at close range. I confess e carving disappointed me, though I don't ave much appreciation for that sort of ing. The leopards didn't look much like opards to me; they were sort of rectangular d the heads seemed out of proportion. hat's the new tendency in art, I suppose. ut the jade itself was beautiful, and even if hadn't been carved by a master artist, I new it was very valuable. It was a perfect lock, without a single flaw, something you ldom see in Oceanic jade. It was soft and apy to the touch, and it was composed of lmost pure Prehnite.

"I reminded Stewart that his son had got s far as the river in his attempt to take the ning, but the man wouldn't listen to me. nd then I realized that this was the climax f an obsession, that during the entire trip tewart had lived only for this moment. I uppose it was a kind of father and son ish-fulfillment. His boy had lost his life n a project that he now was completing for im posthumously."

Henderson placed his empty glass on the able and closed his eyes in retrospection.

"Stewart died there at the river shore," he vent on. "Just as we were pushing out into he current, a Sumpit blow-dart whispered ut of the jungle, and the next minute he vas slumped across the thwart of the canoe, oughing his life away.

"That's about all." Henderson's voice was ard and curiously without emotion. "I man- ged to get away downriver. There was pur- uit, of course, and for a time it was touch nd go. But we made it, and with the Scar- lotti. Naturally, I saw right away that if the Indonesian government knew I was taking an article of such value out of the country, there'd be all sorts of objections. And even if permission to remove it were granted, the customs office would take a good share of its value. I did two things. I covered up my

trail, tried to keep my natives from talking and all that, and I contacted an agent I know in Singapore who handles that sort of thing and arranged to have him take it off my hands. I was taking a chance, of course, but no one listens to the Samarinda wireless any- way; but just before I went aboard the *Sela Luang* I learned that one of my boatmen had spilled the beans. We got away before the investigation could start, but the chances are ten to one I'll be subject to an investigation the minute we reach port. Figure it out for yourself. Transferring the Scarlotti to an- other ship was my only alternative. Captain Fenner was—er—good enough to see with me, eye to eye."

The silence that fell after this long talk was embarrassing. Henderson lit another cheroot, and I said, "Scarlotti—the artist chap—what finally happened to him?"

The big-game hunter shrugged. "Oh, he had died there of leprosy years ago. In a way it's a good thing he did. You see that makes that carving doubly valuable now. Of course," he added quickly, "I don't want to be selfish about it. When I've disposed of it, I fully intend to send a part of the profit to Stewart's widow. And anyway, it's only a matter of beating the customs' people, and that's being done every day."

That night in my cabin, with the air hot and thick as moist gauze, I went over Hen- derson's story, detail for detail. There was no good reason why it should concern me, but the more I thought about it, the more it struck me that it was too pat. There was too much Stewart and not enough big-game hunter. Henderson's role of casual observer was hardly in keeping with the man's extro- vert qualities. As for Captain Fenner, his conniving acceptance of the whole plan told me two things: that Henderson was paying him liberally and that he was nothing more than the blowsy ruin of a man I had always suspected him to be.

THE *Sela Luang* continued to plough its way west by northwest, and the heat steadily became more oppressive. I picked up storm warnings from the British Naval Station as S'pore, but there seemed to be no indication that the blow would hit us. At mess Henderson attempted to start a conver- sation with Mr. Jarvis, but the Second barely answered him.

"He's too smooth," Jarvis said to me, aside. "He reminds me of a windfall apple; nice exterior, rotten inside."

The morning of the twelfth dawned hot and bright, but off to the east a thin wafer of greenish cloud gave promise of bad weather. With the time nearing for our meet with the *Java Queen*, I got to worrying about Stewart again. Worrying, I say, and yet it was silly troubling my head over a dead man. Twice I was prompted to ask Henderson to let me see the jade Scarlotti, but each time I rejected the idea after a moment's thought. At three bells the big-game hunter came up on deck and advanced to his customary place at the rail. There was perceptible in him an attitude of complacent satisfaction as he stood there gazing into the distance. His very stance seemed to flaunt contempt and sardonic defiance toward his fellow man. I watched him for a while, and then abruptly a latent thought crept up far back in a corner of my mind.

THE thought grew and developed and clarified. Now it had blanketed my brain, crowding aside all else. How strange that it had never occurred to me before. And then I realized how cleverly insignificant detail, had been piled on detail, masking the truth so that I couldn't see the woods for the trees. I left the bridge and went down to the cabins under the house. Before the door to Henderson's room I drew up, hesitating. I could be wrong, of course, but—— The door was locked. Impulsively I jerked out my pocket knife and fitted it into the antequated opening. Inside I went directly to Henderson's duffel bag and began a careful search through it.

Beyond a few personal articles there was nothing of interest. The shelves of the locker contained shaving kit, comb, brush and a metal mirror, and a canvas holster containing Henderson's automatic revolver, an old-type British Navy regulation Webley-Scott. On the table beside the bunk still lay the open box of cheroots. Beside it was a fine Lorenzo watch with a heavy chain and a small gold-cased compass in lieu of a charm. The trunk next, much-battered and scratched from heavy service. Halfway across to it, I stopped short, frowning.

What was I looking for? What did I expect to find here, rummaging through an-

other man's cabin like a sneak thief? After all, I had only a chance word here and the upon which to base my suspicions.

I opened the trunk. It contained generous amounts of underclothing, a pair of expensive mosquito boots, a rubber poncho and several lightweight suits of whites.

Suddenly I jerked erect, listening. Foot steps had sounded, advancing down the outer corridor. My pulse raced as they approached the door of the cabin, as the seemed to slow there and hesitate. But the steps passed on without stopping, and I realized with a sigh of relief that it was Mr. Jarvis returning to his cabin.

I returned to the duffel bag, felt for false bottom, felt into each of the side pockets of the lining. There was another box of cheroots there, apparently full and unopened, but as I was about to replace it I noticed that the seal was broken. I lifted the cover, and there it was—a small leather bound notebook, with the initials *D. S* burned on the top surface. I turned to middle page and read the following in an even precise script:

July 18. Approximately three days from village. Weather hot and humid One of the Dyaks stepped on a *krak* thorn at last night's camp. Leg badly swollen.

I flipped the page impatiently.

July 20. We are approaching the village. As yet I have said nothing to Henderson save that foolish talk of mine two nights ago. Hope he has forgotten. Oven heat during the day, but the nights are cold. Sighted a small party of Pennihings on left bank today. They seemed friendly.

Two pages farther on there was a single notation, heavily underlined. It read:

QTI Henderson QTI QTI.

Something like a blow in the face struck me as I stared down at those words. I continued turning pages, scanning notations, reading prosaic remarks about the weather, about the jungle. Was the significance behind Stewart's terse entry what I thought it

.? Well toward the back of the book I
.e upon another single sentence:

Henderson QTE QTE QTE

I could feel the sweat ooze out of my
.ds. With trembling fingers I turned to
last page. There it was, scrawled in
.ky letters as if written under violent
:ss of emotion:

QRR QRR Henderson QRR QRR

I closed the book and placed it in my
:ket. I zipped shut the duffel bag, left the
.in very quietly and made my way topside.
Henderson was sitting in one of two can-
. chairs on the bridge wing, a place Cap-
.n Fenner was in the habit of reserving
. himself for a brief siesta after the noon-
.y mess. Under the awning the big-game
.nter was smoking his perpetual cheroot.
. nodded casually as I took the chair
.reast of him.
"The *Java Queen* should be coming into
.ht in an hour or two," he said. "Have
.a spoken with her lately, Sparks?"
I nodded. "She's standing by, waiting for
."
A smile of satisfaction crossed his lips.
'll be glad to be rid of the thing," he said.
. piece of jade that size and a Scarlotti at
.at isn't the easiest thing to lug around
.ese seas."

WATCHED him for a moment. "This
. partner of yours—Stewart—interests
.e," I said. "Tell me more about him."
His eyelids flickered: "Why, there's noth-
.g more to tell. He was killed out there in
.e jungle, poor devil. I suppose I haven't
.ghtly got over the shock of his death yet,
.d it'll be years until I accustom myself to
.s loss. He was a good man."
I lit my pipe. "He was an American, I
.lieve you said?"
Henderson nodded. "Australian born and
.ved quite a number of years in Sidney, but
.e spent his youth in the States."
"Was he interested is radio?"
The hunter eyed me contemplatively for
.veral seconds. "Now that you speak of it,
.believe he was. I remember he told me
.nce that he had operated his own trans-
.itting set in Boston, a 'ham' set, I believe

you call it. That was a long time ago, of
course. Why?"
I answered his question with another.
"Out there in the jungle, at the native village, was there any argument at all as to how
the profits from the Scarlotti carving would
be divided between you? After it was sold,
that is."
A change came over Henderson. Though
his body still remained slack, a perceptible
tenseness entered his face. I could see his
eyes grow hard and glittery again the way
they had when Jarvis had ordered him off
the bridge.
"That's a damned strange question. There
was no argument whatsoever. We always
divided our profits fifty-fifty."
I knocked the ashes from my pipe and
braced myself. "Then why did you murder
him?"
Had a blow struck him he could have
been no more startled. His jaw gaped open;
he stared; then he burst out laughing, a hollow mirthless laugh.
"So that's what's been sticking in your
craw. Well, Sparks, I don't know how you
arrived at that conclusion, but your deduc-
tive powers are all wet. I didn't kill Stewart.
I didn't steal the jade Scarlotti from him.
And even if I did either of those things, I
rather think you'd have a tough job proving
them. Stewart is buried far up the Mahakam
River, and if you've been receiving some
crazy reports passed on by my Dyak boatmen—well, I think you know no one accepts
the word of a Dyak."
"I've received no reports," I said. "But I
do have this." And I drew out Stewart's
notebook.
"Been going through my luggage, eh?
Well, there's nothing in that book either.
It—"
"It gives me all the proof I need, Henderson. I think you admitted that Stewart was
a former radio amateur. Now if you'll look
on several pages of this notebook, you'll
find three series of letters preceded or followed by your name: QTI, QTE, and
QRR."
The hunter's face had paled. "What of
it?" he snarled. "They don't mean a thing.
I'm familiar to some extent with the wireless code, and there's nothing incriminating
about those letters. As a matter of fact, it's
a sort of slang Stewart used all the time. He

had a trick, for example, of shouting 'QRM' when he wanted the natives to stop their jabbering."

I shook my head. "Not slang, Henderson. 'Q' signals. They're abbreviations known and used by every radio operator. Take a look at the first combination of letters, QTI. Translated, it means: '*What is your true course?*' The implication is obvious. Stewart suspected you, but at the time of that writing a doubt remained in his mind.

"Again several pages farther on we find the letters *QTE*. QTE translated means '*What is my true bearing in relation to you?*' Stewart obviously wrote that after you and he had escaped the village with the Scarlotti.

"And finally—" I paused and shoved my hands in my pockets—"there are the letters *QRR*. That clinches it, for QRR is the radio amateur's danger or distress signal, the signal used only when serious trouble is directly at hand. Coupled as it was with your name, that signal can mean only one thing. You've admitted that Stewart was a capable man. You were a fool not to see that he knew what you were going to do, but realized it after it was too late to help himself."

A muscle had begun to twitch on Henderson's cheek. Under his lower lip a tiny bead of sweat formed. His eyes were wide open now, staring. When he spoke his voice was husky.

"And just what are you going to do with that information?"

"I'm going to inform the operator of the *Java Queen*," I said coldly, "the ship we're going to meet presently. I'm also going to advise the *controlleur* of the Indonesian Po-lice at Batavia. The matter is out of hands."

Henderson sat there motionless a lo moment. Then he slowly got to his feet. "I think I'll go below," he said.

CAPTAIN FENNER was in the cha house when I came up a few minu later.

"Sir," I said, "I have a question I'd li to ask you."

He regarded me curiously. "Go ahe Sparks."

"It's this. Suppose two men had be friends for years, had gone through thi and thin together. Suppose together th came into possession of an article worth large sum of money. And suppose one them by a process of slow premeditati killed the other so that he would be able keep both halves of the profits. What you think would be his reaction wh confronted with absolute evidence of h guilt?"

Captain Fenner was silent a moment. " white man?" he said at length.

"A white man, yes."

"I should think that he would take t quickest way out—that he would——"

Abruptly from below decks a sound sp the silence. It was the hollow muffled thun of a revolver shot. Both of us stood qui still as the sound went echoing through t bowels of the ship.

"In heaven's name, what was that?" cri Fenner.

"That," I said, "was the quickest wa out."

DEATH'S OUTPOST

In the Papuan Jungle, a Human Devil Spawns a Diabolical Saurian Menace!

By

CARL JACOBI

Author of "Murder for Medusa," "Head in His Hands," etc.

Relentless, the monster came on

TOWARD evening Callahan wakened from his sleep under the stern awning of the gasoline launch and gazed ahead at the open spot in the jungle where a rude stockade encircled three *nipa*-thatch huts. Ambunti at last! The Union Jack hung above the post like a limp dishcloth, and a white man with a freshly-chalked sun helmet stood waiting on the little jetty.

Callahan scowled. By all rights he should be relieved at reaching his goal. Two hundred and thirty miles up the Sepik in the midst of New Guinea's rainy season was no picnic. But the post before him looked anything but an end to a rainbow. It resembled rather another native burial place, at least a dozen of which he had sighted along the shore.

The Chinese boatman swung the tiller. Two minutes later the launch was secured to the bollards, and Callahan leaped to the planking.

"You're Andrews, district officer in charge," he said, extending his hand. "I'm Callahan, your new assistant. You've been expecting me, I suppose."

"Glad to know you," Andrews said, shaking the hand vigorously.

He was a heavy-set man with little blood-shot eyes and a lobster-red face which would never accustom itself to a tropic sun. Scars of ancient insect bites stood out on either cheek. He drew two whitish cheroots from a breast pocket, offered the newcomer one of them, and waved his arm hospitably.

"Come inside, and I'll fix you a drink and show you around."

The showing around didn't take long. Ambunti, the most remote interior outpost in the mandated territory, was all the officials on the coast had warned Callahan it would be: Three thatch huts, one for the D.O. and his assistant; a slightly larger one for the five native police-·····ys; and a windowless storage shack. On three sides thick jungle brooded. On the fourth was the river, dark and sullen.

But Callahan had been in the wilds before, and he knew it was neither the isolation nor the forlorn location that oppressed him. Over the post an atmosphere of evil seemed to hover, as existent as the miasma that drifted over a morning swamp.

"What's that smell?" he asked Andrews as they returned to the main hut.

The district officer shrugged. "Crocodiles maybe," he replied. "I don't notice it myself, but the shores are thick with them a mile upstream. By the way, the launch starts back for the coast in an hour. If you want to write, you'd better do it now. After that we'll be cut off and alone—alone, that is, save for Trakert and Fenley."

"And who," asked Callahan, frowning, "are Trakert and Fenley?"

TRAKERT, Andrews explained, was a map survey man, a cartographer, employed by the Australian government to chart both geographically and geologically the Sepik River, mouth to source. At present he was a short distance in-country examining sedimentary rock formations. Fenley—

"Fenley's a pest," Andrews said. "He's a missionary, so he says, but about all he does is stir up trouble among the natives."

After that Callahan went to his assigned room, splashed water on his wrists and face and proceeded to change his clothes. Close-knit mosquito screening covered the two windows, but a horde of insects had crawled in from somewhere and were scurrying across the floor, table and chair tops.

As he stood there, slowly removing the articles from his canvas duffle bag, Callahan felt it again, a definite yet unexplainable aura of menace that brooded about him. He frowned, then started as an old-fashioned ship chronometer on the wall abruptly rang four bells—six o'clock.

He returned to the main chamber just as the veranda door opened, and a tall good-looking man entered. Dark-faced, and with a high forehead, he carried a small geologist's hammer at his belt, and in his hand he held a large clamp-board, the paper of which was filled with notations.

"Lans Trakert, Callahan, my new assistant," Andrews introduced. "Trakert is the survey chap I told you about, Callahan. He knows more about rocks and rivers than any man in the country."

Trakert smiled as he shook hands. "Welcome to hell," he said sarcastically. "This place is the world's worst jumping-off spot, in case you haven't heard."

The truth of the surveyman's words were brought home to Callahan an hour later when they sat about the table for the evening meal. An electrical storm, which according to Andrews was a nightly occurrence at Ambunti, sprang up from nowhere, and in a trice the compound and surrounding jungle was a raging inferno. Lightning zigzagged through the stifling heat. Wind rattled and shook the sago palms. Rain thundered incessantly on the thatch roof.

In the dingy light of the oil lamps Andrews ate his food stolidly, seemingly untroubled by the battling elements. It was not until cigars had been passed around that Callahan looked across at the district officer and said quietly:

"It strikes me that this is rather a useless place for an outpost. Just what constitutes your biggest work here? Suppressing head-hunting outbreaks?"

Andrews lit his cigar, blew out a cloud of smoke and dropped the match in a dish before answering. His eyes slowly narrowed in his moon face. "Ambunti is here for a number of reasons," he replied. "Primarily, of course, our job is to collect taxes from controlled villages. We also settle native disputes and check tribal fighting. Head-hunting is of course a big angle, but of late it's gone beyond that. Our greatest threat right now lies in the Sangumenke."

"What," Callahan asked, "is the Sangumenke?"

It seemed for a moment that Andrews was desirous of avoiding the question. He swiveled the cigar between his fat lips and coughed nervously.

"IT'S a native secret society, he said at length. "No one knows much about it, though vague reports have filtered in to the officials at Moresby and Madang for months. The general belief seems to be that it's some sort of a religious organization that practices killing for ritualistic purposes. Sort of a mafia, y'know. The hell of it is, whenever you ask a Papuan about it, he either gets scared stiff and won't talk, or else he fills you with so much poppycock the information's worthless.

"According to the few natives I've managed to pump at all, the Sangumenke have developed head-hunting to an art. They hunt heads in the old way, of course, and they dry and

cure 'em, but their treatment of the decapitated head is rather unique. Mind you, I'm only quoting what I've been told. The natives who belong to this society are supposed to have a process whereby they can graft onto the decapitated body the head of a crocodile and still maintain life."

A blinding lightning streak flashed outside the windows, and an explosion of thunder vibrated the hot air. Callahan looked across at the district officer with perplexed eyes.

"But—but surely you can't believe such idiocy as that?"

Andrews met the gaze, and his eyes wavered. "Callahan, when you've been in these evil smelling jungles as long as I have, you're ready to believe anything. Life here is a bit different than it is on the coast. We're surrounded by primitive people who have primitive methods and beliefs. Besides, Trakert, here, has seen the living proof."

The survey man brushed a hand through his wavy hair uneasily.

"I thought I saw it at any rate," he said deprecatingly. "It was horrible. I was three miles upstream, returning from a study of the delta caused by a small tributary there. The sun had gone down, and it was pretty dark, but the thing stood on the shore and simply looked at me. I—I wanted to scream."

"A native with a crocodile's head?" Callahan asked slowly.

Trakert nodded. "The thing was hideous. It had a native's tattooed body, shell loin cloth and spear in its hand. But the head was the head of a crocodile. The mouth was open, and I could see the teeth."

Even after he had gone to his room that night and undressed for bed, the survey man's words lingered in Callahan's brain. Was Trakert one of those impressionable people who, after once hearing a story, imagine it is an experience encountered in his own life? But no, Trakert didn't seem that type. He was calm and deliberate, even to the point of coldbloodedness.

The room was a sweating oven. The storm had passed on now, leaving clammy heat in its wake. Outside Callahan could hear the drone of insects, the occasional call of a night bird.

For an hour he lay there, unable to court sleep. Then finally he dozed off into a restless, dream-filled slumber.

When he awoke it was still dark, and the radium hands of his watch told him it was exactly two hours after midnight. The hut was silent save for the intermittent snoring that filtered through the bamboo partitions from Andrews' room at the other end of the corridor. Callahan lay there, listening.

SOMETHING had jarred him into consciousness, something foreign to the usual jungle night. He slid out of the .cot and moved across to the window. Starlight made the compound a vague place of blue shadows. But the intervening space between the hut and the stockade wall was empty.

Yet as Callahan stood there, he heard the unmistakable creak of the stockade gate slowly opening. Into his restricted path of vision a vague form moved slowly.

A chill stole up Callahan's spine. The gate should be closed at this time of night with a native police boy guard keeping a ceaseless vigil beside it. Quietly the assistant turned, picked up his revolver from the table and passed through the door that opened into the corridor leading to the main room of the hut.

In the center of the veranda. he stopped. He saw the shadow again, moving silently across the compound.

Callahan inched the screen door open, stole down the steps and began to close in. He had covered half of the distance when the shadow whirled abruptly, leaped forward and faced him.

It is not to be listed to Callahan's credit that he did not scream. Rigid, jaw agape, he stood there, frozen with horror, brain refusing to believe what his eyes saw.

The naked body of a Papuan native was revealed in the starlight. The long arms hung apelike at its sides, and the naked feet were spread wide in defiance. But what held the assistant there, galvanized to inactivity, was the head. Not a native head! Not a human head! But the flat, scaly head of a crocodile!

The huge mouth was partially open, disclosing rows of teeth, and white flaccid flesh. The lidless eyes were chips of agate. A hybrid growth it was, half man, half saurian. By sheer force of will Callahan whipped his revolver upward.

He had no opportunity to use it. With a hiss the monster sprang, hurled itself on the body of the assistant. He went down with a thousand terrors converging in his soul.

The monster seemed in no haste. It fought deliberately, forcing Callahan's struggling hands slowly downward, bringing its foul head inch by inch down toward the helpless white.

Just how the events arranged themselves after that Callahan could never be sure. His agonized eyes caught the glint of his fallen revolver on the ground three feet away. With a last frantic superhuman burst of strength he twisted sideward and stabbed out his hand to grasp it.

He jerked the gun around and fired. Sobbing, he continued to pull the trigger again and again, long after the hammer had clicked down on an empty cartridge. Vaguely he was aware of his assailant leaping away in the gloom, of lights appearing suddenly in the officer's hut. Mercifully then he felt a great inner weariness, and fell back into oblivion. . . .

CALLAHAN came to in the main room of the hut with Trakert and Andrews standing before him. Andrews had just finished pouring whiskey down the assistant's throat, but the district officer set the glass down on the table now, and said:

"Take it easy, son. Don't talk until you feel you can."

The liquor restored his strength quickly. But it was a quarter of an hour before he sat upright in his chair and told his story to the two men across the table.

Curiously, Andrews seemed to accept it without undue amazement. Trakert, at the district officer's request, went out to round up the five police boys and search the compound. The surveyman came back to report almost immediately. Four of the police boys insisted they had been sleeping until awakened by the sounds of the shots. The fifth, detailed to guard duty that night, was nowhere to be found. Only a pool of blood marked the spot where he usually stood sentry duty near the stockade gate.

Andrews took a big pull from the whiskey bottle when he heard this information and slumped into a chair. "That settles it," he said. "Either the government moves this post a hundred miles nearer the coast, as I've repeatedly demanded they should, or I get out. A man can stand just so much of this; no more."

The rest of the night passed quietly, though Andrews insisted on sitting on the veranda, revolver in hand, watching—watching for he knew not what.

But morning brought three visitors to Ambunti. The first of these lived near and stopped in at the post frequently. The arrival of the other two came as a bombshell.

Harrison Fenley was a hawk-faced, gaunt man with thin lips and narrow, almost Asiatic eyes. He wore a much soiled suit of whites, and he carried a gold-headed cane which Callahan suspected was for display purposes only.

Fenley styled himself a missionary, but when the assistant discreetly asked questions about church affiliations, the man's answers were vague and indefinite. A renegade undoubtedly, who was keeping well away from his past here in the jungle.

"I thought I heard several shots last night," Fenley said smoothly. "I came over to see if there was any trouble."

"No trouble," Andrews replied curtly.

And then as they stood there on the veranda they heard the plane! It came out of the southwest, flying high, a cumbersome biplane, equipped with pontoons. Motor droning, it circled, dipped in salute over the post, then glided down to a jumpy landing on the broad river. Ten minutes later it was working its way slowly toward the jetty.

"It's the government inspector from Moresby," Andrews said. Satisfaction sounded in his voice. "My suggestions that the post be moved have apparently brought results."

Callahan viewed the plane with disgust. "It's a wonder they didn't let me come up here that way," he said. "That dirty launch took more than a week to make the trip."

PRESENTLY the plane was alongside the jetty. The cabin door opened and the government inspector stepped out. And then both the district officer and his assistant stared with unbelieving eyes. Leaping lightly to the planking came a young girl.

A white girl here at Ambunti! It wasn't possible. But it was possible. Tastily clad in a tailored suit of pongee, with a white beret set roguishly over one eye, she stood there staring about her with curious eyes.

"Hello, Davis," Andrews said slowly, in response to the inspector's greeting. Then his emotions went out of control as he glared at the girl. "What in the name of eternal hellfire—"

Davis, a slight man with a toothbrush mustache and fair, almost feminine complexion, smiled. "My daughter, Hope, gentlemen. She insisted on coming along."

In the main room of the officers' hut Callahan viewed the newcomers with misgivings. The government inspector might be efficient in an executive capacity back at the coast, but his thin figure seemed horribly inadequate here. As for the girl—the assistant thought of his experience of the night before, and he shuddered.

Talk then centered down to argument. Slowly and methodically Andrews began to catalogue his reasons why the post should be moved nearer the coast.

"Ambunti is sitting on a dynamite

box," the D. O. summarized. "Only last night Callahan here was attacked in the compound by a member of the *Sangumenke.*"

The conference over, Callahan followed Hope Davis out on the veranda and sat down beside her. She was beautiful, he suddenly realized, beautiful in a delicate yet resourceful way. She didn't belong here at this jumping-off spot where hell itself seemed to be lurking in the background.

"Tell me, Mr. Callahan," she said. "What is the *Sangumenke?*"

He explained as well as he could, but he held back details. She frowned slowly.

"And you really believe these natives have the ability to graft the head of a crocodile onto a human body and still maintain life?"

"Well—" Callahan began. But Fenley, the missionary, moved onto the veranda then and smiled crookedly at them.

"Mr. Callahan not only believes it," he said. "He has seen the living proof of it."

Night came and with it another storm. The government inspector had stated that he and his daughter would remain at least three days until he could make out a complete report. Fenley had not yet left the post, and the six of them sat in the main room, speaking unconsciously in low tones. One by one they left to retire, until once again Callahan was alone with the girl.

The assistant lighted a cigarette and looked at her, content to drink in her beauty.

"You shouldn't have come here," he said at length. "The place is— Well, as Andrews said, it's a dynamite box. We're surrounded by something we don't understand."

SHE made no reply, and Callahan got up and strolled nervously toward one of the windows. It was hot in the room. The bamboo shutters had been dropped to keep out the rain, but the storm was dying now, and he pulled the rope slowly.

Suddenly the cigarette slipped from his lips. In the window he saw. . . .

It was gone in an instant, but Callahan's brain retained a photographic impression of the hideous sight that had passed before his eyes. The head of a crocodile, of a live crocodile surmounted on the neck of a native, staring at him balefully.

Revulsion swept through him as he leaped to the door and raced across the veranda to the outer steps. That window opened on the back side of the hut. He tore open the screen door and, revolver in hand, ran through the drizzle, approaching the opening from the outside.

Nothing. No shadow stood there by the sill. No figure stood ready to attack him. Callahan continued on to the front of the police boys' hut. One of the natives, clad in Sam Brown belt, looked at him curiously.

"Did you see anything—anyone here?" the assistant demanded.

"No, *tuan.*" The native shook his head stolidly.

But Callahan was not content until he had searched the entire compound. Everything, he found, was in order. The stockade gate was closed. An exceedingly nervous police boy guard stood near it.

With matches the assistant examined the ground beneath the window. The ground was hard and wet, but close to the thatch wall where the eaves sheltered it, he thought he made out the print of a naked foot.

At length, bewildered, he returned to the room.

"Nothing," he said in answer to Hope Davis' gaze. "I thought I heard something, that's all. You'd better get some sleep."

Early next morning Government Inspector Davis announced he was leaving for a tour of the neighboring native villages. There were three of them within walking distance of the post.

"If, as you say, Ambunti has become such a danger spot," Davis told the district officer, "I must see with my own eyes the attitude of the Papuans. I'll be back by nightfall."

He left with two police boys as guides, and Callahan frowned as he watched his slight figure march across the compound and disappear through the gate.

The day passed slowly. Trakert, Fenley, Hope Davis and Callahan sat on the veranda, sweating profusely, trying to stifle their emotions in a game of whist.

"I'm really not supposed to play cards, y'know," Fenley, the missionary, said.

But he did play and, as the assistant noted, he played well. Trakert, the surveyman, also played a good game, but the girl kept her attention on the table with difficulty. At intervals she glanced at Callahan, and her eyes were dull with fear.

CALLAHAN played mechanically. A native with a crocodile head, alive, and with the ability to attack! If anyone had told him that story two weeks before, he would have laughed it to ridicule. Now, like a nightmare, the memory of his battle with the hideous thing there in the compound returned to send a cold shudder down his spine.

Five o'clock passed, and still the government inspector did not return. Hope Davis nervously paced the length of the veranda. Pallor began to show in her face.

"You—you don't think anything could have happened to Father?" she said to Callahan. "Oh God, I wish he hadn't gone!"

The assistant shook his head and smiled to thwart her fears.

"Let's walk down to the river," he suggested. "It's beautiful at sunset. You'll like it."

They strolled slowly down the short path to the jetty. Parrots scolded and chattered above them, and bright-colored butterflies fluttered on all sides. The scarlet sun was dipping over the roof of the jungle, but off to the east sullen, low-riding clouds harbingered another storm.

They moved to the end of the jetty, stood staring over the broad river.

When it came the girl shielded her eyes against the sun and went slowly rigid like a slack wire drawn taut. Callahan felt a sickening wave of horror surge over him.

A native dugout canoe was drifting on the current close to shore. In it was a single occupant, propped upright against a flat-bladed paddle. A horrible figure! Callahan went suddenly sick.

The uniformed body of Government Inspector Davis was mounted in the craft like a lifeless doll. But merciful God! The body had been decapitated, and the head was the head of a crocodile! Even as the assistant stood there swaying, the canoe passed them on a swirl of current and continued downstream.

Hope Davis gave vent to her emotions then in a single prolonged scream. Callahan caught her as she fell in a dead faint. He lifted her in his arms and stumbled at a run back down the path to the post. On the veranda he seized Andrews by the arm.

"Davis murdered!" he yelled. "Come on."

Heavy though he was, the district officer responded like a deer. The two men ran back down the trail, fought their way down river along the shore.

But there was no need of haste. The canoe had lodged in a thick clump of reeds. Andrews splashed out, lifted the ghastly body and carried it to the bank. For a long moment the two men stared down upon it. Then Callahan made a careful examination.

"Severed high on the neck," Callahan said at length, fighting back a surge of nausea. "Davis can't have been dead more than a few minutes. But the crocodile was killed days ago. Something was used to stop the flow of blood. Whoever placed the croc head on the body did a crude job of it. Look, sir, you can see the splinters of bamboo jammed into the flesh to hold it in position."

The district officer leaned against the bole of a tree. His lips were moving, but no sound came from them. He was unable to answer.

"We can't let Hope see this again at close range," Callahan said. "I'll send a police boy down to take care of the body. Come, man, get hold of yourself."

ANDREWS was completely unstrung. Silently he permitted his assistant to lead him back down the path to the post. On the veranda Callahan braced himself for an ordeal. Oddly, the veranda was deserted. They went into the main room of the hut. Here, too, there was no sign of Trakert, Fenley or Hope Davis. And then a single object centered itself in Callahan's gaze, and he rocked backward with an oath.

A chair on the far side of the room was overturned. Beside it the mat rug was a twisted heap.

Callahan vaulted forward into the corridor leading to the sleeping rooms. Five feet forward he halted, staring down at the motionless figure of Harrison Fenley. The missionary lay supine, arms outflung, a bloodsmeared welt over one eye.

But the girl, Hope Davis, and Trakert were gone!

Back on the veranda the assistant rushed, to stare about him with frantic eyes. He tore open the screen door and raced across to the police boy hut. Over the threshold he slewed to a stop, heart pounding. A police boy lay dead in his bunk, a knife buried deep in his chest. Of the other native soldier there was no sign.

But at the stockade gate, to which Callahan ran like a madman, there was a single object which seemed to scream back at him in its mute appeal. A girl's handkerchief, splattered with blood, lay on the ground. Five yards farther on along the river trail was a torn remnant of a dress.

Callahan remembered little of his frenzied passage down that trail. It was dark, with the jungle walls pressing close, and the shadows that formed about him were a thousand devils of mockery.

The river trail, he knew, led to the most distant of the neighboring villages. Halfway it dipped low into marshy ground, and it was here that the crocodiles abounded. A nameless fear rose up within him.

Suddenly the trees fell away, and he burst into an open spot, lined with thick *lallang* grass. Ahead he could hear the low soughing of the river.

And then a flare of light materialized out of the gloom, and a flaming torch rose up before him. A man held that torch in one hand high above him. He strode forward, a step at a time, advancing toward the assistant.

In the flickering light Callahan gazed with horror at the monster. The body was that of a native, darkskinned and naked save for a loin cloth, but the head was the head of a crocodile. The jaws were gaping, the eyes . . .

This time Callahan didn't wait for the attack. Whipping up his revolver he fired three times pointblank. Relentless, the monster came on.

CALLAHAN flung the weapon before him with all the strength he possessed. Then he braced himself and closed in. It was a demon of a nether world that received him. A terrific, blinding blow caught him hard over the heart; long, apelike hands stabbed out to coil about his throat.

In an instant his windpipe was shut off, and his lungs were bursting within him. He fought the hold loose, delivered a powerful right into the monster's midsection. Then they were down, rolling over and over.

In meeting the attack the monster had cast aside its torch, and the flaming wood lay in a clump of weeds, flickering weirdly, casting Gargantuan shadows over the surrounding jungle. Callahan's head was pressed back now, his arms pinned to his sides. Terror lent unknown strength to his body. He got his hands free. He lurched upward, seized one of the monster's arms and snapped it backward with a peculiar twisting motion. An abrupt scream of agony split the air. Callahan bent the arm farther, felt bone and sinew give way in a sickening crack. Then the monster fell backward, sobbing moans issuing hollowly from its throat.

The assistant staggered to his feet weakly, seized the dying torch and held it above him. "Hope!" he cried hoarsely. "Where are you?"

A low gurgle guided him twenty feet into the bush. He found the girl lashed to a tree, a gag in her mouth. "Are you all right?" Callahan asked. She shook her head. "All right," she gasped. "I — I —" Callahan led the way back to the clearing, took the rope and proceeded to bind his motionless assailant thoroughly. It was not until then that he tore off the false crocodile head and stared down at the familiar features of the white man before him.

* * *

"YOU see," Callahan said the next morning on the veranda of the post, "it was a carefully worked-out scheme, and the attacks in each case were very much premeditated. Trakert played a lone hand for a big stake, but he lost. It was only the background that he used for a stage setting that fooled us. Do you know what this is, Andrews?"

The assistant held out to the district officer a flat piece of grayish rock. Andrews examined it.

"Mica schist," he replied. "But I still don't see —"

"Mica schist, yes. You remember Trakert was an experienced geologist. I found this rock slab in his room. While studying geologic conditions in this district, Trakert apparently found large deposits of that mica schist. He recognized it immediately for what it was, a strong indication of the presence of emeralds.

"Emeralds, Andrews! Trakert had struck it rich! He knew, however, that if he attempted to mine and take those stones out of the country he would have to pay a high duty to the mandate government. Mining them in secret with Ambunti so close was, of course, impossible. So he reasoned that the mountain must come to Mohammed. Or in other words, the post itself must be moved.

"Trakert built his plot carefully. He suggested from time to time that you demand to the officials that the post be located nearer the coast because of increasingly dangerous conditions here, and he enlarged upon the story of the *Sangumenke*.

"The *Sangumenke* as a secret native society no doubt exists, but not as Trakert would have had us believe. It

was he who appeared in the compound that night with a crocodile head, killed the native guard and attacked me. It was he who stole from his bedchamber with that disguise and looked in the window when Hope and I were in the main room alone. Previously he had killed a number of the reptiles, and dried and cleaned the heads and fashioned those masks out of them. The first time he attacked me the shots from my revolver almost got him. After that he substituted blanks for the cartridges in my gun.

"When Government Inspector Davis came, Trakert realized he must bring his plot to a head. So he left the post, came upon Davis and the two police boys as they were making their return from the village inspection trip and murdered them. Then he fixed up the body in the dugout canoe, sent it floating downriver for the proper theatrical effect. He wanted to impress you, Andrews, you see, that the post must be moved from here, and moved at once.

"He might have won if he hadn't stepped too far. His eye had been caught by the beauty of Hope Davis, and he wanted her as well as the emeralds. Back at the post he managed to send one of the police boys away by subterfuge, then k i d n a p e d Miss Davis. Fenley, the missionary, tried to stop him, but Trakert struck him, leaving him, as he thought, to die. Fortunately it was only a glancing blow, and Fenley will recover. Then to complete the picture Trakert murdered the last police boy at Ambunti and carried off Miss Davis. You know the rest."

ANDREWS, the district officer, lit a cheroot with shaking fingers. "I see," he said. "All right, Callahan, you can take Davis' plane, fly back to Port Moresby and hand Trakert over to the authorities. He'll hang for this, of course. As for you, Miss Hope —"

The girl had risen from her chair and moved across to Callahan's side slowly. She smiled tremulously.

"I think I'll be well taken care of," she said.

LEOPARD TRACKS

By
CARL JACOBI
*Author of
"Holt Sails the
'San Hing',"* etc.

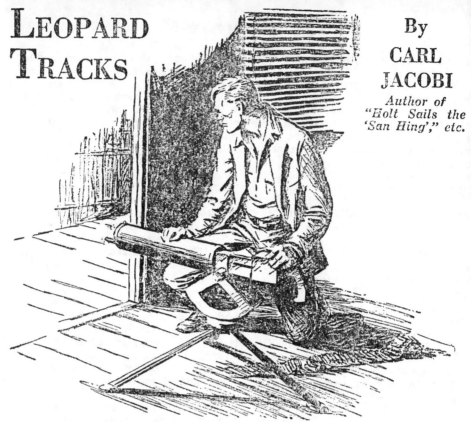

*A Really Good Engineer Doesn't Fancy Himself as Crocodile
Bait—Not At All, in Fact*

STOCKTON was halfway between sleep and consciousness when the train ground to a sudden stop. The wheezy locomotive screamed a protesting whistle blast, and the groans and creakings of the wooden coach gave way to the thick silence of the jungle.

Stockton opened his eyes slowly. Dim light from the car's hanging lamps made a drooling glare of the rain-washed windows. But outside the blackness was unbroken.

There could be no legitimate reason for the train's stopping here. Long Hatap, the last intermediate station lay forty miles behind. Between Long Hatap and Sepitang, his destination, was only jungle.

Up ahead a confusion of yells sounded as Malay trainmen ran forward to inspect the trouble. The door to Stockton's coach opened, and the native conductor hurried down the aisle.

"Something is wrong, Tuan," he said. "Someone has placed a tree across the tracks."

Stockton nodded. Without reply he got to his feet, paced through the entrance and swung down the steps. Rain and wind, the forerunners of the southwest monsoon, smote his face as he advanced quickly to the front of the train.

A moment later he came to a halt in the glare of the engine's headlight. Fifty feet ahead, squarely across the narrow-gauge track, a heavy Seraya tree barred all passage. The native engineer and fireman stood in silence, gazing at the obstruction stupidly.

"Tuan." Kelea, Stockton's Number-One boy, materialized out of the gloom and seized his master's arm. "Tuan, you had best go back in the train. It is the Muruts. They will attack any moment."

A gleam snapped into Stockton's gray eyes as the familiar sight of Kelea's moon-face and the sting of the rain combined to bring back his old alertness. He was a tall, rangy man with an incisive face and a firm jaw. He squared his shoulders now, snapped:

"Run back to coach three and hustle out that gang of Dyaks. Post guards at the end and either side of the train. Move!"

The Malady nodded and vanished in the darkness. Stockton turned to the fallen tree.

HE HAD been warned something like this would happen. Trouble with the Muruts was to be expected, of course. But all the way from Sandakan Stockton had wondered by what miracle this railroad managed to operate. The native trainmen were lax and incompetent. The coaches, dry of oil, developed hot-boxes with maddening regularity. Trestles creaked and trembled. And overshadowing it all was the officials' suave and shrugging indifference. "It cannot be helped."

Stockton's job was to see that it was helped. Employed by the company's London stockholders, he had come here to British North Borneo for a double purpose; to improve the present two hundred miles of trackage and to continue the road forty-five miles farther into rubber-rich Sepitang jungle.

From the beginning, since he had arrived on location, he had been advised repeatedly both were impossible. More than that, on the night before he had boarded the train for the interior the warnings had come to a sinister head. A pistol shot had missed him by inches as he strode along a waterfront street.

Stockton was puzzled. He knew some dark motive lay beneath it all. But up until now he had only vague innuendos to support his suspicions.

Running footsteps sounded behind him, and ten or the thirty Coast Dyaks he had hired for construction-labor shambled forward.

"Move the tree!" Stockton ordered. But even as he spoke, it happened.

Back in the jungle a drum began to boom. Simultaneously from the underbrush close at hand a sharp *thwack* sounded, and a feathered shadow whipped across the open space. With a gurgling scream one of the Dyaks pulled the poisoned dart from his throat and plunged headlong.

It was open hell then, without preamble. Muruts—North Borneo's savage headhunters—rushed onto the right-of-way. With fiendish yells they went at the Coast Dyaks with parangs.

Stockton's revolver was spitting fire. Deliberately he stood, back to the little teakettle engine, making each shot count. But they couldn't stay here. They would be wiped out.

In Malay he shouted an order to the Coast Dyaks to retreat to the coaches. Then, pistol empty, he directed his attention to the leader of the attack, a squat, naked Murut crouching half in the undergrass. At intervals the native raised a *Sumpit* blow pipe and sent a dart streaking into the struggling mass.

LIPS a grim line, Stockton circled out of the path of the headlight, threw himself forward in a flying tackle. He struck the native low, sent his fists pounding outward. The Murut gave a yell of surprise.

Then they were rolling over and over, clawing for each other's throat.

A breath-taking blow caught Stockton hard in the midsection. Twice he felt gouging fingers rake across his face, tear at his eyes. Struggling frantically, the native utilized every savage trick he knew to overcome his white man opponent. They rolled over and over in the tall grass, pounding each other mercilessly.

Suddenly the native whipped his hand to his bark loincloth, brought it up with a glint of steel. It was a kris, and the blade bit deep into Stockton's arm. He recoiled, let his hold slip. Like an eel the native jerked free.

And then abruptly as it had begun the attack ended. The raiding Muruts turned and with hoarse cries of defiance sped into the jungle.

Weakly Stockton got to his feet, staggered back to the locomotive. Four of the ten Coast Dyaks lay dead on the right-of-way. The remaining six huddled in a close group, gazing at the dark foliage where their assailants had disappeared.

"Kelea!" Stockton yelled. "Get that tree off the track. There's nothing to fear now. They've gone."

"Tuan hurt bad?" The Malay eyed Stockton's bleeding arm anxiously.

Stockton shook his head. "Not bad, Kelea. See that the train is moving in ten minutes."

After that the American engineer made his way slowly back to his coach. He opened his canvas luggage bag, drew forth a small but compact medicine kit. The kris had not touched the bone, he knew. But the wound was deep, and he was taking no chances of blood poisoning.

II

THREE hours later the train reached Sepitang, the rail-head. Here, as if to demonstrate the futility of jungle con-

struction work, a single shack on piles served the triple purpose of freight shed, station and residence for Winston Traynor, Sepitang's District Officer.

Left arm well bandaged, Stockton leaped across the pool of mud and water to the *nibong* platform. A smoking carbide lamp threw down a circle of light, and in its glare, hand outstretched in welcome, stood Traynor.

"So you're Stockton," the District Officer said after a house-boy had taken the engineer's bag. "Welcome to the world's jumping-off spot. Come inside, and we'll have a drink."

Stockton slid a bulldog pipe between his teeth and glanced back at the motionless train. "I've got thirty Dyak laborers here," he said, "or did have when I started. They'll have to be put up for the night."

A perceptible frown crossed Traynor's face. "Thirty, eh?" he repeated. "Well, there's an abandoned *kampong* a quarter mile through the bush. They can stay there. Who's this?"

"Kelea, my Number One boy. He bunks with me."

Five minutes later, after he had seen the last of his Coast Dyaks move down the trail, Stockton took the proferred chair in the main room of the District Officer's shack and came to the point abruptly.

"Just how many men," he said, toying with his glass, "had this job before me?"

Traynor took a moment before replying. He was a big man with a large, round face and a tooth-brush mustache. His eyes were clear and friendly. Yet behind his constant smile there lurked an air of caution, as though he were weighing each word he spoke.

"Three," he answered. "Didn't they tell you in Sandakan?"

"They didn't tell me much of anything in Sandakan, except to predict I'd be back in a month."

Traynor laughed nervously. "You *will* too," he said, "or follow your predecessors. Hawley died of fever. Irving was killed by Muruts, and Granson gave it up as a bad job."

FOR a moment Stockton sat in silence, palms pressed hard against the wicker arm-rests of the fan-back chair.

"As I understand it," he said, "a single track is to be laid from here to Laudang, a distance of forty-five miles. The survey maps show the country to be heavy jungle, but all comparatively high ground, with the exception of a half mile strip of swamp. I don't quite see——"

"You don't see why it would be such a difficult job, eh?" Traynor interrupted. "Well, it doesn't happen to be a case of physical trouble. It's something a little harder to understand. The leopard tabu."

The District Officer got to his feet and crossed to a large map mounted on the wall. With his pencil he drew a small circle in the center of it.

"Three miles west of here," he went on, "is the beginning of leopard country, a district supposedly overrun with cats, both spotted and black. The Muruts believe an invisible magic boundary surrounds the tract, and that as long as man does not attempt to cross it, the leopards will remain there, and the *kampongs* will be safe from their attacks.

The magic boundary was brought into creation by a powerful witch doctor. A year ago maulings and killings by leopards was a regular occurrence. Since then, strangely enough, there has been practically no trouble."

Stockton's brow furrowed. "Magic," he repeated slowly. "You mean the Muruts will try to prevent construction work through that section?"

"They'll fight tooth and nail to stop it," Traynor replied. "And beside that, there's Lorgan and Mace."

"Lorgan! Not Britt Lorgan, the rubber man who used to be in Sumatra?"

"The same." Traynor's eyes shifted slightly. "He and Mace have a big plantation surrounding the tabu grounds. Im-

ported Brazilian trees. Mace says no damned railroad is going to cut through his property."

The two men drank another gin pahit, and then Stockton, with an abrupt yawn, rose to his feet.

"I'm done up," he said. "Think I'll catch a little shut-eye, if you don't mind."

Followed by Kelea, he went to his assigned room. Inside he carefully bolted the door, saw that the bamboo shutters on the window were secured. Undressed, he slid his revolver under his pillow and lay back on the bed heavily. From his cot on the other side of the room, Kelea waited his master's order to extinguish the lamp.

But Stockton had no intention of sleeping for the moment. He wanted to think, to prepare a plan of action. It was no wonder, he mused, that the men before him had failed in their attempt to place the railroad on a paying basis. No wonder the stockholders back in England were complaining.

YET from where he stood he could see only a mixture of troubles to confront him. Beneath those troubles and linking them together lay some sinister activity, the nature of which he could only guess at.

Nor was Traynor as friendly as he appeared. The District Officer had told Stockton only what he wanted to tell. It was obvious the man was concealing something.

"But he seems all right at the core," Stockton told himself. "I'd bet my arm there's something hanging over his head."

It had been interesting to watch the District Officer's reaction when informed of the attack on the train by Muruts. Traynor had gone white for a moment, then laughed hollowly. He was very sorry, he had said, but such things were to be expected. After all, Sepitang was pretty much jungle.

The engineer turned to Kelea.

"Kelea," he said slowly, "you know of a

Tuan-besar who calls himself Lorgan— Britt Lorgan?"

The Malay boy's eyes narrowed. "Yes, Tuan," he said. "An evil man."

"How long has he been here?"

"A year, Tuan. He joined the man called Mace, and together they are becoming very rich. But they are cruel to their natives."

Stockton nodded. He signaled the light to be extinguished and closed his eyes to sleep. In the morning he would take the river trail to Lorgan's plantation.

III

UNDER ordinary circumstances Stockton would have called himself a light sleeper. The years he had spent back of beyond in New Guinea and Upper Burma, and more recently in the unexplored interior of the Celebes had taught him to awake at the slightest intimation of danger.

Tonight, however, wearied by the jolting train ride and by the sudden change from the comparative coolness of the coast to the humid heat of the interior, he fell into a deep slumber.

He awoke with a start. The room was in blackness, and there was no sound save the steady breathing of Kelea.

Stockton strained his ears. All at once it struck him that Kelea's breathing did not sound normal. It was less regular than a man in natural sleep. Even as he listened, it became fainter. Simultaneously there swept into the engineer's nostrils the unmistakable odor of chloroform.

He inched his hand under the pillow, drew out his revolver.

His eyes were accustoming themselves to the gloom now. Abruptly two shadows formed before him. One was creeping toward his bed. Deliberately Stockton shifted his position until the springs creaked.

"Hold it," he said quietly. "One move, and I fire."

There was a startled intake of breath, and the nearest figure hurled itself forward. Stockton fired point-blank. Then massive hands clawed for his throat, and a heavy weight landed upon him.

An instant later it was two against one as the second assailant closed in from the opposite side of the bed. Heavy blows rained upon the American's face. A cloth soaked with chloroform was clamped over his nostrils. He tore it away, wrenched his revolver hand free.

He pumped two shots in quick succession, leaped from the bed and delivered a bone-cracking blow on the jaw of the nearest figure. There was a howl of pain and a frantic attempt of the attackers to regain the advantage they had lost.

Back somewhere in another part of the house a door slammed, and a rush of feet sounded. The two figures turned, ran for the window. One last shot Stockton fired as they ripped the shutters open and vaulted into the night. A scream of pain told him he had scored a hit. Then heavy blows sounded on the door, and Traynor's voice could be heard yelling, "Stockton, are you all right? Open up."

Stockton paced across to the door. But before he slid back the bolt, his fingers moved swiftly across the locking device. A dry exclamation came to his lips as he touched a slender steel band that had been forced between the door and the frame. So the assailants had entered from the main room of the shack, had they? That was interesting.

A moment later, the lamp lit and Traynor firing questions in a steady stream, Stockton bent over the supine figure of Kelea. Cold water applied to the Number One boy's wrists and forehead brought him around slowly. But a long five minutes passed before Stockton elected to talk.

He swung around then, faced the District Officer with hard eyes.

"I thought Sepitang was pretty much a controlled district," he said icily. "Do you make a habit of inviting night visitors to the guest room?"

Traynor's lips quivered. "It must have been Muruts from Kinabatangan country, deep inland," he said. "None of the tribes near here would dare——"

"Muruts from deep inland," replied Stockton, "don't arm themselves with cloths soaked in chloroform. And they aren't exactly experts at opening a locked door."

A moment later Stockton took up a flashlight and went outside. But the window of his room opened on a wooden walk, and he could find no footprints. He walked around to the front of the shack. Here he could see the twin rails of the narrow-gauge track stretching into the jungle gloom. The train had departed hours ago for the coast.

"Pleasant job I've taken over," Stockton muttered to himself. "I haven't even started work yet, and the attempts to get rid of me are coming fast."

MORNING, and he found his plans abruptly changed. He had intended to go downriver by *prahu* to Lorgan and Mace's plantation. But when he emerged from his room into the main chamber, he found the two rubber men waiting for him.

Lorgan was a huge man, bearded, with deep-set eyes and an ugly knife scar across the left side of his face. He wore dirty duck trousers, a singlet, and a solar topee, the puggaree cloth of which was torn and yellowed. Mace was smaller, with a swarthy complexion. Neither of the two men rose from their chairs to greet him.

"We heard you were here," Lorgan spoke up, swiveling a whitish cheroot to the other side of his mouth. "So we came over to give you a little information. I suppose you figure on running trackage up toward Laudang. Well, Mr. Stockton, you're out of luck. It can't be done."

Stockton helped himself to the coffee on the table. "A lot of other people seem

to have the same idea," he said. "Just what are your objections?"

"My objections are plenty. First of all, I'm not takin' any chances of losin' native labor by arousin' fear and suspicion of the leopard tabu. Second, if you run that trackage forty-five miles farther, you'll pave the way for every fly by-night planter in British North comin' up here and cuttin' in on our business. We're

doin' all right now without that damned railroad. We ship our stuff by the river, and it gets to the coast in plenty of time."

Stockton eyed him quietly. "I'm afraid all that won't make any difference," he said. "The Company—the Government, that is—has granted me complete power to lay tracks from her to Laudang. We start today."

For a moment tense silence filled the room. Then, with a snarl, Lorgan lurched erect. "Oh, you do, hey?" he snarled. "Well, you trespass on my property, and there'll be trouble. The same kind of trouble the last guy found that came up here with big ideas."

HE swung on his heel and with Mace trailing puppy-like behind him, stalked out the door.

Traynor, the District Officer, who had watched the drama in silence, shook his head. "I'm afraid you're biting off more than you can chew," he said. "Those men are powerful in the district."

His breakfast eaten, Stockton dispatched Kelea to the abandoned *kampong* to round up his crew of Dyak laborers. Then, armed with a Winchester 50-110, he walked down the tracks and headed into the jungle.

The tracks ended within a few yards at a bumper switch. Protected there by a canvas covering was a small gasoline-motored hand-car. The hand-car was oiled and fueled and apparently kept there by Traynor for a quick exit in the event native conditions became out of control.

A rough right-of-way had been surveyed a quarter-mile past this point, Stockton knew. Beyond, he would have the triple job of surveying as he advanced, planning road-bed and overseeing construction. As he strode along now, avoiding vines and creepers, he made a mental note, with satisfaction, that at least there would be no difficulty in obtaining ties. The Taphang, Palapak and Seraya trees which would have to be felled would take care of that with lumber to spare.

A mile Stockton trekked through the dense bush. He was approaching the outer boundary of Lorgan and Mace's plantation, but an indefinable urge kept him going. Suddenly he halted, gazing at a large sign nailed to a tree:

PRIVATE GROUNDS
TRESPASSERS WILL BE SHOT!
BRITT LORGAN.

Stockton smiled grimly. What lay beneath all this? Fear that the district's rubber market would be spoiled? But no. Continuation of the railroad's trackage and running trains on regular schedule would enhance rather than depreciate Sepitang's wealth.

He pushed past the sign, continued marching due east. The jungle about him was unbroken as yet with no sign of planted rubber trees. A hornbill screeched in the tesselation of growth above.

And then the foliage thinned to an open spot. Snaking its way across the center of it was a muddy stream.

Like a slowly-drawn piece of wire the engineer went rigid in every nerve and muscle. Across the stream, on the opposite shore, a bamboo pole angled upward from the water's edge. Fastened to its top end was—a human head.

It was not the type of head Stockton had so often seen dangling from the ridge poles of Dyak long-houses. It was shriveled, it was dried and cured, yes—but—it was the head of a white man!

IV

FOR a long time he stood there, staring at it. Then, lips tight, he waded into the stream and crossed to the other side. It was not difficult to understand the presence of that head—and yet it was. Traynor had said Irving, one of the three men who had undertaken this job before him, had been killed by Muruts. The thing then constituted one more threat in the many hands-off warnings that blocked his way.

But who had put it here? Lorgan? If so, how had the man obtained it from the natives? And why had Irving been murdered at all?

Back at the Sepitang station Stockton found his Dyak laborers waiting impatiently to begin work. The iron rails had been piled alongside the track, and competent Kelea had already distributed picks and shovels.

"Okay," Stockton said. "Let's go. Kelea, I'll want ten men for tree cutting."

A loud sing-song chant went up as the Coast Dyaks leaped to their tasks. Sweat streaming from under his helmet, the engineer strode ahead, marking each tree that would have to be felled.

By nightfall the work was well under way, and the vague fears which had loomed before Stockton faded somewhat. He made his way back to the District Officer's shack.

The evening meal over, he sauntered over to the wall map, studied it a long time.

"Traynor," he said, "you say these leopard tabu grounds are three miles west of here. Can they be reached by river?"

The District Officer nodded. "They can," he said, "but you'll be on Lorgan and Mace's property. You see the forbidden district begins in the western side of Lorgan's plantation and extends a short distance beyond."

"Has Lorgan done any planting in the tabu district?" Stockton asked casually.

"No," Traynor fumbled to light a cigarette. "The leopard spots act as a wedge across the western side of his plantation. "But——" The officer's eyes widened as Stockton picked up his helmet and began to strap his revolver belt around his waist. "You're not going out there now?"

"Just a little look-see," Stockton replied. "I want to give the place the once-over."

He passed out the door and headed across the clearing in the direction of the river. Once the *lallang* grass had closed about him, he stopped short and turned, watching. As he had expected, the door of the shack opened again, and Traynor's native house-boy emerged. In long fast strides he ran down the overland trail toward Lorgan's plantation.

Smiling grimly, Stockton continued to the river shore. He found a one-man dugout, took up the paddle and pushed onto the black stream.

For an hour he guided the clumsy craft up the inky waterway. Lights filtering through the leaves told him at length that he was abreast of the Lorgan house. He continued silently past the log-landing, moored the canoe in a clump of tall reeds.

On shore long, symmetric rows of rubber trees loomed before him. Stockton got a flashlight out of his pocket and advanced to examine the nearest tree.

A LOW whistle came to his lips as his eyes took in the smooth, unbroken trunk. If Lorgan and Mace were operating a rubber farm, they had a funny way of doing it. The trees showed no signs of recent tappings.

Tree after tree he inspected. All were the same. With the flash casting a white beam ahead of him, the engineer moved deeper into the forbidden plantation.

Abruptly the regular corridors came to an end. Rising up before him, a solid, unthinned wall, was jungle again.

The leopard grounds!

Silently Stockton slid his revolver from his holster and pushed into the wall of growth. Twenty feet forward, he switched off the flash. On and on he forced his way, advancing with the greatest caution.

But no danger presented itself. Even the insects seemed to have stopped their monotonous drone, and he felt as if he were walking blindfold through a great void. He drew up at length, scowling in the blackness. His hunch had been wrong. There was nothing here.

And then as he turned to go back, he suddenly stiffened. Voices had drifted to his ears. Low voices and the muffled popping of what seemed to be a gasoline motor. Stockton darted forward. He dropped to hands and knees, wormed past a last fringe of bush—and stared.

A circular man-made clearing opened before him. Suspended from wires stretched between bamboo poles were four gasoline lanterns. The place was ablaze with a whitish glare.

A line of recently built nipa-thatch huts dotted the far side of the clearing. Before them, like some elongated water spider, a corrugated iron runway reared its bulk upward.

And in the center of the illuminated space stood three men, Lorgan, Mace, and a naked native. Lorgan was talking:

"This time we've got to do the job and do it right. In two days Stockton and that damned railroad of his will have reached the outer boundary of our plantation. In two more the tracks will be pushing here into tabu grounds. He's got to be stopped and stopped cold."

Mace nodded. "Do you think he suspects?"

"It don't make any difference whether he suspects or not. We'll finish him before he has a chance to make a report. LaGahi, how many Muruts can you gather by the morning's sun?"

THE naked brown man considered. "As many as the bees over a cone of honey, Tuan."

Lorgan spat. "Stockton keeps his Coast Dyaks in the abandoned *kampong* near the Sepitang station. You and your Muruts will steal upon the village at dawn and kill them. You will then go to the railroad tracks, seize the iron rails and throw them into the quicksand of the *klubi* swamp. Do you understand, La Gahi?"

The brown man licked his lips. "It will be done, Tuan."

A cold wave darted up Stockton's spine as he heard these words. Cautiously he inched his way closer.

"What about Traynor?" Mace demanded. "He hasn't talked so far, but I don't trust him, and—"

"Traynor is my job," Lorgan replied. "I'll take care of him in my own way."

The two rubber men turned abruptly as a fourth figure darted into the clearing. Like a flash Stockton recognized Traynor's house-boy. The native would bring information of his presence!

Revolver in hand, Stockton acted. He strode into the clearing.

"Don't move," he said quietly. "Lorgan, pull your gun and drop it before you."

There was an instant of motionless tableau. Feet braced wide, Lorgan stared with open eyes.

"Your gun!" Stockton repeated. "Drop it!"

Slowly the weapon appeared from the man's belt, fell to the ground. Mace lifted his arms skyward.

"Now," Stockton permitted a grim smile to touch his lips, "now, Mr. Lorgan, I think your plans are going to be somewhat changed. You're going to the Sepi-

tang station, but you're going there to make a confession. After that, unless I'm mistaken, you'll be escorted to Sandakan for trial."

Lorgan's first start of surprise had passed on. He gazed back defiantly. And suddenly he laughed.

With that laugh came the American's first intimation of trickery. He gave a heaving lunge, threw himself sideward. Too late—powerful hands closed about his throat from behind. Even as he felt his windpipe jam closed, the two rubber men leaped forward.

Something hard and heavy came down on the engineer's head. The world before him shut off in a curtain of darkness.

V

HOURS seemed to have passed before he opened his eyes. His skull ached, and there was a clot of dried blood on his forehead. He moved his lashed wrists to touch a wall of nipa-thatch, and he saw, as he had expected, that he was a prisoner.

A prisoner in one of the huts facing the corrugated iron runway. He understood the significance of that runway only too well now, and he knew he must free himself and get back to the Sepitang station before dawn.

The words sounded mockingly in his brain. Try as he would, he could not separate his hands. His ankles too were securely bound.

The radium dial of his wrist watch showed him it was five minutes after midnight. In a few hours blood-thirsty savages would swarm down on his unsuspecting Coast Dyaks, massacre them. And Traynor——!

Even though evidence was piling up to condemn the District Officer, there was something about the man that touched a chord of friendship far back in Stockton's brain. Deliberately he fell to work on his fastenings. At the end of twenty minutes he lay back exhausted. And then his keen ears detected a sound outside the hut.

He lay rigid, listening. Stealthy footsteps came nearer. A voice whispered: "Tuan Stockton. Are you there?"

The American gave a gasp of relief.

"Kelea," he answered. "In this hut, quick."

A moment later the Malay Number One boy skillfully finished untying the knot, and Stockton stumbled unsteadily to his feet.

"When you did not return, Tuan," Kelea said, "I knew something was wrong. I followed you to the Lorgan landing, and I trailed your tracks inland."

Stockton nodded. It was not yet one a. m. There was still time. He strode out of the hut, and with the Malay at his heels, headed at a fast pace for the river.

THE Sepitang station was in darkness when he reached it. On the platform Stockton hesitated, swung about to face the faithful Malay.

"Hurry to the *kampong*," he ordered. "Round up the Coast Dyaks. Bring them here. But don't take the regular trail; cut through the bush!"

Then he went inside to the door of Winston Traynor's room and rapped loudly. No answer. Scowling, Stockton twisted the latch, pushed across the sill.

A wave of dismay swept over him. By the lighted lamp he saw that the room was empty. An overturned chair and twisted bed clothes bore mute evidence of a struggle.

For a moment he stood there, unmoving, face a grim mask. Then his eyes fastened on the opposite wall. There was a map there, a map similar to the one in the main room, showing the Sepitang district drawn to scale. But at the bottom a small section had been torn out, leaving a triangular opening. Stockton stepped closer. And then he saw something else that galvanized him to attention. There was a smear of blood on the map next to the torn section.

In one quick moment he had the whole picture. The point of that tear ended at the marking of a river junction a short distance downstream. Traynor, unobserved, must have left this trail-mark before being dragged from his room.

But why there? There was nothing at the river fork save an impenetrable reed-choked swamp and— He rocked backward as a thought struck him with full significance.

Securing a fresh revolver from his luggage, Stockton turned, ran out. Caution to the winds, he raced back to the river shore, leaped into the dugout and began to paddle madly downstream. As his powerful arms moved back and forth, digging the blade deep, his eyes studied the black shores. But he saw nothing.

The river turned, and in the darkness he sensed its widening. Swamp grass rustled against the keel.

On he raced, keeping midstream. There was something uncanny about it all. The water purled and sighed beneath him. Back somewhere in the flanking wall of gloom a leopard coughed as it made its kill.

And then all at once he became a ramrod in the dugout. On the southern shore a light flashed behind a network of intervening trees. Stockton backwatered, twisted the canoe and headed toward it.

Five minutes later he was fighting his way toward higher ground. The light was a short distance ahead of him. Emerging on a well-worn trail, he darted forward silently.

Abruptly he caught sight of his quarry.

There were four natives, faces hideous with war-paint, and a white man. The white man was Winston Traynor. Half carried, half dragged, the District Officer moved between them, still pajama-clad.

Britt Lorgan's cold-blooded plans struck Stockton like a whip-lash. He had delivered Traynor over to these Muruts with instructions to feed him to the crocs. There was a swamp pool at the river junction where the saurians fed. Once the District Officer was out of the way Lorgan would have full rein to pursue his plans as he wished. It would be a long time before Government red-tape would send another magistrate to the section.

Stockton whipped out his revolver and fired. Two shots in quick succession sent two natives writhing to the ground. The remaining two hesitated an instant, then plunged off the trail into the dense bush.

"Kelea!" Stockton yelled in Malay to no one, "after them! Cut them off before they reach the river!"

The ruse worked. Crashing footsteps pounded in frantic diminuendo. Stockton rushed to Traynor's side. The District Officer leaned against a tree, face white, blood trickling down his cheek from a knife slash on his temple.

"Are you all right, old man?" Stockton demanded.

Traynor nodded. "I'm all right," he said slowly. "The blighters pummeled me a bit, but——"

"Then put your arm around my shoulder. We've got to get back to the station —pronto."

O N the platform of the District Officer's shack twenty-four Coast Dyaks worked in frantic haste. A breastwork, waist high, of green bamboo and the sawed sections of heavy Taphang trees, was being erected. Kelea stood in the center of the confusion, shouting orders. In the doorway Stockton labored at top speed to mount on its tripod a forty pound short-range Maxim machine gun.

Slumped back in a Singapore chair, the District Officer watched the preparations in silence. The first streaks of dawn were climbing in the eastern sky.

At length Stockton rose, crossed to Traynor's side.

"Unless I'm wrong," he said, "Lorgan and Mace will be here in a few minutes. They'll have regimented a tribe of Muruts from Kinabatangan country, and they'll have guns. When they discover my Coast Dyaks are no longer at the abandoned kampong, they'll direct their attack here. It's going to be war!"

"War, yes," Traynor stroked his jaw slowly. "And we've got only a few rounds of ammunition. Stockton, you don't know——"

"I know more than you think," the engineer replied. "I know this isn't a jealousy fight by a couple of rubber men or a rebellion incited because of violation of the leopard tabu. It goes a long way farther than that."

Traynor's eyes widened. "Then——" His voice faltered.

"For more than a year Lorgan and Mace have had interests other than rubber," Stockton continued. "As for the leopards in the tabu district, that was just a story they cooked up to keep away curious natives.

"Blue grounds, Traynor! Silty clay hiding one of the richest mineral deposits in the world. The tabu sector in the Lorgan and Mace plantation is the hiding place of a diamond mine!"

Traynor put a cigarette between his lips, chewed it nervously.

"It was quite a scheme," Stockton went on. "Mace must have discovered the deposit and sent for Lorgan to help him mine it. They started on a big scale, enlisted the operators of the railroad to help them. Lorgan knew that mining was strictly a government monopoly, controlled by the British North Borneo Company. But as long as that railroad was kept in its present miserable condition there would

10

be few visitors to this section. As long as it was prevented from penetrating the plantation, the secret would not be discovered."

The engineer paused, shot a glance across the clearing. Heat waves shimmered before him. The air was tense, pregnant with menace.

"The uncut diamonds were shipped to the coast in disguised rubber drums and slipped by the customs. Lorgan killed Irving, one of my predecessors, because he feared interference with his plans. He planned to do away with me in a like manner.

"But what I want to know—" Stockton's eyes hardened—"is where you fit into the picture. Why——?"

THE question was never finished. From the wall of underbrush on the other side of the clearing a rifle roared suddenly. A Coast Dyak at Traynor's side clutched at his throat and crashed to the platform floor.

An instant later the attack began. Into the open space a swarm of naked savages poured, mouthing wild yells. Bullets and blow pipe darts thudded into the newly-built barricade. Muruts — headhunters from the deep interior, they were. And most of them were armed with modern rifles.

Stockton swiveled the machine gun. His teeth were clamped about the stem of an unlighted pipe, and his face was grim as a ripping staccato roar vibrated into the morning air. Back and forth he swung the Maxim. Muruts fell like pushed dominoes.

And the hail of death had its effect. The attack broke. Turning, the natives beat a retreat to the jungle.

"The devils are up to something," Stockton said to Traynor. "If they can't smoke us out by gunfire, they'll try trickery."

Even as he spoke a flaming streak lifted out of the undergrass, whipped through

the air and slammed into the front wall of the station shack. Quickly Traynor jerked the fire-spear out of the wood and ground it out under his heel.

Stockton retaliated with a burst of shots from the Maxim. He could see his fusilade lance its way through the foliage. He could hear intermittent screams as the steel-jacketed bullets found their mark. But no native showed himself.

The sun was mounting higher. Sweat began to pour down Stockton's face. He began to fire more slowly as the attacking shots lessened. Three more cartridge belts lay beside him. When those were gone— for the moment he preferred not to think about that.

And then, as suddenly as the first, a second attack began. They came from three sides this time, closed in on the station in a half-circle of thunderous gun-fire. A bullet tore along Stockton's cheek, left a hot trickle of blood.

Suddenly the engineer motioned Traynor to his side.

"We can't hold 'em," he yelled. "Take the gun. I'll try and get out the back way."

The District Officer shook his head. "You can't do it. There isn't another white man within——"

"Take the gun!"

An instant later Stockton was inside the shack, striding to the rear entrance. Two Coast Dyak guards stood there, armed with parangs. He pushed past them, peered out into the open space.

No living thing showed itself in the undulating stretch of lallang grass. Were they out there, too, waiting for him? Stockton knew he must chance it.

He gripped his revolver, bent low and leaped down the steps. Ten feet forward he dropped flat and began to crawl. An eternity of nerve-grinding caution, and then at length he had reached the jungle. In a wide circle now he moved past the station toward the far side of the clearing.

The rattle of the machine gun, the yells

and the intermittent shots seemed hollow and distant as he fought his way through the undergrowth. At last instinct told him he was behind the raiding natives, approaching them from the rear.

Abruptly every nerve of his body jerked taut. He listened. A footstep sounded close at hand.

And then roaring close at hand came the crash of a revolver. The bullet screamed past Stockton's ear. Two more slugs in quick succession slammed into the trees at his side.

The American dropped. Ahead through the intervening foliage he caught a momentary glimpse of a familiar figure. Britt Lorgan! The renegade darted behind a tree, firing as he moved.

A second figure, that of Mace, appeared for a split instant. Stockton snapped the trigger of his own gun, but the slug went wild.

As the shots continued to hammer around him he realized grimly that he was cut off. It was only a question of time before Lorgan or Mace would pick him off.

And then a flash of hope streaked into his brain. A heavy *nageva* vine hung before him, dangling from the branches above.

Lips tight, Stockton wormed his way toward it, as a new fusilade of lead lanced the undergrowth around him.

In Indo-China five years before he had seen a vine of that type used for a bizarre and bloody kind of duel. There had been two vines then, with a man suspended from each. Swinging, the two combatants had slashed at each other with knives.

Now the American acted. He grasped the vine, crawled backward until it was stretched taut at a forty-five degree angle. With a heaving lunge he threw his weight upon it, shot into the air, a human pendulum.

Two shots from two guns thundered forth. A hot slug ground into the American's shoulder. Then he was swinging abreast of the two renegades; releasing his hold, he dropped.

He dropped hard upon the crouching figure of Mace. The renegade reared like a cornered animal. Stockton brought the butt of his revolver down on the man's skull in a smashing blow.

And as Mace relaxed and went limp, Stockton leaped erect to meet the attack from behind. Ten feet away Britt Lorgan lunged from behind the tree, pistol flaming. Again Stockton felt a slug hit, this time penetrating deep into the calf of his leg.

Then he threw himself forward. The two men clinched, went down, exchanged blow for blow.

A cruel kick caught the engineer hard in the groin, sent a wave of nausea surging through him. He hammered back grimly, drove his fist hard over his opponent's heart.

And then, at last, an opening presented itself. Lorgan spat blood, twisted free and poised for a final thrust. Like an enraged tiger he lunged, clawing for Stockton's throat.

Stockton pivoted at the precise instant. He brought his right fist catapulting upward against the renegade's jaw. With a gasp Lorgan dropped and lay still.

But even as the engineer stood there with the two prone men before him, a chorus of yells farther back in the bush and a renewed burst of shots told him his work was but half completed. The Muruts were massing for a last attack. With his ammunition almost gone District Officer Traynor would be helpless.

Stockton's lips squeezed in determination. He stifled the moan of pain, bent down and lifted the inert figure of Britt Lorgan to his shoulder.

And then, staggering under the weight of his burden he began to fight his way through the jungle. In a wide circle he moved, keeping well to the rear of the rifle shots.

Penetrating the last fringe of bush he

emerged abruptly on the railroad tracks. Here, still covered by its sheet of canvas, was the gasoline handcar. Stockton whipped off the covering, dropped the unconscious Lorgan upon the seat.

"You're going to take a ride, my friend," he said huskily. "Not a long ride, but if my guess is right it'll bring results."

Red spots were swimming before his eyes as he gave the motor a last look. He switched on the ignition, twisted the crank. There was no response, and his strength was fast ebbing.

Again he spun it, fought the dizziness that was overwhelming him. The motor caught with a roar. Stockton flung the gear into forward.

And then as the handcar with its motionless passenger began to move down the rails toward the Sepitang station, he felt his legs slowly buckle beneath him.

IT WAS noon of the next day before Stockton opened his eyes. He sat up in bed, found himself back in his room in the Sepitang station, gazing at Winston Traynor, who stood at his side, smiling.

"How do you feel?" the District Officer asked.

Stockton felt his bandaged shoulder, swallowed hard. As in a haze memory returned to him.

"Lorgan and Mace"—he began. "The Muruts—did they——?"

"Lorgan and Mace are on their way downriver under guard to Sandakan,"

Traynor replied. "They'll stand trial, and unless I'm wrong they'll be locked up for a long time. But I wouldnt' be here at all if it hadn't been for that handcar stunt of yours."

"It was a neat job," he continued. "The natives, full strength, were advancing into the clearing. And then, like a bolt out of the blue, came that handcar with Lorgan sprawled unconscious across the seat. The Muruts took one look and ran. They knew that with their white leader gone, they were lost."

Stockton nodded. But his face still wore a puzzled frown.

"You want to know why I didn't tell everything in the first place," Traynor said slowly. "Well—that isn't so easy to explain.

"You see my son who is in Government service also served as District Officer here at Sepitang when I was in Sandakan, recovering from fever. That was when Irving, one of your predecessors, was here in the interests of the railroad. As you know, Irving was murdered, probably by Lorgan, but Lorgan, by trickery and cunning, falsified evidence so as to place the guilt of the crime on my son.

"Lorgan held that evidence over my head, forced me to shield him and Mace. I should have refused, of course, but—my son——"

Stockton leaned forward, gripped the District Officer's hand.

"I would have done the same thing, Traynor," he said quietly.

DECEIT POST

By Carl Jacobi

A crooked game that wasn't in the pictures.

JOE KLAY was leaning against one of the upright piles of the little wharf, smoking his pipe, when the sampan came into sudden view around the bend in the river. The sun had just sunk into the roof of the jungle. Klay was there to watch the steaming day slide into the Borneo night.

There was a single white man and two Dyak polers in the sampan. Even as the boat turned and headed toward shore, the white man got to his feet, waved his arms and shouted:

"Hello, there! Is this Menda Laong?"

Klay carefully studied the stranger, but made no reply. He waited until the sampan thumped to a landing, and the man, leaping out, asked again:

"Is this Menda Laong?"

He was young, but tall and muscular, with square shoulders and a lean face. Travel-stained whipcord breeches ended under leather boots. A neck-protecting puggree cloth hung down from his sun helmet.

"The natives call it that," Klay replied shortly. "Otherwise known as Klay's Trading Post. I'm Joe Klay. Come up from Tumbang?"

"Straight through from Long Iram." The man smiled and extended his hand. "My name's Prescott. Advance surveyor for Van Helst Rubber. I'm heading for the headwaters of the Kapuas and Bukat country to look over new grounds. Can you put me up for a spell?"

Klay turned his gray eyes to the waiting Dyaks and the sampan before answering. He nodded slowly. "Guess I can. You leave your natives and luggage here, Prescott. I'll have N'Gaia come down for them later. This way."

The fat trader turned and strode down the wharf to the shore, where a trail led inward through the jungle. Prescott followed. For five minutes they picked their way silently up toward higher ground. Then the trail ended before an oblong bungalow set on stilts in the midst of a bamboo grove.

"Come in and make yourself comfortable," Klay invited. He went up a narrow ladder, ushered the way across the veranda into the inner room. Two steps over the threshold Prescott halted, surveying his surroundings.

The room was large, with mounted tiger and leopard skins adorning the four walls. A Winchester .50-110 express rifle hung above a collection of Malay krises. Over a grass cot in the rear a punkah fanned the air gently. And by the center table, sprawled back in wicker chairs, sat two men.

It was toward these two men that Prescott, eyes suddenly narrowing, held his gaze. Dressed in dirty whites, they stared at him coldly.

"Meet your shipmates," Klay said, waving a beefy arm. "Beretsford, and this is Hawley. They got here just this morning. They're laying over until the Dyaks north of here quiet down."

Prescott's voice was hard and quiet as he acknowledged the introduction. The man called Beretsford was hawk-faced, with thin lips and heavy brows over little pig eyes. He wore a wide ornamented cartridge belt with a holstered automatic. Hawley was shorter, lantern-jawed.

Klay moved across to a row of shelves, brought out four glasses, filled them with gin and passed them around. He drained his own glass quickly, filled it again. "And now," he suggested cordially, lowering himself into a chair, "let's talk. Prescott here is a rubber man. You two are after gold, going into the same district. Ought to be a bond of interest somewhere."

THE trader lighted his pipe and waited. But conversation was not forthcoming. A few remarks passed across the table. After that there was silence. Klay frowned as he watched. Something strange here. The three men professed to be strangers. Yet an invisible barrier seemed to lie between them. It was a long five minutes before Beretsford cleared his throat and broke that barrier clumsily.

"I don't see," he said, nodding toward Klay, "how you stand it alone here with the constant danger and the infernal jungle. We—Hawley and I—have been away from the coast only three weeks. I'm dead sick of it already."

Klay smiled, folded his hands across his paunch. "Those things don't bother me," he replied. "I've worked up a nice profitable trading business with the natives along the river. Always treated 'em honest, and it's brought results. As for the loneliness—I've got entertainment here. Plenty of books, plenty of liquor, and something you wouldn't expect to find any place south of S'pore."

Hawley looked up curiously. "Gramaphone?" he asked with a slight sneer. "The damn things only get on my nerves."

"No, not a phonograph. Something better. Something different. A moving-picture machine."

Quiet followed the statement. A sudden half-concealed gleam entered Beretsford's eyes. Across in the other chair, Prescott stiffened and leaned forward.

"A moving-picture machine?" Beretsford repeated slowly. "Here? With real films?"

"One film," Klay corrected. "Two reels. It's an old one called 'Tattered Hearts,' and part of it is torn. Bought the machine in Samarinda one time when I was down gettin' supplies. I'll run it off for you, if you'd care to see it."

There was a moment's hesitation during which Hawley smiled significantly at his companion. Beretsford nodded. "Bring 'er on," he said.

Darkness had closed in on the post now. Outside a macaque screamed loudly. Joe Klay got to his feet, paced across the room and disappeared through a doorway into the adjoining corridor. A moment later he returned, carrying a box and a roll of dirty white canvas. He set the box on the table, opened it and drew out a small projection camera. Cheaply made, it consisted of an unpainted metal case, a crank, a lens tube, and a carbide lamp.

From the box the trader also took out a spool of film which he clamped into position on a bracket. Then he stepped across to the wall and draped the canvas from four hooks.

"There's a little crack in the lens," he apologized. "But it don't bother the picture much. Once this carbide begins to generate, it works real well."

He darkened the room. A square of light played on the canvas. Klay focused the lens and began to turn the crank.

Then for a quarter of an hour the four men watched the picture flicker jerkily across the improvised screen. It was small, scarcely three feet across. The story was old, concerning a girl and the usual love triangle. But parts were dark and blurred. Sequences had been cut and the two ends glued together. Only the scenes of civilization made its presence here in the jungle a luxury.

WHILE he turned the crank, Klay carefully studied his waiting audience. Beretsford looked on with crescent eyes and a smile of expectation. Hawley cast sidelong glances from time to time into the empty box that had contained the machine. Prescott, a troubled frown lining his brow, chewed an unlighted cigarette.

The film came to an end at length. Klay lighted one of the room lamps.

"That's the first reel," he said. "The second isn't so good. It——"

Beretsford rose to his feet slowly, his face betraying a mixture of emotions. "This is the only film you have?" he asked.

Klay nodded.

"No local views? Nothing else?"

"No. Sorry." Klay's eyes darkened slightly. "But the second reel is——"

"Save it for to-morrow night." Beretsford stifled a yawn. "I haven't had a decent night's sleep in three weeks, and I'm ʲᵒⁿe up."

He drained the last of his gin, slapped the glass back on the table. "Coming, Hawley?"

The second prospector stretched, nodded. Together the two men slouched across the room and without further word disappeared into the corridor toward their assigned sleeping room.

When they had gone Klay stood silent a moment, looking after them. Then with a sigh he began dismantling the camera. He packed it and the film in the box, stowed the box under the grass cot. That done, he filled his pipe again and sank into a chair. For a long time he sat there, smoking, staring blankly into space. Abruptly he jerked around and faced Prescott.

"Prescott," he said evenly, "this little game has gone far enough. I may be more or less of a hermit, cut off as I am, but I'm not entirely a fool. Suppose you tell me who you are."

For an instant there was silence. Then Prescott started as though struck. "What do you mean?"

Klay smiled thinly. "I mean simply this. The Van Helst Rubber man went by here two months ago. He came in the official launch. I also happen to know that with prices as they are, the company isn't interested in looking over new grounds."

Rigid, the man in whipcord breeches stood there while a slow flush mounted into his face. He sucked in his breath, strode quickly forward.

"Not so loud," he whispered, glancing over his shoulder. "Those men in there—— Isn't there somewhere we can talk?"

TWO minutes later, seated across from the trader on the veranda, separated from the main section of the post by a heavy matting curtain, Prescott stared out into the blackness and twisted in his chair.

"You're—you're right," he began haltingly. "I haven't anything to do with rubber. I only said that because—well, because I wasn't sure I could trust you. My real reason for going into Bukat country is a lot more important. Ever hear of a man by the name of Martinson—John Martinson?"

Klay coughed oddly, but shook his head.

"Martinson," Prescott continued, after a moment, "worked for the same outfit I do, the Pacific Film Co. He left Samarinda August 1st, heading for a point on the Kapuas River far beyond all explored territory to find a certain tribe which has never been in contact with whites. If native rumors can be believed—and you've probably heard them—this tribe has a high state of culture and a religion that is not Dyak, but a form of Taoism. According to the garbled reports there is a huge wooden temple there, somewhere in the foothills of the Müller range, where all sorts of strange rites are practiced. What is either a white man or a freak albino native is supposed to rule them.

"Martinson was a camera man. His mission was to go among those natives, film their life and habits, photograph the interior of the temple and make a different sort of travel picture."

Prescott paused, glanced at Klay. The big trader remained silent.

"Originally, of course, we were to do the trip together. But right at the start I got bit by a poisonous water spider. Next day my leg was so swollen I couldn't move. Martinson decided he'd have to go it alone. A delay would mean getting caught in the rains.

"Every week during his trip up-river Martinson communicated with me in Samarinda by carrier pigeon. The last message said he was within a day's travel of the tribe and everything going fine. Then the pigeons stopped coming."

In the darkness Prescott's lips tightened and his face grew suddenly hard. He slumped lower in the chair.

"At first I thought he was too busy to write. But when three, four, and finally five weeks went by without a word, I knew there was something wrong. I hired guides and started inland to find him.

"Anything might have happened to Martinson, of course. But I felt pretty sure he had taken his picture and started back. He photographed his way across Sumatra, and he was experienced in handling natives. This film, if it ever was photographed, would be worth a fortune. Any booking office would fight to get it. But if Martinson died, then it's simply salvage, the property of the first finder. And that's where the trouble comes in.

"When I stopped off at Long Iram I learned that two men were preceding me upriver. They claimed to be prospectors. But prospectors don't go this far inland. And they don't travel night and day. Obviously some one had got wind of what I was after and was trying to head me off."

Prescott dropped his hands slowly. "That's about all," he finished. "I've got to find what happened to Martinson. I've got to find that film. But Beretsford and Hawley, I know, are after it, too. And they'll stop at nothing."

For a long moment Klay made no answer. The trader drummed his fingers reflectively on the chair arm, chewed on his pipe. At length he turned.

"And I suppose," he said quietly, "when I brought out my little camera, you thought I might also have the film you're looking for?"

"I did at first, yes. Then I realized that if Martinson had come this far, he would have written me. He carried plenty of carrier birds."

Joe Klay nodded. "If your man does get through on the Mahakam," he said, "he'll have to stop here. North, the Dyaks are bad enough; but south, where you passed, no white man can get by now. Rice-feast tabu. You'd better figure on staying a while."

"And Beretsford and Hawley?" Prescott put the question blankly.

The trader smiled. "Don't worry about them," he answered. "I'll see that they stay here, too."

HALF an hour later Klay sat alone on the veranda. Prescott had gone to his room. Ahead in the jungle blackness there was only the drone of insects and the distant wash of the river. Klay rubbed his chin thoughtfully.

Had Prescott told the truth? Did he actually represent the film company as he claimed, with a legal right to the missing film? Or were Beretsford and Hawley the rightful owners, and Prescott merely a shade shrewder, undermining them with suave talk and a claim to innocence. Men who came here usually couldn't be judged by their speech or appearance, that was certain.

There was another item. Granting that all three of the men were after the same thing, none of them seemed to have taken into consideration the possibility that this man,

Martinson, did not by necessity have to return down the Mahakam at all. From Bukat country he could cross into Apo Kayan, lay over at the garrison, then continue down the Kayan River to Bulungan on the east coast. A somewhat longer route, but infinitely less dangerous.

"Which means," the trader told himself, "the last message from Martinson didn't say he was *near* the tribe and *hoped* to get the picture. It must have said he already *had* the picture and was on his way back —this way. But why didn't Prescott tell me that?"

He shrugged perplexedly and leaned back, closing his eyes. For another half hour he sat there, making no move. Then he got to his feet, slipped like a shadow into the main room. In the darkness he felt his way slowly to the cot in the far corner, reached under it and pulled out the box containing the camera and the film he had shown a short while before. He removed the film, pushed the box back under the cot. Then, gripping the spool, he stepped softly to the opposite wall. There he groped a moment, found a small teak cabinet level with his eyes.

It was a medicine case, that cabinet. Klay swung the door open, placed the film spool on the top shelf, shoving it far back behind the first-aid kit.

Then he stole noiselessly back to the veranda.

He was waiting now, waiting for developments he felt sure would begin immediately. Five minutes snailed by. Ten. He stirred impatiently. Then from the inner corridor came the sound of a slowly opened door and stealthy footsteps. The footsteps advanced slowly into the room. Again there was a pause. Then a match was scratched, quickly passed to the table lamp. A short,

bulky figure stood outlined in the faint glow.

On the veranda behind the matting curtain Joe Klay smiled grimly. The invader was Hawley, fully dressed, a revolver in one hand.

Hawley ran his eyes about the room, looking from wall to wall. He moved the lamp to the edge of the table and slid open the table drawer. Carefully, making no sound, he began rifling the contents. He searched for a long time before he shoved the drawer closed again, muttered an impatient oath.

A second smaller table came under his examination next. There was no drawer here, but Hawley felt of the woodwork, ran his fingers along the edges as if searching for a concealed compartment. He lighted a cigarette, rose with a snarl of frustration.

Then he saw the cabinet.

He strode across to it quickly, wrenched open the door and fumbled through the shelves within. Suddenly a smile of satisfaction came to his lips, and he drew forth the spool of film.

H E shut the cabinet door, moved back to the table and extinguished the lamp. Joe Klay had just time to dart behind a chair at the far end of the veranda before the matting was shoved aside and Hawley came out. An instant the man hesitated there, listening. Then he crossed to the door, eased it open and descended the ladder. Seconds later his footsteps died off along the trail to the wharf.

The trader made no move to follow. Instead he returned quickly to his place at the edge of the curtain and continued his watch.

The second interruption came almost immediately. Again softly moving footsteps entered the dark room. Again the lamp was lighted. Beretsford stood there, the brass filigree on his cartridge belt glowing dully.

The man did not search the room as his companion had done. His eyes fell at once upon a significant object on the edge of the table: Hawley's cigarette, the end still burning, which in his haste the first man had forgotten. A snarl of understanding welled to Beretsford's lips. He turned and lunged for the door.

The game of blindman's buff was repeated. Joe Klay was well-hidden in the shadows when Beretsford rushed out on the veranda. The self-styled prospector saw no one. He ran down the ladder and disappeared into the inky jungle, heading toward the river.

Smiling, Klay returned to his veranda chair. He lighted his pipe, sucked on it thoughtfully while he weighed the situation.

"Mutiny in the enemy's camp," he muttered to himself. "Interesting. Well, a house divided against itself cannot stand. Also a fire ignited at both ends burns out in the center."

He grinned at his proverb speech, settled back to smoke and to wait. Silence lay heavy about him now. A quarter of an hour passed. Then suddenly Klay sat bolt upright. A short, high-pitched scream had come to his ears from the river bank. Twice it was repeated in quick gurgling succession.

Klay swore, strode to the veranda rail and peered out into the blackness. For five minutes he remained there, scowling, seeing nothing. Then abruptly he jammed his pipe into his pocket and ducked around to the protection of the chair back.

Footsteps were returning up the river trail. An instant later the door opened, and a shadowy figure stumbled onto the veranda. It was Beretsford, alone. No sign of Hawley. The pseudo-prospector stood there in the half light, swaying. His face was bruised and bleeding, his clothing torn, plastered with mud.

But in his right hand he gripped a familiar object—a spool of moving-picture film!

Lurching, Beretsford shoved aside the curtain, crossed to the table within, blew out the lamp and moved unsteadily into the corridor. Klay heard a door click shut, the bolt snap into position. For a moment the trader stood there motionless, eyes hard. Then slowly he followed to his own room. He undressed and lay down upon the bed. But it was a long time before he let himself be overtaken by sleep. To a certain extent events had shaped themselves as he had expected they would. But they had gone farther than he had thought—much farther. The little game of three-point hypocrisy for which the post had found itself a stage had developed into something more than a game. With set lips Klay lay there planning a course of procedure for the coming day.

NEXT morning, when Klay entered the main room, Prescott was sitting by the center table, closing the last buckle of his leather luggage bag. Prescott got to his feet heavily.

"I'm leaving," he said. "Leaving right away. Martinson may be dying in some native kampong. I've got to find him."

Klay shrugged. "You can try it, if you want to," he replied. "But if you take my advice, you'll stay here. The rice feast is going full strength now. The river is impassible either way. You wouldn't get by the first village."

Prescott frowned, hands opening and closing in indecision. But before he could answer a step sounded in the corridor doorway behind him. The trader swung about. Beretsford, showing no signs of the night before, stood there, tobacco sack dangling from his teeth, deftly rolling a cigarette. An almost imperceptible gleam of mockery lurked in his eyes.

"If that's true," he said slowly, running his tongue over the paper, "then I hope Hawley didn't run into any difficulty. He left during the night, you know, upriver, bag and baggage. We had an argument, and the fool thought he could do better alone. You don't really think he'll be in serious danger, do you?"

Klay studied the man closely, shrugged and said nothing. He turned quietly, paced toward the kitchen in the rear to instruct N'Gaia, his Dyak cook, concerning the morning meal.

Breakfast over, the trader rose from the table abruptly, left the room and returned with a canteen and a small knapsack. He removed two rifles from their wall mountings, took a box of cartridges from the table drawer and began to fill a canvas cartridge belt.

"There's a black leopard been seen close to the post," he explained. "Big fellow. I've tried to get a shot at it several times, but up to now— no luck. Care to have a try with me, Prescott? Beretsford, I'm sure, won't mind staying alone here a few hours."

Prescott hesitated. He still was undecided whether to go on with his search for Martinson or accept the trader's apparently sincere advice to wait until the rice feast was over. Something in the trader's eyes made him determine upon the latter. He nodded quickly.

Leaving Beretsford on the veranda, the two men went down the ladder, strode through the bamboo grove to a small trail leading northward, parallel with the river. They trekked a quarter mile in silence before Prescott drew up, faced Klay questioningly.

"What's this all about?" the film man demanded. "You tell me the river is impassable. Yet Hawley seems to have gotten through. He didn't come back, so apparently he found no trouble. Now you head directly for the district which is supposedly tabu."

K LAY dropped the stock of his rifle and leaned on the barrel. His gray eyes were slits now, his face grim.

"That's not quite right," he said slowly. "Hawley didn't get through."

"Didn't——"

"Listen, Prescott"—the trader's voice was filled with quiet earnestness—"Hawley ransacked the post last night. He had the strange idea that Martinson's film is here with me. He found a film and hurried down to the wharf, hoping to take one of the boats and escape with it alone downriver."

Prescott's eyes slowly widened.

"Unfortunately for him, Beretsford discovered what he was up to and followed. There was a fight at the river shore. Beretsford killed Hawley. How, I don't know. Probably with a knife. But the body never will be found. Unless I'm mistaken, Beretsford threw it to the crocodiles, then sneaked back to the post with that film."

"But——"

"No." Klay shook his head. "Both of those men were fools. Even if I did have a film in my possession as valuable as the one they thought it to be, I wouldn't keep it in a medicine cabinet. Right at this moment, unless I'm wrong, Beretsford is running the film off on my camera and getting pretty much of a surprise. The thing they fought over, you see, was simply the first reel of the 'Tattered Heart' picture I showed you last night."

The trader marched ahead in silence after that. Rifle in readiness he swung easily along the trail, peering from side to side. At length the trail turned, ending at an open spot on the river shore. Anchored here to a stake in the sand was a small dugout canoe, paddles lashed to the sides.

An emergency exit, Klay explained. If the natives ever attacked the post the boat could be used for a quick get-away.

There were marks of leopard here, imprinted in the sand, where the animal had come down to drink. But they were several days old.

Klay suddenly untied the mooring line, slipped free the paddles and, with the knapsack still over his shoulder, took his place in the dugout.

"Going upstream a ways," he said. "There's another likely watering place farther on. You stay here and watch. If I see anything I'll come back for you."

Before Prescott could disagree, the trader pushed off into the river. Prescott sat down on a log, lighted a cigarette and frowned. He was quite sure Klay had other reasons for leaving him alone. He was quite sure the hunt was mere subterfuge. And in that assumption he was entirely correct. Paddling cautiously upstream, Klay entertained no thought of leopards, either black or spotted. He was heading for a certain point on the river just within the territory of the next tabu village, and he was keeping well in the reeds of the right bank where there was less chance of detection.

THE trader was gone the better part of an hour before he returned. He beached the dugout and stepped toward Prescott with a shake of his head.

Back at the post they found Beretsford sitting on the veranda, sullenly playing solitaire. The man's sardonic attitude was gone now. His face was a mixture of bafflement and restrained rage.

Inside, the trader found what he had expected. At first glance the post seemed in perfect order. A closer scrutiny revealed that every movable object had been carefully searched. The bamboo case containing the collection off krises had been removed from the wall and replaced slightly askew. The grass rug had been torn loose from the floor. And the projection camera in the box under the cot was still warm from recent operation.

Klay kept these discoveries to himself. He puffed his pipe thoughtfully, sucked it to the heel, then strolled aft to the kitchen where N'Gaia was working with pots and pans.

"N'Gaia," Klay said, moving closer, "I've got work for you. Something out of your regular cooking routine. Something which is going to tax that thick skull of yours." Klay smiled and tossed a package of cigarettes to the Dyak.

"Yes, tuan."

"Listen closely then and get this straight."

For the next two minutes the trader spoke steadily in low tones. At the end of that time N'Gaia was nodding his head in complete understanding.

Later, at the evening meal, Klay

talked more, for the benefit of his two guests. Covertly watching Beretsford the trader launched into an endless recitation of his past hunting expeditions and experiences with the natives.

"Murder," he said casually, between swallows of hot tea, "is the one crime even the natives don't tolerate here in the jungle. Of course there's head-hunting outbreaks occasionally. But that's between two rival tribes and has a religious significance. If one Dyak should kill another of his own village, justice is quickly dealt. I remember——"

He stopped short and turned. "What is it, N'Gaia?"

The Dyak cook had rushed in from the veranda and stood now, eyes wide, at the trader's side.

"Tuan," he began excitedly, "Tuan, two Long Glat warriors outside. Come downriver from north. They have news, tuan. News of a dead white man."

Klay pushed back in his chair. "Bring 'em in," he ordered shortly.

A MOMENT later the two Long Glat pushed into the room, staring about them curiously. One of them immediately began a tirade of Malay.

Across the table Beretsford, a strange glitter in his eyes, got to his feet, dangled one hand close to his holstered automatic. "What's he saying?" he demanded hoarsely.

"Nothing that will interest you," Klay replied. "This is for you, Prescott. These Dyaks claim they found the sun helmet and the duffle bag of a white man lying on the river bank next to a dugout paddle. Undoubtedly it's Martinson. They say there was also a strange black box which the water could not pene-

trate and which they did not touch, fearing evil spirits."

Beretsford kicked aside his chair and sprang forward with an oath of satisfaction. His right hand clawed out the automatic.

"Martinson, eh?" he snarled. "That's fine. And that black box must be the container with the film. Ask those natives where the spot is, Klay. Talk fast or I'll drill you."

Brows turned upward in surprise, the trader hesitated. "But I—I don't understand," he said slowly. "This film is——"

"—the property of the first finder," Beretsford finished, with an ugly grin. "I mean to find it. Back in S'pore there's plenty of places I can get rid of it for a high price. Now ask those natives where they found the stuff."

For an instant Joe Klay glared across the table with eyes of steel. Then his shoulders sagged and, turning, he shot the question at the waiting Long Glats. The reply came in Malay without hesitation.

"Mile and a half north of here," Klay said quietly. "On the right bank. The Dyaks stuck the paddle upright in the water to mark the spot."

With a smile of satisfaction Berestford strode across the room, seized a lantern hanging on the wall, stepped to the veranda door.

"I'm goin' after that film, see," he said. "You two are stayin' here. And you"—he shifted the automatic to cover the Dyaks—"are comin' along and directin' me to that spot."

He herded the natives through the doorway, took three steps backward. Then suddenly a smothered exclamation of rage from the other side of the room stopped him. Prescott, unmindful of the automatic, threw himself across the floor, hands clawing for the renegade's throat.

Beretsford roared profanity and tried to throw off his assailant. Prescott fought with grim desperation. Back and forth they surged, exchanging blows, while Klay looked on quietly.

For a moment it was silent struggle. The prospector shot two blows straight into Prescott's midsection. He followed with a haymaker to the jaw and a short, quick jab to the heart. Prescott, blood streaming from his lips, reeled backward. He quickly recovered and slammed back with a powerful left. The blow went wide. Beretsford, right hand free, lunged forward, lifted the automatic high in the air and brought it down upon the other's head with a sickening crunch. For an instant Prescott stood there, swaying, face a sickly white. Then with a low moan he sank to the floor.

Beretsford planted a kick in the prone form and hitched his trousers with a grin.

"That'll teach him I mean business!" he snarled. "You, Klay, if you know what's good for you, you'll stay right where you are."

He went out, the two Long Glats before him. An instant later the screen door slammed, and their footsteps died off in the jungle.

MORNING of the next day found Klay seated on the veranda, working a wisp of plait grass through the stem of his pipe. Prescott, eyes dark with defeat and disappointment, stood quietly in the doorway.

"I don't see," he said bitterly to the trader, "why you let Beretsford get away so easily. You might at least have given me a hand."

Klay raised his eyes, frowned. "I never resist a loaded revolver," he replied. "Beretsford had the upper

COM—8B

hand last night—or thought he did. To-day, I'm rather inclined to think he's changed his mind."

Prescott studied the trader curiously. "What do you mean?"

"What do I mean?" Klay stood up, reached for his revolver on the table and buckled on his cartridge belt. "Come along, and I'll show you."

He led the way to the wharf, slipped free the moorings of a long, narrow canoe and motioned Prescott to take his place in the stern. Both men plying the paddles, the boat shot out into the current. Once midstream, the trader did a strange thing. He turned the canoe about and headed downriver instead of upstream.

For half an hour they moved slowly down the winding, silt-heavy river. Then abruptly Klay jerked his head about, shaded his eyes and turned the canoe toward the right shore.

Seconds later they slipped through an overhanging wall of foliage and grated on the beach. Prescott looked about him, stared, and felt himself growing suddenly sick at the pit of his stomach.

Two feet away a sampan floated, caught on a projecting root. Inside, lying in a pool of his own blood, lay the body of Beretsford. A native parang was thrust to the hilt in his neck. And still gripped in his hand was a moving picture film spool, unwound, with only a torn five-foot remnant of the celluloid trailing from it over the side into the water.

Prescott seized the spool, stared down at it, then with a low cry flung it into the river.

"Gone!" he said bitterly. "Gone for good. The rest of the film is somewhere at the bottom of the river. Beretsford found it and was caught trying to make his get-away by the Dyaks of the tabu village. The Long Glats deserted him at the first sign of danger, and the dugout floated down to here."

Klay nodded silently. Without further word he pushed the canoe out into the river and headed back for the post.

ON the veranda again, a long time later, the trader sat across from Prescott, slowly sipping lime juice. With somber eyes he gazed out into the surrounding jungle. Prescott sat slumped in his chair like a man drugged.

Presently Klay rose and went inside the post. When he returned he carried a package wrapped in red rice paper.

"For you," he said quietly, dropping it into Prescott's lap. "Just a present, you know—with my compliments."

Prescott looked up, eyes widening. Slowly he began to remove the paper wrapping. It took him a moment, but when the contents lay revealed he leaped to his feet.

"A film! Three reels! But I don't understand."

Klay smiled. "It's the film you were sent to get," he replied, hooking his hands around one knee. "Martinson's travel picture."

For an instant Prescott leaned weakly against his chair. Then he crossed to the veranda rail, unfurled a six-inch strip of the film from one of the three spools, held it up to the glaring sunlight. He swung around slowly.

"But that other film. Beretsford had——"

Klay filled his pipe, passed a match over the bowl.

"Three weeks ago," he said slowly, "a man by the name of John Martinson came here. He came on foot through the jungle. He was sick, almost gone with fever.

"I tried to pull him through, but it was no use. Between spells of delirium he told me of his escape from the natives, who had become infuriated when they learned the real meaning of his camera, of constant pursuit, and his ever-increasing fever. Before he died he gave me the film, explained its value and told me to keep it until the right party came upriver."

Two feet away Prescott was nodding with jaw agape. "I see," he said. "And Beretsford——"

"I told you before Beretsford was a fool. More of a fool than Hawley, the man he killed. He made all that fuss last night without questioning the word of the natives. Those Dyaks weren't Long Glat men, but quiet Punas, employed here at the post. Beretsford raced upriver to find something he might have seen without trouble. A film, of course, but a very old one: the second reel of that "Tattered Hearts" picture I bought in Samarinda.

There is only one way to pay a gentleman's debt of honor — D e Horn's way.

JUNGLE WIRES

By CARL JACOBI

THE gasoline launch turned midstream under the watchful guidance of the Dyak steersman and headed for shore. Slanting rain pelted the broad river. Ahead, the jungle loomed dark, wet, and forbidding.

Bancroft, who until now had been drowsing in his canvas chair amidships, peered out under the soggy awning flaps and breathed a sigh of relief. The post was reached at last. He could see it clearly, the little jetty protruding into the silt-heavy water and the shack-on-piles showing a veranda through the thick foliage.

Five minutes later the launch nosed to the landing place, and Bancroft, a black poncho shielding his suit of duck, stumbled out. He stretched his legs wearily, waited for the Dyak to secure the painter and toss up his single bag of luggage. Not a particularly inviting place, this. But after the grueling trip he had had, any port was a welcome one. Even in a government launch an eight-day trek upriver in the midst of the rainy season is no health excursion.

His sun helmet partially shielding his face from the driving downpour, Bancroft paced hurriedly the length of the slippery jetty to the clearing just beyond. At the shore edge a dripping, weather-scarred sign greeted him. It read:

DUTCH EAST BORNEO
TELEGRAPH CO.
STATION No. 5

Bancroft paused a moment to smile at the incongruity of English wording in a Dutch enterprise in the midst of a Malay-speaking world. They were lonely holes, these telegraph relay outposts. Twelve of them, at evenly-spaced intervals, stretched across the Borneo jungle from Bandjermasin to Bulungan. Two operators were stationed at each. It was their duty to prevent the Dyaks from tearing down the wires and insulators and to keep the Dutch government informed of ·native conditions and the all-too-frequent head-hunting outbreaks.

Bancroft braced his shoulders under the poncho and strode to the entrance ladder of the shack. Before he reached it, the door above burst open and two men appeared on the veranda.

"Hullo, there, Van Tromp!"

Bancroft chose to disregard the mistaken welcome until he had climbed the six bamboo rungs and let himself in the screen door. He stamped the water off his feet, shoved his helmet far back on his forehead, and said tersely:

"Van Tromp's laid up in Samarinda with a bad case of fever. I'm taking his place until he's on his feet again. The name's Bancroft.

You're Stockbridge and De Horn, I believe?"

There was a moment of surprised silence during which the two men glanced at each other significantly. Then the shorter and younger man moved forward.

"I'm De Horn," the youth said, extending his hand. "This is Stockbridge. You sort of surprised us. Not used to strangers, you know. Come inside and have a drink."

IN silence Bancroft shook hands and followed the two men into the inner room, removing his poncho as he walked. He accepted the whisky that was poured for him, sipped it slowly and stood looking at his surroundings.

Over in a far corner a telegraph sounder rattled in a sounding box. Above the instrument desk, bracketed on the wall, a dismantled Hotchkiss machine gun gleamed dully. There were two bunks, two tables, several Singapore chairs, and a large cabinet which apparently contained everything from food to a rack of six revolvers. The side walls were covered with old magazine illustrations.

Bancroft put down his glass, accepted the proffered chair and came to the point abruptly.

"Eight days ago," he said, "you reported over the wire that trouble was brewing in the native villages in your district. That's why I'm here now instead of next month, when the regular government inspector usually makes the trip. What's the story?"

Stockbridge, a bulky, hawk-faced man with oily hair, beady eyes, and thin lips, slid a cigarette into his mouth and spoke for the first time.

"De Horn sent that fool message," he said. "I didn't. You came up from Samarinda on a wild-goose chase. There're only three villages here and nothin' doin' in any of 'em. The Dyaks are quiet as they've ever been."

"Quiet. Yes," De Horn agreed almost hurriedly.

Bancroft frowned. "You also reported queer messages coming over the wire, messages that suggested line tapping. Have you a copy of one of them which I could look over?"

De Horn gnawed his upper lip nervously. "I'm afraid that report was a mistake," he said. "There have been some different messages, but they were simply code quotations on rubber prices coming down from Bulungan. I got a bit drunk one night, and I guess I wasn't exactly responsible for what I told the Samarinda operator. I flashed him the next day and told him to forget all I'd said. But it seems you'd been sent in the meantime. Sort of rotten for you—but you don't realize how the loneliness of this place——"

The young man was lying, there wasn't a doubt of it. Bancroft studied with interest the clear blue eyes, eyes that avoided his gaze, but showed no trace of alcohol, the strong jaw and the wide forehead. Something definite was wrong here. In the first place, rubber reports were seldom sent at this time of the year from Bulungan.

"How long you expecting to stay in the district?" Stockbridge put the question carelessly, as he shoved across the table a box of white cheroots.

"Not long," Bancroft replied. "You're sure everything is peaceful? No head-hunting? No sickness?"

Stockbridge shook his head. "Everythin' quiet," he said again. "Not even a wire torn down or an insulator swiped for I don't know how long. The Dyaks are afraid of us since I turned that machine gun on 'em a year ago."

"Then"—Bancroft leaned back apparently relieved—"I'll simply give the villages a look-see to-morrow, fill out a routine report, and head back for God's country. This is as far up the Mahakam as I'm detailed to go, thank heaven."

OUTSIDE, the darkness was thickening. The rain coming down even harder now, drummed the thatch roof like distant thunder. For a quarter of an hour Bancroft smoked his cheroot and chatted with the two operators.

The cheroot consumed, he rose to his feet and reached for his canvas bag.

"Think I'll spruce up a bit," he said. "I always do at sundown. Makes the day seem shorter."

He paced quietly down the little corridor to the spare room in the rear that had been assigned to him, entered and closed the door. For a moment he stood there, feet braced far apart on the uncarpeted floor, brow furrowed in a deep frown. Then slowly he filled a basin with water, washed, and donned a fresh shirt.

"Odd," he murmured, as he knotted his tie. "Damn odd. De Horn and Stockbridge don't want me here any longer than necessary, that's clear. But they're both clumsy liars, and De Horn seems to have something on his mind."

He brushed his damp hair, gazing unseeing at his reflection in the cracked mirror.

"Neither of them would mind getting out of here in a hurry," he continued to himself. "With the kid it might be social starvation. But Stockbridge is too experienced for that. Yet it was De Horn who sent that message."

He shrugged his shoulders perplexedly and strode back to the door. At the threshold he halted long enough to draw out his Webley revolver, glance carefully at the magazine and return it to the waist holster, Then, eyes narrowed, he returned to the main room.

The evening meal, an hour later, was held under the glare of a double carbide lamp. Stockbridge, made garrulous by several helpings from a bottle of whisky, punctuated his eating with a steady flow of talk. But it was strained talk, aimed apparently to thwart any questions Bancroft might ask.

"Twenty days' sampan travel to the coast," Stockbridge said thickly. "Nothing but jungle, heat, fever—and rain. Two operators in a relay station cut off from the world. It's hell, I tell you. Me, I'm gonna quit soon."

De Horn said little, ate even less, and nervously smoked one cigarette after another.

They went out on the veranda. The two operators took chairs. Outside, the rain had stopped, and Bancroft stared into the dripping blackness before him. Presently he excused himself, turned and strode back to his room in the rear.

TWO minutes later Bancroft was bent over the little dressing stand, unpacking something that lay wrapped in oilcloth at the very bottom of his canvas bag. He removed the cloth carefully, examined the contents. A curious object was revealed—a telegraph sounder. Also, there were two coils of insulated copper wire, each with a weighted contact clamp at one end. Bancroft shoved the sounder into his coat pocket where the bulge would show least, then uncoiled the wires and began to

wrap them loosely about his waist, pushing them under his shirt.

With a last glance at his appearance in the mirror, he turned out the lamp and returned to the veranda.

"Going down to the launch," he said, as he stepped to the door. "Want to see how Sahar, my Dyak, is getting on. He has to sleep there, you know."

He went down the ladder and strode toward the jetty, whistling noisily. A quick glance over his shoulder showed that Stockbridge had risen from his veranda chair and was moving into the inner room. At the edge of the clearing Bancroft stopped his whistling, slipped into the underbrush and began to pick his way silently parallel to the river shore. For a hundred yards he continued. Behind him the yellow glow from the lighted station shone fitfully through the dense bush.

When that glow had disappeared entirely, Bancroft drew from his pocket a flashlight and sent a white ray stabbing the darkness above him. Back and forth he moved it, outlining the vines and creepers overhead. Suddenly he murmured an exclamation of satisfaction.

There they were, two black threads running from tree to tree through the inky jungle: telegraph wires that connected Bandjermasin with Samarinda and Samarinda with Bulungan on the east coast. The white insulators seemed strangely out of place in the maze of green.

Bancroft fell to work quickly. With the aid of the steellike vines he lifted himself up a near tree, climbed until his outstretched hands reached the taut wires. Using a pocketknife he scraped off two lengths of insulation and then, removing the wires from his waist, slipped the copper contacts over the bare sections and pressed the clamps securely. He trailed the wires down to the ground, hiding them as well as he could in the vine entanglement. A hollow log came into the glare of the flash next. Bancroft carefully took out his sounder and placed it under this wooden protection, connecting the wires to the binding posts.

Immediately the sounder broke into a rapid series of clicks. With the flash resting on the log, Bancroft got a notebook and pencil from his pocket, his ears strained to catch each word of the coded message.

Two minutes later the sounder stopped, and he stared down at his scribblings. They were short and significant.

—is here now but suspects nothing. Will probably stay two days, three at most. Sampan of samples well hidden in village. Can place at least a thousand more for high price. But hold all shipments until I advise you.

A LONG time the government inspector sat there, mouth screwed tight while he read and reread what he had written. Then slowly he disconnected the sounder, snapped off the flash and headed back for the post.

Morning, and the rain began again. The odor of damp rot, which Bancroft knew so well and hated, rose up like a fog from the floor of the jungle. Concealing his impatience at the forced postponement of the village inspection trip, the government inspector strolled out on the veranda.

De Horn was there, slumped in a wicker chair, cleaning a long-barreled Luger automatic. Inside, in his bunk, Stockbridge still snored loudly.

"Gets pretty monotonous here with nothing to do," Bancroft said.

"Suppose you'd like it better if the Dyaks weren't so quiet."

De Horn looked up and smiled shortly. "I'd hardly say that," he answered. "But this way it's like sitting on a dynamite box. You never know when the natives will change their minds. They hate the idea of these relay stations being here in their country. And they hate the Dutch military outposts along the river even more. They'd be only too glad to wipe them all out."

"Have they ever attacked here at No. 5?"

"Once." The youth fumbled nervously for a cigarette. "That was a year ago, before I came. Stockbridge was here alone then. He killed hundreds of them before they could get within striking distance. Parangs or blowpipes don't exactly compare with a machine gun, you know."

Bancroft nodded. "It's a good thing," he said, looking sharply across the table, "that they haven't rifles. There'd be a different story then."

De Horn started and a slow flush mounted in his cheeks. He dropped his eyes, started to reply, then broke off, listening. From the inner room had come the sudden chatter of the telegraph sounder.

"That was Munpore talking to Samarinda," De Horn explained, a moment later when it stopped. "Munpore is a couple of hundred miles east of here, deep in Taban territory. The operator was reporting bad flood conditions in his district."

Bancroft crossed his legs thoughtfully. He didn't offer to inform De Horn that he understood code as well as Dutch or Malay. But this time the young man was speaking the truth.

AT noon, with tropic suddenness, the rain ceased. Bancroft donned a pair of mosquito boots and made ready for his trip of inspection. Two of the villages were within walking distance, but the third and largest was five miles upstream. He took the launch.

He spent only an hour in the first two kampongs. The first, on the south bank of the river, was quiet and fairly clean. The second, on the north shore, was an odorous collection of huts and filth. In both villages he was received without question. Yet Bancroft was struck with the feeling that the peacefulness was only a mask fashioned with native cunning to trick him.

The third village was thriving under the tribal rule of Kota Noh. Kota Noh had been warned twice to desist in his attempts to gather heads, especially white heads from the military posts downriver. A few hideous native skulls still adorned the outside of the long house, but otherwise everything appeared in complete submission to the Dutch government.

The old chief pompously escorted Bancroft into each thatch hut, grinning suavely. He was greatly disappointed that the government inspector could not stay in his village for the night. He was disappointed that the government inspector did not care to share a gourd of native rum with him. And he hoped very much that the government inspector would return soon.

All of which Bancroft took with a large grain of salt. He noted as he went down to the launch that the Dyak chief apparently had forgotten to include in his tour a small hut set apart from the others.

Smiling grimly, Bancroft ordered Sahar, his steersman, to let the launch drift downstream until a bend in the river hid them from sight. Then, choosing a spot where the shore reeds massed thickly, he directed the native to head for the bank. He leaped out, fastened the painter to a shoot of bamboo and plunged on foot into the jungle. Kota Noh didn't know it, but his kampong was to undergo two inspections that day instead of one.

An hour passed before Bancroft returned to the launch. His clothing was torn, and his face and hands were scratched from the dense bush. In his eyes was a grim look.

Once more he ordered the launch downriver, docking at the telegraph station jetty.

Neither of the two operators was in sight on the veranda. Bancroft paused a long time, filling his pipe, making sure his movements were unobserved. Then he darted across the clearing and pushed his way through the foliage to the hollow log that housed the sounder.

Connected, the instrument remained silent. Bancroft waited impatiently. He was working on a hunch. Hunches were rare with him, but when they came they usually brought results. Ten minutes passed.

Frowning, the government inspector slipped back to the clearing and cast a hasty glance toward the shack. But his arrival had gone unnoticed; the place brooded in silence.

He returned to the sounder, checked the wires. Then without warning the instrument broke into a spasmodic rattle.

When, seconds later, the message was completed, he puffed his pipe thoughtfully and sat there considering. The second message was as short as the first. It read:

Three sampans with one thousand ready to leave here as soon as you advise. If all goes well, can you meet me at Kampong Nanaoh? Then overland to Sambilioen and a ship. Remember we split fifty-fifty.

A slight smile touched the corners of Bancroft's lips as he disconnected the sounder and stood up. The situation was clearer now, considerably clearer. There remained, in fact, only a few details to complete it. He went back to the telegraph shack.

RAIN came again while the three men were eating their evening meal. It descended in a torrent of fury from a thunder-split sky, and De Horn hurried to let down the canvas shades on the veranda. With all outside drafts cut off, the air in the station became sweltering.

Stockbridge poured himself a stiff drink from the whisky bottle, drank it, and wiped the sweat from his neck.

"Filthy weather," he said. "No rain until the rainy season, then there's so much of it, it get's into a man's soul. I tell you these jungles are no place for whites. Even in Sumatra it ain't so bad. There's roads there, and you can get back to civilization. Here you can sit and rot for all the company cares. Well, I'm quittin' soon, and I'm gettin' out. Sidney maybe, or Wellington. Any place just so's it's——"

"Money?" interposed Bancroft softly. "You'll need money, you know."

Stockbridge swung around. "I'll have money," he snapped. "And I'll know how to use it, too. No drink, no gambling until I'm outa this rotten country. Then I can raise hell."

For a long time Bancroft sat still, thinking. He rose presently, walked to his room in the rear and returned with something clenched in his hand.

"Just remembered I had this along with me," he said. "Did either of you two ever play *main pó?* I haven't all the pieces, just the cubes and the die. But we can make a board easily enough. What say to a game?"

Stockbridge glanced across at the brass cube and smiled with the eyes of an experienced gambler. De Horn shook his head.

"I never played," he said.

Accepting the ensuing silence for agreement, Bancroft cleared off the rough table, shoved it directly under the carbide lamps and marked off a four-foot square, dividing the top into four triangles by means of two diagonal lines. He numbered the triangles from one to four. Then he turned to De Horn and quickly explained the rules of the Malay game.

With only half interest, Stockbridge began by placing a stack of coins on number three. Bancroft spun the brass cube, picked it up and dropped the smaller, inner cube out, exposing the red-and-white die. Stockbridge lost.

"What odds?" the operator snarled angrily. "And how high do we go?"

"Three to one," Bancroft replied, smiling. "Make your own limit if you wish."

FOR two hours the three men sat there, sweating in the sultry heat, watching the little colored die as it dealt out the tides of fortune. When the game finally ended Bancroft was unconcerned over the fact that his loss had been considerable. He was far more interested in the methods the two operators had used against him.

Stockbridge had played recklessly from the beginning, betting wildly, yet with a certain system, accepting his occasional losses in bad humor.

laughing coarsely when he found he had won. Once, when he thought neither of his opponents was looking, he had called a five, a four. De Horn, on the other hand, had played an honest, conservative game throughout. Yet he had not hesitated to take a long chance when Bancroft had him in a corner. These facts were most interesting. To Bancroft they were an excellent piece of character portrayal. He knew where he stood.

The government inspector sat on the veranda for an hour after the two operators had gone to their bunks. He pulled up the canvas flaps. The rain had ceased and starlight filled the sky. Twice he filled and lighted his pipe. At length he knocked the ashes from the bowl, rose and strode to his room in the rear.

He undressed quietly, donned pajamas and lay down on the cot. For another hour he lay there wideawake. The rain stopped, and from the main room of the telegraph station came the sounds of two men breathing heavily in sleep.

Not until the hands of his watch pointed to two thirty did Bancroft show signs of action. Then he rose and, barefoot, moved lightly to the door. He lifted the latch, slid the barrier open an inch at a time, listening. Silence, broken only by the occasional cry of a hornbill somewhere in the surrounding jungle, met his ears.

Slowly Bancroft made his way down the short corridor to the center room. He stopped at the threshold, peering through the semidarkness at the shadowy outlines of the two bunks. The breathing continued regularly.

Like a shadow the government inspector melted across the floor to the instrument desk. Before him,

indistinguishable in the gloom, the sounder, switches, and key were silent pieces of brass.

He moved his hand forward, felt for the switch, pushed it open, and grasped the knob of the telegraph key. He flashed a last glance over his shoulder, listening to the men's breathing. Then quietly he began to tap out a message.

It was short, composed of only two call letters, and Bancroft repeated it three times at spaced intervals. Then he closed the switch, muffled the armature of the sounder with his finger and waited.

Almost immediately the sounder answered, repeating the call letters, spelling out: "Go ahead."

There was a glint of excitement in the government inspector's eyes as he seized the key again. His lips were clamped tightly together.

Arm motionless, fingers moving by only the flexibility of his wrist, he resumed his careful tapping. For many moments he continued, spelling out words and sentences, forming a coded message with an experienced touch.

The interruption came without warning.

"Get away from that key!"

BANCROFT whirled to see a bulking shadow rise from one of the cots, jerk erect, and begin to approach.

"Get away from that key, you damn sneak!"

Bancroft answered quietly:

"The game's up, Stockbridge. I just informed the Kentsan operator of the whole game of blindman's bluff that's been going on here for the past weeks. Kentsan, you know, is the Dutch military outpost downriver. It happens to be quite near where your accomplice tapped the wires and made arrangements to send you one thousand rifles. That accomplice and those rifles will be in the hands of the Dutch government before morning."

Stockbridge drew up short and jerked in his breath heavily.

"Rifles," Bancroft continued in a steady voice. "British Lee Enfield rifles, Mark VI, short magazine improved type—better guns than the Dutch police has. It was quite a game, Stockbridge, but you played too high. I saw the samples in Kota ·Noh's kampong yesterday. Pretty things, they were, and I'll wager the natives were ready to pay a pretty price for them. No wonder you were planning to give this country the go-by. One thousand armed, blood-thirsty Dyaks wouldn't make this station any health resort. But once away, you didn't care what happened. Stockbridge, you're under arrest!"

For a moment the figure in the gloom stood rigid. Then with a roar he closed in.

The operator struck Bancroft hard in the abdomen, shot his hands upward, clawing for the government inspector's thick throat. Bancroft coughed as the wind rushed out of him. He stumbled to the floor. In an instant the two men were rolling over and over, exchanging blows. Bancroft was no weakling. He had kept his weight down to a wiry one hundred and eighty pounds, and he had kept away from native rum. Yet the man who sought to kill him now was a caged tiger with a tiger's strength in his arms.

Back and forth they surged, Stockbridge panting hard as he flailed his arms.

"You may have spoiled that gun deal," he snarled. "But you'll never get back to Samarinda to crow about it."

Bancroft snapped out his right fist, followed quickly with his left. A brutal kick struck him in the groin, sent a wave of nausea surging through him. Vaguely as he fought, the government inspector was aware of De Horn standing in the darkness beside his bunk, watching them like a wooden image.

Lips cut and bleeding, Bancroft waited for an opening. And presently one came. Stockbridge slipped his iron hold, lunged sidewise in a frantic attempt to plant a finishing blow on the inspector's jaw. With a quick movement Bancroft rolled over twice and leaped to his feet. He jerked backward, rested against the instrument table, waiting for the second attack.

Four feet away the gun-runner operator swayed clumsily as he staggered erect. He spat blood from his mouth and roared profanity. Then he whirled and lunged for the near wall, one arm extended above him. A moment he clawed there, jerked at something that seemed fastened on a level with his head. He ripped it clear and stood framed in the doorway. Soft light from the sky gathered around him to reveal what he held in his hand: a native parang, the curved blade gleaming.

Bancroft stared with a sudden loss of hope. He knew that running or lunging to one side would be futile. A thrown parang reaches its mark quickly. And Stockbridge had spent enough time in these jungles to learn the proper method of handling one.

For an instant Stockbridge poised motionless, gloating over the opportunity that was his. Then he spat blood again and jerked his arm back for the throw.

But he got only halfway. A deafening roar split the silence of the station. A streak of orange flame spewed through the darkness, coming from the direction of the wall bunks.

Stockbridge seemed only surprised at first. He stood there, the parang raised in his hand, his legs stiff. Then, with a low moan, he swayed and crashed heavily to the floor.

Even as he fell, Bancroft leaped to his side, wrenched away the native knife and pinioned the man's arms to the floor. Stockbridge struggled, then fell back limp. A bullet had struck him in the shoulder almost at the base of the throat.

The government inspector struck a match and lighted the carbide lamps. His hands were trembling slightly as he turned and looked across the lighted room.

Five feet away, still by his bunk, stood De Horn. The youth's face was dead white. A curl of smoke was rising upward from the bore of his Luger automatic.

"Is—is he dead?" he asked huskily.

Bancroft shook his head. "No, not dead," he replied slowly. "But the fight's all taken out of him. Thanks, son. I won't forget this."

MORNING of the next day found Bancroft and De Horn on the veranda. Outside, the rain was falling again. Inside, Stockbridge lay in his bunk, his shoulder swathed in bandages, his feet manacled to the wall.

"I knew about those rifles eight days before you came," De Horn was saying. "I'd noticed Stockbridge acting queerly, sending strange messages over the wire for some time. Then one came through to us. Stockbridge broke the circuit so that it wouldn't continue farther down the line, and I knew by the touch to the brass that it wasn't any regular station. The natives in Kota Noh's village were growing impatient, too. The old chief and three of his warriors came up here and demanded to talk to Stockbridge in private. I listened in, found he had promised to sell them a large number of rifles sent to him by an accomplice nearer the coast. He had already delivered a sampan load of samples to their kampong. But the big shipment had been delayed.

"I worried myself sick about it for two nights and finally reported the matter to Samarinda."

Bancroft nodded as he slowly filled his pipe and ran a lighted match over the bowel.

"And you didn't mention Stockbridge's name in your report, not wishing to be a snitch. You figured you could scare him out of it, make him turn straight before an official investigation came. That's clear enough. But why did you still hold out on me when doing so placed you under suspicion, too?"

For a moment De Horn looked across the table. Then he leaned back and pressed his finger tips together slowly.

"A long time ago," he said, "when I first came here, Stockbridge saved my life. It happened out there on that path leading from the clearing to the jetty. A thirty-foot python dropped from a tree and wrapped itself around me before I could get out of its way. Stockbridge shot the thing. It was——"

Bancroft nodded gently as he blew out a cloud of fragrant tobacco smoke. "It was a gentleman's debt of honor," he said. "I would have done the same thing, son."

HOLT SAILS
THE
"SAN HING"

By CARL JACOBI

overlord or government, would not open up till night. But even now it was the worst possible place for a man who was admittedly on the beach.

Tall, lithe-limbed, he followed the street to its ends, turned into a smaller side-alley and drew up before a faded sign:

PON MOY TRADING COMPANY
JEROME KINDAIR, AGENT

Holt knocked the ashes from his pipe and smiled grimly. He too was beginning to look what he was. His duck suit, washed thin, and his faded blue cap, clean but obviously land-stained, spoke plainly of a seaman down on his uppers. Even with the best of luck the Pon Moy Trading Company would have little if anything to offer. But it was his last chance.

He pushed through the door. Inside was half-darkness, a faint smell of camphor, and an American-made roll top desk.

S INGORA looked what it was—a third rate coastal town of the Unfederated Malay States. The narrow cobblestone street was deserted to the afternoon heat, and Holt, striding up from the waterfront, felt strangely friendless and alone.

He knew of course that Singora's gambling holes-in-the-walls, undisciplined by

Behind that desk sat a florid faced man, wearing horn-rimmed spectacles.

"Mr. Kindair?"

"That's my name."

Holt drew a long breath and plunged into his appeal.

"John Holt. Master's papers in steam," he began tersely. "Skipper of the *Rogenta*. You heard about her, I suppose. Ran into a typhoon two days out of Saigon and broke her steering gear. Limped into Pattani and found every blessed plate strained, though she was only eight years old. The insurance people had an agent in Pattani, and he condemned her. Then Old Man Jardin, of the owners, Jardin and Peigh, died in S'porte, and I was left high and dry. I'm looking for a ship."

The man behind the desk did an odd thing. He leaned back in his chair and laughed softly as though he had been expecting just such a story and as though he didn't believe a word of it.

"Can I see your watch, Mister Holt?" he said.

"My watch?" With a puzzled frown Holt hesitated, then reached in his pocket and drew forth his timepiece, an engraved Swiss repeater, which he had bought just before his last cruise. He unhooked it from its chain and handed it across.

JEROME KINDAIR took the watch, turned it over and over in his hands and studied it closely. Then he returned it and drew from a pigeon-hole of the desk, a large manila envelope.

"You'll find your instructions here," he said. "Obey them implicitly, and you'll receive your money when you reach your destination. The *San Hing* is at the wharf with a crew aboard. Talk to no one. Get going."

Bewilderment seized Holt. He gaped. "But I——"

And then, as he stood there, it happened. Behind him a step sounded, and the street door banged open. Pivoting, Holt saw a man leaning comfortably

against the door frame, a revolver in one hand. Clad in dirty whites, his face was hidden by the yellowed puggree cloth that hung down from his sun helmet.

Even as Holt realized what it meant, the man fired. The trading agent crashed to the floor. The man with the gun looked at Holt, then turned and ran.

Rigid for a startled instant, Holt saw that the bullet had struck Kindair squarely between the eyes, killing him instantly. He yanked out his Browning, ripped open the door and lunged in pursuit.

Down the street he raced. Ahead the fleeing figure ran in long, leaping strides, did not look back. Holt fired twice, aiming over the runaway's head.

"Stop!" he yelled.

The man was heading for the waterfront. Two natives shambled from a doorway into his path. Like a juggernaut, he bowled into them, sent them spinning to the cobblestones. Twisting, he sent a single shot screaming past Holt and dived into the shadows between two buildings.

With slackening pace, Holt followed. But when he reached the narrow, refuse-strewn passage he found it deserted. He climbed over a fence, mounted a low hut. Twenty yards beyond the jungle began abruptly.

A man could elude a regiment there.

SLOWLY Holt returned to the street. What did it all mean? What sort of a mess had he stumbled upon? Only one fact in the swift movement of events stood out with any clarity. The agent who had been killed had first mistaken him for someone else.

The street before him was still steeped in silence. A half-dozen Malays stood in a huddled group just beyond. But there was no evidence of excitement. Pistol shots apparently were a common enough occurrence in Singora.

He halted in the glaring sunlight and took stock of the situation. These were the Unfederated States, yes, but there must be a British official in the vicinity, and British officials had a way of being obstinate. It struck the ex-skipper forcibly that when the dead agent was found, his story, that a third man had done the killing and fled, would sound pretty thin. In the eyes of the law he—Holt—was a man on the beach with no particular reason for his presence.

He remembered the letter then, still gripped in his left hand. The envelope was blank, and the flap unsealed. Holt pulled out the paper and began to read slowly:

This letter will give you complete authority as master of the "San Hing." You will proceed down coast at once to Saiburi where you will pick up 200 bundles seedling sugar cane consigned care of Pon Moy Trading Company to Palembang, Sumatra. You will sign on man named Saja Marak as supercargo at Saiburi. Marak will wear a piece of red string around his left wrist. *San Hing* must reach Palembang no later than 25th.

'A wave of exultation swept over Holt. He had a ship at last. For a full minute he stood there, lean incisive face alternately lighting and clouding. Then he swung about and headed at a brisk pace for the waterfront. Mistake or not, Lady Luck had smiled at him at last, and he wasn't going to disappoint her.

The *San Hing* was a frowsy-looking hooker, sadly in need of paint. Holt went up the gang-plank, pushed past a knot of Malay seamen who eyed him curiously and looked around. An old tub, as he had expected. These Chinese let a thing run to wrack and ruin fast. Decks needed a good scrubbing. Boats sunblistered and probably leaked like sieves.

But he found the captain's cabin snug enough. There were shelves of books, some comfortable furniture and the papers were in order. The *San Hing* was a two

thousand tonner out of Shanghai under Chinese registry. She carried no wireless.

Holt descended to the engine room, and here he drew up short in surprise. Diesels! The *San Hing* was faster and more powerful than she appeared. As for the crew

Holt had not seen a white man in the lot. Lascars and Straits-Chinese, they accepted his presence without comment.

Not until he sounded a call to pipe all hands on deck did he sight the white officers. Two men slouched up to him then, one tall and heavy set with an olive complexion, the other red-haired with small, beady eyes.

"I'm Melrose," the dark man said. "Acting first. Barwin here is second. We don't carry a third. I'll see your identification, if you don't mind."

Holt surveyed the two men narrowly. He handed over the manila envelope. Melrose extracted the paper, read it. A long time passed before he looked up, nodded.

"All right," he said, "we clear for Saiburi immediately, I suppose. Your name is—?"

"Holt. Signal to start the engines, Melrose."

The lines were cast off, and a gong clanged. The *San Hing* slid slowly out into the Gulf of Siam. Holt, gazing shoreward, realized he had acted without a moment to spare. A red-faced man, in the immaculate whites of a British official, came running down to the beach. His hand was aloft, and he was shouting something.

When the man realized the *San Hing* was out of voice range, he jerked a revolver from his pocket and sent two shots echoing over the water.

Grimly Holt turned and made his way to the bridge.

SAIBURI lay farther down the Malayan coast, the last port in the Unfederated District. Though he knew these waters, Holt studied the chart and laid out a course with care. He then looked at the sky, glanced at the barometer and frowned thoughtfully. The glass was dropping.

Alone in his cabin Holt let his thoughts run wild. Who had killed Jerome Kindair, the trading company agent? Was there any connection between his death and the manila envelope? Why was the *San Hing* equipped with Diesels when by outward appearances she was just another Chinese-owned, coastwise tub?

He was tamping tobacco in his pipe when he heard a sudden stealthy footstep in the outer passage. Quickly he drew his Browning, paced noiselessly to the door. He inched it open, looked out.

Four cabins opened onto the passage. The door of the last was slowly swinging shut.

Something sounded a warning in Holt's brain. He moved forward warily. He had reached the door and was pushing it open, when he suddenly realized he had been tricked. A board squeaked behind him. A terrific blow crashed down on his head.

Reeling, he twisted about, swiveled the Browning. He fired twice. Then a fist ground into his jaw, and another seemed to rip open his skull. He slumped to the floor.

As in a dream he felt himself lifted bodily, carried into the cabin and thrown to the floor. The door slammed shut.

HOW long he lay there he didn't know. His vision cleared at length, and he stumbled to his feet. Waves of pain pulsed

through his head. He moved across to a water basin, soaked a cloth and pressed it gently against his scalp.

"Nice," he muttered. "I get conked on the head, and I don't even know who hit me."

Then, and not until then, did he see the dead man. He was lying in a bunk bracketed to the farther bulkhead, and his eyes were open, staring. Protruding from his chest was a short, black-handled knife.

Dead! Holt stepped closer and stared down into the waxen face, controlling himself with difficulty. There was something strangely familiar about those features, something that stirred a faint sense of recognition far back in his brain.

He bent down, ran his hands through the dead man's pockets. They were empty of anything of value save a few coins and a watch.

The watch was a duplicate of his own!

Pieces of the puzzle were dropping into their respective slots now. His thoughts rushed back to that night months ago when he had walked along the Singapore waterfront. He had wandered into a dingy jewelry store run by a slant-eyed Eurasian, and he had browsed through the shop idly while a customer already there bought a watch.

The watch the man had finally chosen had caught Holt's eye. After the customer left, Holt had laid his wallet on the counter and demanded one just like it.

The rest wasn't clear, but the skipper thought he could see the answer. The dead man here and the man who had bought the watch were one and the same. He recognized him by the clipped bristle mustache, and the small mole on the left cheek.

In some way that watch was to have identified this man as the new skipper of the *San Hing*. For—why else would the Pon Moy agent have demanded to look at Holt's timepiece? The *San Hing's* present mission—whatever it was—had necessitated hiring the new captain in secret.

When Holt had displayed a similar watch, the agent had mistaken him for this man. It was mixed up, but it made sense.

HOLT replaced the watch in the dead man's pocket, then moved across to the door. It was locked. He turned and sank into a chair.

"Funny," he muttered, "they must have waylaid this poor Johnny and murdered him to get that manila envelope and sailing instructions. When they found he didn't have them, they figured Kindair was pulling a fast one, and they went to get him. They probably thought that after the agent was dead they could ransack his office when things had quieted down. Something must have been damn valuable that——"

A key rasped in the lock, and the door swung open. Melrose entered, an automatic in one hand.

"Awake, eh?" he said. "I thought you'd be. There's a blow coming up. You're going to take charge."

The man was even more ruthless-looking than he had appeared on deck. There was a raw blemish on the side of his neck which spoke of an old knife scar, and his eyes under bushy brows were dry and glittery.

"Charge," he repeated. "That means you're going to have full run of the navigation. But if you try anything funny you'll wish you hadn't."

An inch at a time Holt let his right hand slip toward his coat pocket. Melrose, sighting the movement, only gave a short laugh.

"Do you think I'm a fool?" he said. "Your gun's topside. Get going."

With the automatic prodding his spine, Holt marched out of the cabin, up the companionway, to the deck.

"On the bridge," Melrose snarled.

They went up the port ladder, strode into the wheelhouse. Barwin, the second, stood at the wheel, a whitish cheroot hanging limply from his lips.

"She's getting dark quick," he commented.

Holt had already noted the sky. An ugly mass of black nimbus was climbing out of the east. The water was dark green. Melrose fingered his automatic. "All right, Holt," he said. "Listen close. We're taking this hooker down the coast to Saiburi. There we pick up two hundred bundles of sugar cane. We also pick up a native named Saja Marak. We——"

"I know all that," Holt said lightly.

Melrose scowled. "Here's something you don't know. Saja Marak is more than just a native. His real name is Rajah Mahmud Lahar, and he's a native prince, rich as sin, in the Unfederated District. He's traveling incognito for a definite reason. The natives Rajah Mahmud rules have been threatening a mutiny for a long time. Taxes too high, they said, but Mahmud is forced to impose those taxes by the British government. Couple of months ago they killed five of his personal bodyguard, rose up in revolt.

"Rajah Mahmud knew his goose was cooked. So he figured he'd skip the country. He looked around, and the Dutch in Sumatra offered him protection. Mahmud then made arrangements with the Pon Moy Trading Company, chartered the *San Hing* to take him secretly to Sumatra along with the shipment of sugar cane."

"But——" Holt's eyes slowly widened.

"Until we had that envelope we didn't know what port he was going to sail from," Melrose went on. "But for a native he was pretty clever. We know that that sugar cane will look like ordinary seedling sticks for experimental planting. Actually, hidden in each bundle will be the Rajah's royal jewels, rubies, emeralds, diamonds, amounting to five hundred thousand dollars."

FOR a long moment Holt stood motionless, digesting this information. He regarded Melrose quietly, got out his pipe and began to pack it.

"Just where do I come into the deal?" Melrose smiled. "I'm laying my cards flat on the table," he said. "Neither Barwin here nor I know a damn about navigation. When we came aboard we chucked the native first and second officers overboard. We can read a compass, but that's about all.

"All you have to do is run this ship to Saiburi, pick up Rajah Mahmud and his sugar cane, and we'll take care of the rest. We divide the stuff three ways, and you get a sixth. What say?"

Blunt anger rose within Holt. Barratry, was it, not to mention murder? And then his eyes narrowed, and his anger gave way to cunning. He nodded slowly.

"I don't want any part of the jewels," he said. "But as for the rest, I suppose I can't help myself."

Barwin laughed, and Melrose said, "That's the stuff, Cap'n. Now how about this storm?"

"Batten down the hatches," Holt said. "See that everything is tight."

SWINGING on his heel, he left the bridge, went down to the mess cabin. His head still ached, and there was a tight, empty feeling in his stomach. But after the Chinese steward had served him food, he felt better.

For once in his life, he hoped the storm would strike soon and hard. He didn't know how, but he felt sure that in the confusion of a typhoon he could get the upper hand. Malay deckhands paraded down the passage, as he sat there, returned a moment later, carrying the body of the dead man with the watch. Holt's fists clenched.

His meal finished, he went back up to the chart room, took another look at the chart. South of Saiburi the map showed Kuala Mang, a tiny port in the Federated area. If he could manage to pass Saiburi he would be off strictly-enforced British territory, protected by colonial courts of law. Then——

Outside there was a sudden drone of wind, and the *San Hing* heeled over under its impact. A deluge of rain detonated against the charthouse.

Holt ran out, headed for the wheelhouse. The wind was terrific. Breathless, soaked to the skin, he ripped open the door, found Barwin, nervously gripping the wheel.

"Ain't we got any quartermasters for this job?" Barwin whined. "It's thicker'n bloody hell out there."

Like a well-oiled machine Holt acted, taking the renegade by complete surprise. His left arm coiled around Barwin's throat. He twisted the man around, sent him reeling to the wall. Then his right hand smashed outward.

Barwin took the blow full on the jaw, and slumped in a heap. Quickly Holt spun the wheel two points to the left, set the automatic steering gear.

"One," he muttered. "Now for Melrose."

THE *San Hing* was wallowing like a drunken thing now. Huge waves rolled over her well decks. The wind and the rain were a deafening roar.

He found Melrose on the bridge wing, clawing at a life preserver, lashed to the rail. The first officer spun about, face streaming water.

"Do something!" he yelled. "This damned tub will sink and——"

"I'll do something," replied Holt, and swung. His fist buried itself in Melrose's face. But the man was not to be taken as Barwin had. He reeled backward, and came at Holt like a madman.

Back and forth they struggled. Pressed hard, Holt slowed his attack, placed each blow where it would count most. A cruel kick caught him in the shins. Melrose stiff-armed him over the heart, aimed a swinging haymaker at his left ear.

Buffetted by the storm, they exchanged blows. Melrose was no coward, but he was a dirty fighter, and he did not hesitate to hit foul. Then Holt saw his chance. He drove in hard.

But he got only halfway. Behind him a revolver crashed. A stab of agony lanced into the skipper's life arm, slammed him against the rail.

He saw Barwin standing there, holding the gun. The second's jaw was bloody where he had hit him.

Melrose staggered forward, slapped an open palm across Holt's jaw.

"Try that again," he snarled, "and I'll do for you. If I didn't think I needed you, I'd kill you now."

Holt was left alone on the bridge wing, his arm bleeding profusely. Five minutes he remained there, fighting to gather his strength. Then he left the support of the rail and stumbled below. In the captain's cabin he found a medicine cabinet, disinfected and bound his arm and drank a pannikin of rum. Lowering himself on a settee, he lit his pipe and sat staring into space.

He had failed this time. As for the storm, they must have passed through the tail end of it, for the glass on the wall was already rising.

Melrose and Barwin had laid their plans well. They had only to let events take their natural course, and the loot would be theirs. They would force Holt to navigate them across to Saigon, and when near enough to the Indo-China coast, they would do the same to him and to Rajah Mahmud as they had done to the *San Hing's* original first and second officers.

A glance at the compass screwed to the bulkhead showed him the ship had been moved back on its course.

SAIBURI drifted out of the morning mist, a ramshackle settlement with a couple of copra godowns and a sprawling collection of shacks with corrugated-iron roofs.

Half an hour later the fore and aft lines were twisted around the bollards. Melrose went ashore with a triumphant stride. He was gone twenty minutes. Presently a line of sarong-clad natives came padding down the wharf, each carrying two bundles of cane stalks. Holt was a prisoner in the wheelhouse. Opposite him Barwin sat on the settee, smoked a chain of cigarettes, and said, "Don't move, Cap'n. We can take care of this ourselves."

One by one the cane bundles were brought aboard. Melrose reappeared and oversaw their transportation to a spare cabin amidships, which, fitted with a steel door, served as a strong room. Then a thin dark-faced man in colored sarong and singlet walked across the plank. Rajah Mahmud.

An hour later the Malayan coast was a smudge in the distance. The *San Hing* headed north by east toward Cape Cambodia.

Released by Barwin from the wheelhouse, Holt headed below. Halfway down the companionway he heard a thud and a groan. Quickly he singled out the one possible cabin, open the door. On the threshold he stopped rigid.

Rajah Mahmud lay on the floor, blood trickling from a cut under his eye. Over him stood Melrose, swaying on the balls of his feet.

"He tried to get funny," Melrose said. "Wouldn't tell me which of the bundles has the stuff. Well, it won't take long to go through them."

The first officer turned and strode out the door.

When he had gone, Holt helped the half-conscious Malay to his feet, propped him into a chair. He took a bottle from a locker, poured whiskey down the dark man's throat. Then he stepped across and shut the door.

"Listen," he said, "we're in a bad way. But it's two against two now that you're here. I'm your friend. If we join forces maybe we can fight them."

Rajah Mahmud nodded his head weakly. "With the aid of Allah," he said.

AFTER that life on the *San Hing* centered down to routine. Through force of habit Holt filled out the rough log, and once he shot the sun. At four bells, the end of the second dog watch, Melrose took the wheel. The *San Hing* was running through a choppy sea at a brisk eighteen knots.

Several times Holt thought he was going to be locked in his cabin. But Melrose, although he knew enough navigation to keep the ship on its course, evidently depended on the skipper for any emergency that might arise. More than that, he apparently assumed that with his attempt at escape ending in failure, Holt must now be resigned to the situation.

Through the night the *San Hing* drove on, her deck lights off, her riding lights in darkness.

Midnight came and went, and Holt sat in his cabin, thinking hard. There were a number of things he might do. He might raid the ship's locker, send up a Very light. But the single flare would probably bring little result, and either Melrose or one of the crew would get him before he could light a second. He might run up the international distress signal flags, N and C. But here again chance of escaping discovery was thin.

"Looks pretty black," Holt admitted. "I'd hate to write my own ticket of insurance right now."

Sheer weariness overwhelmed him at length, and he fell asleep in his chair.

When he awoke the electric lights in his cabin were out, but through the open port

was visible a faint gray of coming dawn. A strange, ringing silence lay all about him.

He sat still a moment, then bounded from his chair. The engines were stopped. The *San Hing* was wallowing without steerageway.

Even as he leaped across the cabin, the door opened and Rajah Mahmud entered. There was an ugly bruise on the Malay's cheek, but his eyes gleamed in triumph.

"What happened?" Holt snapped. "What——?"

The Malay silenced him with a finger to his lips. "I have stopped the engines," he said. "I did not have time to damage them greatly. But there will be a delay before they are repaired."

"You——?" Surprise and a sudden admiration claimed Holt's voice. "How in blazes——?"

"I have been to England and studied engineering," Rajah Mahmud explained simply.

"And the Chink engineers?"

"Two were asleep. I managed to overcome the third after a short struggle."

It was a moment, Holt realized, for action, but what action? Within a few minutes Melrose and Barwin would be aware of what had happened. As it was, no watch had probably been kept, for the simple reason that the two renegades didn't know what a watch was. Barwin undoubtedly was at the wheel and had fallen asleep.

"I have been in the forecastle, talking with the crew," the Malay went on. "Half of them are my own people and are willing to help us. The other half is Straits-Chinese and all for Melrose. There is also in my luggage something I've been intending to tell you about. Two pistols that——"

"Pistols!" Holt's eyes suddenly opened wide. "Why the devil didn't you say so?"

"Wait," the Malay continued quietly. "They are pistols, but in appearance only. Two gold mounted dueling pistols in a walnut case given me as a gift in England. They are fired with powder and ball."

Holt's hopes died, then suddenly leaped again. Topside he heard a shout, Melrose shouting profanity.

"Listen," Holt snapped. "Get those pistols, give me one of them. There'll be plenty of confusion below decks until those engines are repaired. See how many of the Malay deckhands you can organize and send them up to the bridge in five minutes. Tell 'em to bring knives, anything they can lay their hands on. Soon as the engines are started, you drift below and keep those Diesels going. Shoot anyone that attempts to go below the grating. Got that?"

A glitter showed in Rajah Mahmud's dark eyes. He nodded, smiled, and led the way out into the passage.

Five minutes later, gripping a carved and gilded weapon Holt, with the Malay following, climbed the companionway cautiously to the main deck, went up the port ladder and lay flat in the shadows of the port wing.

SO FAR their presence had passed unnoticed. Below, they could hear Melrose's raging orders to the Chinese engineers repairing the Diesels. In the wheelhouse Barwin's figure was visible against the light of the rising dawn. The second officer was evidently holding his post, awaiting instructions from his companion.

Five minutes dragged into ten, into a quarter of an hour. And then suddenly the familiar vibration began anew and the propeller spun. The *San Hing* was again under way.

With a nod Rajah Mahmud moved forward and melted down the ladder. Holt counted sixty seconds five times, then eased himself onto the bridge and headed for the wheelhouse.

Dueling pistol primed and ready, Holt was halfway across the bridge when he was seen. The house door banged open then and Barwin emerged.

For a space of seconds neither man moved. Then Barwin clawed forth his gun and yanked at the trigger. Holt made a desperate lunge to the side even as thought struck him that he must not waste the single shot he had in return. He followed the roar by throwing himself forward in a spinning tackle.

The impact of his body carried Barwin's feet out from under him. The renegade's revolver jumped from his hand, clattered to the deck.

In and out Holt pumped his fists, striving to end matters as fast as he could. He was treading on counted time. A fist jacknifed against his cheek bone, bludgeoned his head against the wheelhouse door. He retaliated with a right and a left and another left. Suddenly Barwin leaped to his feet and came at him with a rush.

Erect, Holt leaped nimbly aside and drove out his fist with all the speed and precision he could call to arm. The second pitched forward on his face.

Panting, the skipper bent down, and scooped up Barwin's gun. He saw then that Rajah Mahmud had not failed him. Swarming up the two ladders came the Malay deckhands, lips split in eager grins, armed with knives and krisses.

"Hold the ladders!" Holt commanded. "Don't let anyone up. Where's Melrose?"

As if in reply a hoarse voice hailed him from the fo'ard well deck.

"Holt, you damned sneaking rat, I'm coming up there. I want to talk to you."

THE skipper strode to the rail and looked down. Daylight was about him now. A red ball of fire was climbing out of the east.

"Stay where you are, Melrose," he said quietly. "I'm armed, and I've got eight men up here. I'm heading this hooker straight back down the coast to S'pore where I'm going to hand you over to the authorities. You can't stop me. I've got a man below decks, and if you or anyone else gets in his way you won't live long."

It took a moment for the significance of his words to reach their mark. Holt could see the expression of rage and surprise that swept the first officer's face. The skipper grinned in spite of himself. Fight, was it? Well, so far he had taken all they had to offer. And now——

How long he could last, there was no telling. Melrose was armed. Beside that he had probably confiscated the ship's arms. The odds were pretty high.

Even as he stood there a gun roared, and a slug tore through the canvas weather cloth of the bridge. Deliberately Holt fired at Melrose, aiming low for the legs. He missed, but he came close enough to send the first officer darting for cover.

Sinster silence dropped down on the *San Hing*. And then with a rush the Straits-Chinese tried to take the bridge. Up the ladder they came. Revolvers crashed. A lascar screamed and fell.

Holt was at the port ladder, clubbing yellow heads as fast as they appeared. Below Melrose fired three times in quick succession. The last shot tore through Holt's coat. Native knives were driving in and out. But above the uproar Holt voiced a taunting laugh.

"Come on, you yellow devils," he panted. "Come and get me."

His gray eyes were dancing with eager excitement. At a command from Melrose the Chinese abruptly fell back, and the firing stopped. Melrose's voice rose up at him.

"Holt! How about a truce for a min-

ute? Will you call those rats off and hold fire if I come up?"

Holt chuckled grimly. "Come ahead," he responded. "But I won't promise anything."

He motioned the lascars away from the ladder and backstepped to the break of the bridge. He slid a cold pipe between his teeth and waited. Presently Melrose stood before him.

"Keep your gun down," the skipper ordered crisply. "And stand where you are. What do you want?"

The renegade first officer ran his eyes about him, saw the unconscious figure of Barwin, took the situation in at a glance.

"You're a double-damned fool, Holt," he snarled. "All this won't get you any place. Come on down to the cabin, and we'll talk things over."

"I'll stay where I am, thank you," said Holt. "You'd better throw down your gun."

"But, you fool, I told you I'd give you a sixth. I'll make it better than that. Barwin's out anyway, so we'll split it two ways. There's five hundred thousand dollars worth of jewels down there, and——"

"Those jewels are consigned care of the Pon Moy Trading Company to Palembang, Sumatra," Holt replied evenly. "I intend to see they get there. Throw down your gun."

A smile of cunning crossed Melrose's lips. He let his gun fall heavily to the planking, crossed his arms and stood as in defeat. Holt kept his own weapon leveled and began to pace forward. But if the renegade thought his actions had tricked the skipper he was wrong. Below decks Holt heard a muffled shot and a scream. The engine room gong clanged twice. Mahmud—— .

With a lurch Melrose dropped to one knee, retrieved his weapon and jerked the weapon to quick aim. He fired.

The slug seared across the calf of Holt's leg, but the skipper had been expecting that very play. His gun exploded even as Melrose made ready for a second shot. Up went the first officer's hands. He staggered and pitched forward on his face.

Holt shouted an order in Malay to the lascars. Then with the eight of them at his heels he leaped down the ladder straight into the massed Chinese on the deck.

It was open hell here. Pistols roared around him, and the Chinese screamed as they fought. Below decks Holt could hear bangings and thumpings and intermittent yells. Mahmud then was taking care of his end. Holt slammed his fist into another yellow face and grinned.

TWO nights later the lookout of the Dutch K. P. M. ship, *Rannswark*, Saigon to Batavia, sighted the masthead light of a Chinese freighter off the port bow. The freighter was passing on an even keel at full speed, but she drew up when the *Rennswark* signaled her with the Morse light from the bridge semaphore.

"Who are you?" the *Rannswark* signaled.

"'Sang Hing' out of Singora for Palembang," came the winking reply.

The Dutch skipper stared.

"For where?"

"Palembang, Sumatra."

"Aren't you off your course?"

Up on the bridge of the *San Hing* Skipper Holt chuckled as he smoked his pipe and rattled the contact key.

"Was off," he flashed. *"On now. Had a little trouble aboard. Mutiny. First and second officers in irons. Three members of crew dead. Everything under control."*

The captain of the Dutch ship was horrified.

"Do you want any help?"

"No thanks. Everything okay. So long."

And with that Holt left the key and made his way to the wheelhouse where Rajah Mahmud Lahar, bandaged but smiling, was for the first time in his life, minding helm.

QUARRY

By Carl Jacobi

When his last cunning ambush failed, when the jungle wall before him was a trackless hell and the shadow of the gallows darkened the path behind, Kramer crouched waiting, listening. Somewhere out there another white man was following—the man he had to kill!

FOR the fifth time in an hour Kramer halted his paddling, turned in the dugout and looked back. The Mahakam, as far as he could see, was devoid of life, a blazing, copperish band, winding through the jungle. No foreign object marked its surface or the jungle shores.

Yet the feeling persisted. It was a feeling Kramer had known before in this business of living by his wits, and without questioning its source, he recognized it for its full warning. He was being followed! Followed by someone who slowly but surely was lessening the intervening distance.

Scowling, he lit a cigarette and for a long moment sat there, face hard, massive body wet with perspiration. Abruptly his hand moved under his shirt and reached for a small chamois sack that hung from his neck by a leather cord. With a jerk of the drawstring he permitted five green crystals to fall

135

into his palm. Emeralds! He rolled them back and forth, looked down at them in satisfaction.

"Let 'em follow," he muttered. "They'll get tired of it soon enough, and if they don't, they'll wish they had. Me, I've got plans. So what am I worryin' about?"

Kramer's plans went back more than a month, to the time he had sat on the hotel veranda in Bandjermasin and listened to a voluble Dutch trader tell the latest Borneo gossip which had not yet found its way into the *Hongkong Weekly* or the *Sidney Bulletin*. A bubonic outbreak in Sandakan, illness of a forest conservator in Kuching, and —casually—the coming trip of the son of the wealthy Sultan of Kotei.

It was that last that made Kramer move to the edge of his chair and forget his gin-sling.

"Trip?" he had repeated.

"*Ja, Mynheer,*" the trader nodded. "The boy, he iss gedding older, and the father has decided to Oxford to send him to study. With five of the royal jewels of Kotei he comes. In Singapore he will change the jewels into expense money. Expense? It is a fortune!"

From that moment Kramer had dulled his ears to further conversation while an idea began to simmer far back in a corner of his brain. A day later he brought his maps out of storage, consulted a couple of mining men about in-country conditions and got his equipment ready.

When the time came, everything worked like clockwork. The Sultan's delicate-looking son arrived in Samarinda via government launch from the palace at Tenggarong. The next K.P.M. ship was not due for ten days, and as Kramer had hoped and expected, the boy took quarters in the house of a Malay friend in the native quarter.

Kramer waited patiently. On a black night he made his way to the house, jimmied open the rear door and entered,

armed with a hammer wrapped in cloth. A single blow in the darkness. A quick search through a bamboo dressing-stand. And a hurried but cautious passage through back alleys to the waterfront.

When it was over the body of the Sultan's son lay in the mud of the river bottom, and Kramer with his five emeralds headed into the interior.

IT SOUNDED simple, but it was planned simplicity. *Corpus delicti* —no body in evidence—would thwart the Dutch police for a time. Even when they did begin to unravel their threads—as ultimately of course they would—they would not suspect an ordinary criminal of being mad enough to attempt escape by way of the jungle.

Kramer, however, was no ordinary criminal. Three years back he had gone up the Mahakam with a hunting expedition. He spoke Malay. He understood the Dyaks. And he knew how to take care of himself in the bush.

Aware of his abilities, he had proceeded on fixed schedule. Five days hard paddling had brought him to Long Iram, where he had joked with the officer-in-charge, asked more questions about interior conditions and replenished supplies. He was now approaching the Boh River junction. A week on that waterway, and the monsoon would definitely break. Kramer planned a layover until the rains were past, then overland through Apo Kayan to the Kayan River, and on to Bulungan on the east coast, from where final escape would be a simple matter. A trip through hell, he fully realized, but for the emeralds it was worth it.

Again he stopped paddling and shot a glance behind.

How many of them were back there —one, two, three? By now he was sure the body must have been found and evidence fitted together. Probably it was some young R.N.I.A. trooper, fresh from Bandjermasin, detailed to bring him back to justice.

He threw away his cigarette and smiled. Dipping the paddle, he turned the dugout midstream and with a few powerful strokes headed for shore. At the east bank he fought his way to solid ground, pushed into the dense brush.

An argus pheasant skuttled off before him. Ahead somewhere a *wah-wah* ape uttered its strange cry.

Kramer stopped before a taller Seraya tree, slung his rifle over one shoulder, his cased binoculars over the other and began to mount upwards. At the end of ten minutes he had climbed to a point where an unbroken view of the Mahakam lay beneath him. Focusing the glasses, he looked toward the south. Abruptly he stiffened.

Far off a Dyak *prahu* had crept into sudden view, advancing around a bend in the river. It was a *prahu* with three occupants, two Dyak boatmen and a white man. As it drew nearer he saw that the white man wore the drill uniform and puggree-wrapped helmet of the Royal Netherlands East Indies Army.

"Damned if it ain't Barret," Kramer said aloud. "Frank Barret. They sent that young fool after me. Me . . . !"

He knew Barret. A quiet, thin-faced kid—more British than Hollander—who a year ago had been sent to the Long Nawang garrison and who had come back with a case of nerves. Come back simply because of a run-in with a half-grown python—so the story went. Since then he had been stationed at coastal barracks, training Sea-Dyaks and border Kenyahs to become soldiers.

The man in the tree leveled the rifle. The boat came on. Now it was well within firing distance. But Kramer did not fire.

The easiness, he reflected, robbed the whole game of its zest. Without pursuit, the long trek ahead, the hardship, the

jungle would pall on him. He needed something to keep him going.

In an instant he had changed his mind. He squinted down the sights and took careful aim, not at Barret, but at the foremost of the two Dyak boatmen. A report—and below a naked brown figure suddenly stiffened, threw up his hands and pitched overboard.

Without haste, without emotion Kramer let himself quickly down the tree, returned to the dugout and headed upstream.

THREE hours later the sun dropped into the trees. Selecting an open spot in the shore reeds, he landed and made camp. He cooked and ate his meal slowly. About him now the night was black and alive with the drone of insects. A leopard snarled somewhere close at hand.

Smoking one cigarette after another, Kramer leaned back and mused over the situation. He would have to tighten up his schedule. Not much. Just enough to prevent Barret from getting too close in the event he chose to continue pursuit. Meanwhile there would be time and occasion to have a little fun. Kramer grinned.

When he left camp the following morning his idea of "fun" had entered its first stage. A bamboo pole was propped in the ooze of the river shore and upon its top where the metal was sure to catch the sun's rays was mounted a label-stripped can.

Within the can Kramer left a torn leaf from his notebook. It bore the penciling:

KEEP COMING, YOU FOOL. IF YOU FOLLOW ME YOU'LL LAND STRAIGHT IN HELL!

By noon the words seemed a prophecy. The sun beat down upon the river, transforming it into a shimmering, eye-searing mirror. The air was like hot gauze, still, breathless without the slightest breeze. Shirt wet, a fresh nipa-leaf in the crown of his helmet, Kramer paddled steadily on.

Midafternoon of the next day saw him entering the mouth of the Boh River. He was now a full twelve hours ahead of his planned schedule, but his eyes showed no satisfaction. This was Kayan country, swarming with savages. Headhunters, whose hate for the white man was a tradition. Moreover the dreaded monsoon showed signs of breaking sooner than he had expected.

He passed two *kampongs* without trouble, then took time out for a much-needed rest. As he squatted in the *lalang* grass he opened the chamois sack once again and gazed admiringly at the emeralds. They were big fellows, all right. He didn't know much about stones. But it was easy to see that these were large enough to buy him a life of ease for a long time to come. Many deals as he had transacted in recent years—most of them shady—none had ever offered as high stakes for as little risk. Drowsily Kramer's eyes closed, and he lay back.

He awoke with a start. Some inner warning sent him stumbling to his feet, hurrying to the river bank. There, behind a fringe of bush, he jerked rigid, staring.

In clear view advancing toward him came a *prahu*. Barret's *prahu*. The white man and his remaining Dyak were paddling with long, sweeping strokes.

Kramer rubbed his unshaven jaw and spat savagely.

"You're a glutton for punishment, ain't you?" he growled. "Okay, soldier, you asked for it."

But again as he brought the rifle to shoulder he hesitated. Better to spare Barret and kill the native. Without a guide the kid must then turn about and head for Samarinda. And there he could tell the Dutch commandant just what kind of a man his quarry was.

S p a n g! A scream, a splash, and once more Kramer was grinning triumphantly.

After that he moved upriver at an even faster pace.

THE tributary began to narrow. Now it was but a sullen creek winding under a tunnel of dark overhanging growth. From either shore came the hot, humid odor of decay. Long floating logs that were crocodiles mottled the surface. Proboscis monkeys came out of nowhere to gibber at him.

Once he heard drums throbbing far off, and once when he passed a larger village natives rushed to the water's edge, shouted imprecations and shot Sumpit darts at him. But they made no move to follow and Kramer paddled on steadily.

He began to take quinine. Fever, he thought, had entered his system. Then he realized the symptoms of an even more serious malady. Dysentery! Cursing, he rummaged through his medicine bag and changed the quinine for *Dover's Powder,* a compound of opium and ipecacuanha root.

Another day, the morning of the second since he had entered the tributary. Kramer looked back and glimpsed something which brought a slow scowl to his lips. That slender thread of smoke rising above the trees far to the rear marked a white man's campfire. Barret had not turned back then. He was still coming. Coming like a persistent, nagging dog.

With a snarl Kramer twisted the dugout and headed for shore. There would be no more playing this time. Even as he landed, a plan to end pursuit for once and for all took form in his brain.

He drew his revolver and lurched into the bush. A few yards and he came upon an erect sapling. Into a crotch of this he jammed the weapon. Next he tore free a ten-foot length of vine, secured one end to the trigger. On the trunk of a nearby tree he fastened a torn remnant of his shirt.

Back at the bank he broke off a handful of reeds, scattered them in the water.

It was child's play. Barret would sight the landing place and would stop to investigate. A touch of the taut vine and a bullet would do the rest.

Not until one more day had come and gone did he discover what this trap had cost him. He had left Samarinda with a rifle and a Webley revolver, but in his hurry had packed only cartridges for the pistol. With the smaller weapon now miles behind he was without arms. Kramer spat an oath and flung the useless rifle into the river.

More than that, the trap, for some unknown reason, had failed to work. Barret was still coming. Kramer didn't know how he knew that, but again he knew it was true.

"Damn snivelin' pup," he muttered. "Thinks he's goin' to offset his bad record by catchin' me. Thinks he's goin' to get a little glory. Well, he won't."

He wiped the sweat from his face and continued his machine-like strokes. Blisters were forming on his hands from continued use of the paddle. The lower part of his body ached dully. His throat was dry and burning.

The rain came. A blinding sheet, at first of cloudburst proportions, it quickly settled to a soaking downpour. Landing, Kramer resignedly made a pack of those supplies he could carry and which were necessary for his existence, and set out through the bush on foot. He moved parallel with the river, but at intervals he halted to listen. Twice he muttered profanity, and an hour later he set his second trap.

Similar to the first, it consisted of a sapling, bent double, with his hunting knife lashed securely to the end. A dead log was moved in such a position that the slightest touch would release the knife and send it hurtling forward. And

upon the log, in plain view, Kramer left an empty cigarette package.

Hate for Barret and all that he stood for rose within him as he stumbled on. Aloud he cursed the Samarinda police, the R.N.I.A., the dead Sultan's son. But not the emeralds. Feel of the chamois sack against his chest reassured him and gave him renewed strength to push on.

THE compass told he was heading due east. Shortly then he would reach the higher ground of Apo Kayan, and the going would be easier. But the jungle floor, instead of rising, dipped steadily lower with more miasmatic pools of water and denser growth.

Abruptly the pools merged into a huge bog that stretched in either direction as far as he could see. Kramer hesitated, stared out at the roily water, then looked above. Yes, a man might go on by taking to the trees. It would be grueling, man-killing work, but such a course would leave no trail for the man behind. On the other hand, if he attempted to skirt the swamp it would mean a serious loss of distance and time. Kramer decided to spend the night here and begin the arboreal trail in the fresh of morning.

But before going aloft next day he set his third trap. There was no need for it, of course. Barret must have given up or been caught by the knife long ago. Yet a vague uneasiness lurked in Kramer's brain, and he stifled his pride by telling himself it was well never to take chances.

With his belt axe he cut a circle of bark, coiled it so that it looked like a log and fastened the two sides together with twigs. Upon one side he strapped his sun helmet. Then he threw the bait before him out into the water.

The synthetic log struck with a splash and floated quietly, helmet up. Kramer gazed down at this, his latest invention and laughed aloud. He had tested that particular patch of water the night before with a long stick, and he knew what lay beneath the surface. Quicksand! Capable of sucking the strongest man under. Fool's luck might have saved Barret twice before, but it wouldn't this time.

The bog seemed endless. Spots began to whirl before Kramer's eyes as, apelike, he fought his way through the trees. The ache in his stomach increased to a searing pain, doubling its agony with each move. He climbed high above the water, advancing along branches with the aid of vines and occasionally swinging across dizzy caverns of space from one tree to another. At intervals he halted to rest his laboring heart.

And then, like a vision, he saw dry ground beneath him. With a hoarse cry he dropped downward, ripped open his pack and began to wolf food.

But his elation was short-lived. Midway through the meal a sound brought his head about with a jerk. A furtive stare entered his eyes. An instant later he had scooped up his supplies and was racing madly through an almost impenetrable sea of rip grass.

As he ran, questions pounded at him. Barret—was it really he he had seen, or but a moving orchid, a vagary of his fevered brain? How had the man missed the traps? How had he crossed the bog?

The rip grass possessed a thousand razor edges, and before he had gone a hundred yards, Kramer found his hands and arms dripping with blood. He wiped them on his shirt and began cutting a trail with his belt axe. At the destruction of their home, insects swarmed about his head in stinging clouds.

A full hour passed before he emerged free of the grass. He turned then, clothing in shreds, panting hard, and shook his fist.

"Damn your dirty soul," he gasped. "Come on. You'll never catch me."

He drank a long draught from the canteen which still hung at his belt and pushed on—now walking, now at a stumbling lope. All day he fled due east. At sundown he had barely sufficient strength to build a fire and throw himself exhausted beside it. The fire smoked and sputtered as rain drizzled down through the canopy of foliage. Kramer stared into the flames, bit his lips.

He must reach the Kayan River. Once there, he knew, Barret would give up the chase. Kramer exhaled a streamer of smoke and twisted his lips savagely. A few hours before he had thought of ambushing his pursuer as he had ambushed the two Dyak boatmen. But in his weakened physical condition the odds would be definitely on the other man's side. No, the only way was to keep going, fight off the dysentery and perhaps leave another trap.

It was in that quarter-hour before complete darkness closed in that his eyes, staring up into the dripping foliage, saw something which stiffened every nerve in his body.

Motionless he lay there, watching. Above him a long brownish shape was slowly gliding along a lower branch. A hooded head moved restlessly to and fro. A forked tongue lanced the air.

Kramer's eyes dilated. It was that snake of snakes, the hamadryad. Even as his hand slid downward toward his belt axe the reptile poised to strike.

K RAMER rolled over twice, leaped to his feet. He had but a split second to act. The hamadryad shot downward.

Came a mad impulse to turn and run. But he knew such a move would be fatal. His only hope was to face the snake and hope to outwit it. Again it came at him, moving like an arrow through the long grass. And again Kramer, terrified, escaped by the narrowest margin.

It was a game of blindman's bluff. By every trick he knew Kramer sought to place a tree between himself and his adversary. The last attempt the fangs came closer; for one horrible moment he thought they had reached his leg.

He ducked backward, tried to circle to the left. Giving no quarter, the hamadryad cut him off. Like a released spring it whipped forward. Back and forth, with light rapidly blurring into darkness, they moved. Panic had seized Kramer now. His heart was racing, his eyes bulging in their sockets. In a dim sort of way he realized that the snake was but withholding its strength for the final attack.

Once more Kramer jerked sideways, escaping the deadly tongue by inches. And then he found an opening. With a single movement he ripped free his shirt, rolled it, clenched it in both hands and threw himself downward. His draped hands clawed wildly, seized the reptile's neck and clenched hard. Hanging on grimly, he reached for his belt axe.

For two long mad minutes he tried to twist the head into striking position. The writhing tail had fastened itself on one of his arms and was exerting pressure. Ground, grass, trees seemed to whirl round and round in a spinning circle.

He raised the axe, poised it—struck. The blow reached its mark. A terrific contortion of the brownish coils, and they jerked away from the severed head. Panting, Kramer staggered five feet, slumped to the ground and lay prone.

For a long time he did not move, knowing only a deep inner feeling of numbness. Gradually his heart quieted, his breathing returned to normal, and his muscles untensed. When at length he moved, it was to sit up abruptly, stare at the dead reptile and break out into a long peal of harsh laughter.

As suddenly as that he had decided upon his fourth and final trap!

There would be no mechanics this time. Nature herself would constitute the whole of it, nature and the mating habits of the hamadryad.

He threw more wood on the fire, stood quiet, listening. Then, arranging his packsack, axe and compass in an orderly pile, he staggered across the little glade into the underbrush.

In a very short time Barret, still continuing his pursuit, would sight the fire. He would find the supplies and reason logically that Kramer had left camp to find fresh water. Barret would draw his revolver and wait. And then . . . .

And then a second hamadryad would come in search of its dead mate! It was inevitable. Always traveling in pairs, the king cobra's one peculiar instinct is faithfulness. Kill one, and the other will come to seek revenge.

Kramer dug his hands into the cool earth and chuckled through swollen lips. Ingenious as the four previous plans had been, this outranked them all.

A man strode into the glade cautiously. By the light of the fire, Kramer, looking through a curtain of leaves, made out the soiled uniform, the helmet, the young but determined face.

Revolver in hand, Barret stood there quietly. He looked at the fire. He dropped to his knees, examined the trampled grass. A low whistle came to his lips as his eyes fell upon the dead snake. Frowning, he knelt there, mentally reconstructing the struggle that had taken place a short time before. He lifted the hamadryad with the toe of his boot and kicked it into the bush. Then he moved away from the firelight and squatted, revolver ready for instant action.

Kramer, watching, found it difficult to repress his emotions. In spite of the ache in his bowels, he longed to laugh. Barret thought he was waiting for him. Instead he was waiting for his own destruction.

TIME snailed by. The jungle night was still. The fire diminished to a few reddish coals and died.

Once Kramer let his mind drift away from his surroundings. Everything was going to be fine from now on. At Bulungan he could rest, recover his health and wait for some coastal steamer. He would go to Manila, perhaps cross over to Saigon and buy himself a plantation.

It wouldn't be long now. The hamadryad, never separated long from its mate, would be entering the glade soon. If only there weren't this infernal darkness he could see rather than guess what was happening.

The rustling continued. Closer at hand. Kramer twisted one leg cautiously to brush aside a more persistent mosquito. The mosquito left, but his leg came into contact with what seemed to be a sharp thorn, jerked away. He changed his position, continued his unseeing watch.

It was odd the way things developed. The mating habits of the hamadryad—they must have killed many in past ages. But who—who else had ever thought to use them as a means of defense?

Vaguely Kramer was aware that a pulse was tapping under the joint of his knee. He stretched the limb farther outward, felt a curious warmth move up along his thigh into his groin. Bad business, these thorns. Might cause an infection. He must cauterize the wound later. But all this when he had time.

He turned his head slightly, and sudden amazement claimed him. His head felt detached from his body, seemed to be floating higher in space.

Kramer swore, shifted again. And then . . .

And then like a flash of light he realized what had happened. With a wild scream he leaped to his feet and plunged forward into the glade. Five steps he ran, yelling insanely.

But before he reached the blackened fire the ground seemed to open up before him. He felt himself falling—falling into a bottomless pit of oblivion.

IT WAS three days later before Lieutenant Frank Barret reached the point on the Boh River where he had left his *prahu*. Bailing out the rain-water, seized the paddle and pushed out into the current.

Not until he was well midstream did he halt his strokes to let the craft drift. He reached in a pocket of his uniform then, drew out a chamois sack and let five green crystals fall into his open palm. Emeralds! He stared down at them curiously.

"You were a fool, Kramer," he said slowly. "They weren't worth it."

He took up the paddle again and dug it into the water. And a grim smile came to his lips, for he realized that in spite of his earlier record, a new man was heading downstream.

TRIAL by JUNGLE

By
CARL JACOBI
Author of "Tiger Island,"
"Balu Guns," etc.

T HE "Kid" got off the K.P.M. boat in the rain, and the first thing he did after being passed through the Samarinda customs was to check over his baggage. There was a huge pile of it on the wharf. As Bascomb remarked later, it looked as if the Kid were arriving at a summer hotel, rather than Dutch Borneo, southeast coast.

From his shelter under the eave of

Even in the Wilds of Borneo a Canny Greenhorn May Be Triumphant Over Case-Hardened Old-Timers!

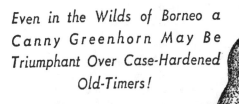

The Kid side stepped, nimble as a ballet dancer, jerked out his big Spanish pistol and fired point blank

a copra godown, Bascomb smoked a cheroot and eyed the newcomer with appraising eyes. He saw a thin, gangly man in his late twenties with a skin as yet uncolored by a tropic sun, wearing a gabardine bush-jacket, light colored breeches and brand new mosquito boots.

Bascomb knew he wasn't alone in his observations. Farther down the wharf, unmindful apparently of the drizzle, another white man slouched against an empty hogshead and watched the Kid's every move. Pierre de Cleyne made it a point to inspect the disembarking passengers of each monthly steamer.

The Kid's baggage included a Winchester 50-110 express rifle and a Fox No. 12 smooth-bore shotgun. There was also a large drill tent with collapsible iron poles, folding cots and three pebble-leather gripsacks of the Gladstone variety.

"Real dyed-in-the-wool explorer," de Cleyne muttered sarcastically. "Probably intends to go upriver in a government launch and write a book about the dangers of the jungle. Well, *tiens*, anything for a change."

But before he could reach the Kid's side, Bascomb strode forward, cutting him off. He touched the Kid's arm, flipped up his hand in what he hoped was a casual salute.

"My name's Bascomb, Captain Mark Bascomb, formerly of the India army," he said. "I see you've just come in. Is there anything I can do to help?"

The Kid looked up.

"Hello," he greeted. "If you can help me get this stuff to a hotel, I'd be obliged. That is, if there is a hotel."

Bascomb permitted his most winning smile to play across his lips.

"There's a hotel of sorts. I'll get you a coolie."

He sauntered around a corner, called something in Malay and singled out a Cantonese boy from the half dozen that scrambled forward.

A moment later the two of them were walking down the wet cobblestones, with Pierre de Cleyne, defeated for the moment, mouthing silent profanity behind.

BASCOMB was a quick worker, and he knew just the remarks to make to weave a cloak of sincerity about himself. Long before they had reached Samarinda's ramshackle hotel, he had learned most of what he wanted to know.

The Kid's name was Steve Pottager. He was an American, and his father, John Pottager, was a Texas oil man. But the Kid wanted it understood he wasn't a tourist.

He was here in Borneo to travel up the Mahakam River into the interior. As an ethnologist, he desired to make a study of the various upriver tribes: Punans, Kenyahs, and Kayans. Also—and this Bascomb managed to pump out of him by a few casual but carefully pointed questions—Pottager, as a side issue, was interested in the location of a certain workable gold deposit in the vicinity.

"Have you ever," the Kid asked, "heard of a man, an explorer, named Charles Fail?"

Bascomb's teeth bit deep into his cheroot.

"Fail?"

"Yes. You may remember he went upriver a year ago, prospecting. He was accidentally shot by one of his native carriers. Before his death he found this gold deposit; but when his effects were brought back to the coast, the map which he was known to have made, was not included."

"And you have that map?" Bascomb restrained the avarice in his voice with difficulty.

"Yes. You see Fail sent it back to Samarinda by carrier pigeon. It was returned by the Assistant Resident to Fail's relatives. How I obtained it is a personal matter. But I intend to locate that deposit and later perhaps sell the claim to some mining concern."

Later when Bascomb emerged from the hotel into the street, he was in high spirits—until he saw the figure that waited for him just beyond the doorway. Pierre de Cleyne barred his way.

"*M'sieu* Bascomb," he said, smiling under his trim mustache, "you are one jump ahead of me, no? I think it wise we join forces."

"What the devil do you mean?"

"What do I mean? I mean I have discovered this Kid—the name, I believe, is Pottager—the same time as you. I see by your eyes you have taken a job with him as guide. Me, I think I will be guide too. Otherwise. . . ."

"Otherwise what?" Bascomb's lips trembled in stifled rage.

"Otherwise, *M'sieu* Pottager will learn things of considerable interest."

Bascomb shrugged. "Okay," he said. "Walk along, and we'll talk it over. . . ."

FIVE days later they passed Long Iram without stopping, and Bascomb congratulated himself that the Kid was undoubtedly the most delicious specimen of greenhorn it had ever been his good fortune to run up against. It seemed incredible that a man could be so idiotically dumb as to head incountry without even a knowledge of Malay or to wonder if they would have any luck bagging a tiger. Bascomb could have told him that tigers didn't exist in Dutch East or in any other part of Borneo for that matter, but he didn't.

He was content to watch the Kid focus his camera and snap picture after picture of the jungle river. He was content to sit in the *prahu*, listen to the *chunk-swash* of the paddles and eye the Kid with a cat-and-mouse gaze, while he luxuriously contemplated the future.

The fact that de Cleyne had forced himself to be included in the party and that he knew what they were searching for, did not concern Bascomb particularly at present. True, the Frenchman's presence meant another cut from the spoils, but long before that time Bascomb meant to remove him from the picture entirely.

It was the morning of the sixth day that trouble struck first.

They were camped on low ground at the mouth of a nameless tributary. The Malay boatmen had taken down the tent and packed most of the equipment in the *prahus*. De Cleyne had strolled several yards down the muddy shore, idly smoking a cigarette.

Suddenly he stood stockstill, frozen with horror. Directly before him was a coiled brownish shape with an inflated hood. De Cleyne needed no one to tell him that this was the hamadryad, the King Cobra, whose bite meant sure and agonizing death. The man stood petrified with terror.

The snake's head was weaving gently back and forth. Its mouth was open, and the deadly fangs lanced the air like a whip lash. Cold sweat broke out on de Cleyne's brow. Every muscle of his body seemed turned to stone.

"Don't move, de Cleyne," a voice said. "Don't move an inch!"

At the sound of the voice the hamadryad whipped around like a released spring. Which was what the Kid wanted. He had his revolver leveled, and he fired three times in quick succession. Two slugs hit. The hamadryad fell in a writhing heap.

De Cleyne exhaled, walked back to the camp and slumped down on a rock without a word. His face was white, and his lips were trembling. It was a long time before he could shake the Kid's hand and mumble his thanks.

But that was the startling part of it. Pottager looked up and smiled. "Was it poisonous?" he asked.

The only shadowy detail of the whole setup was the fact that Pottager as yet had neither shown his map nor revealed even vaguely where the gold deposit lay. Bascomb assumed, of course, that it was somewhere in the Mueller range, but he suddenly realized that he and de Cleyne had been so intent on beating each other, they had made no attempt to check the Kid's word.

Each day Pottager named a village or a landmark which was to be the destination for that stage of the trip. He then left the finding of that landmark to the two guides entirely. Bascomb stood it as long as he could, then voiced his thoughts.

"If this gold deposit is worth the trouble of refining, why don't you work the claim yourself, instead of selling to a mining company?"

Pottager smiled. "I've already told you that gold is a minor incentive for this expedition. Ethnology is my main motive. Also, I intend to gather material for a book, explaining the death of Charles Fail."

De Cleyne tugged at his lower lip. "About your map, M'sieu. Hadn't you better show it to us now? After all, it is not right that we travel blind."

The Kid slowly filled a pipe from an oilskin pouch. "The map is no longer in existence," he stated calmly. "I destroyed it after committing it to memory. Have a terrible habit of losing things, you know. But it wasn't a map in the true sense. Just a list of *kampongs* and landmarks Fail passed through. I know the names of the places, but I don't know where they are. But I can tell you this much. We're heading for Apo Kayan."

De Cleyne stared, then restrained an oath. Considering the fact that Apo Kayan was a district with boundaries about as clearly defined as the Indian Ocean, he knew less than he did before.

Upriver they continued. The shores seemed to grow thicker and darker green, out of which drifted an earthy smell of decay and parasitical growth. The villages were barely friendly now, and they stopped to renew supplies with the utmost caution.

It was, of course, familiar ground to Bascomb and de Cleyne, and they said nothing when Pottager photographed a Wah-Wah ape or a particularly gorgeous argus pheasant, or when he ordered the paddling halted to point his camera at some solitary Dyak standing imagelike on the shore. Roll after roll of film Pottager used, and when he was not photographing, he was scribbling in his notebook.

But the Kid was also stubborn. In Samarinda he had refused to listen to arguments and had insisted that all of his equipment be taken along. Now in the interior with space becoming more of a premium each day, he still would not permit any one article to be left behind.

It was de Cleyne who voiced his impatience at last.

"*Mon Dieu*," he snarled, "how long are we to stand this infernal nonsense. Tents and folding chairs and water filters. It is driving me crazy. Why don't we get rid of the Kid and find the gold ourselves?"

BASCOMB scraped a leech off his calf with a jacknife and shook his head.

"You forget that he has the map in his head. Also that Fail changed his natives so often it is impossible to tell where he went. Pottager may be a fool all right, but he's so much of a fool he won't trust anyone, not even us!"

De Cleyne, however, was not content to sit back and let developments take care of themselves. He decided to force the issue. Quietly as they made their way upriver he formulated a plan, mulled it over in his mind. Next day he spoke again to Bascomb.

"What this idiot needs is a scare," he said. "He's had things too much his own way so far. If we can make him believe we are frightened and want to turn back, thus leaving him without guides, he may decide to talk."

They camped that night by a small Kenyah *kampong* with a very old log-house. Radiating out from the central clearing, paths dissected the jungle in every direction. De Cleyne followed two of those paths a short distance before darkness set in. One, he found, led down to the rice paddies. The other, by a matter of luck, ended at a tabu trail.

Now your Dyak tabu trail may have one of a hundred reasons for existence. This one was reserved for the tomb and after-death spirit of a former chieftain. The tomb, a ramshackle construction of *nipa* thatch, stood in the middle of an open space. The trail was marked by two grotesque totem poles, each with a dried, shrunken head mounted to its top end. In the half light de Cleyen dared go no nearer, for he knew to be seen meant instant death from the natives.

But that night when the Dyaks were milling about their fire, drinking *tuak*, he found occasion to slip back into the path unnoticed and with the aid of a flashlight, return to the site of the tomb.

Stealthily he stood there, listening. A hornbill gave forth its hollow cry, but there was no sound of pursuit. De Cleyne strode forward, reached up the nearest totem pole and yanked down one of the dried heads. Then, moving across to the tomb, he broke over his knee a Sumpitan blow pipe which had been placed on the platform for the use of the dead man in the afterworld.

The defilement complete, he placed where it would be easily seen, a piece of cloth which he had previously managed to rip from Pottager's shirt.

And at dawn, just as de Cleyne had expected, the attack began.

Neither he nor Bascomb were worried as to its final result. They had remained awake, guns in readiness all night. They had chosen a village that was small, with most of the warriors away on a hunting trip. And they had quietly seen that everything was ready for a hasty departure.

The attack began with a wild yell back of the *kampong*, in the direction of the tabu trail. Swiftly it was caught up by twenty throats. Then the drums began to pound, and with a concerted rush a dozen natives headed for the white men's camp on the shore.

DE CLEYNE took command instantly.

"To the canoes, quick!" he yelled. "Spread your fire. Don't waste shots. Pottager, go on!"

The Kid apparently had been wakened from a deep sleep and was not yet fully aware of what was happening. He struggled into his clothes, fumbled for his cartridge belt.

They ran for the last of the dugouts. The two other canoes, loaded with frightened Malay boatmen, were already moving into midstream. Bascomb climbed into the stern; Pottager took his place amidships, and de Cleyne came jogging up, his eyes alone betraying the satisfaction he felt at the success of his plan.

But the Kid was destined to be more than an audience. Just as de Cleyne broke through the reeds and emerged onto the shore, his foot caught in a sink hole, and he plunged heavily forward.

His head struck a partially buried rock, and the blow knocked him out completely. He lay there motionless with the infuriated natives from the village closing in from behind.

"Shove off!" Bascomb yelled in Malay.

The order was never obeyed. Pottager leaped out of the dugout and ran lightly across the beach to the fallen man's side. He passed one arm around de Cleyne's shoulders and lifted him to his feet. Before he could move, the foremost of the attacking Dyaks was upon him.

He was a big brute with massive shoulders and a heavy *parang* in one hand. With a savage yell he swung the knife straight for Pottager's throat. The Kid sidestepped, nimble as a ballet-dancer, jerked out his big Spanish pistol and fired pointblank. The Dyak's body seemed to collapse within itself.

De Cleyne was slowly coming to. Pottager half carried, half dragged him toward the *prahu*. And then, halfway to the water's edge, two more Dyaks came charging up. Pottager's first shot drilled the foremost through the temple. The second native's hand coiled around the Kid's gunwrist, wrenched the weapon free with savage force.

In a moment they were down, rolling over and over. Pottager may have realized his life was at stake, but he didn't lose his head. While Bascomb crouched low in the dugout, firing steadily, he pounded his fists in and out deliberately, making each blow count. Pressed hard, he seemed about to go under, then found an opening.

Swinging his right arm upward in a sweeping haymaker, he connected hard with the native's jaw. Twice he struck in rapid succession, utilizing every ounce of strength he possessed. The brown hands relaxed their grip, and the Kid leaped to his feet. He gave the still bewildered de Cleyne a mighty push forward and hurled himself into the dugout.

"Paddle!" he yelled.

A cloud of darts whizzed after them. But with oars working like pistons the Malay boatmen sent the dugout spinning out from shore. They darted into the protection of overhanging liana vines and raced upstream.

That night de Cleyne said:

"I think, *M'sieu*, we — Bascomb and I—will go back. It is impossible that we go farther without knowing more facts. Also, as you have seen, it is too dangerous."

Pottager looked up from the camera lens he was polishing and nodded.

"I'll pay you now then for your services," he said. "I'll write you a draft on my Singapore bank which you can cash in Samarinda."

Bascomb stared. "But you!" he exclaimed. "You don't mean you expect to go it alone.

The Kid shrugged. "I'll have some of the boatmen, and I know the names of the places along the trail. I ought to be able to pick up a guide at one of the river villages."

But Bascomb and de Cleyne didn't go back. Bascomb scowled and muttered something about "a bargain being a bargain," and said he would stick to his end. And de Cleyne smoked cigarettes chain fashion and lasped into sullen silence.

THE Kid accepted the change of decision without comment. Within a day, however, he added a new procedure to his travel itinerary which served to irritate the two guides even more.

At each and every *kampong*, no matter how difficult of access, Pottager inisisted on stopping and palavering with the *kapala*. Unable to speak Malay, he impressed Bascomb into the job of interpreter.

"We follow the trail of a white *tuan* Charles Fail, who journeyed up this river a year ago. Do you know of such a man? Have you heard how he met his death? Were any of his carriers enlisted from your village?"

And a hundred other questions, all relating to the dead explorer.

In this manner after repeated delays they finally reached Long Tuju. Here the Kid announced they were to leave the river and trek inland. They were to head for a place known as Senglah marsh. Did either of the two guides know where it was? De Cleyne did, but instantly decided on another trick to force Pottager to reveal his final destination before going any farther.

As he explained it to Bascomb the first night inland, it was simple. The Kid had only a list of landmarks and the general direction Fail had taken to guide him. He knew approximately where he was, but that was all. They had only to steal his compass which he had been glancing at all day. Without the direction-finder Pottager would be forced to depend on them entirely.

Next morning the Kid delayed starting for an hour while he looked for his compass.

"Foolish of me to take only one of the things," he said. "And I can't understand you fellows not having at least one between you. Well, it's fortunate we haven't much farther to go."

They were in dense forest. *Seraya* and *palapak* trees towered above them, and a tesselation of vines and lianas shut off the sunlight. The undergrowth in places was so thick two Malays had to go ahead, cutting the way.

But as they continued, the Kid seemed less and less affected by the loss of his compass. Occasionally he halted to glance at the sun or to look at his pocket watch. It was he who was leading the way now, and without variation he kept a course due east.

"I heard once," Bascomb said to de Cleyne, "that a man can tell direction by pointing one hand of his watch, if its running, toward the sun. Halfway between the two hands is north, or something like that. Do you think that's what Pottager's doing?"

De Cleyne shrugged. "He's a fool!" he said.

THEY were moving down into lower ground. Gradually the earth became resilient under foot.

Rip grass appeared and water in pools, and by noon the way before them was blocked by Senglah marsh.

Pottager called a halt. The Malays set about making a meal.

"Well, what's the next landmark?" Bascomb demanded. "If you expect to find a way through that marsh, you're crazy. Dyaks call it the field of the devil, and nothing on earth can make them enter it. There's no trail, and the thing's bottomless."

"Yes," agreed de Cleyne. "Besides we're going farther away from the mountains. This isn't gold country."

Quietly smoking his pipe, Pottager swung around and gazed at the Frenchman.

"How far from the river was this man, Fail, when he was shot?" he asked.

"How far? He was two days from the mouth of the Merasi, in the foothills of the Mueller range. But . . ." De Cleyne paused and tugged at his lip. "That's what I heard at any rate; that's what I heard in Samarinda."

Pottager nodded abstractedly. "We've got to cross this swamp. The next landmark is on the other side. Let's get going."

Within an hour de Cleyne and Bascomb were bathed in perspiration. The going through the marsh was even worse than they had expected. The Kid strode in the lead, picking his way carefully. In places a misstep to the right or to the left would have meant instant death in the sucking quicksand.

Insects droned about them in hordes. Bascomb and de Cleyne had let down the netting proection from their sun helmets, but that did little good. Pottager, his face gleaming with liberal applications of citronella oil, alone seemed untroubled.

Two miles into the swamp, and the Malays drew up, jabbering amongst themselves. This was evil ground, the place of bad spirits, their leader declared. They would go no farther. The white *tuans* could continue, return and meet them here. But they would not go on.

Bascomb tried to look over the sea of grass, hoping to sight a rise of hills, which logic told him must be the Kid's destination. But marsh miasma coiled about him, reducing vision to a few yards.

"What is this landmark?" he growled as they left the Malays behind and pushed on alone. "It strikes me that—"

"A high ridge running in a northerly direction beyond the swamp," Pottager replied. "It should be easy to find. By the way, Fail was laying over to cure an attack of fever when he was shot, wasn't he?"

"Yes, he—" Bascomb clipped off his words and sent a quick look at the Kid.

Nightfall found them without carriers deep in the morass, camped on a small island, surrounded by a sea of green water and tall razor-edged reeds. The sounds of the frogs and insects was deafening. De Cleyne poured a bottle of hydrogen peroxide into a deep wound on his forearm, a cut from one of the rip grass stalks, and scowled.

"Do you realize," he said to Bascomb, "that we are following this idiot like two blind men? Guides, my foot! We don't know where we are going, and now that we're here I, for my part, don't even know how to get back without his help."

THEY built a heavy smudge to ward off the mosquitoes, then spread their blankets on the soggy ground and lay down to sleep.

Hard though he was, Bascomb found himself exhausted by the day's hardships, and he fell into a heavy slumber almost at once. He awoke to broad daylight, with de Cleyne prodding him in the ribs.

"Look!" de Cleyne said. "Look!"

Bascomb rubbed his eyes and stared. The scene before him was arresting in its strangeness and yet startling in its simplicity. In the gladelike open space of the island Pottager had placed three logs, one on either side, ten yards apart; the third some distance in the foreground—all in the form of a triangle. On the ground midway between the three logs lay the Kid's big Ruby revolver. Two other guns, Bascomb's and de Cleyne's, lay on the front log, which stood upright.

And back of that third log Pottager stood bareheaded, like a judge about to impose sentence.

Bascomb's hand instinctively reached for his empty holster. With a snarl, he lurched to his feet.

"What the hell's the idea?"

The Kid lit his pipe and smiled. "If you will take places there"—he indicated the two separated logs—"I have a few things I'd like to say to you. I wasn't so sure you'd be willing to listen, so I took the liberty of relieving you of your guns. Take a seat, please."

He lifted one of the revolvers and leveled it before him.

"What is this?" de Cleyne snarled.

But the Kid's weapon did not waver. Bewildered, the Frenchman followed Bascomb to one of the assigned logs.

"Now then"—Pottager's voice was terse and brittle—"a few facts first. I told you the truth when I said Charles Fail had come through here. He did, but he retraced his steps and found the gold deposit as you suggested in the Mueller range near the headwaters of the Merasi. Fail did send a tissue paper map back to Samarinda by carrier pigeon. It came into my hands because I had been his best friend for years."

"You—" Bascomb twisted restlessly on the log.

"Yes. Fail and I went to college together. Our original intention was to go on that prospecting trip together. Then it was decided I was to meet him here in Borneo six months later. As you know, he was murdered before he could make his way back to the coast."

"Shot by one of his native carriers,

yes," de Cleyne said uneasily. "But, M'sieu, what has all this to do with us?"

THE Kid stiffened, and a glitter suddenly entered his eyes. "It has everything to do with you. Fail sent more than that map by carrier pigeon. He also sent a letter, stating that he was being followed by two white renegades. That twice within two days those white men had attempted to bushwack him in the hope of discovering the location of that gold deposit. They had learned from Dyaks on the river of Fail's discovery, but the information was vague and they had no knowledge where the site was.

"Fail was not shot by a native carrier. He was murdered in cold blood by those two white men. They failed to find the gold because Fail had made a practice of changing his carriers frequently, and he alone knew the course he had followed."

"That's a lie!" Bascomb, face drained white, leaped to his feet. "If you're insinuating—"

The Kid's revolver spun to cover him. "Stay where you are. You're going to hear this to the end, you murderers.

"You were the two white men who killed Fail. You trailed him upriver, ambushed him. Then failing to find the gold, you returned to the coast and spread that story about his being accidentally shot.

"Since the day I met the two of you in Samarinda I knew who you were. But I wasn't quite sure. I brought you in here; I even saved your life so that I could obtain absolute proof. That proof I now have. Your own statements were a damning testimony. We are now in the direct center of Senglah marsh, from which there is but one way out—Fail's trail, the way by which we came. I alone know that trail.

"I'm offering you one more chance. If either one of you has anything to say which might show his innocence, say it now. Otherwise—"

Abrupt silence clamped down on the little glade. Pottager stood there motionless, his eyes closed to crescents, a nerve twitching perceptibly in his cheek. Bascomb and de Cleyne were like wooden images.

And then Bascomb acted. Before him on the ground, midway between the three logs lay the Ruby revolver where Pottager had so conveniently placed it. With a single leap Bascomb vaulted across the intervening space, seized that weapon and swung it toward the Kid.

Two shots thundered through the swamp mists. A streak of red appeared like a ribbon on Pottager's neck. But Bascomb, with a gurgling cry, threw up his arms and staggered backward. He tottered and crashed heavily to the ground.

In the split second drama de Cleyne had sat stunned. Now he lurched erect and threw himself forward in a flying tackle. Pottager's gun spat fire again, but the slug went wild, and de Cleyne struck, outstretched arms coiling about the Kid's waist. The two men went down like blocks of wood.

Over and over they rolled. De Cleyne worked his fists in fury, screaming profanity. The Frenchman was small, with short legs, but he was built like wire, and years in the open had hardened his muscles to iron. He drove a grinding uppercut to the jaw, then slammed his heavy boot deep into the Kid's groin.

A WAVE of nausea swept over Pottager. Fighting deliberately, he worked his fists in and out, directing his blows where they would count most. Twice he felt his left connect hard with bone and flesh. Twice, in retaliation, de Cleyne drove a knee into his mid-section.

It was brute struggle with no holds barred. The Frenchman's hand clawed upward, clamped about Pottager's

(Concluded on page 104)

cil. "I'm writin' a note about where to find the money—in case I ain't here when yore daddy comes home."

"But you mustn't go anywhere," said Mamie in distress. "You're tired. You have to rest up for our trip."

"Yeah," he mumbled. "That's right —kid. I have to—rest up—for—my trip—"

On the back of the circular he had scrawled:

The money for this reward goes fer Mamie here fer her operation. Whoever gits here first better see to it. Black Tor.....

It was dusk when Sheriff Maxwell returned to his house. Everybody, including Paquita, was thronging around the bank, jabbering and marveling. Before setting out on the trail of Black Torry, the sheriff went home to see how his little girl was.

As he entered the bedroom, before he could flash a gun on the figure of the man sprawled at the table, Mamie placed a finger on her lips.

"Sh-h-h! You'll wake Uncle Hiram, Daddy. He's tired and he's sleeping."

Sheriff Maxwell cautiously approached the figure of Black Torry. A brief examination was enough. Jim Hawk had not died in vain. A Winchester bullet plays hell with a man's innards.

Black Torry was no longer tired, but he was sleeping—sleeping the sleep of eternity.

TRIAL BY JUNGLE
(Concluded from page 91)

throat, closing off his windpipe. Gasping, Pottager gave a supreme effort, twisted free and leaped erect. There he stood back, poised—waiting. De Cleyne came up like an enraged bull. For a brief instant they faced each other. De Cleyne charged again, but nimbly the Kid darted sideward and propelled a terrific triphammer blow squarely to the jaw. The Frenchman's rush was halted in mid-career. With a slow exhalation of breath, he rocked backward and collapsed.

Six weeks later a bronzed, grim-eyed man sat in his room in the Samarinda Hotel, writing a letter. It read:

Dear friend Alice:

I'm back at the coast after a short trip into the interior, and everything turned out as I expected it would. Had no trouble following the map of your brother, Charlie, and found the gold deposit as he had marked it near the headwaters of the Merasi in the lower Mueller range. I've filed a claim all in order in your name, after staking the grounds, which Charlie neglected to do.

I'm sorry to report the death of Charles a fact. He was killed by two white renegades as we both feared. But I can assure you of one thing. The two men have paid for their crime. They have been tried and brought to justice in what, let us say, was the equivalent of a court of law. . . .

—POTTAGER.

HAMADRYAD CHAIR

By CARL JACOBI

The right arm rest had come alive!

Challenging, forbidding, waited the dread guest chair of Kayan Plantation— the chair whose touch meant death!

THE chair was really an inconspicuous thing, and Bradley and I didn't notice it until the night of our second day's lay-over at Long Senla. We had come up the Mahakam in easy stages, intending to reach the Apo Kayan district before the rains. Long Senla was just another forlorn rubber plantation hacked out of the jungle.

On the veranda that night, Van Haefner served us a round of gin *pahits* and spoke in his quiet voice about the monotony of life this far from the coast. Presently the moon moved around the bungalow eave, casting an ellipse of blue light across the compound.

Bradley put down his glass and stared. "I say," he said slowly, "is that a chair out there?"

I saw the thing myself then, and a shudder ran through me. The compound stretched before us in a rough half-moon, ending in the stockade that enclosed the bungalow and the three long huts comprising the native quarters. Midway between the veranda steps and the stockade gate squatted a solid piece of rough-hewn furniture.

It was a chair, large enough to seat two men. The thing was carved out of *nibong* wood, grey and weathered from the sun and rains . . . all save the two arm rests. And it was upon those arm rests that my gaze centered while my pulse quickened within me.

"Let me show it to you, *mynheeren*," Van Haefner said, rising and moving toward the screen door. "I think even big game hunters like yourselves will find it of interest."

He led the way down the steps and across the gravel, moving with an erect, graceful stride. Even then I found myself wondering how this cultured gentleman came to have cast his lot in this sink hole. With his trim Van Dyke and lean, incisive face, Van Haefner looked like a fashionable medico from Fifth Avenue. The incongruity of his presence here was overshadowed only by the breath-taking beauty of his wife.

When we reached the chair, Bradley drew in his breath in a slow whistle. "Horrible looking thing," he said. "Who made it?"

The chair was clearly revealed in the bright moonlight. In spite of the solidity of its construction, there was a quality of latent animation about it, as if it were alive and watching us with malignant eyes.

The left arm rest was made of bone and fashioned from the skeleton of a man's arm. The right one . . . .

A piece of ice stabbed up my spine. The right rest was carved of wood in the likeness of a snake. But so perfectly was it carved that a squirming, writhing serpent seemed poised there, ready to strike.

"Dyak work," Van Haefner said, tapping the chair with his pipe. "This

chair was made in a Kayan *kampong* a mile upstream. You couldn't make a Kayan Dyak sit in it for all the gold in the Indies."

"Why not?" Bradley demanded.

"It was built for a Dyak *kapala* who was a cripple," Van Haefner explained. "He couldn't walk, and he lived in it all his life. Then he killed the hamadryad. The rest is Kayan superstition, pure and simple.

"According to the native legend, this *kapala* killed a hamadryad without reason. Threw his *parang* at it while he sat in the chair. The deep inland Kayan, you know, looks upon the king cobra—the *naga bungarus*—as an object of veneration. He is permitted to kill it if it attacks him, but to do so otherwise supposedly brings down upon his head all the wrath of his multiple gods."

Bradley grinned and lit a cigarette. "I get it," he said. "The mumbo-jumbo spirits changed the chief's arm into a snake, and from then on he went around scaring all the native kiddies."

Van Haefner frowned.

"Not exactly, *mynheer*," he replied. "The *kapala's* right arm was changed miraculously into a live hamadryad, as you say. But according to the story, he died in utter agony, and when he did, his serpent arm turned as to hardened wood. The natives thereupon hacked off both arms and placed the chair out of sight in one of their devil-devil houses. I was fortunate enough to obtain it without difficulty."

"Fortunate?" I looked at the Dutch planter curiously.

An odd glitter had entered his eyes.

"It makes an excellent whip, *mynheer*. I have but to threaten forcing one of my rebellious Dyak laborers to sit in it, and he becomes the most docile person in the world.

"You see, a strange belief has grown up around that chair. The Kayans believe anyone who sits in it will have his arm changed to a hamadryad, and his soul will thereafter become the soul of a snake."

BACK on the veranda, talk drifted into other channels. Freda, Van Haefner's lovely wife, appeared for the first time since tiffin, and Bradley, the idiotic fool, immediately made a play for her.

Freda was a gorgeous creature, as unlike most planters' wives as you could imagine. The heat of the tropics seemed to have left no mark upon her rich olive features. Dark-haired, dark-eyed, she wore an outmoded, tight-fitting dress of white that only enhanced her beauty.

We discussed the reports we had heard on the coast of trouble among the up-river tribes. They had heard the stories of the impending mutiny, but placed no stock in them. The Dyaks of the interior were always being reported on the war path.

All the while Bradley was brazenly making eyes at the woman. But Van Haefner sat smoking his pipe, paying no heed.

"And what do you think of the chair?" I said presently, striving to break an embarrassing silence.

My words were electric. Freda Van Haefner stiffened like a slack wire drawn taut. Her face became the color of wood ash. Sahar, the Kayan houseboy, who at that moment was leaving the veranda with a tray, swung on his heel and flashed me a glance that was heavy with unmistakable fear.

"The chair, *mynheer?*" Freda repeated hoarsely: "I . . . I hate the chair. I hate it with all my life and soul!"

The houseboy still stood in his tracks like a graven image. A cruel-looking little devil, I thought, with his undersized, misshapen body and deep-set eyes.

For a full moment he remained there. Then, with a clucking sound of his lips, he paced across the threshold into the inner room.

I glanced back at Freda Van Haefner. Her eyes were strangely dilated, and she was staring out through the mosquito screening at that silent bulk in the center of the compound.

AT MIDNIGHT, Bradley and I went to our assigned room, across the corridor from the planter's and his wife's quarters.

Sahar slept in a room in the back, near the kitchen.

For a while I lay there, restless and uneasy, stifled by a sickeningly sweet odor that drifted in the open window. The smell had been noticeable since we landed at this plantation, but it seemed a hundred times stronger now.

I slept finally, to awaken, as was my custom, an hour later. In all my years of jungle travel, this mid-sleep awakening was a habit I had never been able to overcome. The only remedy for it was a stir in the night air and a pipe.

I slid a bush jacket over my pajamas and made my way to the veranda. Insects droned like some distant generator. The moon was low in the east, tesselating the compound with long, tenuous shadows.

For some time I sat there, musing over the weird story I had heard earlier in the evening. Before me, like some giant squatting in the gloom, I could see the chair.

Then abruptly footsteps sounded in the inner corridor. A moment later Sahar, the houseboy, stole silently across the veranda, unlatched the screen door and entered the compound.

He had passed without seeing me. Struck by the stealth of his actions, I moved to the veranda railing and watched him pace slowly toward the stockade gate. But he wasn't heading for the gate. He turned, and on an angle approached Van Haefner's hamadryad chair. Five feet away, he suddenly raised his arms in supplication and began to mutter a low, droning chant.

A chill passed through me. There was something unearthly about sitting there in the darkness, watching this jungle native make obeisance to his heathen gods.

The chant continued only a moment. Sahar picked up a small stick and began to draw a circle in the dirt about the chair.

He turned then and made his way to the stockade gate. Without attempting to unlatch it, he clambered up the piles and dropped to the ground on the far side.

Odd, I thought. Did Van Haefner know of this night promenade of his houseboy? And what was all that business before the chair?

I won't say it struck me all at once. Rather, it grew upon me gradually—an unconscious, subtle desire to leave the veranda and look upon the chair again at close range. It was as if some powerful lure were urging me forward.

At length I got up and gave in to inclination. My feet were dead things as I crossed the expanse of gravel. The drone of insects had ceased now, and silence engulfed me.

The moment I came abreast of the chair, the moon above slid behind dark clouds. For an instant only there was blackness. Then the light returned, and a cry of horror spewed from my lips.

The right arm rest of the chair was alive! A writhing, twisting serpent was there—a deadly hamadryad!

I could see the needle fangs dart in and out, the beady eyes glitter. The underside of the body was a leprous white, the upper side a greyish brown.

Transfixed, I watched it glide across the chair seat, move down one of the *nibong* legs and head slowly toward me. Nameless horror swept through my brain.

Now it was but five feet away. I could see the shimmer of the blue light on its dry, hard body. It reared, preparatory to striking, and the sinister hood slowly inflated.

And then a series of events happened in quick succession. Above me the moon slid behind clouds again. Inky blackness dropped over the compound. Simultaneously, from the interior of the bungalow there sounded the sharp crack of a revolver shot.

Not until the light returned could I wrench myself away from that spot. The incredible fact that the hamadryad was no longer there, that I was staring now at a motionless, carved chair, failed to register on my brain. I swung and raced for the bungalow.

In the corridor, Van Haefner, pajama-clad, was already moving forward, gripping a flashlight.

Back of him, his wife, Freda, stood in a revealing night dress.

The planter and I reached my room together. Ripping it open, we saw Bradley half crouched by the table. He had lighted the kerosene lamp, and in the yellow glow his face was a mask of terror. His trembling hand gripped a revolver.

"It was a snake or something," Bradley gasped. "It was . . . crawling up my arm. I shot at it in the dark, but I can't see it now."

The three of us made a thorough search of the room. The mosquito screens were tight; there were no holes or crevices in the baseboards. And the ceiling was made of close-fitting insulation board.

We found nothing.

"You must have been dreaming, *mynheer,*" Van Haefner said at length. "No snake could possibly have entered here. You will forget it in the morning."

It was a long time before I fell asleep. Questions unanswerable pounded through my brain; questions which so far I had elected to keep to myself. Sahar's night movements . . . the optical illusion by the chair in the compound—for optical illusion it must have been . . . the queer, drawn look on the face of Freda Van Haefner . . . that damnable sweetish odor that permeated everything . . . and lastly, the thing which I had not dared to mention to Bradley and which he hadn't seen . . . *the curious blemish-like mark, like a tiny snake, which had suddenly appeared on his right forearm.*

MORNING, and Van Haefner offered to show us his plantation.

"You may as well finish out the week here," he said. "The rains are a long way off, and there's no other civilization point beyond."

The plantation was larger than I had expected. The trees were all imported Brazilians and stretched deep into the cleared jungle back from the river. But the grove, though tapped with care and mulched with *crolotaria* bush, gave the impression of running to seed. Here and there windfalls blocked our way, and mape vine had been permitted to run wild.

At the farthest end of the grove the trees gave way to a vast savannah. And here, rippling like a great sea in the sunlight, were millions of scarlet flowers—poppies. The sweetish smell was strong here, but it seemed different than the odor I had noticed about the bungalow.

"I've been intending to plant more trees here too," Van Haefner said. "But with the prices on rubber what they are, I've been forced to retrench."

At that moment an incident occurred which was to bring home to me the true nature of this hell spot into which we had blundered.

Van Haefner had just introduced me to Colburg, his plantation foreman, who had suddenly appeared through the trees. Colburg was a giant of a man, swarthy, with a week's growth of black beard and predatory eyes. He had two natives with him, Dyak rubber laborers, clad only in loin cloths.

As Colburg reached forward to shake hands, one of those Dyaks suddenly spat. He was chewing betel nut, and the crimson liquid splashed directly on the foreman's canvas mosquito boots.

The white man said nothing for an instant. He took out a handkerchief, leaned down and wiped off his boot. His face was impassive, but there was a glitter in his eyes as he spoke two short words: "The chair!"

The Dyak went berserk. Face contorted with fear, he groveled in the dust; mumbling over and over again his apologies in frightened Malay.

Colburg seized him by the arm and dragged him off in the direction of the bungalow. Long after he had disappeared among the trees I could still hear his pitiful moaning.

Van Haefner shrugged. "I told you the chair served as a whip," he said. "But I wish Colburg would be a little less severe with the natives. He insists on ruling them with an iron hand."

On the way back we passed the smokehouses and drying huts where the rubber latex was prepared for shipping to the coast. Natives were stirring and sieving the milky liquid and adding quantities of the necessary formic acid.

But two of the larger huts were deserted. I noticed that the windows were carefully boarded up and the door padlocked —also that sweetish smell was almost unbearable here.

When we re-entered the compound, the native was sitting strapped in the chair, full in the glare of the blinding sun. Bradley clenched his fists at the sight, but Van Haefner gave him a warning glance.

"I know how you feel, *mynheer*," he said. "But I must have no trouble with Colburg. He is a good man, even if he is cruel. Besides, the native will come to no harm. He will be frightened by a silly superstition, but that is all."

ALL during the noon meal I couldn't get the matter off my mind. Even in the bright daylight there was something weird about this plantation. A breath of evil seemed to lie over everything.

There was an old-fashioned horn phonograph in the bungalow, and Freda Van Haefner started it playing *Liebestraum*. But the record was cracked, and the wheezy music only added to the tension of my nerves.

Bradley sat next to me. The sleeves of his shirt were rolled high, and the mark I had seen on his arm wasn't there, although I thought I could make out the faint outlines of it.

Bradley seemed to have forgotten his experience of the night before. He kept his eyes on the planter's wife, and he addressed his remarks only to her.

Over cigars I turned to Colburg and asked deliberately, "How long are you going to keep that native in the chair?"

"Until his arm changes to a hamadryad," he replied, scowling.

"You mean until he's thoroughly frightened by the legend?"

"I mean what I say!" Colburg's voice rose to an ugly snarl. "You hunters are all alike. You skip inland from the coast for a few weeks, and you regard yourselves as authorities on the country. Live here in the interior year in and year out, and you'll change your mind.

"What you call legend happens to be fact. These Kayan Dyaks are primitive people, yes. But their religious beliefs are untouched by the taint of civilization. They live close to the earth, and their gods are all-powerful. In one hour that native's arm will begin the change."

He said it without emotion, and the horror that dropped upon all of us was mirrored in Freda Van Haefner's eyes.

Bradley lit a cigarette.

"That's sheer hogwash," he said.

For answer Colburg flew into a rage. "You think I lie, eh?" he snarled. "Come and I'll show you."

On stiff legs he led the way out into the compound. Before the chair he leaned forward and pointed at the native sitting there.

"Look!"

The Dyak was like a dead man. His eyes were open wide, his lips clenched shut. A heavy leather strap had been passed around his middle, preventing his escape.

At first, beyond the awful fear that was revealed in the native's eyes, I saw nothing unusual. And then . . . a wave of loathing swept over me. My imagination, of course, but for an instant I thought I detected a change in the Dyak's right arm. Wasn't it darker brown in color on the top side, graying underneath?

Colburg took a rubber-tree gouge from a sheath at his belt and jabbed it into the native's arm.

The blood spurted, but the Dyak didn't move a muscle.

But I had seen enough, I walked slowly back to the veranda, an inner sickness welling over me. What damnable witchcraft was this that could be embodied in a wooden chair? Was I going mad, or had that attack of fever which had struck me on the river returned without my being aware of it?

That night we again discussed the trouble among the natives farther in-country. Van Haefner said the Resident in Samarinda should see that such rumors were stopped as they had absolutely no basis of fact. He said there wasn't the slightest danger of any of the tribes starting a head-hunting mutiny.

While he talked, Freda and young Bradley smiled behind the planter's back, and once I saw them boldly lock hands.

At ten o'clock Colburg sauntered across the compound and released the native in the chair. For many moments the Dyak did not seem to realize he was free.

Then a shudder passed through him. He rose and began to move toward the quarters of the rubber laborers.

But half way, he crumpled to the ground. And then I felt the hair slowly rise on my scalp. For that Dyak was *crawling* the remaining distance, wriggling forward inch by inch like some great saurian.

Van Haefner shook his head and scowled. "Colburg should use that chair only as a threat," he said. "That Dyak actually believes he is turning into a hamadryad. It's strange, the power of mind over matter."

AGAIN, as on the night before, I woke an hour after dozing off. This time, without knowing why, I lay there in a cold perspiration. That sweetish odor seemed to be crawling down my lungs like a bulbous thing alive.

Abruptly I realized I was alone in the room. Moonlight, filtering through the window, revealed Bradley's cot unoccupied.

But even as I slid to my feet and moved across to the door, I heard his whispered voice in the corridor.

"Take only the barest necessities," Bradley was saying. "I'll meet you at the jetty in ten minutes. I'll have a dugout loaded and ready to go."

The words staggered me. Could it be that Bradley was planning to run off with Freda Van Haefner? I heard two pair of footsteps move off, and a moment later the veranda door close softly.

Savagely I twisted the door latch. It was locked! Bradley had taken no chances that I would awaken to thwart his plans.

But what then? Was I to sit here helpless and permit this travesty to continue? Headstrong, foolhardy though he was, Bradley was really not a bad sort. I knew this infatuation was but the result of long weeks of social starvation, of grueling river travel, of heat and jungle, of one pretty white face in the midst of the wilds. On the other hand, common decency demanded that I must not waken Van Haefner.

I worked twenty minutes on that latch before I got it open. Ripping down a Malay kris from its mounting on the wall, I ran silently to the veranda and across the compound. The stockade gate yawned open. Into the blackness of the river trail I stumbled, heading toward the jetty.

The bungalow was set sufficiently far back from the river to allow for floodwaters, and it took me ten minutes more to reach the shore.

Nothing! There was no sign of the planter's wife nor of young Bradley. A dugout was drawn up against the jetty, moored to the bollards. In it I made out piles of duffle and luggage.

And then, as I turned to retrace my steps, two high-pitched screams tocsined into the heavy night air. The screams of a man and a woman—filled with stark terror!

I headed up the trail again at a run. Again and again as I fought my way up over the uneven ground, those screams reached my ears. The black tree boles on either side seemed to leer at me, waving their lower branches like plumes. The trail was an endless treadmill upon which I moved without advancing.

But abruptly the stockade loomed before me, the gate still open. I plunged into the compound and drew up short.

The hamadryad chair was occupied! Young Bradley sat in it, rigid as a sphinx. Moonlight revealed the heavy leather strap, buckled behind his back, which held him prisoner, revealed too the deathly pallor of his face.

Before him, spread-eagled to the stockade wall, stood the planter's wife, Freda Van Haefner. She was dressed in hunting breeches and boots, but her long black hair hung in wild disarray. Her eyes were wide with terror.

Yet, beyond the fact that the girl's arms were pinioned to stout pegs in the piling,

I saw nothing to account for their cries. The compound between the chair and the bungalow was deserted.

It was the staring eyes of the captive man and woman that drew my gaze toward the gloom of the native huts. A dislodged pebble rattled there. Naked footsteps padded toward me, and as I stood staring, I made out a dark figure slowly advancing parallel with the stockade wall.

Not until the figure was twenty feet away could I discern any details. Then, like an uncapped bottle spewing forth, a scream rose to my lips.

It was the Dyak rubber laborer whom Colburg had forced to sit in the chair. His eyes were open wide, staring, and he paced forward mechanically, a step at a time, like a figure on a wire. His arms were thrust out horizontally before him, and . . . .Merciful God! . . . that right arm was an arm to the elbow only!

The rest was a twisting length of horror. A full-grown hamadryad had merged at the elbow. Where the hands and fingers should have been, the head of the king cobra now weaved to and fro, the hood fully inflated, the fangs darting in and out.

A step at a time the thing advanced, and Bradley watched it like a man mesmerized. The snake-arm, sighting its victim, prepared to strike.

Now the fangs were almost within reach of the helpless man in the chair.

I must have gone momentarily mad then. With the Malay kris gripped in my right hand I threw myself forward. Even in that moment of horror I had sense enough to time my lunge. As I collided with the Dyak and he reeled backward, I brought the kris hacking down, intending to decapitate the serpent.

The blow missed. The hamadryad jerked like a whip and stabbed its fangs directly at my eyes. Horror welled over me. Then, under my weight, the Dyak stumbled and went down.

I slashed the kris downward with every ounce of strength I possessed. The blade ground dully as it severed skin and sinew. The head hung by a ribbon, and the hamadryad gave a last convulsive twist.

Weakly I staggered erect and moved toward Freda Van Haefner. But as I reached the stockade wall, some inner warning prompted me to swing and look back toward the bungalow.

A lone figure stood halfway out from the veranda steps, holding an upraised revolver. Before I could leap to the side, the gun spoke, and accompanying the report something hot and burning stabbed into my thigh.

I had practiced for years in the handling of the East Indian kris. As the figure deliberately took aim again, I lifted the kris, handle foremost, and threw!

The knife shot across the compound and struck as the second shot sounded. I heard the slug whine past my head, thud into the piles of the stockade. Then before me Van Haefner slowly slid to his knees.

B RADLEY and I placed most of it together ourselves. Colburg talked a little, as did Sahar, and Freda Van Haefner knew the whole story. But in her shocked condition we didn't feel we should subject her to any more strain than was necessary.

Van Haefner was behind it all, of course. From the odds and ends Bradley and I picked up, we fitted together a picture of his true character, and it wasn't pleasant. The man was a fiend!

He had spoken truthfully when he said the chair served as a whip. He had utilized the superstition behind that chair to make himself an absolute power there in the jungle. And to make the legends seem real, he had gone to considerable mechanical pains.

Most interior outposts and plantations, of course, have an underground passage, leading beneath the compound to a point outside the stockade, near the river. It's almost an essential emergency measure against native attack, but somehow I'd never thought about that.

He had placed the chair directly over the passage. In the underground chamber beneath, he fed and kept several hamadryads. Almost blind from never seeing the light, they were comparatively easy to handle.

He had hollowed out one of the *nibong* legs of the chair and arranged it so that a hamadryad had just enough room to slide up from the underground passage. That snake was always secured with a wire with sufficient slack to permit it to move a few feet but no farther.

When he perceived that Bradley was falling in love with his wife, he became almost mad with jealousy. He tried a warning first, entered Bradley's room while he slept, left that mark upon his arm and the impression that a snake was somewhere in the room.

But he soon realized that the matter had gone farther than that.

Conceive, if you can, the diabolic cruelty of a man who will lash a venom-spitting snake to the arm of a helpless native— order him to go forth and murder.

"But why did the native respond?" Bradley asked me. "Why didn't he—?"

"Attempt to escape? That's a little more difficult to explain. The only answer I can give is that Van Haefner must have had hypnotic — psychological — powers over his natives. It was not difficult, therefore, to implant in the Dyak's already fear-crazed mind, the obsession that he was a hamadryad, and that the man in the chair was to be his victim. So strong was that hypnotic suggestion, that even being bitten by the snake himself would not deter that native from his purpose.

"As for Colburg—he obeyed Van Haefner's orders and didn't ask too many questions. You see, Van Haefner was growing and selling rubber all right, but he was doing more than that. Remember those poppies we saw beyond the grove, the boarded-up huts, and that queer sweetish smell?

"Van Haefner was manufacturing crude opium and smuggling it to the up-river tribes. In return he was growing rich on native gold. The fact that this smuggled opium was slowly causing unrest and was preparing the way for a concerted head-hunting mutiny didn't concern him a bit."

That's about all, I guess, except for two things. The sole reason for Sahar's leaving the house that night was to visit his lady friend in a neighboring *kampong*.

As for Van Haefner—until he woke up on the river, one arm bandaged in a sling, the other manacled to the dugout thwart, he never guessed I was anything more than a big game hunter. Even Bradley didn't know I held a *carte blanche* commission from the government to track down the source of that native trouble.

A Film in the Bush

is worth a man's life in a jungle—
in this particular case

By CARL JACOBI

KENNEDY climbed out of the dugout onto the rickety wharf and stood gazing at the *nipa*-thatch shack twenty yards beyond in the jungle foliage. It was a government rest hut beyond a doubt. The mildewed flag of the queen hung above it, and *lallang* grass grew undisturbed to the water's edge.

But what Kennedy didn't like was the curl of smoke issuing through the hole in the roof.

Lips tight, he loosened the revolver in his belt holster, strode forward cautiously. He was halfway to the shack when the door opened, and a man stepped out.

"Howdy!"

Clad in dirty whites, with a sweat-stained sun helmet pushed far back on his head, the man was thick-set and swarthy. A long scar disfigured one side of his face.

Kennedy nodded a reply to the greeting.

"Bill Kennedy," he said shortly. "Come down from Long Nawang and

Apo Kayan country. Room for me to put up for a spell?"

The man opened the door wider and extended a beefy hand. His pinched eyes glittered, and his lips turned in a loose smile.

"Glad to meet you. Plenty of room. Shove in."

For a moment Kennedy hesitated, while a small voice far back in his brain sent out a call of warning. But the interior of the shack loomed cool and inviting, and the long hours he had spent on the steaming river had dulled his usual quick perception of danger. With a sigh, he pushed his cramped legs over the threshold.

Inside, he stopped short, surveying his surroundings. A second man sat sprawled in a wicker chair in the middle of the room. There was a whisky bottle on the table at his side, and his face was flushed from drink. For a brief space none of the three spoke.

Then Kennedy shifted uneasily and cleared his throat. "I'm heading down-river," he said. "Expect to reach Bulungan day after to-morrow, if the rains don't set in. But I don't want to crowd you and——"

The last of his words died before they were spoken. A sudden, unmistakable click sounded behind him. Pivoting slowly, Kennedy found himself staring into the bore of a revolver.

"Sit down," the first man said. "And no tricks, or I'll plug you sure!"

With a quick movement, the man plucked the gun from Kennedy's holster and flung it into a corner of the hut.

Quietly Kennedy stood there, fists clenched. He was a fool! After two weeks of caution, of doubling in his tracks, of grueling night travel, always with the knowledge that he was being followed, he had walked blindly into a trap.

But were these two men his pursuers? Had they managed to pass him during the long trek downstream, confident

that he must go this way to reach his destination? Did they know—as Kennedy feared they did—the value of his tin-boxed cargo back in the dugout?

The first man's finger tightened perceptibly on the trigger of his gun. With a shrug, Kennedy walked across to a chair and slumped into it.

"What do you want?" he said.

THE second man in the wicker chair came to life now. He strode to the door, slammed it shut and drew the bar. Then he leaned against a wall and grinned sardonically.

"I'll tell you what we want, and I'll tell you who we are," he said. "The names are Durhan and Lodge, in case you're interested. I'm Durhan, the same Flash Durhan mentioned on the reward posters in Samarinda. Right now, you're going to hand across that travel film you took up in Apo Kayan."

A gleam shot into Kennedy's gray eyes. He eased his lean, muscular body back into the chair and shook his head.

"I don't know what you're talking about," he said.

He knew very well what they were talking about. Employed by the Pacific Cinema Corporation, Kennedy had come inland to photograph a travel moving picture of the Dutch East Borneo interior.

By easy stages, he had pushed into Apo Kayan, forbidden head-hunting territory. Then, two weeks ago, Kennedy had stumbled upon something that had changed his plans abruptly.

He had heard, of course, of the Dutch explorer, Jan Van Treller, who had preceded him along this same route a year before. Up there in Apo Kayan, Van Treller had located an almost pure platinum deposit of untold value.

The explorer had reported his discovery to government officials in Bandjermasin by carrier pigeon, withholding only the exact location. He had then headed back for the coast to organize a mining expedition.

The rest had become a legend. Suddenly the carrier pigeons stopped coming. Van Treller disappeared completely and without trace. And with him his discovery had died a secret.

A secret until Kennedy, by the merest stroke of chance, had left the Kayan River and spent a day photographing one of its lesser tributaries.

Durhan took a step forward now, lips twisted in a sneer of triumph.

"Two weeks ago," he said, "you spent the night at the Dyak *kampong* near where Van Treller found his platinum. Because you saved the village *kapala's* life from snake bite, he told you something no other member of the tribe knew about. That is the exact spot where Van Treller had done his digging. You found the place and staked a claim. Then you photographed a full reel of film, showing various landmarks, so that the site could be found again. Right, isn't it?"

"Where did you get that information?" Kennedy's jaw set hard.

Durhan guffawed. "Where? Do you think we're traveling up this stinking river for our health? Ever since Van Treller disappeared, we've been looking for that platinum. When you dismissed your natives and decided to continue to the coast alone, you made a big mistake. We found your chief guide and made him talk. He couldn't tell us everything, but he told us enough to let us know we were on the right track. Now —where is that film?"

Kennedy helped himself to a cigarette from the package on the table and lighted it deliberately. Outwardly he appeared calm, but inwardly his brain was racing.

To give up that film meant to lose everything! Kennedy's resources had dwindled to the last few guilders. For months now Pacific Cinema had held back his pay. With rumors of the firm's bankruptcy and with a girl back in the States, Kennedy had looked upon his discovery as a very necessary ace-in-the-hole.

He killed the cigarette on the table-top. "I guess you've got me," he said, slowly. "O. K., we'll make it a fifty-fifty proposition. I'll——"

Durhan gave a snarl of rage and jammed the revolver hard into the photographer's middle.

"Fifty-fifty, nothing! You'll show us where that platinum is, or I'll blast a hole through you!"

Slowly, Kennedy's shoulders seemed to sag in defeat. "The film is in the dugout," he said. "In the box marked X-3. You'll find it next to my duffel bag."

Durhan nodded with satisfaction and glanced at Lodge. "Go get it," he said shortly.

THE door opened and closed. Tense, Kennedy waited until he could hear Lodge's footsteps echo hollowly on the wharf. Then he acted.

The photographer's right hand was resting on the table, close to the whisky bottle. Casually now, he grasped the bottle and filled the glass next to it. Durhan, watching, kept the revolver at a steady aim.

The next instant, Kennedy's arm was shooting forward, flinging the contents of that glass straight toward Durhan's eyes. Simultaneously, the photographer hurled himself out of the chair in a flying tackle.

A single shot thundered into the confines of the shack. A slug whined past Kennedy's head. Then the two men struck like blocks of wood.

For an instant Durhan, blinded by the whisky, flailed both hands upward to his eyes. Kennedy seized the man's gun wrist, wrenched the weapon from it. After that it was give-and-take, with Durhan roaring profanity.

The two crashed against a wall, upset a skillet and a pile of tin dishware. They went down on the nibong floor, pounding each other mercilessly. Twice, Durhan brought a bent knee grinding into Kennedy's abdomen, sent a wave of nausea sweeping through the picture man's vitals. Then the photographer saw his chance.

He fell backward as one of the renegade's fists slammed hard into his jaw. Then, as Durham reared forward, hands outstretched for his throat, Kennedy brought his right arm around in a sweeping hay-maker.

There was a dull thud and a gasp of pain. Durhan went out cold.

In a flash, the photographer was on his feet, lunging for the open door, scooping up the unconscious man's revolver. Lodge had heard the shot, he knew. The only possible way out was to continue the attack.

Outside, the path and the wharf were deserted. Kennedy, gun leveled, began to advance cautiously toward the water's edge. Ten feet forward, he jerked to a halt. He saw nothing.

And then, like a fleeting shadow, a figure leaped up ahead of him in the *lallang* grass. A long arm snapped backward, and a heavy rock catapulted through the air, straight for the photographer's head.

A bomb seemed to explode in Kennedy's skull. He clawed his gun hand upward, tried desperately to press the trigger. But blackness and a swirl of colored lights closed in on him, and he felt himself falling.

WHEN he opened his eyes, Kennedy was lying on the floor in a corner of the shack. Durhan, a heavy welt on one cheek, sat in the wicker chair, glaring at him savagely. Across at the table Lodge had stacked up five tin boxes of film and was prying with a hunting knife at the lock of the one marked X-3.

The knife blade snapped as he exerted pressure, and, with a snarl of rage, he flung it down and wiped the sweat from his face.

"Where's the key?" he demanded of Kennedy, striding forward. "Talk fast, or I'll——"

Weakly, Kennedy lifted himself upward, drew a key ring from his pocket and handed it up.

"I told you the film was in the X-3 box," he said quietly, "but I'm afraid that information isn't going to do you any good. Go ahead, open it if you want to."

Silence filled the room for an instant. Then Durhan swung around, blood-shot eyes gleaming.

"Isn't going to do any good," he repeated. "What the devil do you mean?"

Kennedy was sitting upright now, staring at the lashings on his ankles. His wrists too were bound, and the rope was heavy Malaysian hemp. A third rope, knotted tightly around his waist, held him prisoner to one of the stout bamboo wall posts.

"Well, you see"—Kennedy lingered on each word, stalling for time—"those five boxes contain approximately twenty thousand feet of film. I came up here to make a travel picture, you know, and I photographed quite a bit of jungle scenery between here and the west coast. There are shots of various Kayan and Punan *kampongs*, some fine scenes of a fight between a leopard and a python and——"

"Never mind that, you fool!" Durhan roared. "Why——"

"Each of those five boxes contain roughly four thousand feet of celluloid," Kennedy continued quietly. "I imagine you're going to have quite a job finding out which strip of film is a photograph of the landmarks surrounding the platinum—especially since none of the films are developed."

For two long minutes Durhan sat there, digesting this information. Then, slowly, a cruel smile rose to his lips.

He got up, walked across to the opposite side of the room. Like all government rest huts this shack was not equipped with a stove.

It had, instead, a wide piece of corrugated iron, flanged on the sides, and laid on the floor beneath a smoke hole in the roof. A small fire was glowing on this makeshift fireplace now.

Durhan bent down, jammed two heavy sticks under the sheet iron and, balancing it carefully, carried it back across the room to a point a few feet away from Kennedy. With his sun helmet, he fanned the fire into life. Then, with deliberate efficiency, he began to unlace Kennedy's boots.

Lodge, who had been watching with puzzled eyes, grinned as he understood. "Put his feet in the fire, eh?" he said. "Sure, that'll make him talk!"

The photographer compressed his lips. An instant later his teeth ground together, and his face contorted with excruciating pain. Durhan had thrust the tender soles of his feet deep into the glowing coals.

Once more, the renegade repeated the process. Then he leaned back calmly.

"Does that change your mind, or do you want more?"

COLD sweat streaming from his brow, Kennedy shook his head. "You win," he said. But even as he spoke, a plan took form in his brain.

Durhan swept the fire aside and moved back to the table. He scooped up the film box marked X-3, shoved the key in the lock and opened it.

"Now fix that film so we can see it!"

Kennedy swallowed hard. "I'll have to have my developing kit," he said. "It just happens I carried a small one along to make light tests on my work. The kit's in the dugout, packed with the camera."

Durhan hesitated, half suspicion in his eyes. Then he shrugged. He went out to the dugout and returned a few minutes later with a large, canvas-wrapped object.

"O. K.!" he snarled, untying the photographer's wrists and ankles. "Do your stuff. But remember, no tricks."

Slowly, Kennedy struggled to a standing position. He bent down, removed the canvas and lifted out his camera and a small leather-covered case. The camera he placed carefully out of the way in a corner. Unseen by Durhan, he managed to remove the lens and slip it into one pocket.

Kennedy opened the case, revealing a series of small bottles and a shallow tray. From an earthen jug on the table he filled the tray with water, then began adding the contents of the various bottles.

"Metol-hydroquinone solution," he said quietly, as he stepped across the room and draped the canvas over the single window. "I've got to have darkness, and I can make only a rough development of the negative, of course. I'm out of sodium sulphate crystals, which are necessary in the tropics; but after the film has had a hypo bath, you should be able to make it out."

For ten minutes there was no sound in the shack, save the two renegades' hoarse breathing. Face a mask, Kennedy did his work silently. Foot after foot of film, he carefully immersed in the solution.

And then abruptly a while later he stopped and nodded.

"The landmarks are shown here. If you look closely, you can see the river shore, the Dyak kampong and the inland trail to the platinum deposit."

Animal greed leaped into Durhan's eyes. "Rip it off!" he snarled. "And tear off the rest of it, so I won't make any mistake!"

Without a word, Kennedy complied. Durhan snatched the film, tore the canvas off the window, and stared at the film in the sunlight.

"I know the place!" he cried. He seized his sun helmet, crammed it on his head. "Lodge, your job is to stay here and watch this fool—until I get back. If it's the right place, I'll come back and pick you up. If not——"

He glared at the photographer significantly and went out.

But Kennedy was smiling quietly to himself. The ruse had worked! Temporarily, at least, he had lessened the odds.

AN hour passed before Kennedy found opportunity to put the rest of his plan into operation. Lodge picked up a hunting rifle then, gave the photographer's lashings a quick survey, and strode to the door.

"Going after a little fresh meat," he said. "You stay put."

And ten minutes later, Kennedy was free. It was simple. The camera lens he had slipped into his pocket was a special magnifying glass, used for long-distance pictures. Placed in the shaft of sunlight streaming through the open window, it had burned through the ropes with ease.

The photographer was massaging his wrists back into circulation when it happened. A stealthy footstep sounded outside the shack. Came the wheeze of restrained breathing——

A rifle shot roared close at hand! A bullet slammed into Kennedy's left shoulder, sent him reeling against a wall.

Cursing his lack of foresight, the photographer twisted madly forward, lunged for the door, slammed it shut, and yanked the bar over. Of course, Lodge would be clever enough to look in the window before reëntering the shack.

Even as Kennedy threw himself face to the floor a second shot screamed over his head. Crouched there, close beneath the window, Kennedy heard Lodge's voice rasp through the stillness.

"Open that door, damn you, or I'll blast this shack to hell!"

The photographer's shoulder was pulsing feverishly, but he knew it was only a flesh wound. An inch at a time, he began to worm his way parallel with the window toward the back wall.

Kennedy reached it, began to dig frantically at the *nipa* thatch. Deep into the vine lattice work he dug his hands, rapidly widening a hole. Dry thatch jammed under his finger nails, gashed his arms and wrists cruelly.

But at length the opening was large enough for him to pass through.

Kennedy wriggled out, after securing his gun, and continued crawling through the tall *lallang* grass. Then, guessing Lodge's direction, he moved in a wide circle, heading back for the front of the shack.

An instant later the photographer leaped to his feet, spoke quietly.

"Drop that gun, Lodge. I've got you covered."

The renegade whirled. He pivoted his rifle, jerked the trigger once. But the roar of his shot was accompanied by the sharp staccato of Kennedy's pistol. Lodge flailed his arms wide, gave a hollow cry and crashed backward.

NINE days' furious paddling had carried "Flash" Durhan far up the Kayan River. He had passed the imaginary boundary into that forbidden district which the Dutch refer to on their maps as Apo Kayan, and he knew he was nearing his destination.

At intervals he let the dugout drift, seized the spool of moving-picture film and held it up to the light. Durhan confined his attention now to those scenes which showed the landmarks on the river shore: a giant tree bent snakelike over the water, a Dyak *kampong* with a notched-log ladder leading up toward higher ground. When he sighted them, the renegade knew he must leave the dugout and cut through the bush.

Durhan's face was flushed with approaching fever, and there was a dull pain in the region of his heart from the many capsules of quinine he had taken. Sweat streaming from under his sun helmet, he worked at the paddle. The sun above him was a molten ball of fire. The river was a glittering mirror, over which oven heat pressed thick and moist. Crocodiles drifted by.

It was noon of the ninth day when Durhan sighted the tree. Since dawn, he had been pushing up a narrow tributary of the Kayan, a muddy, roily stream whose narrow shores formed a tunnel of vegetation above him.

Now, with a low cry, he twisted the blade of the paddle, sent the dugout gliding in toward the left bank. He found a notched-log ladder leading to the native village, carefully avoiding it, and headed into the jungle, moving due east.

"Smooth as silk," Durhan muttered to himself, as he stumbled through the dense underbrush. "I find old Van Treller's platinum, I stake a claim, and then I race it back to Bulungan to have the claim recorded. Lodge can wait with that fool. Kennedy at the shack forever, if he wants to. If he wants to talk, let 'im. It's their word against mine."

The renegade chuckled at his cleverness, drew forth his hunting knife and began to hack at the thick vines which barred his passage.

At mid-afternoon, Durhan sighted his third landmark, a wide swale, dividing the jungle from north to south. The platinum deposit lay on the other side. Once again, Durhan studied the roll of film carefully. Then he pulled down the sleeves of his shirt and headed into the man-high rip-grass.

Before he had gone a hundred yards, the renegade's clothing was in shreds, and his arms and legs were covered with blood. The rip-grass possessed razor stalks which slashed back at him like a field of knives.

NIGHT was closing in on Durhan when he reached high ground again. But here the renegade took one look and gave a hoarse cry of satisfaction. He had reached his goal! At his feet was the beginning of a rocky terminal moraine. Ahead, a huge tree towered upward. Nailed to its trunk was a crude sign:

William P. Kennedy

June 1st, 1937

Durhan grinned, slid a cigarette between dry lips and exhaled triumphantly. Two men had been here before him. First Van Treller, then Kennedy, and now himself. Two men had discovered this treasure, only to lose it.

But he—Durhan—wouldn't lose! He would stop here only long enough to stake a claim, tear down Kennedy's markings and dig enough of the metal to be assayed. Then he would hurry on to the coast and——

He stiffened, jerked his hand suddenly to his holster. A sound had reached his ears from out there. Durhan swung around, listening.

And then, illuminating the jungle about him in a great white circle, came a blinding flash of light. For one brief instant, the surrounding wall of trees stood forth in vivid relief. Then blackness clamped down again, and Durhan, blinded, could see nothing.

A familiar voice rose out of the void. "Don't move, Durhan! Don't move an inch!"

"Kennedy!" Even as Durhan mouthed the word, he acted. He hurled himself sidewise, clawed forth his revolver and pumped two shots into the gloom. Then madly, blindly, he closed in.

Chance sent the renegade's outthrust

fist connecting solidly with Kennedy's jaw. The photographer staggered back, blood trickling from his lips.

In an instant, Kennedy was charging forward, driving his arms clean and hard from the elbows. His right fist struck Durhan over the heart; his left —an uppercut—slammed into the renegade's right temple.

In the blackness they fought, stumbling over the rocky, uneven ground. Long hours of paddling a native dugout canoe had hardened Kennedy's arms to limbs of steel, yet the man before him was an enraged tiger, with the animal's strength in his blows.

Abruptly, Durhan whipped his hand to his belt and yanked forth a short-bladed Malay creese. Cunningly he feinted, then drove hard for the photographer's throat.

Kennedy sensed the attack as it came. He leaped, felt cold steel rip through his sleeve. He threw himself forward, seized the knife wrist and gave it a sharp twist.

The renegade's cry of pain was cut off by a smashing, battering-ram blow to his jaw. Kennedy put every ounce of strength he possessed into that blow. And Durhan, with a hoarse intake of breath, sagged slowly to the ground— unconscious.

THREE weeks later, a dugout bearing three haggard white men crept down the broad river and slipped to a mooring at the Bulungan jetty, Dutch military headquarters on the Kayan.

Two of these men sat helpless in the prow, securely bound. The third, his left shoulder swathed in bandages, carefully lifted a moving-picture camera and five boxes of film to the wharf, then climbed out weakly.

Kennedy stood looking down into the dugout a moment, a grim smile on dry lips.

"You see, Durhan," he said, "there are several ways of prospecting in this bush country. A revolver might be one of them, but I think you'll agree it doesn't compare with a camera. Without that little box on a tripod I'd probably be lying at the bottom of the river, crocodile food now."

Durhan glowered, said nothing; but Lodge, the second man, uttered a stream of profanity.

"You haven't got a thing on us!" he snarled. "You forget it's our word against yours!"

Kennedy jerked the dugout's painter around the bollards, shook his head.

"You're wrong," he said quietly. "I told you a camera was better than a revolver, and in more ways than one. It was camera flashlight powder that blinded you, Durhan, when you thought you had won. Simple powder I use occasionally for taking night still shots. It didn't harm you, but it gave me the temporary advantage I needed.

"But there's one other item both of you have overlooked: I took moving pictures of the platinum deposit, all right, so that it could be located again. I also took pictures of something else.

"When you first learned about that platinum deposit, you did it by capturing one of Van Treller's carrier pigeons. Then you made Van Treller prisoner, and tried to force him to give you the information you wanted. When he refused, you shot him. When——"

Durhan's face had suddenly gone white. He reared upward, lips twisting back over yellow teeth. "You're lying!" he screamed. "It's not true!"

"It is true. You left Van Treller there in the jungle, supposedly for dead. He did die a few hours later, but he lived long enough to draw his knife and carve all the details of the crime on the smooth trunk of a tree.

"I photographed that tree, Durhan. I rather think the pictures of it will convict you in any court."

REDEMPTION TRAIL

By
CARL JACOBI

Author of
"Trial by Jungle," "Black Passage," etc.

Through the Grim Dangers of the Borneo Jungle, Officer Rutland Follows a Murderer He Does Not Want to Capture!

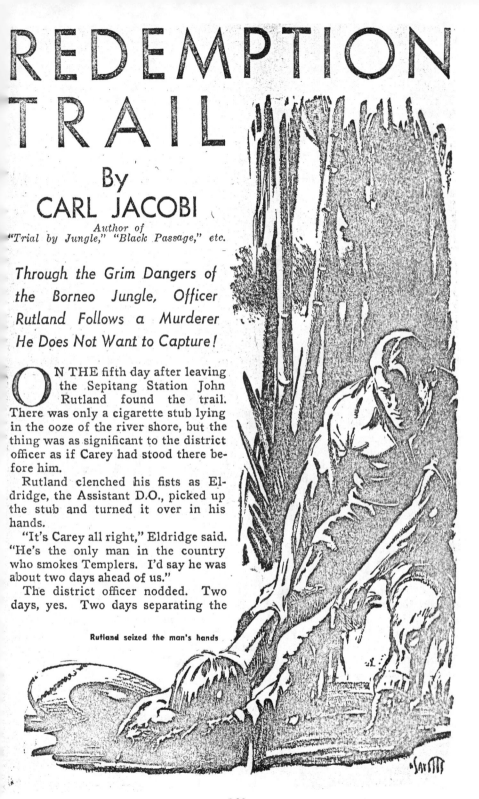

Rutland seized the man's hands

O N THE fifth day after leaving the Sepitang Station John Rutland found the trail. There was only a cigarette stub lying in the ooze of the river shore, but the thing was as significant to the district officer as if Carey had stood there before him.

Rutland clenched his fists as Eldridge, the Assistant D.O., picked up the stub and turned it over in his hands.

"It's Carey all right," Eldridge said. "He's the only man in the country who smokes Templers. I'd say he was about two days ahead of us."

The district officer nodded. Two days, yes. Two days separating the fleeing man from arrest and inevitable conviction. And what irony that he—Rutland—should be the arm of the law reaching out to pull him back!

He took out his pipe and filled it mechanically as a storm of ugly thoughts crowded down upon him.

Five days ago at the Station he had laughed and joked with Frank Carey, listened while the man spun yarns of his innumerable experiences. It had been a long time since they had been together like that.

From buddies in the same Philippine regiment, they had shipped here to Borneo, had shared "beach bungalows" during a temporary period of insolvency, had divided luck, good or bad. In the course of time they had drifted apart—Rutland to take over the district officership of the Sepitang area, Carey to become timber cruiser for the British North Borneo Company.

"None of your red-taped government posts for me," Carey had said. "I want a job without strings I can handle my own way."

He had handled it his own way. Today there wasn't a cruiser in British North Borneo with a comparable record of tracking down cuttable areas of hard wood or dickering with native *kapalas* for the necessary native labor.

BUT Carey had seemed different somehow as he sipped his gin-slings on the Station veranda. Eldridge had noticed it too and had showed no surprise when a week after the man left, the letter came.

The letter came upriver by Chinese pinnace. It was from the Resident in Sandakan, and Rutland now knew its damning words by heart:

Sir:

I have to inform you that one Frank Carey reported to be in your district, is wanted here in Bandakan for murder. On the sixth of this month at the Murut *kampong* of Paleyo, Carey engaged in a fight with a trader well known on the Kinnebatangan, Gale Hearne. Hearne was shot through the left lung and died here in Sandakan after telling his story. I also have additional evidence which I consider unimpeachable.

You are hereby ordered to trail Carey and return him to the coast for trial. Take all precautions; this man is dangerous; but spare no effort as native conditions, under influence of this crime, will be intolerable if justice is not dealt.

(Signed)   David D. Cleyne,
Resident.

That was the letter, and it had struck Rutland squarely between the eyes. For not only was Carey his friend, but—and this is what hurt—there was an unpaid debt between them.

It all went back to the time when Rutland was on his yearly inspection trip, and Carey, coming down from the foothills, had joined up with him for a day before continuing on to the coast.

Hacking their way through dense bush to a remote inland village, Rutland had thrust his hand into an innocent appearing mass of *trelip* vine. The eight-inch Krait had struck without warning. Carey had sucked the deadly venom from the wound and then carried the district officer forty miles to medical aid.

"And now," Rutland muttered aloud, "now I've got to come and get you."

As in a dream he stood there, watching Eldridge move up and down the shore, examining the ground, studying each reed and bush. At length the assistant turned, a questioning look on his face.

"We might as well get going," Rutland said.

They made their way back to where the dugout and the six Dyak boatmen were waiting. A moment later they were paddling down the wide river.

RUTLAND sat amidships, watching the thick green shores drift past. Under the brim of his sun helmet his steel-gray eyes were hard and lusterless, his lips tight. He heard Eldridge's voice vaguely, hardly heeding the other man's words.

"He'll probably turn up some

smaller tributary, follow that as far as he can and then take to the bush," Eldridge said. "We ought to be able to catch up with him before he reaches Saputan territory."

Unmasked zeal showed in the assistant's face. Tall, broad-shouldered, but with a certain weakness about the mouth, he was a young man, new to his job and full of the apprentice's ambition.

Rutland, of course, was due any time for an advancement to a more important post nearer the coast. Eldridge, providing his record was a good one, was slated to take over the Sepitang district-officership when the opening was thus made.

"I've studied the maps and survey reports," Eldridge went on. "Until the monsoon sets in, most of these streams are barely navigable. If the rains will hold off, we may even come up with him before he reaches the headwaters."

For three hours they continued up the roily waterway. The air was hot and moist, heavy with the smell of jungle growth. Macaws screeched on the banks and proboscis monkeys like so many old men peered out at them from the foliage. At sundown they were abreast of a nameless tributary that branched into the main stream when Eldridge suddenly leaped erect in the dugout.

"Look! By that rock," he said excitedly. "What do you see?"

Rutland had already seen, and a nerve twitched perceptibly by the side of his mouth. A large water-spider web was spun between two rocks midstream. But the silken strands were broken as if they had been struck by a paddle, and a section trailed into the river.

A low laugh of triumph came from Eldridge. Heavily Rutland spoke a command in Malay. The dugout turned and, propelled by the Dyaks, headed up the tributary.

They found their first positive evidence half a mile farther on where an aisle of broken water lilies led them to shore. Back on higher ground was the cold ashes of a fire, an empty tobacco tin.

But there was something else which stabbed out at the district officer like a cruel knife. Fastened to the bole of a *Seraya* tree was a scrap of notebook paper, covered with penciled writing. It read:

> Rutland:
> I know you're after me, and I know what you want. But it's no go. I never was meant to rot in jail. Go back, Rutland. This is where we part.
>
> Carey.

Eldridge tore the paper down with a scornful laugh.

"Damned murderer!" he growled.

FOR a moment Rutland sucked his cold pipe to conceal his emotion. "Those are strong words," he began slowly. "After all, we don't know yet if—"

"We've got the Resident's letter, haven't we?" Eldridge demanded. "We heard the Murut's story in their own words when we stopped off at that last village. Carey had been drinking *tuak*—native rum. He picked a quarrel with Hearne without reason and then shot him before the man could defend himself.

"He left Hearne there to die, escaped downriver and stopped off at the Station as if nothing had happened. Then, when he thought he had prepared an alibi, he doubled back and headed upriver again, probably slipping past that village at night. What more do you want?"

What more? Rutland wanted a lot more. In spite of this evidence, he still wasn't ready to accept the word of a Dyak inlander or of Gale Hearne against Carey. Hearne! His teeth grated at the thought of the man. If ever anyone deserved killing, it was Hearne!

He was a trader, yes, a trader in drugs, in smuggled rifles, in anything he could slip past the customs and carry incountry to the Dyaks. A brute of a man, he had been haled into court three times in as many years for man-handling his native carriers. Each time his smooth lies and ready tongue had won him his freedom.

A camp was made in the same spot where Carey had rested a few hours before. The evening meal over, El-dridge rolled up in a blanket and was asleep almost at once. Rutland lit his pipe and moved slowly down to the river bank. He stood there in the darkness for hours, alone with his black thoughts.

Dawn found them on the trail again. But trouble, Rutland knew, lay ahead. Carey was aware he was being followed, and Frank Carey wasn't the kind to give up without a fight. With a kind of grim pleasure the district officer awaited the obstructions he felt sure would block their path.

They came upon the first at high noon when, fighting their way around a bend in a suddenly increased cur-rent, they realized the roar in their ears had been no fancy. A sixty foot waterfall barred their way. To right and left the banks rose sheer, form-ing a narrow cut, within which spray and mist were thick as fog.

DRAWN up on the south bank, wedged between two rocks al-most at the foot of the falls, was a one-man dugout. On the opposite shore a nature-formed stairway of protruding rocks was clearly visible, leading up the escarpment. Eldridge seized a paddle and began swinging the canoe toward the stairway.

"Wait!" Rutland lifted a warning hand. "There are two trails! See— by that dugout? That series of ledges leading up parallel with the falls. Carey might have gone that way."

As he spoke, the district officer's brain was working hard. Admittedly, Carey would have a full appreciation for the tracking abilities of his pur-suers. Why then had he left his dug-out here instead of casting it adrift?

Even as the thought came, he had the answer. The fleeing timber-cruiser knew they would have fol-lowed him this far. He knew too, by first-hand experience, this entire area as far as forbidden Saputan territory. Now, with ironic disregard for his own safety, he had left the dugout to mark the only safe trail.

But Eldridge, hesitating only a mo-ment, continued to paddle toward the bank with the stairway.

"That dugout's just a blind," he said over his shoulder. "Carey left it there, hoping we'd try to follow him that way. Then he swam back across to this shore and took the easy trail."

They reached the cliff wall. With a dry feeling in his throat Rutland watched the Dyaks take up the canvas supply bags, change their roles to car-riers. Then they were mounting slowly upward.

Twenty minutes later it happened. The rock here was smooth and slip-pery with moss and moisture. Mist rose in thick clouds about them. Three quarters of the way up the rock stairs opened onto a narrow shelf that fol-lowed the face of the cliff directly over the falls.

Suddenly Eldridge gave a hoarse scream. Rutland saw the assistant's feet whip out from under him, his body catapult forward.

Eldridge thrust out his hands, claw-ing for support. Down, down he went toward the edge of the abyss. His feet dug frantically into shale, found no foothold. Like a plummet he gath-ered speed, carrying an avalanche of small stones and rubble with him.

Then as the lower half of his body shot into space, with a final outward thrust of his hands his fingers closed around a pinnacle of rock. Desper-ately he clung there, poised over eter-nity.

"Grab hands!" Rutland ordered the Dyaks. "Make a chain."

The seconds that followed seemed hours. With the natives clasping hands and supporting him, the district officer inched his way down the treacherous incline and seized Eldridge's belt. Sweat stood out on Rutland's forehead as he pulled the dead weight slowly upward. Once his moist fingers slipped, and a dull horror assailed him.

"Steady!" he panted. "Keep yourself limp."

He gave a last jerk that seemed to pull his arm out of its socket, and then they were back on level footing.

For a moment neither man spoke. The assistant's face was white, and he leaned weakly against the cliff wall, breathing hard.

Rutland forced a smile. "I'm going to have a look-see at what you missed."

He left the trail and mounted a higher eminence from where he could peer down into the cleft. Fascinated, he stared there in silence while a chill crept up his spine. The hidden chasm was like an elevator shaft, a sheer drop with sides smooth as glass. At the bottom water creamed and boiled around a jagged rock centerpiece. And on that rock, like so much refuse, lay a bleached pile of broken bones.

ONE more day passed before they came upon another note from Carey. The trail was less distinct now, hidden in places by every jungle trick the timber cruiser had at his command. Twice Eldridge was baffled, and twice Rutland with an ache in his heart pointed out the way their quarry had taken.

Across an open savannah, into jungle so thick and dark they seemed to be moving inside a huge mattress they fought their way. The spoor was always there, mocking them, leading them on. Now it was only a freshly broken reed, now an axe mark on a low-hanging branch. Only the fact that Rutland had traveled the game trails with the Muruts and Ibans enabled him to continue.

The note this time was wrapped in a piece of foil from a cigarette pack-

age. It was mounted atop a length of bamboo at a point where the jungle dropped into a watery expanse of reeds and shimmering lallang grass:

Rutland:
    You are entering B'Lungan swamp. Your natives will quit you here, for they are Ibans, and to an Iban this district is tabu. Only one man, the Belgian explorer, Renburg, has ever crossed this area and come out alive. I have his map. Go back, Rutland. I will not be caught.
                                    Carey.

The message was a prediction. Even as Rutland finished reading, the Dyaks stared out over the marsh, began jabbering excitedly among themselves. Their leader approached, a strange gleam in his eyes.

"*Tuan*," he said, "we can go no farther. This place is *lagayia*. Evil spirits are here."

Rutland nodded quietly. Could go no farther, eh? For a moment he almost welcomed the words. Mentally he saw himself back at the Station, writing a report to the Resident: "Proceeded far as possible. Refusal of carriers to continue forced expedition to end in failure."

But Eldridge seemed to read his thoughts. He turned on the Dyaks and began to heap abuse on them. Were they so many old women to heed such fool's talk? Were they frightened by so much mud and water? Stoically the natives listened, but continued to shake their heads.

"Let them go," the assistant said with a snarl. "If Carey can make it alone, so can we—map or no map."

Not for an hour after the carriers had left did the loneliness of the place close in on them. They were well into the swamp then, and the blazing sun on their shoulders and the air in their faces were solid with furnace heat. They moved slowly, advancing by a series of muddy hummocks which projected above the water.

The trail was vague here, only an occasional bootprint in the soggy soil. Yet as they went on, Rutland saw that Carey was heading almost directly due east and that he seldom varied from his course.

NIGHTFALL found them on a small island deep in the morass. Eldridge pulled out his jackknife, began scraping leeches off his legs. "Carey's a fool," he said. "Even if he does cross this swamp, he'll run straight into Saputan country, and I wouldn't give a Straits' dollar for a white man's chances there alone. The Saputans are the most treacherous Dyaks in Borneo. They'll take his head and hang it over the doorway of one of their longhouses."

Rutland nodded heavily. He had been thinking the same thing. And there was something else which he alone had observed and which was hurting him now like a wound in his own flesh.

Carey was sick! In the swamp grass not far from where they had found the last message, the district officer had picked up a small medicine bottle. Dover's Powder! Opium and ipecacuanha root. It meant that Carey was fighting fever now as well as the jungle and the relentless law.

With the first rays of the sun they were on their way again. And now in the trail Rutland could see the struggle the man ahead was putting up. Carey was throwing precautions to the wind. But before the sun was halfway to the zenith Eldridge for a second time found himself facing death.

Again there was no warning. The district officer in the lead, they were slogging slowly across a narrow aisle of yellow ground when abruptly Rutland heard a loud sucking sound behind him.

He whipped around to see Eldridge waist deep in a pool of clinging slime. Even as he watched, the assistant settled slowly deeper while his arms flailed helplessly for some support.

Rutland leaped forward, seized the man's hands and pulled, utilizing all his strength. But the quicksand covered a wide area, and he could feel the ground give way beneath his own feet.

He looked around frantically, saw a long snake-like object trailing across the ground. A dried length of *trelip* vine, strong as wire and capable of supporting great weight.

Even with the vine, it was touch and go for long enervating minutes. But at length Rutland stood back panting, and Eldridge lay where he had crawled, mud-covered, face white and drawn.

He got to his feet shakily and burst into a stream of profanity.

"Carey did that," he snarled. "He left that trail, hoping one of us would fall into that death trap. If only I could get my hands on that blasted murderer!"

Rutland lit his pipe. What good to tell Eldridge that that length of *trelip* came from farther back in the swamp, that none of it grew here on this barren hummock. It *was* Carey again! Once more the timber-cruiser had stretched out a hand to save them from disaster.

A MILE farther on an empty duffel bag lay beside the trail. The assistant's lips twisted crookedly.

"It won't be long now," he said. "His food is gone, and he'll have to depend on game. It'll slow him down."

The swamp was endless. Mile after mile the two men pushed on, following a trail that grew plainer all the time. In spite of the citronella oil they had applied, their faces were a mass of insect bites, and haggard from approaching exhaustion. The sun blazed mercilessly in a cloudless sky. The wind complained with its burden of the impending monsoon and brought no relief.

Then miraculously the mud and water fell behind, and they entered dense jungle again. Eldridge took the lead, for as they whittled down the intervening miles, Rutland found himself waging a battle to continue. What a cold-blooded thing British law was! It made no distinction, demanded a life for a life. Scales of justice? Fixed dice rather, in which the player had lost before he threw.

Two hours later they came upon the bridge.

In a calmer mood the district officer would have marveled as he always did at the engineering skill which had enabled the natives to sling these bamboo cat-walks across a chasm. The bridge crossed a deep ravine that stretched in either direction as far as the eye could see.

But both white men stopped short as a voice called out to them from the opposite side. At the far end of the bridge stood a familiar figure—Carey!

The timber-cruiser spoke again, his voice floating huskily across the gorge.

"Stay where you are, Rutland. I'm cutting the bridge!"

Rutland stood rigid. Before him he saw the timber-cruiser sway weakly as he fumbled for an axe at his belt And then before the district officer realized what was happening, Eldridge jerked his Webley revolver from its holster and leveled it at Carey.

Rutland threw himself forward. "Put up that gun, you fool!" His hand clamped around the assistant's wrist as a sudden hard light of determination flashed into his eyes. "Put up that gun. This has gone far enough. I'm in command here. Do you understand?"

Astonishment and rage curled Eldridge's lips in an ugly sneer.

"Going soft, eh?" he snarled. "Just because he's a pal of yours—"

He tore his arm free, whipped up the gun and fired. The descending blow from the timber-cruiser's axe and the bullet seemed to reach their mark simultaneously. A dull vibration followed the report. Severed, one side of the bridge sagged down at a crazy angle. Carey grabbed at a crimson spot on his leg and fell back with a hoarse cry.

"Got him!" Eldridge's yell was filled with triumph. "The bridge'll hold. Come on!"

ON LEGS that were dead things the district officer followed the assistant onto the swaying catwalk. The bridge was tilted at a forty-degree angle now, and only by gripping hard on the hand line could they keep from being precipitated into the ravine below. On the opposite side Carey was sitting up dazedly, gripping his wounded leg. His face bore a look of defeat.

But halfway across Rutland froze with horror. The bridge was slipping. Even as he and Eldridge stood stock still, the single remaining support gave way with a series of jerks.

Now Rutland could see the woven cable where it was fastened around an outcropping of stone. The line had broken, and only the wedging of the rocks kept the end from running free.

Eldridge advanced a yard more cautiously. The structure under the strain slipped another six inches.

Then Carey twisted around painfully, and dragging his useless leg behind him began to crawl slowly to the brink. His hands seized the bridge end; his left boot dug firmly into a cleft in the rock.

"I'll hold it, Rutland," he gasped. "Damn you, I've got to save you!"

Night had closed in on the jungle, and the three white men sat huddled about a sputtering fire—listening. Somewhere in the black foliage a skipping-on-the-ice bird sounded its queer *tok tok tok*, and far off a leopard coughed as it made its kill.

But there was another sound which reached their ears only at intervals when the wind changed. A dull booming sound—the throb of drums!

For an hour they had heard them, and for an hour they had known what they meant. This was Saputan country—the Saputans were a race by themselves, vicious head-hunting savages whose hate for the white man was a tradition.

It meant that the situation was almost funny. They had Carey, but their escape was cut off. The bamboo bridge lay shattered at the bottom of the ravine where it had fallen when Carey, his strength failing him, had released his hold an instant after Rutland and Eldridge had crossed.

Now Carey sat propped against a tree, his leg crudely bandaged with strips from the district officer's shirt. The man's face was twisted from pain, drawn from fever. Yet he had shown no emotion when Eldridge, a note of victory in his voice, had said, "Frank Carey, I arrest you for the murder of Gale Hearne."

There was a dull empty feeling at the pit of Rutland's stomach now. The drums sounded a rhythmic accompaniment to his black thoughts.

"Why did you do it?" he asked abruptly. "Why did you kill Hearne? You must have had a reason—"

Carey shook his head. "Does it matter?" he said.

IN THE pause that followed the drums sounded nearer. Eldridge put a cigarette between his lips, began chewing it. He stirred uneasily as he listened.

"We can't stay here," he said. "The place will be alive with those slinking devils and—"

His voice clipped off as a feathered shadow whipped out of the black void and thudded into the tree above Carey's head. The palm-rib dart embedded itself there, vibrating softly. Rutland stared at it, then jerked to his feet, revolver drawn.

He pushed into the undergrowth, nerves taut. Cautiously he made his way, moving in a wide circle. But he found nothing and returned to the fire.

"We've got to get out," he agreed. "Those Saputans have their own way of fighting. They'll wait out there, trying to wear down our nerves. Then they'll pick us off one by one." He turned suddenly on Carey.

"Renburg's map! The one that led you across the swamp. Maybe it shows a way—"

Carey shook his head. "No," he said, drawing a crumpled piece of oiled cloth from his pocket, "Renburg penetrated this far in thirty-eight all right, but he went back the way he came. The only reason he wasn't bushwhacked was because the Saputans were at war at the time with the Ibans." He studied the map in silence. Then: "Hold on—"

Painfully Carey dragged himself into the brighter light of the fire. His hands tensed.

"There is another trail marked," he said. "It— Look here, Rutland, it goes due north into the foothills of the Sinsiang range. And there's something else written here I didn't notice before. It says: 'Narrow cut, presumably passage through to Mahabu tributary.' The Mahabu runs into the Kinnebtangan."

With a quick movement Rutland strode forward and took the map.

"The passage begins a mile north of here," he began slowly. "A mile— Well, we'll have to try it. Eldridge, scatter that fire."

But even as he gave the order, the district officer sensed the antagonism in the assistant. Eldridge's hands opened and closed convulsively. Feet braced wide, he stood there, listening to the drums. A sudden gleam had entered his eyes, he flung away his cigarette, gnawed his lips.

"You figure on carrying him?"

Rutland looked up sharply as he recognized the significance of the words.

"Of course. He can't walk."

"It'll slow us down. We'll never get through that way."

"Listen," Rutland said. "I'm taking Carey with us. Now scatter that fire."

Like a cork spewing from a bottle

Eldridge cast aside all pretense then. He strode to the canvas luggage bags, seized one of them and threw it over his shoulder.

"You can dally along with that carrion, if you want," he snarled. "Me, I happen to value my head, and I'm getting out alone. Hand across that map."

A WAVE of contempt swept over the district officer. For the first time he was seeing Eldridge's full craven soul revealed without any veneer. The assistant had been brave enough when spurred on by the thought of self-aggrandizement and by the knowledge that the odds were on his side. Now that the situation was reversed. . . .

"You can go," Rutland said coldly. "But the map stays with us."

Out of the jungle a second Sumpitan dart shot, to miss Eldridge's body by inches. The assistant recoiled, then jerked out his revolver.

"I said, hand across that map."

Rutland heard the snick of the gun hammer. He saw the wild gleam in the man's eyes as Eldridge advanced a step nearer.

Then the district officer swung into action. Leaping sideways, he lunged for the assistant's gun hand. But Eldridge fired before he was halfway across the intervening space. A hot stab of agony shot through Rutland's shoulder. He seized the revolver barrel and with a sharp twist wrenched it free.

Unarmed, Eldridge clawed desperately for Carey's map which protruded from Rutland's pocket. Simultaneously he drove up his right boot in a cruel kick to the stomach, followed with a swinging haymaker. Again he reached out, tearing at Rutland's pocket.

But Rutland was fighting for his very life now. That map was his last ace-in-the-hole. Without it escape would be cut off. He fought off the nausea that was surging through him and traded blow for blow. Vaguely as he struggled he could hear the drums booming in his ears.

Eldridge thrust out his foot in an attempt to throw Rutland off balance. Both men went down, rolling over and over.

And then the district officer found an opening. Feinting, he brought up his fist with every ounce of strength he possessed and drove it against the assistant's jaw.

Eldridge gave a hoarse cry and fell back unconscious.

Six weeks later a *prahu* bearing four men floated slowly down the Kinnebetangan River toward the government jetty at Sandakan. Rutland, face gaunt and haggard, paddled from the stern. He had lost his *topee* somewhere in the miles behind, and his shirt was in ribbons.

Amidships Carey lay, one leg supported on a rude sling of *nibong* wood. By his side Eldridge gazed at the nearing shore and smoked a cigarette sullenly. The fourth man who wielded a paddle in the prow was a native, an Iban Dyak.

They slid alongside the jetty. Rutland whipped a hemp mooring line around the bollards, then carefully lifted Carey to the planking.

"Listen," Eldridge said, "can't we forget all about this? You've got what you wanted, and I'll make it worth your while—"

The district officer pointed to the white portals of the Government House clearly visible through the foliage farther up the hill and shook his head.

"It's out of my hands now," he said. "Get going."

TWENTY minutes later they sat in a cool airy room facing the Resident across his flat-topped desk. Overhead a *punkah* swept to and fro gently. The Resident studied the faces of the three men, then opened a humidor and took out a whitish cheroot.

"Well, Rutland," he said. "I see you've brought back your man. But it looks as if you went through hell to get him."

Rutland nodded. "There's quite a lot to report, sir," he began. "In the first place Carey isn't guilty of murder. Oh, he was at Paleyo village all right, and it was his gun that killed Hearne. But there's a lot more to it than that.

"You see, sir, Hearne was beating his number one boy, accusing him of having stolen trade goods from his loaded *prahu*. The boy was undersized, and Hearne had already broken his arm when Carey stepped in. Hearne drew a gun, and they both struggled for it. In the mixup the gun went off, hitting the trader in the chest.

"Carey wanted to help him, but Hearne was a brute of a man and didn't seem to know how bad he'd been hit. He took his natives and headed upriver, swearing to return for vengeance."

THE Resident stared. "But the Muruts at Paleyo," he objected. "We have an official report with evidence given by the *kapala* of that village and—"

"The Muruts were superstitiously afraid of Hearne," Rutland explained. "He had established himself among them as a virtual white god. Carey knew they would never give evidence against the trader, and he knew too that Hearne would live to reach Sandakan and that his last words would be to convict him. Don't you see, sir?

It was stacked cards. Carey was fighting odds he couldn't defeat."

For a long moment the Resident puffed his cheroot in silence. Then: "I'm afraid I'll have to have proof," he said slowly.

For answer the district officer jerked to his feet and strode across the room. He opened the door to admit a short Murut native, clad in only a loin cloth.

"Here is your proof," he said. "This is the native Hearne was manhandling when the trouble took place. After the shooting he became frightened and took to the bush. We came up with Carey in Saputan country and got out by making a raft and floating down the Mahabu tributary to the main stream. But before we came on to the coast we doubled back to the Iban villages near Paleyo. We found this Murut in one of them. The story he'll tell will prove Carey's innocence in any court."

Quietly the Resident leaned back and flipped the ash of his cheroot. He was an emotionless man, and the six years he had spent in Borneo had prepared him for anything.

"I'm glad the matter has worked out as it has," he said. "Hearne was a menace to society, and with the law satisfied the slate will be cleaner than it was before. Is there anything more, Rutland?"

The district officer hesitated and glanced at assistant Eldridge. "There was," he said. "There was a matter of insubordination I wanted to take up with you. But on second thought I think I'd rather handle it myself."

What Do You Think of
THRILLING ADVENTURES?
Please write a letter or postcard giving your opinion of this issue and address it to The Editor, THRILLING ADVENTURES, 10 East 40th Street, New York, N. Y. Thank you!

Black Passage

Command of the "Bamba Queen" Falls to Sam Kellogg,
Stranded in Port Moresby—and the Vessel Proves
a Plague Ship, with Murder at the Helm!

A Complete Novelette
By CARL JACOBI
Author of "Tide of Terror," "Beach of Death," etc.

CHAPTER I
A Proposition

KELLOGG has just climbed the ladder and entered the veranda of his corrugated-iron bungalow when he heard heavy steps approaching from behind. He shot the bolt on the mosquito-screen door, turned and waited. In Port Moresby at night it was well to be cautious of strangers.

A moment later a hulking figure strode out of the gloom and approached within speaking distance. "Just a minute there. Are you Sam Kellogg? If you are, I'd like a word with you."

Kellogg reached in his pocket, pulled out a small flashlight and sent a white ray stabbing forward. His eyes narrowed as the light centered on the man before him. He was dressed in a dirty suit of white drill with a sun helmet pushed far back on his head. A long scar ran across one side of his brow, and the lower part of his face was dark with a week's beard.

Scratching a match, Kellogg lit the gasoline lamp suspended from the ceiling, then moved back and unlocked the door.

"Yes, I'm Kellogg," he said crisply. "Come in. What's on your mind?"

The man stepped over the sill, extended his hand. "Heron's the name," he said. "Bill Heron. I got a proposition to make to you. You are a sea-faring man, aren't you?"

A HUNDRED yards down the hillside, the last street light of Port Moresby gleamed like a yellow eye. Farther on a brighter radiance marked the waterfront and the native quarter. Kellogg nodded slowly. "First officer of the *Markella*," he replied. "She went down in the Papuan Gulf two months ago. Why?"

Heron drew forth a cheroot, lit it and blew out a mouthful of smoke. "I heard about that," he said. "I also know you're out of work and not liable to get any in this hellhole. How'd you like a ship?"

Kellogg surveyed the man with greater interest. He waved him to one of two wicker chairs, took his place opposite.

"A ship," Heron repeated. "I got a crew—everything. Everything except a skipper. I need a man who—"

Regretfully Kellogg shook his head and smiled. "You called at the wrong address, I'm afraid," he said. "I haven't my master's papers yet, and I can't—"

"Papers be hanged!" Heron twisted around, leaned forward. "I'll lay my cards straight on the table, Mr. Kellogg. I'm a man of few

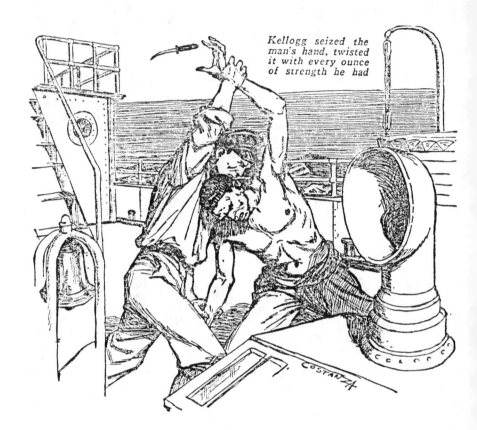

Kellogg seized the man's hand, twisted it with every ounce of strength he had

words, but I know a man I can trust when I see one. In the first place, my knowledge of navigation wouldn't fill a thimble. In the second place, have you seen that hooker that came in this morning, the *Bamba Queen?*"

Kellogg stretched his long legs out in front of him, brought one hand up to his lean jaw. "The *Bamba Queen?*" he said. She's that two-thousand-tonner out of Darwin, under British registry. Quarantined for bubonic and—"

"Right." Heron licked the end of his cheroot and nodded. "One of her crew is dead. Another's dying at the native pest-house up the line. In a day or so she's to be fumigated, but in the meantime"—his piglike eyes closed to crescents—"in the meantime I mean to do a few things."

He paused, waiting for Kellogg to reply. The other remained silent.

"Here's the whole of it in a nut-shell," Heron continued. "Bubonic means a long wait, and the skipper and white officers of the *Bamba Queen* didn't like the idea. So all three of 'em left ship last night and sneaked ashore. It seems the skipper has a relative working at the copper mine up by Rona Falls. They went there, figured on laying over until the quarantine period was past. Of course there'd be the devil to pay when it was found out, but the skipper knew the officials are lax in this port. The whole thing'd blow by shortly." Heron smiled.

"Now my plan is this. All that's aboard that ship right now is the crew. Lascars in the fo'c'sle. Straits Chinese below. With you and your knowledge, it's simple. We row out to the *Bamba Queen*, fill her full of steam and slip out to sea. The government will raise all hell, of course. But from outward appearances, it's simply a case of breaking quarantine. The real skipper won't **show** himself for three weeks. Once away from the coast—"

He stopped abruptly. With a muttered exclamation Kellogg leaped to his feet.

"You mean steal the ship?" he demanded aghast. "Why, you fool, even if I was that crooked, no one could pull a stunt like that. You must be mad!"

A smile on his lips, Heron kept to his chair. "Afraid of bubonic?" he asked. "You needn't be. One percent of quicklime is perfect disinfectant."

He spat, wiped his mouth and continued: "The *Bamba Queen's* carrying a cargo of munitions—rifles, principally — consigned to Rabaul in New Britain. They've had an uprising there, back in the interior, and they want to put it down quick. Now, once away from here, we head up the New Guinea coast. West of the Fly River there is plenty of native coastal villages where we can sell those rifles for a high price. What do you say?"

Kellogg stared. Here was a man calmly offering him a hand in high seas piracy, or what amounted to as much, and not batting an eye as he did it. Along the China coast perhaps one might expect such things, but in these waters— He strode to the door, kicked it open.

"Get out," he said shortly.

Heron appeared unruffled. "We split fifty-fifty," he persisted. "That is fair enough and—"

"Get out!"

With one powerful hand Kellogg seized the man by the collar of his coat, jerked him to his feet and sent him reeling down the ladder. He slammed the door shut.

"Next time you have any more fool ideas," he snapped, "look up someone else!"

Heron picked himself up and burst into a stream of profanity. "All right," he snarled. "But no man treats Bill Heron like that, see? I'll make you sweat if it's the last thing I do." He strode away into the darkness.

Kellogg turned out the veranda lamp and wandered thoughtfully into the bungalow. For a moment when Heron had mentioned a ship, he thought his luck had turned. Two months he'd been here in Port Moresby—ever since his former ship had gone down, and he had escaped, the only man alive. With his last few guilders Kellogg had rented this ugly iron shack, a roof over his head.

HE went into the bedchamber, sat down on a cot. Cunning, this man Heron. It took brains to hatch such a plan, and Heron was just the type of scoundrel willing to try it. An ex-plantation-owner, probably, who had lost everything in a few games of fan-tan and now was ready to take a long gamble to return to power.

Kellogg undressed and turned in.

He had been asleep for an hour or so when a low sound awakened him. He sat up, listened. It came again after a moment's hesitation, the low rasp of a knife cutting through the screening of his veranda door.

Cautiously he slid into his clothes, groped across to the dressing stand and seized his revolver. An inch at a time he opened the bedroom door, slipped across the main room of the bungalow and advanced toward the veranda.

Darkness lay before him. The knife had stopped now, but someone was fumbling with the latch. A voice whispered hoarsely.

Kellogg ducked behind the protection of a chair, pointed his revolver toward the ceiling and fired a single shot. Instantly cries of confusion rang out. The door shot open, and a shadow lunged forward. Kellogg fired again while his brain whirled in perplexity. Robbery? He had nothing of value here. All Port Moresby knew him as a man forced on the beach. What—

The shadow darted to the side of the main room entrance, out of range. Outside below someone hissed an order. And then Kellogg heard a step from behind.

He whirled, brought the revolver upward as a club. A grinding blow smashed hard into his face. An instant later they were upon him. He swung his fists, lashed out into the darkness, traded blow for blow.

But the struggle was shortlived. Something hard and heavy crashed down on his skull. The room spun in a vortex of colored fire. With a low moan he felt himself falling backward into unconsciousness.

CHAPTER II

Shanghaied

 DAYLIGHT was shining through a round aperture in the side wall when Kellogg opened his eyes. His head still throbbed dully, and there was a hot, dry feeling far back in his throat.

For a moment he lay there, trying to fit in their proper position the events of the night before. Then he saw he was in a bunk protruding from a bulkhead. The circular opening at his side was a port, and the familiar vibration could mean only one thing—a ship at sea.

Kellogg slid from the bunk and stared about him perplexedly. He was fully dressed. His blue cap lay on the table before him. Beside it was a bottle of whiskey and a glass. Only the dried blood on the back of his head told of his recent struggle.

Weakly he poured out a peg of whiskey and sipped it. The liquid sent new life surging through him. Stumbling forward, he tried the door. It was locked.

What did it all mean? If he were on a ship—what ship? And who were the men that had attacked him? He forced himself into a chair and tried to think. Knocking about these Eastern seas for as long a time as he had, a man might barge into a lot of scrapes. Yet he had never run into anything quite like this before. There seemed no reason—

Steps sounded in the passage outside. A moment later the door was unlocked, and a man entered the cabin. Kellogg looked at him, stiffened, and fought hard to conceal his emotion.

Bill Heron, face alcohol reddened, strode to the chair opposite. His lips were twisted in a smile of satisfaction.

"Hullo, Mr. Kellogg," he said. "Maybe you'll see now I'm not a man to be laughed at."

Kellogg compressed his lips. "Would you mind telling me why I'm here?" he asked. "Or is this some new kind of a joke?"

"No joke." Heron drew out a cheroot. "The idea is, I asked you to join up with me. You refused. There being no other man in Port Moresby whom I cared to entrust with the job, I had to change your mind."

A light was beginning to break in Kellogg's brain. "I see," he nodded coldly. "You shanghaied me, and now I'm to navigate the ship. Is that it?"

"Right." Heron blew smoke circles toward the deckhead. "We head up the New Guinea coast, as I said before. We get rid of those rifles, and then—"

"You can sail to hell for all I care," Kellogg snapped. "I won't budge."

"Oh, yes, you will," Heron sneered. "I figured you'd be in bad sorts when you woke up. So, until you decide to play, you don't get a bite of food. When you change your mind," he finished, "I'll be up on the bridge."

He rose unsteadily to his feet and went out, leaving the door open behind him. Kellogg rubbed his jaw.

Wild a scheme as it was, Heron had already put it halfway to completion. Some time during the night he had boarded the *Bamba Queen*, forced the native crew to heed to his command and stolen out to sea. The harbor officials would be wild at the quarantine breaking, but there would be no pursuit. Not until the rightful skipper came down from his interior hideaway would the plot be discovered.

Kellogg got out his pipe, packed it slowly. He was in a fix proper.

If he continued to be stubborn, he'd simply be starved into submission or forced to obey at the point of a gun. Undoubtedly it would be wiser to yield and wait for a turn of the cards.

He left the cabin, followed the passage to the companionway and gained the deck. The sun rode high in the sky. Kellogg ran his eyes about him quickly.

The *Bamba Queen* was a two-decked well-deck tramp. Coal smoke, not oil smoke, issued from her funnel. She was old and dirty, weather-scarred and typically British in design. But Kellogg got his first start when he glanced up at the masthead.

It wasn't the Union Jack that floated there, but the Dutch tricolor, the flag-of-the-queen. How Heron had contrived the change there was no telling. Kellogg scowled, turned aft, made his way to the taffrail and looked over. He gave a low whistle. Doing it up brown, they were!

The words, *Bamba Queen*, had already been painted out and a fresh legend crudely supplanted. To outward eyes the ship was now the *Hellendoorn*, a Dutch packet out of Macassar.

IT was clear Heron had not lost a moment in turning his plans into active play. Nor was he losing time in getting distance between himself and Port Moresby. Water creamed at the bows. The wake was a green-edged mass of foam.

"Eleven knots at least," Kellogg muttered. "The stokehold gang must be breaking their backs." He turned and made for the bridge. In the charthouse he found Heron bent over the fixed table, parallel rulers held clumsily in one hand, dividers in the other. Two other white men stood beside him.

"Changed your mind, eh?" Heron said with a triumphant grin. "Meet your partners, Rigori and Lobeck. They'll act as First and Second."

Kellogg surveyed them coldly. They weren't a lovely pair; dock-rats, probably, whom Heron had picked up in some Port Moresby waterfront dive. Rigori was a Por-tuguese, dark, with evil, penetrating eyes and thin lips. Lobeck, a heavy-set man, had a bullet-head and wore a revolver at his waist. It was evident neither of them would stop at anything.

"You're the skipper as far as navigation goes," Heron said. "You'll have freedom of the ship. But one funny move, and I shoot. Now where are we?"

Kellogg hesitated a moment, lips tight. Then, with a shrug, he glanced at the rough log. As he had expected there was no entry. He took up a sextant, went out on the bridge, shot the sun. After glancing at the chronometer in the gimbals he swiftly figured the position.

"Well across the Gulf and heading for the Torres Straits," he said quietly.

Even as he made this statement, it occurred to him that he might steer the ship toward Thursday Island, the Three Sisters, or some other of the many atolls just ahead. But Heron seemed to sense the thought.

"We head in closer to the coast," he growled. "I'll put a lookout on the fo'c'sle head to see we stay in open sea. Meanwhile, here's where I want to go." He pointed a finger at a general area of Dutch New Guinea coast line. "Lay a course and finish out the watch. But no tricks. Remember, I can read a compass."

Kellogg watched the three of them go down the port ladder, swore softly.

Just exactly how much knowledge of navigation they had between them there was no telling. But it was clear that Heron, drunk with newly acquired power, would pursue his plans to the end.

And beside all that there was the danger of bubonic. The ship had not yet been fumigated. All of the crew had been exposed. Time alone would tell whether they would be-come a raging plague ship, carrying the most feared malady of Oriental seas.

"Nice prospect," Kellogg muttered. "I'd hate to write my own ticket of insurance right now."

Throughout the long afternoon watch he stayed on the bridge, making no attempt to converse with the stoic Malay quartermaster at the helm. He had had no food, and his stomach began to gnaw hungrily. The charthouse clock had long struck eight bells before Lobeck came up to relieve him.

"Keep her as she goes, eh?" Lobeck asked, biting off a chew of plug tobacco.

"As she goes," Kellogg nodded. Without further word he went down the ladder and headed for the mess cabin. He was going to look up the ship steward and demand food. If he didn't get it, he told himself, there was going to be trouble. But halfway down the passage he stopped, changed his mind abruptly.

Ahead, from the direction of the skipper's cabin, came loud yells and the sounds of a struggle. An instant later there was a shattering crash, and Kellogg leaped forward.

HE reached the closed door of the cabin, pushed it open. On the threshold he stood, gaping inward. In the center on the floor, Rigori, the Portuguese, lay sprawled face downward. A broken whiskey bottle lay beside him, and blood oozed slowly from a gash on the back of his head.

Slumped in the swivel chair by the desk sat Heron. Eyes wide, he was staring down at a package in his hand. Greed, surprise were written across his face.

"What the devil—" Kellogg began. Then he stopped short as he saw the contents of the box in Heron's hands. Lying unprotected on a piece of cotton was a pile of gleaming crystals. Yellow and blue fire radiated from their prisms.

Heron looked up, coughed huskily.

"Found this in the safe," he said. "I had to rap that rat, Rigori, on the head or he'd have taken 'em."

"Diamonds," Kellogg said slowly. "I don't understand—"

"Neither do I. No mention of 'em on the manifest. They were in the

safe in this box marked fragile, consigned to Hoggard-Mark and Company, Rabaul. Case of secret shipment to avoid duty, I suppose. Even the former skipper didn't know what was in that box. If he had, he'd never have left ship."

Kellogg bent over the box, examined the largest diamond, moved his finger back and forth over the others.

"What're they worth?" Heron asked. "Figurin' roughly."

For a long moment Kellogg did not reply. His brows contracted, and his lips screwed tight as he stared down at the stones. "Figuring roughly," he said at length, "I'd say somewhere around a hundred thousand dollars."

"A hundred thousand!" A glitter shot into Heron's eyes. "You sure?"

"No." Kellogg moved one of the gems nearer the light. A good diamond weighing about one carat is worth around three hundred dollars. These are all big and above average."

Heron tilted back in his chair, wiped his brow. "A hundred thousand dollars," he said slowly. "I could live on that a long time. I could get out of these rotten islands and go back to God's country. I could—"

He swung around sharply. In the open doorway stood a squat Chinese, dressed in the dirty white coat of a steward. His almond eyes were staring inward.

"Tea," he said shortly. "You come dlink 'em now?"

Heron snapped the cover back on the box with an oath. He got to his feet, nodded and slammed the door. Then he turned grimly.

"Now there *is* gonna be hell. Wu Fong'll tell the whole crew."

Kellogg's face was grave. "A fortune here, and rifles in the hold," he said. "I'm afraid that spells trouble, all right. Just what do you plan to do?"

For answer Heron looked at the diamonds again. "The rifles can go hang now," he said. "These stones are enough for me."

There was a stir from the floor,

and Rigori stumbled to his feet. He swayed unsteadily for a moment, clutching at the back of his head.

"Rigori, you're going to keep your hands off, see?" Heron snarled.

"When we get ashore, we'll split up evenly."

Rigori rearranged his clothes sullenly but made no reply. Kellogg strode to the door.

"It's no concern of mine," he said with a lightness he didn't feel. "But I advise you to hide those stones in a better place than the safe, Mr. Heron."

He stepped into the passage, halted a moment to light his pipe. As he passed a match back and forth over the bowl, stealthy footsteps sounded ahead of him. Kellogg darted forward silently, raced to the companionway in time to see Lobeck disappear onto the deck.

More trouble. In a short while there'd be hell popping. Neither Rigori nor Lobeck would be content with a share of the diamonds, and it would be a case of survival of the strongest and most cunning. But where in the tangled picture did he fit?

He went to the mess cabin, ate in silence the food Wu Fong served him, then found the cabin in which he had awakened. For an hour he sat there, trying to plan a way of action. Keeping in to the coast would mean they would pass to the east of the Aroe Islands line and therefore out of all regular ship lanes. New Guinea west of the Fly offered nothing. It was all steaming jungle coast with only a few native settlements here and there.

He was in the midst of his thoughts when the door opened and Lobeck entered. The man nodded, glanced back into the passage, then crossed over and sank into a chair.

"Want to talk to you," he said. He helped himself to the whiskey bottle, downed a stiff drink. "You don't like Heron?"

"I haven't any love for him," Kellogg replied coldly. "Or for you or Rigori, either. Being shanghaied isn't exactly—"

"I know, I know. But all that was Heron's idea. Now listen. Rigori's a snake. Heron means to keep those stones for himself. Suppose you and me take things in hand ourselves?"

"What do you mean?" Kellogg asked.

"What do I mean? Heron is helpless without you. He don't know a thing about navigation, and he's depending on you to run the ship. We simply team together, that's all. I'll take care of those two swine, and after that we simply divide the stones between us."

Kellogg pretended to consider the matter. He kicked back his chair, paced across the room, returned.

"I'll think it over," he said at length.

Lobeck nodded. "You do that," he advised, moving toward the door again. "Play with me, and we'll both profit."

CHAPTER III
Death at the Helm

DARKNESS had closed in, thick and heavy, before Kellogg left his cabin. On deck he stood silent, gazing out into the black Arafura sea. The engines still throbbed steadily, but the *Bamba Queen* ploughed forward without lights, a blacker shadow in the night. All ports by Heron's orders had been closed. Even the nagivation lights were turned out.

Presently Kellogg turned, paced across the well-deck and advanced to the fo'c'sle scuttle. He hesitated a moment, then passed in. Might as well have a look at the deck crew. One of their number might be intelligent enough and willing to act as an ally.

A smell of unwashed human bodies assailed him as he stared forward in the dim glow of a single drop light. Curious eyes answered his gaze. An instant later, lips twisted in a frown, Kellogg was on deck again. There would be no

help from that quarter, he told himself. The brown men, without an
exception, were a cutthroat lot.

On the bridge, Heron and Rigori
stood side by side at the for'ard
rail. The Malay quartermaster was
still at the wheel.

Kellogg glanced at them, turned
and made his way upward. At the
top of the ladder he paused
abruptly. The voice of the Portuguese
came to him, suave and quiet.

"It is understood then. We divide the stones between the two of
us the moment we sight shore. Kellogg and Lobeck are to be locked
below. We open the valve, sink the
ship and take to the boats."

Heron uttered a warning whisper,
and then Kellogg was at their side.
"Do you want the course kept as
is?" he asked, trying to keep his
voice casual. "We'll be through the
Straits and off Dutch territory before long."

HERON'S pig eyes shut halfway,
and he nodded slowly. "Want to
get well past the boundary first," he
said. "I ain't takin' any chances of
extradition." He spat over the rail
and hitched his trousers.

Kellogg nodded, walked away a
few paces and stared over the rail.
So Rigori and Heron planned to kill
him, did they? They had patched
up their recent quarrel, and Lobeck
was to be done away with too, all
as part of the game. The situation
was thickening.

Kellogg was still standing there
two minutes later when the interruption came. Stumbling steps on
the port ladder whipped the three
white men about. Lobeck, breathing
hard, raced forward.

"The Chink steward!" he gasped.
"It's got him. Got him cold!"

Heron stared. "What are you
talking about?" he demanded.

"Wu Fong." Lobeck's face was an
ashen mask in the gloom. "Half an
hour ago I was talking to him. Now
he's lying dead in the cabin. It's
bubonic."

Even before the dread significance of the words reached him Kellogg felt a cold ripple move up his

spine. Bubonic, the worst plague in
the East, the most horrible malady
of all times. With mechanical steps
he followed the others below, entered the mess cabin.

Wu Fong lay by the door, face
upward, eyes staring. His legs were
twisted under him as if contorted
in a last dying agony. But his face
was not spotted, marked with any
tumorous pustules or signs of fever.
Kellogg shouldered his way forward, bent down. Now that the first
shock of Lobeck's statement had
passed, he realized it couldn't be.
Bubonic strikes quickly, yes, but not
within a period of thirty minutes.

His brain raced as he unbuttoned
the Chinese steward's coat and
glanced at his chest. His teeth came
together with a sharp click as he
saw what had happened.

Should he pretend to fall for the
ruse? Directly over the steward's
heart an almost imperceptible smear
of blood was oozing from a tiny
puncture in the skin. The man had
been stabbed with some thin wire-
like instrument. He had not been
killed in this room. The marks of
dragged heels were plain on the
floor.

Yet Kellogg decided to play for
time.

"It's bubonic, all right," he said
shortly. "Seen it before in Soera-
baya. We'd better throw the body
overboard right away."

Beads of sweat stood out on
Heron's face. He swallowed,
clenched his fists.

"One of the Lascars will do the
lousy job," he said. "But no one
lets on what's happened, understand?
That black gang know too much for
their own good now."

For an instant after that the three
white men stood in mute silence,
staring at one another. Then with
an oath Heron crammed a cheroot
into his mouth, turned and made for
the skipper's cabin. Lobeck followed him. Rigori headed down the
passage for the companionway and
the deck. Alone in the room, Kellogg slumped slowly into a chair.

He saw the answer clearly enough.
It was Rigori. The Portuguese's hand

was clearly marked. He had sneaked into the skipper's cabin some time before, searched for the diamonds. Wu Fong, bent on the same mission, had accidentally discovered him. A struggle had followed. Rigori had killed the steward, probably with a very thin stiletto, in such a way that plague would appear to be the cause of death.

His purpose was twofold. He did not want Heron to learn of his treachery, and he hoped that the fear of bubonic would bring sufficient confusion to enable him to search again.

"But how about Lobeck?" Kellogg mused. "Is he tied up with Heron or Rigori, or is he really planning to fight away from both of them? The whole thing's a pretty kettle of fish."

There were several things he could do. He might take rockets from the ship's locker, send up a Very light, hoping to attract the attention of some vessel. But such a move probably would have no result save to bring the wrath of the three renegades down upon his head.

HE might steer the vessel farther away from the coast, try to get in the regular traffic lane of the Manila-Thursday Island run. But that act too would no doubt be discovered in short order. A man did not need to be an authority on navigation to read a compass.

Scowling, Kellogg was about to leave the cabin when a thought swung him around. Quickly he bent over the body of the dead Chinese, searched his clothes. His frown changed to a grim smile as he drew forth a small, snub-nosed revolver.

"Luck," he whispered softly.

Then he went into the passage and headed for the companionway. On deck the night darkness had softened a little. Away off the starboard bow a ghost of a moon wove in and out through a fringe of thinner cloud. The sea was flecked with phosphorescent fire.

For several moments Kellogg stood motionless by the rail, contemplating the scene. Then, with the revolver hidden in his hip pocket, he went up on the bridge and advanced to the wheelhouse.

In the dim light of the binnacle he saw that Rigori had replaced the Malay quartermaster at the wheel. The Portuguese stood motionless, bent slightly forward. An unlighted cigarette hung from his lips.

Kellogg jammed his cold pipe between his teeth and glanced at the compass.

"Better give her a half point east," he said to Rigori. "There'll be a slight variation between this and the standard compass, but no need to check it."

Rigori made no reply. Kellogg's teeth bit hard on the pipe stem. He was anxious to head in for shore now. There had come in his mind a vague hope that he might anchor within immediate Dutch jurisdiction where a patrol boat would be in the vicinity.

"Turn her, man," he repeated. "Don't you—"

An exclamation jerked from his lips. Below him, hidden machinery clanked loudly. Beside him one of Rigori's hands slid silently from the wheel. The man's body seemed to slump within itself. He swayed a moment, fell to the floor.

"Damnation!" Kellogg cried. "You too?" He bent down, pressed his hand against the man's chest. There was no heart beat. Rigori was dead!

Two minutes later as an icy calmness began to replace the first shock Kellogg tried to place this new piece into the growing puzzle. Rigori had been killed by a terrific blow on the back of the head. The steam steering gear had been set, holding the ship to its course. Rigori's body had been propped up before the wheel in a lifelike position! But why?

"It's Lobeck this time," Kellogg muttered. "This is the last straw. I'm going to have a showdown."

Lips tight, he strode out of the wheelhouse, drew his revolver from his pocket and headed below. At the head of the ladder he stopped abruptly. He stared into the semidarkness. A shadowy form was moving in the port wing. A dark face seemed to surmount a pair of naked shoulders.

Kellogg's finger tightened on the trigger. He leaped forward, groped into the blackness and suddenly came into contact with hot, sweaty flesh.

Simultaneously he felt cold steel rip through the left sleeve of his shirt and bite viciously into his arm.

Kellogg seized the knife hand of his assailant and twisted it with every ounce of strength he possessed.

Relentlessly he closed in, striking blow after blow.

One last smashing blow, and the unseen one crashed to the deck with a hoarse cry. Kellogg stood over him breathing hard. He reached in his pocket for a match, lit it and looked down. A low exclamation came to his lips. The unconscious man was one of the Strait-Chinese from below decks!

Mutiny? Where then were the others? Why was the fo'c'sle so quiet?

The partial answer to his mental questions came abruptly. From below, the steady rhythmic pulsations suddenly died. A ghostlike silence settled over the *Bamba Queen.*

The engines were stopped.

Kellogg whirled, leaped back to the ladder, peered over. Racing upward, noiseless on bare feet, came a line of yellow men, their faces in the thin moonlight wild with fear and panic.

"Back!" Kellogg snapped. "Where the devil do you think you're going?"

Silent, unmindful of his command, they swept forward. Kellogg got his gun around, fired once, saw a rat-faced figure claw at his throat and pitch forward.

An instant later and they were upon him.

A spanner whizzed through the hot air.

The heavens over Kellogg's head seemed to explode and rush downward.

He coughed, clutched at the rail, fell.

CHAPTER IV
Distress Signal

AN eternity seemed to have passed before he returned to consciousness. His first thought was for the ship. The *Bamba Queen* was rolling in a heavy swell without steerageway. But no longer was he on the bridge wing.

A dim light from an oil lamp illuminated the room in which he lay. It was the skipper's cabin, and at the desk at the far side of the room Lobeck sat, bent forward, moving heavy fingers over a pile of white crystals spread before him.

Kellogg gritted his teeth, stood up weakly. His shirt was soaked with blood from the knife wound; his head ached and his legs trembled beneath him. At the sound of his movement Lobeck raised his eyes, twisted around and nodded.

"Been waitin' for you to come around," he said. "I'm clearin' out, and I need you to show me the way."

Left arm dangling, Kellogg walked forward to the desk.

"Heron?" he asked slowly. "Where is he?"

"Dead." Lobeck's voice was without emotion. "Dead as a herring. Told you I'd take care of him and Rigori. I'm boss now, and you're going to do what I say whether you like it or not."

Kellogg's brain was clearing rapidly. He looked about him, sent a quick glance toward the door.

"The engine crew—" he began, bewildered.

Lobeck scowled. "Gone. Someone must have heard me say Wu Fong died of bubonic. The Chinks came from below, put you out of the way and jumped ship. The Lascars tried the same thing. I got one. The others are locked in the forepeak. You've been out a long time."

Kellogg compressed his lips as he sought to digest all this information. Mechanically he crossed over to the first-aid cabinet, applied half a bottle of hydrogen peroxide to his wound and bound it as well as he could. The knife thrust was not deep, but he was taking no chances of blood-poisoning.

"We'll go to the galley now," Lobeck said, after watching him in silence. We'll get some supplies and take one of the boats. The coast can't be so far away. If you act nice, maybe I'll give you one of the diamonds. If you don't—" He tapped the revolver in his belt significantly.

From the galley shelves Lobeck took down two tins of biscuit, several cans of tomatoes and bars of chocolate. On deck he dropped his armful of supplies to the planking.

"I'll let four men out of the forepeak," he said. "That's all we need to man the boat. You go up on the bridge, figure out how far we've got to go. Remember, Heron and Rigori are dead, and you're not armed. You might just as well take it easy."

Kellogg got out his pipe, crammed tobacco into the bowl. Black night still enveloped the *Bamba Queen* as she rose and fell drunkenly in the trough. Ahead in the scuppers lay the body of the Lascar Lobeck had shot.

The renegade headed forward. Kellogg began to think fast. Heron dead? Probably so, yet Lobeck had seemed too ready to disclose this fact. Abruptly Kellogg darted down the companionway and paced silently along the passage.

H E was working on a hunch. Hunches were rare with him, but when they came, they usually brought results.

Six cabin doors opened on the passage. The last of the six, the first officer's room, was closed. Kellogg tried the latch, found it locked, and called out softly through the panels.

"Heron!"

No answer for a moment. Then something thumped within, and a voice answered:

"Here. I'm tied up."

In an instant Kellogg had leaped to the cabin across the passage, retrieved the key. He snapped it in the lock of the closed door, twisted. Then he groped his way to the side of the bound man.

"Listen, Heron," he said. "Lobeck's got the diamonds and is ready to jump ship. Rigori's dead. Together we've still got a chance. If I free you, will you play straight?"

Heron mumbled an eager assent.

"Straight," Kellogg continued. "That means if we get in control again, we head back for Port Moresby, hand over the ship and see that the diamonds are delivered to the authorities. Agreed?"

"Anything," gasped Heron. "Only cut me loose."

With his pocket knife, Kellogg reached out, began to saw on the bindings. He knew well enough that Heron was a treacherous scoundrel whose word meant nothing. Yet in the present situation, an ally was necessary, and by his own judgment Lobeck was the greater of two evils.

Released, Heron staggered to his feet.

"The deck crew?" he asked abruptly.

"Locked in the forepeak. The engine room gang have already gone —afraid of bubonic. But we're not armed."

"I'll fix that. Come on." Heron strode to the door, paced quickly to the skipper's cabin which was still dimly illuminated by the emergency oil lamp. He went to the desk, tore open a bottom compartment and took out two Webley Scott British Navy regulation automatics.

"Where's Lobeck now?" he demanded, handing one of the weapons to Kellogg.

"For'ard, letting enough men out of the hold to man one of the boats. He thinks I'm on the bridge."

"Oh, he does, does he?" Heron's face was wreathed in smiles at his sudden turn of fortune. "Well, he's going to get a big surprise."

Cautiously they made their way to the companionway, gained the deck. No sound met them. Lobeck must still be in the hold, having difficulty in persuading the Lascars that only four of their number was to be released.

The two men ran up the port ladder to the bridge.

"Douse the binnacle lamp," Heron ordered. "When Lobeck discovers what's happened, there's going to be a lot of lead flying."

Behind the protection of the wheelhouse, they waited. For two minutes there was only the noise of the sea. Then a medley of grumbling voices came up from the open fore hatch. Four Malays appeared in the gloom of the well-deck. After them, a lighter shadow in the darkness, appeared Lobeck.

Kellogg stepped to the for'ard rail.

"Lobeck!" he called suddenly.

The renegade below turned, and laughed in satisfaction. "All set," he called back. "I've got 'em. We are comin' up and lower a boat."

"Lobeck, stand where you are!" Kellogg commanded. "There's two pistols here with a dead bead on your head. Heron's and mine. Throw down your gun and come up alone."

THERE was a second of silence as the significance of the words sank in. Then Lobeck snapped a low order to the four Malays. With three of them at his heels, he plunged forward, crouched behind the main hatch. The fourth native leaped into the open fore hatch and disappeared. Three revolver shots raced up to the bridge.

"The dirty rat!" Heron muttered as he leveled his own automatic and fired twice in reply. "He's going to release the rest of the crew. They'll break open the cases, mount the rifles, and it'll be two of us against an armed mob."

Kellogg said nothing. Automatic in hand he waited. A pause followed the initial burst of shots. From below decks came the hollow rending and splintering of wooden cases. A moment later more men issued from the hatch.

Muttering profanity, Heron then crouched low and fired five times in quick succession. Cries and yells followed the reports. A Malay pitched forward. Rifles began to respond as the Lascars spread wide in the darkness. Streaks of orange fire stabbed the night. A slug whined past Kellogg's ear.

While he raced to insert a new clip Heron turned breathlessly. "Get Lobeck!" he snarled. "If we don't, they'll rush us."

His words were a prediction. Kellogg, firing deliberately and slowly, saw the Lascars suddenly divide into two groups, heard Lobeck urge them on with quick inaudible commands. Lurching forward, one group headed for the port ladder, the others for the starboard.

Up they came, firing the hastily-mounted rifles, shouting Moslem curses. And then Heron saw Lobeck.

The two renegades stopped short, firing pointblank. For a split second Lobeck stood swaying, a ghastly look on his face. With a liquid cry he threw out his hands and crashed to the deck.

Heron grasped the situation instantly. In the surprised lull of firing that followed his voice shouted loud in Malay:

"Cease firing, you rats! Stand by to man the boats. We're leaving this hooker right away."

The words were magic. They spelled the desire of every brown man in the lot—to get away from this pestilence ship with its threat of bubonic and white man murder. As one man they threw down their rifles, raced onto the boat deck abaft the bridge. They bent over the davits and began to work at the falls.

Kellogg whirled and strode forward. "You treacherous scoundrel!" he cried. "You agreed to turn back and head for port. You agreed to—"

Heron's face was a twisted mask of triumph. "Yeah?" he snarled. "I may have said a lot of things. It's what I say now that counts. I'm gettin' out with those diamonds, and nobody's stoppin' me!"

He bent over the body of Lobeck, ran his hands through the dead man's pockets and presently gave a cry of satisfaction. In his hands was a small leather tobacco sack. Heron ripped it open, let a cascade of tiny objects fall into his hands. "A hundred thousand dollars!" he said. "Enough to put me on easy street for a long time. Enough to—" Kellogg charged. Fists doubled before him, he threw himself across the intervening space, struck the renegade hard in the jaw. Heron uttered a surprised oath, whipped his revolver up in defense. In the moment before Kellogg struck again he pulled the trigger. A thunderous burst of flame, and a hot sword of agony shot through Kellogg's side, sent him reeling backward.

Again Heron fired, and again Kellogg felt the slug hit, this time penetrating deep into his left leg. For an instant the night swirled before him in confusion. Then by sheer force of will Kellogg heaved his body forward once more.

With one hand he seized the renegade's weapon hand, twisted the revolver loose. He struck twice in quick succession. A brutal kick struck him in the groin. In maddened fury Kellogg jerked back his right first and ground it with battering-ram force straight into the face before him.

Heron's head snapped backward. Blood spewed from his lips. He gave a hoarse cry and sank to the deck.

FIVE days later the Australian inter-island steamer, *Queensland*, steamed into the harbor of Port Moresby, bringing in tow the derelict freighter, *Hellendoorn*, which had been sighted eight degrees south of the line, drifting without steerageway in an offshore current.

The *Hellendoorn*, to the master of the *Queensland*, was a bit of a puzzle. Despite her name, her articles showed her to be the *Bamba Queen*, out of Darwin. From her signal yards floated the International Code flags, "N" and "C," the distress sig-

nal. Aboard her there were but two living men, one securely tied and bound on the bridge deck, the other lying on the chartroom settee, unconscious from two bullet wounds.

It was two weeks before Kellogg was able to leave the Port Moresby hospital and enter the presence of the lieutenant governor. He handed across the diamonds then, sat stiffly on the edge of a chair, and told his story from beginning to end.

"The Chinese and the Lascars probably landed somewhere in Dutch New Guinea," he finished. "There was a smooth sea, and they should have had no trouble in reaching the coast. They'll turn up in some Dutch port shortly."

Through it all the lieutenant governor sat in silence. The narrative completed, he nodded quietly, rose to his feet, and left the room. When he returned a moment later it was to hand Kellogg a large envelope.

"What's this?" Kellogg asked with a frown.

The lieutenant governor lit a cigar and smiled. "That," he replied, "is your share of the salvage. We're proud to thank you for your services, Mr. Kellogg—the mandate government as well as the owners. I hope we'll meet again some time."

Kellogg shook hands, mumbled his thanks and reached for his cap. Clutching the envelope, he moved slowly toward the door.

"There is just one thing more, Mr. Kellogg. Am I right in saying you are anxious to leave Port Moresby?"

"Leave?" Kellogg swung around sharply and clamped his teeth hard together. "Leave?" he repeated. "By the Lord Harry, I'd swim if I could. But—"

"Then I suggest you call at the consulate immediately. The *Bamba Queen* is putting out again with a new crew and a new skipper. If I'm not mistaken, there's an empty first officer's berth, and I don't think you'll have any trouble signing on."

Spider Wires

*Weaponless, Doyle Uses
Cunning to Protect that
Human Totem Pole
of Death*

By JACKSON COLE
Author of "Gunfire Gold," "Trapped," etc.

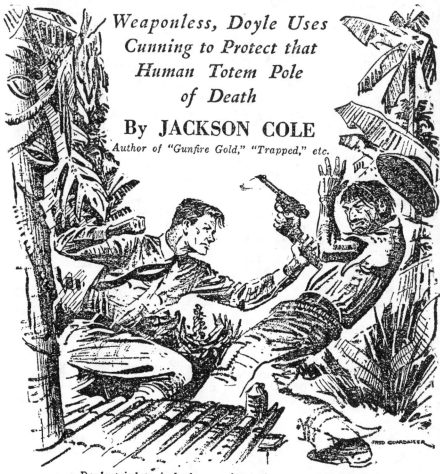

Doyle tried to jerk the gun from the renegade's hand

OYLE bent over the instrument desk and tried it once more. Tensely his hand pounded the key, repeated call letters over and over again. Then he closed the switch and sat staring at the sounder.

It was no use. Both wires were down. He was cut off.

An hour ago he still had the east wire connecting him with Tabin, Malsung, and Tandjong-Selor on the east coast. Now, in the same mysterious manner that the west line had gone dead six days before, the east circuit was broken.

And Stuart, who should have located the trouble by now, still had not returned.

Scowling, Doyle kicked back his chair, strode across the main room of the nipa-shack and went out on the veranda. It was raining again, a monotonous steady downpour that had been coming down for as long, it seemed, as he could remember.

Ahead, across the little clearing, the jungle was a dripping, composite wall. To the right, a bamboo mast projected from the shore of the yellow river to flaunt the sign:

DUTCH EAST BORNEO TELEGRAPH
COMPANY
STATION NUMBER 5

Doyle got out his pipe and packed it slowly. They were lonely holes, these telegraph r e l a y stations. Twelve of them, at evenly spaced intervals, stretched across the Borneo jungle from Bandjermasin to Bulungan. Two operators were stationed at each, and it was their duty to keep the Dyaks from tearing down the wires and the Dutch Government informed of native conditions, headhunting mutinies, etc.

Six days ago, while serving his night trick at the key, Stuart, Doyle's assistant, had received their last communication from the west coast. Quotations on rubber prices, routine forestry reports, and an official warning, signed by the Samarinda Resident, notifying in-country *controlleurs* that Kite Steadman, fugitive from justice, wanted for murder, was heading upriver.

EVEN as this message was completed, the circuit had broken. "Native swiping insulators again, I suppose," Stuart had grumbled. "Means one of us will have to trek downstream and fix the break."

At dawn Stuart had donned mosquito boots, taken his Winchester and Luger and paddled off in the station *prahu*. Assuming he had found it necessary to travel as far as Kampong Naoha, which marked the limit of their wire-jurisdiction, he should have been back before this.

Doyle glanced at his watch uneasily. He was a tall, well-knit American with a lean open face bronzed by years under a tropic sun. He wore trousers of cool pongee, a loose knit *chabla* shirt and a short, black tie knotted carefully at the collar. The tie was a strict Company regulation. Order Number Fourteen: "No operator while on duty will go about in a state of semi-undress. Ex-

perience has shown this induces a lowering of morale."

Doyle strode nervously across the room and peered aimlessly out the window. Abruptly he went rigid in every nerve and muscle.

In the jungle wall at the edge of the clearing his keen grey eyes had caught a moving palm frond. Beside it he saw a glinting blue-steel shaft, slanted upward.

Doyle watched that shaft come to rest in a direct line with his head. The palm frond moved again. Through the hot stillness came the unmistakable snick of a rifle hammer.

Doyle, with a single movement, threw himself to the floor, flattened behind the protection of the heavy railing.

A moment late a bullet whined through the mosquito screening and thudded into the wall behind him.

Doyle felt a cold ripple race up his spine. He whipped his hand to his belt, swore softly as he remembered he had left his revolver in the inner room.

He rolled over, began to inch his way forward. If he could reach the connecting door—

"Stand up and raise your hands. I've got you covered." The words, intoned in a deep guttural voice, came from close at hand.

Doyle lifted his head, saw a squat, heavy man shuffling across the clearing, rifle outstretched before him. His clothing hung in rags, his filthy shirt glistened with sweat, and his sun helmet bore a knife slash in the center of the crown.

"Stand up," the man snarled, "and no funny moves or I'll plug you sure."

Quietly Doyle stood up, raised his hands. He took in the zigzag scar running across the newcomer's left cheek. The brief description of the fugitive from justice which had come over the wire flashed back to him. This was Kite Steadman!

"Don't budge," Steadman said. "And you might as well wipe that look off your face. I aim to stay here quite a spell."

"What do you want?" Doyle

stalled for time as he measured the distance between him and the inner door. He saw quickly what had happened. Steadman had cut the wire to prevent information of his whereabouts reaching the coast. And Stuart— Had the renegade waited for him to come and repair the damage?

Steadman seemed to read Doyle's thoughts.

"Sure I cut your wires," he sneered. "And I got your assistant too. He's out there, deader'n a door-nail." With a jerk the renegade exchanged his rifle for a short snubnosed automatic. "And you'll end up the same way if you don't do as I tell you. Now get a move on and bring me somethin' to eat."

Half an hour later Doyle stood again on the veranda with the automatic still covering him. He tried to keep his face calm while his brain seethed and plotted to find a way out. Steadman was going after the food he had prepared like a starving animal.

Why had the renegade come here? It was not to replenish supplies. The jungle teemed with game, and any Kenyah or Punan kampong would have kept him from starvation.

OUTSIDE in the clearing the rain was coming from a darker sky. At length Steadman wiped his mouth and pushed his plate away. "How many villages near here?" he demanded.

"Two," Doyle answered.

"Two, eh. One of 'em's got a kapala by the name of Kota Noh, hasn't it?" And when the operator hesitated he snarled, "Answer, damn you, or I'll—"

Doyle nodded. Steadman grinned evilly.

"Okay, I'll tell you what you're going to do. I wasn't sure if this was the place at first. Tomorrow you and me are going out in the jungle, and you're going to take me to the Kallukai image. You've heard of it?"

Doyle stiffened. So that's what Steadman was after! His brain reeled at the possibilities. He had thought the Kallukai image was a three-way secret held by himself and Stuart here at Number 5, the Resident in Samarinda, and the Kenyah Dyaks of Kota Noh's kampong.

His nails dug into his palms. He said, "I don't know what you're talking about."

Steadman guffawed. "Don't, hey? Then I'll refresh your memory. The Kallukai image isn't an image at all; it's a totem post. It's got five emeralds inside of it, along with the bones of old Kallukai, the witch doctor."

With one hand the renegade drew a bamboo flask from his pocket, tilted it to his mouth.

"Old Kallukai," he continued, "was the most powerful witch doctor the Kenyahs ever had. When he died five years ago he was buried in full Kenyah ceremony. Funny ideas these natives have. They hollowed out the inside of a Palapak tree, stuck the corpse in it together with his most valued possessions and then sealed the tree up again. Living tomb, see? Well, after four years they cut the tree down, sharpened up their parang knives and carved the trunk into a totem post. Then they put the thing in the center of their village where it was supposed to ward off evil spirits. Right, isn't it?"

"Where did you get that information?" Doyle's face was a grim block of granite.

"Never mind where I got it. But that ain't all. Up to that time the Kenyahs had been fightin' bloody hell to get these telegraph posts out of their country. When Kota Noh was made *kapala* he got the bright idea peace was better than war. So he lugged the totem post over here and offered it as a token of friendship. Either you or the other operator wired the Resident in Samarinda, and he advised setting the image up in the jungle somewheres near the station and the village. The idea was to play along with the natives, make a big hit with them.

"Now I happen to know," Steadman grinned evilly, "that Kallukai's five emeralds are still inside that block of wood. I been figurin' this out a long time. All you have to do is take me to the thing. I chop it open, and the rocks are mine. If you do as I say, you won't get hurt."

For an instant Doyle sat in rigid silence.

"But you don't realize what you're saying," he said finally. "If you violate that totem post the Kenyahs will consider their peace bond broken. They'll rise up and destroy our station—every station in this section of the country. It'll mean war!"

"So?" Steadman took another swallow from his flask. "That don't concern me. I want those emeralds, and I'm goin' to have 'em. Meanwhile I'll just tie you to that chair so you won't get any funny ideas of runnin' out on me."

With one hand he reached up, tore loose the rattan rope of the bamboo curtain rolled up at the ceiling of the veranda. Clumsily, the revolver still leveled before him, he whipped the bindings around Doyle, secured them to the chair back. Then he pocketed the weapon and nodded in satisfaction.

"That'll hold you," he said.

He moved toward the connecting door, heading for the wall bunk in the inner room. But he got only halfway.

A little brown blot suddenly wriggled through a hole in the mosquito screening, plopped to the floor and darted across the reed carpet. Steadman saw it, gave a snort of fear and lunged backward. The blot poised, then hurtled through the air toward him like a stone released from a sling.

It landed on the renegade's shirt. Long, hairy legs propelled it toward his throat. With a scream Steadman clawed his hand down, knocked it to the floor. With trembling fingers he lowered the automatic and sent three shots thundering into the floorboards.

One of the slugs hit. The brown blot jerked spasmodically, curled up and lay still.

"In God's name," Steadman cried, "what was that?"

Doyle, who had watched the split-second drama with narrowed eyes, shrugged.

"Jumping spider," he said quietly. "The place is full of them."

"Jumping spider?" Sweat stood out on the renegade's face. "Poisonous?"

The operator nodded. "Deadly."

"Why in blazes don't you get rid of 'em?"

A smile crossed Doyle's lips. "If you can suggest a method," he said, "I'm sure the company would be obliged. They live under water, you know, raise their young there, and during the rainy season come up in droves. They've got a bite like a .45 slug."

STILL trembling, Steadman ground his heel on the dead spider. Then he hitched his trousers and moved into the inner room.

A few minutes later Doyle heard him snoring evenly.

The operator stared out at the gathering darkness and the falling rain, cursed his helplessness savagely. Stuart dead! Good old Stuart who had been his friend and sole companion for two years!

If Steadman succeeded in finding the Kallukai image, it wouldn't take a military expert to prophesy what would happen. For months the river Kenyahs had been restless, brooding under the Dutch law that kept them from hunting heads. They hated these relay stations. They hated the white men who operated them. And the image was a hair-suspended guarantee of peace and friendship.

Quietly Doyle went to work. He had been a prisoner under similar conditions before. Once when a wire-repairing expedition had led him far upriver a wandering band of Punans had taken him captive and lashed him upside-down to a bamboo shaft close to shore. They had left him to the crocodiles, but Doyle had managed to work himself free.

Now he strained at his bonds with experienced maneuvers. Steadman had done his work well; the more he moved, the deeper the lashings bit into the skin. And then he lifted himself tentatively upward, and his lips lifted in a smile.

The fan-back chair was old. The arm supports and back rest were loose in their sockets. Five seconds later Doyle stood free on the veranda with the chair dismantled behind him. He slipped across to the veranda door, opened it stealthily and slipped into the gloom.

Halfway across the clearing he stopped to listen. No sound came from the inner room of the station. He pushed into the dense bush.

He was in pitch blackness now, an impenetrable roof of foliage hiding the vague light of the sky. As he advanced along a faint trail a hundred mad thoughts whirled in his brain.

It would be an easy matter to slip down to the little jetty, jump into a dugout and paddle down the Mahakam to safety. Once at Munpore, the next telegraph station along the line, he could wire the coast and get the police.

But if he did that he would be playing into Steadman's hands. The renegade would find the image, get the emeralds and escape. And within twenty-four hours the district would be an ignited powder-box.

He could go to Kota Noh's kampong, demand native aid to capture an evil white Tuan who was wanted for murder by the soldier-sahibs downriver. But such a move might be futile. Kota Noh had grown increasingly sullen of late, and it was likely he would refuse his request.

The jungle pressed thick and close about Doyle. Damp rot assailed his nostrils. Rain sifted through the trees.

Far off a prowling cat coughed as it made its kill.

For half an hour Doyle pushed his way forward. Vines, long dangling creepers with razor edges, tore at his clothing, drew blood on his arms. Leeches, cold and blood-sucking, crawled under his puttees.

Then abruptly the foliage opened before him, and he stood in a small glade. Slowly he advanced across the open space, through the *lalang* grass to the center where a tall shadow loomed before him. Above, the clouds opened slightly, and the shadow resolved itself into a small totem post, grotesquely marked with Dyak carving. The post was mounted on a low wooden platform. Two upright bamboo poles on either side supported a protecting roof of nipa-thatch.

"Insignificant-looking thing, aren't you?" Doyle muttered. "But you mean a lot to these Kenyahs, and if anything happened to you, it would be just too bad for the white settlers. I wonder if the emeralds are really inside."

He knew they were. The Kenyahs had borrowed their burial customs from the Saputans, and the Saputans had taken theirs from the Pennihings. Always, when a man of importance died, his body was buried in a living tree, his life treasures with him. In this case the monument had been made even more lasting, carved into an animistic image.

Doyle reached his hand toward the wooden post. The thought had come to him that he might lift it from its mounting and hide it somewhere in the jungle. Such a move at least would thwart Steadman's plans for a time.

HIS hand touched something soft, silky. Quick as a flash a little furry object sidled out from under the thatch and darted down one of the bamboo poles.

Doyle jerked his arm back. Far back in a corner of his brain something clicked like a final slot in a puzzle. He stood there, staring into the darkness. A dry laugh came to his lips.

After that he moved quickly and deliberately. Striding across the little glade to a small Seraya tree, he braced himself and began to climb. He fought his way to the top branches, felt about him.

Scowling, he took a match from his pocket, lit it and searched again. This time he found them, two thin black strands that stretched on and beyond in either direction, mounted to the trees by heavy white insulators. Telegraph wires connecting Bandjermasin with Tandjong-Selor—the west coast with the east!

He leaned far out, grasped the two insulators, twisted them free. Cutting the wires with his pocket-knife, he trailed them down the tree and returned with them to the totem post.

For several minutes he bent on hands and knees, working furiously. When he stood up, it was to gaze at the totem with new satisfaction.

He made a quick survey to be sure he had left no trace of his presence, hid the wires well in the *lalang* grass, then retraced his steps along the jungle trail. Half an hour later he was back on the station verandah. Steadman's snores still came from the inner room. The temptation to rush in and fight it out with the renegade, hand to hand, swept over Doyle but caution made him resist it. Steadman had confiscated every weapon in the shack, including the kitchen knives, and stacked them beneath the bunk on which he slept. The odds would be terrifically against him.

Quietly Doyle crept across the room to the instrument desk. He slid into the chair, frowned down upon the sounder, switches and key. If only the circuits weren't broken!

REACHING over, he opened the switch to the east wire, bent down and lifted a small panel from the floor. Exposed in the aperture were the twin wet-batteries used to relay the weak signals from the post. Cautiously Doyle unscrewed the binding posts, changed the connections, placing the batteries directly into the east circuit. He knew that the wires were dead either way so he didn't take a chance on trying them. The noise might awaken Steadman.

Cautiously he made his way back to the verandah.

He lowered himself into the chair, slipped his untied bindings into position and pushed the back-rest and arm-supports into their respective slots. Quietly he closed his eyes, and eventually he slept.

Morning came. From a leaden sky the rain still poured, turning the clearing before the station into a pool of mud and water.

After forcing Doyle to make his breakfast, Steadman slid a cigarette between his lips and snarled:

"All right, talk up. How far is it to that damned emerald post?"

"About half an hour's march east." Doyle said. "Probably longer in this weather."

Profanity welled to Steadman's lips. "Half an hour, eh?" he snarled. "Well, I'm not trekking that far in this muck. There's plenty of time. We'll wait 'til the rain stops."

He turned and strode into the room where the guns were. A second later a hoarse bellow of fear, followed by a stream of profanity, burst from the room. Two pistol shots followed in quick succession.

Doyle leaped across the room, stopped short to find himself staring into the bore of the automatic. Steadman, leaning weakly against the bunk, divided his gaze between the operator and an inanimate brown smear on the floor.

It took the renegade a full minute to find his voice.

"Damned crawlin' worms," he snarled. "Another of your blasted jumping spiders."

Doyle relaxed, his eyes became calculating. "I told you the place was full of them," he said. "But they're not as bad here as they are at Munpore. A year ago an operator there was bitten, and he died in the worst sort of agony."

With shaking fingers the renegade lit another cigarette and exhaled a streamer of smoke.

"I'm gettin' out of here," he said, "rain or no rain. This place gives me the creeps. Turn around and walk out that door slow. You're takin' me to the Kallukai image."

Rain streaming from the brim of his helmet, Doyle plodded along the jungle trail toward the glade with the fateful image.

Five feet behind him, revolver still leveled, Steadman followed unsteadily, breathing hard from the exertion. At intervals he ordered the operator to halt while he wiped the perspiration from his neck and cursed the Borneo weather.

"If I find that you're leadin' me wrong," he told Doyle. "I'll shoot first and ask questions afterward."

Lips tight, Doyle said nothing, went on slowly. Once he reached out, plucked something from the branch of a near tree. Quickly his fingers rolled it back and forth, and molded it into the shape he wanted.

The jungle thinned, the ground grew higher, and the glade opened before them. For one short instant Steadman stood in his tracks, staring at the object in the center—the totem post with its protecting roof of nipa. Then he gave a hoarse cry and pulled a camp axe from his belt.

"Got it!" he cried. "It's taken one long year, but I've got it!"

He lurched forward, yet even in his excitement he kept the revolver in instant readiness, kept Doyle in front of him. Ten steps from the totem he stopped short as Steadman waved him back.

"Right where you are," Steadman said. "This is my job, and I don't need any help. Keep your distance."

For a moment then the renegade's eyes turned to linger gloatingly on the image, then, belt axe upraised, he moved under the nipa roof.

Once Steadman's back was turned Doyle acted.

The operator snapped his arm back, poised something in his fingers and threw straight in a short quick throw. Simultaneously he yelled:

"Steadman! Look! On your arm!"

Steadman whirled. His eyes caught the furry object clinging to the sleeve of his shirt, and his eyes bulged in terror. His right hand lashed up, slapped wildly to brush the thing away. As he did so his sweaty palm struck the face of the totem image. An agonizing scream of pain burst from his lips. He jerked rigid, stumbled back like a man who had been shot.

Flat upon the ground Steadman fell. "The spider!" he gasped. "It —it bit me!"

The moment had come. Doyle swung into action. He threw himself across the intervening space, tried to jerk the revolver from the renegade's hand. Panic-stricken, Steadman ground his fist into the operator's face with blind fury. They rolled over. An upraised knee caught Doyle hard in the abdomen, sent a wave of nausea surging through him. He answered blow for blow. The renegade clubbed the butt of the revolver on Doyle's head, screamed profanity as he tried to free the grip. There was power and speed in Steadman's gorilla arms and he was using them with driving ferocity.

But Doyle had one trick left, a trick taught him by the Kenyahs of Potah Noh's kampong in the days when they were friendly. He worked himself back, seized the renegade's left foot and for an instant left his guard temptingly open.

With a bellow Steadman reared upward. Quick as a flash, using every ounce of strength he possessed, Doyle twisted the foot hard, whipped his own body sideward and dealt Steadman a short hammer blow back of the ear.

The renegade's sudden violent exertion plus the double thrusts at two vital spots had its effect. Steadman gave a short cry and slumped back unconscious.

AN hour later, back on the verandah of the telegraph station, Doyle, spic and span again in clean whites, packed his pipe and surveyed his captive quietly. It was Steadman now who sat in the fan-back chair, arms and ankles tightly bound. But Doyle had taken the precaution of nailing the arm rests and back support into position.

Steadman seemed not to realize he was a prisoner. He stared wide-eyed at his left arm, lips moving spasmodically. "I'm dying!" he moaned.

Doyle smiled. "Nothing of the sort," he said. "Outside of that hen's egg on your forehead you're in perfect health. You won't even have that by the time the police arrive here to take you back to Samarinda.

(Concluded on page 68)

something that seemed to rush through his fingers. Instinctively, miraculously, his hands tightened as his brain responded to the feel of that ripping, skin-tearing thing— the rope!

His body instead of completing the full arc of that tremendous throw, stopped short in the middle of it with a sickening jerk. The shortened rope, in that one horrible uncertain instant, collected all of his own strength and all of the immense strength that Corbin had put into that one throw.

The entire force of both men rushed in one direction along the rope—toward Kirkland.

CORBIN'S body rose from the ground as though jerked up by an invisible power, the noose tight about his neck. In the next instant, as his body catapulted toward Kirkland who rolled himself clear by scarcely a foot, his feet began to move madly beneath him in an instinctive effort to give slack to the rope. But so powerful and quick was the force that had been put into play, and so powerful was his own instinctive response to it, that he overran.

Again the rope was fire in Kirkland's hands, tearing away the skin. With all his remaining strength he clung to it. There was a last horrible jerk, different from the last, seeming to come from below—then silence, sudden silence, save for Kirkland's struggle to get air into his bursting lungs.

He hung on, racked with pain, feeling all the muscles of his arms, his shoulders, his back, being agonizingly stretched, as though some great weight were pulling upon them. He began to crawl forward, hand over hand, and the weight, as the rope shortened by inches, grew heavier, tore more cruelly at his muscles, slipped a little. His crawling brought him to a narrow but deep cleft. He looked over its edge; he understood.

He let the rope slip through his hands at last. The dark silent shape at the end of it went down scarcely two feet, touched bottom, crumpled shapelessly.

Kirkland lay for a while on his stomach, waiting for his heart to stop its pounding. The shapeless mass on the bottom of the cleft did not move. Kirkland looked down at it feverishly and at last whispered to the surrounding darkness: "Dead. Hanged—hanged by himself. I—I was his gallows."

Later, once more in the *abbe's* cloister, he said: "My work is done. I'm going home," and fell senseless to the floor.

But home he went, after only one night spent in rest. His welcome was a blur. He found himself in a familiar house, in a familiar room, and suddenly Bess Raleigh was in his arms. He had come back from hell to enter heaven.

SPIDER WIRES

(Concluded from page 53)

"You were a fool, Steadman. If you hadn't thought so much of the emeralds in that totem post you would have seen that the thing on your arm wasn't a jumping spider. Not a spider at all, in fact, but an innocent furry cocoon of a hawkmoth that I plucked from a tree during that walk.

"And the sting, Steadman. I told you the jumping spider had a bite like a forty-five slug, but that's quite different than an electric shock. The thing that hit you was the full charge of my relay batteries at the station passing through those telegraph wires you see overhead. I fastened the wires to the totem post, and when your wet hand touched the two of them you made contact, and closed the circuit."

Doyle knocked the ashes from his pipe.

"Simple, isn't it, Steadman," he said. "But where you're going it won't be so simple. And there won't be any wires there—just ropes and a noose."

TIGER ISLAND

Ganler whipped out a revolver, and turned it toward Simms

Haxton's Conflict With the Pearl Poachers of Papua
Takes Place Where No Man Dare Risk Strife—
Fathoms Deep in a Sea Tenanted by Death!

By CARL JACOBI

Author of "Black Passage," "Dead Man's River," etc.

THE island came into sight off the *Morinda's* port bow at six bells in the afternoon watch. Haxton was on the bridge when Fail, the first officer, strode out of the wheelhouse to meet the skipper who had just come up from below.

"There she is, sir," Fail said, eyeing without interest Captain Gan-

ler's drink-reddened face. "Tiger Rock dead ahead. We slide in to the lee of it, same as before, eh?" He awaited confirmation.

Ganler swayed slightly, jerked the glasses to his eyes. He looked a long time, first at the island and the little cove, then at the horizon. Then he nodded.

"Quarter speed. See if you can

find the same anchorage. Haxton!" he answered thickly.

Haxton, a frown on his lean face, turned and came forward. He hadn't liked Ganler's looks the day he came aboard. Now that the skipper was drunk, he liked them even less.

"Haxton—" Ganler rubbed a beefy hand over his unshaven face and spat over the rail, "haul that new-fangled diving gear of yours on deck and get ready for a dive. Move, damn you! Want to get as many shells as we can before dark. Fail will go down with you."

For a moment while he relit his cigar, Haxton studied the skipper coldly. Then he nodded, stepped to the port ladder and headed below.

Somehow this job, which had seemed such a gift from the gods before, had taken on an unsavory aspect. Not to have accepted would have meant another two months on the beach back in Port Moresby, of course. Pearl fishing was pretty much a closed game these days. A diver out of work couldn't be very choosy.

YET he had known what he was up against when he shipped. The *Morinda* was a dirty, rat-infested tramp. Captain Ganler had a blood-temper that came to a head on the slightest provocation. Fail, the first mate who was to help with the diving, was a hard-faced scoundrel. A nondescript Limey for a Second, Eurasian quartermasters, and a lascar-Chinese fo'c'sle didn't improve the picture.

The *Morinda* had come up through the Dampier straits, taking on copra along the New Guinea coast. But Ganler had discovered something that put copra in second place in his mind. He had outlined the situation to Haxton before sailing.

Just south of the line in longitude 142°19′ E., was Tiger Island. A British possession, uninhabited, with a virgin bed of pearl oyster on the south bank. Outside the Queensland boundaries; therefore open fishing.

"But it's sixteen fathoms and too deep for the natives," Ganler had said. "I need another diver. I'll pay you regular rates and passage back. What say?"

Haxton entered his cabin, opened a chest and began to haul out his heavy diving dress. There was a fly in the ointment somewhere, he felt sure. It was odd for one thing, that a ship of such low tonnage carried a wireless in these seas. Yet that proved to be the one favorable item. For Simms, the wireless op, was the only man with whom Haxton had cared to make friends. There was something about his quiet attitude that inspired confidence.

The diving dress laid out on the floor, Haxton stripped and donned a suit of underwear. He was pulling on his heavy socks when the door opened and Simms entered.

"Hello," the op said. "Understand you want me to handle your lines."

He was a tall man. Clear grey eyes were shining pleasantly under the visor of his blue cap. Haxton nodded.

"Help me carry this stuff out on deck. I'm going down right away."

By the time two Malays on the after well-deck had clumsily helped Haxton into his rubber suit, the *Morinda* had reached a point just within the entrance to the cove. Ganler bawled a command. A gong clanged, and the engines came to a dead stop. The anchor chain shot out through the hawse hole. Beyond, Tiger Island presented its silent, palm-fringed shore.

Fail got into his own suit, a cheap piece of shoddy that had seen better days, and the two divers stood waiting orders.

"Now listen." Ganler looked at them with blood-shot eyes. "Fail, you go down first. Three jerks on the line if it's the right spot, and Haxton follows. It's sixteen fathoms, but you're stayin' below until you get a good load. Remember, we're after pearls, not button shells."

The copper helmet was fastened down on the head of the first mate. He went overside in a stream of bubbles. Almost immediately his line jerked three times. Haxton motioned Simms to his side.

"Ganler's drunk, so I'm depending

on you," he warned. "That pump—" "Don't worry," Simms nodded, as he replied quietly. "If any of these swabs interfere, there'll be trouble." Simms helped the Malays place the helmet on Haxton's head. He gave it a quarter turn, locked it into position. The lead belt and heavy breastplate were already secured. Haxton seized his electric lamp. Native handlers lifted him overside onto the sea-ladder.

For an instant he hung there, the water swishing over his head. Then with a jerk, he began to descend. The water changed quickly from blue to pea green. Air gurgled out the exhaust valve in the back of his helmet. He swallowed several times to relieve the heavy sensation in his ears and throat. Down, down he went, while the pressure against his suit slowly increased.

An eternity, and then abruptly his lead shoes struck bottom.

He jerked his life line once, stood motionless, waiting for that first dizzy feeling to pass. He switched on his lamp and looked about him. Five feet away stood Fail. Magnified by the water, the man seemed twice his ordinary height.

Two large wire baskets settled to the bottom, each at the end of a separate line. With his lamp feebly illuminating his movements, Haxton seized the nearest. Fail stepped to his side; they pressed their helmets together, a method of conversing under water.

"You work here. I'll go farther in. Take the big ones, not those that are too young."

Haxton nodded. He looked down at the oyster bed. No yellow or inferior green-edged shells here. They were pure white. Chances were, it would be rich in pearls.

When the basket was filled, Haxton sent it up, watching it disappear like a fat porpoise in the murk. His eyes had grown more accustomed to the depth now, and he stared about him curiously. Funny no one had thought to fish here before. But of course most British islands lay inside the Australian boundaries.

Five more baskets, and Haxton moved slowly in toward the island. He selected shells with an experienced eye. Abruptly he noticed a darker shape lying on the ocean floor some distance ahead. Curious, he hesitated a moment, began to work his way toward it.

An instant later he was standing rigid, staring down. An inert, armored figure lay there, half-hidden in the marine growth. The figure was that of another diver, his life line and airhose lying in a twisted tangle beside him.

Dead! For a moment Haxton's brain refused to act. Then a succession of thoughts assailed him. A dead diver here on the sea floor— The *Morinda* alone had visited these waters in recent months— Then the man was off the *Morinda* on her previous trip. But what had caused the accident, if accident it was?

Unmindful of Fail who had approached and stood glaring at him, Haxton bent down and examined the rubber-clad body. Wide-open eyes stared at him out of the face-plate. But he saw no mark of violence on the suit.

THIRTY seconds, Haxton like a wooden image, remained transfixed to the spot. Then he seized his line, jerked twice in rapid succession.

Immediately the line tightened, and he was jerked upward. He ascended swiftly to the approximate seventy foot level. There he stopped, swayed with the current, while the necessary period of decompression snailed by.

When he finally gained the deck, Haxton waited until his suit was entirely removed before he answered the skipper's sullen glare.

"Ganler," he said, "there's a dead diver down there. Dead and off this ship. I want to know what it means."

Ganler wiped his mouth, clamped his yellow teeth down harder on his greasy pipe. He glared at Haxton sneeringly.

"Keep your shirt on," he snarled. "That diver was a dirty Malay I picked up in Rabaul. Can I help it if his suit was old and rotten? His line busted, that's all."

"His air hose broke?" Haxton repeated unbelievingly.

"Sure."

"Why didn't you tell me about it before?" Haxton's eyes narrowed.

"I had reasons. Main one is, you blokes are a superstitious crowd, and I wasn't takin' any chances of you backin' out."

Haxton pressed his lips together grimly. He turned without another word, and headed for his cabin. Simms followed. There, while the radio operator looked at him with puzzled eyes, Haxton briefly described the situation.

"It might be true, of course," he concluded. "These Malays are careless as hell. But all the same, I don't like it."

"Fail's a blackguard," Simms replied slowly. "Ganler's worse. He keeps me at the wireless every minute I'm awake. Wants a report on every ship in the district. And if you ask me, it's funny a ship carryin' only copra bothers with a wireless. I signed on the day before you did, you know, and only because my last ship was being scrapped by her owners."

HAXTON nodded, finished dressing in silence. He slid into a suit of white drill, then strode across to the locker and took out an automatic.

"You might need this," he said, handing it to Simms. "Won't hurt to have it along at any rate. I'm going up and have a look at our position."

Haxton made his way quickly to the bridge and the deserted charthouse. With a quick glance over his shoulder he bent over the table and examined the chart which lay upon it. Carefully he traced the *Morinda's* course from Port Moresby. Almost directly on the equator a circle in red ink had been drawn around a pinpoint whose marking read: *Tiger Island*. With the aid of dividers Haxton checked the position.

Frowning, he stood up, drew a cigar from his pocket. The island was in the location Ganler had said, British owned and outside of any restricted pearl-fishing ground. Hax-

ton gnawed his lips, went down the ladder and walked aft.

Fail was up now. He had stayed underwater the full time limit, and his face was white and drawn with pain. By the after-hatch, five Malays squatted on the planking, busily opening the shells which had been brought aboard.

Within twenty minutes the bed proved its value. The Malays extracted three pearls, then two more. Ganler pawed over them greedily.

"Smooth, eh?" he said, turning to Haxton. "A fortune just waiting to be taken up. Tomorrow you dive full time. I've had enough of your stalling."

A flush rose to Haxton's face, but he made no reply. A few moments later, he entered the wireless room. Simms was at the transmitter. He looked up at the sound of steps.

"K.P.M. ship off Halmahera," he said. "Reports a bad typhoon there, but it'll miss us of course. What's new?"

"Nothing new." Haxton dropped into a chair and studied his cigar. "There's pearls here, which makes Ganler plenty satisfied. The position is right, according to the chart. Open fishing. And yet that dead diver—"

Simms got up abruptly, paced to the door and closed it.

"Listen," he said. "Couple of minutes ago I was up for'ard, and I heard two of that black gang talking. Those lascars are a bad lot and have a lingo that beats me, but there were a few words in pidgin English that set me to thinking. One of them said something about 'deep-down fellah off when sea fellah come.' Now what does that mean?"

Haxton smoked a moment, shook his head.

"Search me," he replied. "Might mean anything. But maybe we're worrying our heads over nothing at all. See you at mess."

Haxton slept poorly that night. Sultry heat filled his cabin, and at three bells—one-thirty a.m.—he got up and decided to catch a breath of air.

Pajama-clad, he strolled out on the

for'd well deck. The *Morinda* lay under a vault of blackness. Water slapped rhythmically against the sides. Farther off, waves washed against the island's shore.

All at once, the diver noticed that the regulation anchor light was not lighted. Not necessary in these waters, of course, but still a ship without riding lights— Haxton turned. The aft light, fifteen feet lower, was not visible either.

With a scowl he made his way slowly toward the poop. What possible reason could Ganler have for keeping the ship in inky darkness? Cautiously, he paced on past the after main-hatch. Then voices came to his ears, and he saw the skipper standing at the taffrail, a darker shadow in the gloom. Ganler had night glasses to his eyes. He was gazing seaward.

Haxton hugged the shadows and watched. The voices he had heard, began again. They were speaking Malay, and they seemed to come from beyond the ship, from a point low down near the water.

A moment later two lascars came over the rail. They mumbled something to the skipper and shuffled off. Ganler continued his scrutiny of the black sea. From east to west he looked, long and intently. Chuckling softly, he turned and headed for his cabin. He passed within a few feet of Haxton, but the diver made no sound.

When he had gone, Haxton darted up to the rail, and leaned over. Only dark water below. Then a heavier blot in the blackness met his eyes, and he understood quickly.

A bo'sun's chair had been rigged over the rail. The two Malays suspended in it, had stretched a sheet of canvas across the ship's stern. Nailed down, the canvas completely hid the name, *Morinda,* from all outward eyes.

"Blind ship, eh?" Haxton whistled softly. Something definitely was in the wind. But what?

He stood there in silence a long time. A quarter of an hour later when he went to his bunk, he was no nearer an explanation. He stirred restlessly until the change to the morning watch, when he fell into a troubled sleep.

Morning, and Ganler was drunk again. He stayed in his cabin, not appearing until noon. Then he staggered into the mess cabin, whiskey bottle in one hand, faced Haxton, swaying.

"You dive right away, see," he growled. "You go down, and you stay down until I tell you to come up. We can't hang around here forever."

WHILE he waited for the Malays to get his diving dress in readiness, Haxton stood with tight lips, staring out over the water. He was more perplexed now than before. A few moments ago, when he was sure he was not being watched, he had brought out his sextant, always a part of his luggage, and taken the sun. Checking the longtitude with the chronometer, the result tallied with Tiger Island's location on the chart.

As he stood there, Simms approached. The operator was smoking a cigarette in his calm, deliberate fashion.

"I don't like it," he said in a low voice. "Ganler drunk again, and Fail nervous as a floating cork. Have you noticed the skipper keeps steam up all the time? Funny."

Haxton nodded. "I signed on as diver," he said, "and I suppose I'll have to go down, but—"

Abruptly his words died off. He stiffened, rocked backwards as a thought struck him full force. Turning, he ran up the ladder to the bridge and raced into the charthouse. As he had expected, there was a *Pacific Islands Pilot* book there. He whipped through the pages. Five seconds later he was staring stunned at the printed words:

An island named Tiger was reported by Captain Bristow in 1817 to exist in latitude 1°45'S., longitude 142°19'E., but in 1894 information was received from the German Government that no island existed in this position, and that the so-called Tiger Island was probably identical with Matty Island, now known as Wuvulu, which was discovered by Cartaret in 1767, and which lies in latitude 1°46′S., longitude 142°56′E. Matty Island is a German possession, leased recently to the Dutch fisheries at Macassar. It is low, covered with cocoanut palms, about four miles in length in an east and west direction and—

Haxton's teeth came together with a click. He saw it all now. Poaching. These were Dutch fisheries. The chart Ganler had left on the table for him to see was an old one, out of date. The difference in positions was so close, his sextant had failed to show it. Poaching was a criminal action which would be dealt the limit in any court—which would blackball a diver everywhere.

ANOTHER thought came. The Malay diver had been below on the *Morinda's* first visit to the island, when another ship, probably a Dutch patrol craft, had been sighted. Without compunction, Ganler had slashed the Malay's line and raced seaward. The ruthlessness of the skipper's action was like a shock of cold water. Mechanically Haxton dropped the book, left the chart-house, paced onto the boat deck, abaft the bridge. He could hear Ganler aft now, barking commands at Fail who was getting ready to dive.

Haxton clenched his fists, went down the ladder and headed for the skipper.

"Get in that dress of yours," Ganler roared, catching sight of him. "You damn scavenger, what do you think I'm payin' you for?"

Haxton glanced at Fail, who, helmet off, stood waiting.

"I'm not diving," he said. "For you or anyone else."

"Not diving!" Ganler's sweat-stained face crimsoned. "Why you—What do you mean?"

"We're in Dutch grounds," Haxton continued quietly. "This isn't Tiger Island, Ganler. It's Matty Island. Leased fisheries. My papers didn't say anything about poaching."

For an instant the skipper remained silent, eyes slowly closing to crescents. Then with a bellow he lurched forward. His right fist leaped like a mallet, struck Haxton hard in the jaw. He followed with two more lightning thrusts in quick succession. Haxton, taken unawares, staggered and fell.

"Back, damn you!" Ganler whipped out a revolver and turned it toward Simms as the wireless operator charged forward. Haxton slowly rose to his feet.

"You're goin' down, see," Ganler continued, moving the revolver to cover the two of them. "If you don't, there's a bullet lands straight between your eyes. Into that suit, blast you."

Cowed Malays came forward and helped Haxton into his diving dress. Three feet away, Simms looked on with tight lips. Revolver still in one hand, Ganler slammed shut Haxton's face-plate, gave the order to lift him onto the sea-ladder.

Then once more he was descending. Down he went, the current whipping at his air hose.

The water grew darker. Pressure increased against his suit. A school of tropical fish fled before him. He was on the bottom.

Mechanically adjusting his air, Haxton stood motionless, brain in a turmoil. Whichever way he moved, his way was blocked. In a moment Fail and the baskets would be down. He would be forced to continue poaching. Topside, Ganler with his revolver, would be watching Simms' every movement on the line.

The two baskets came down. Fail followed an instant later. The mate-diver motioned to one of the baskets, lips snarling something unheard in his helmet. Haxton made no move.

"Come on," Fail said, stepping forward to press helmets together. "One funny move outa you, and—" He waved his knife threateningly.

Haxton stepped obediently toward the baskets, but halfway, a storm burst within him. He whirled, and touched helmets.

"I don't poach," he said. "Not if I have to stay down here all day. Put that in your pipe and smoke it."

Eyes gleaming through his face-plate as he heard the words, Fail suddenly brought his right hand up through the heavy water, thrust the knife at Haxton. Haxton had clicked on his electric lamp a split-second before. He caught the movement and heaved his body aside. The knife scratched harmlessly off the side of his suit, just below the breastplate. In an instant Fail was lunging for another attack. Haxton clawed downward, seized the weapon hand, and tried to wrench the knife from its grasp. They clinched.

Sixteen fathoms down, they were, ninety-six feet below man's natural element. For each foot of that depth, a thousand pounds of water pressed down on them, almost fifty tons in all. Haxton knew that the nitrogen being forced steadily into his blood would not stand much exertion.

Fail brought his knee upward into Haxton's abdomen, struck twice below the breast plate with brute strength. Their helmets clanked together. Heart laboring, Haxton answered blow for blow.

Suddenly, he realized that as he was fighting here on the ocean floor, so Simms must be battling for his life topside. With that revolver Haxton had given him, the young op would not submit long to Ganler's inquisition. Even then Haxton felt the air falter in his helmet. The pumps—

Again Fail attacked him with the knife. Again Haxton managed to drive the blade off. And then abruptly the first mate leaped to the side.

REACHING up, he seized Haxton's air hose, jerked it down, and went at it with the knife. A vague horror came over Haxton as he saw the movement. He lurched forward, grasped the mate by the shoulders and yanked him backward. Fail made one last attempt. Knife before him, he charged like a striking devil-fish, came at Haxton in a fury. Three feet he moved, no farther. His life-line, trailing slackly from the struggle, caught between his feet. He tripped, fell. Even as his helmet crashed onto the bottom, Haxton saw an accompanying mass of bubbles shoot upward. Fail had fallen with his knife under him. The blade had penetrated the suit.

But Haxton had no time to look

farther. An instant later he felt his line jerk hard, and he was lifted upwards. Swiftly, while he fought to regain his breath, he was taken toward the surface. No decompression period this time. He had not been down long enough, and besides, as he knew, hell must be raging on deck.

Then he was being hauled overside. Malay handlers lifted the helmet from his head. Simms' voice, cold as ice, snapped into his ears.

"Keep away from that gun, Ganler. One step, and I shoot. Look alive there, you black rats. Get that suit off fast. Okay, Haxton, everything under control."

The wireless op stood by the rail, automatic before him. Ten feet away Ganler, the Limey Second Officer, a crowd of lascars crouched like wolves at bay. Two Malays, grinding steadily at the pump, worked only because they were also in line with Simms' weapon.

"You can stop the pumps," Haxton said, his diving dress removed. "Fail is below dead, a hole in his suit. The game's up, Ganler."

"Like hell it is," the skipper said. "Mutiny, eh? Two men seizing the ship against the crew. Well, it can't be done, you damn wharf rat. I'll—"

The captain's own revolver lay two feet before him on the deck; Simms apparently had ordered him to drop it when he brought the automatic into play. Ganler shot his right foot forward, kicked the weapon within his reach, lunged down. On his knees he pumped three shots at Simms, urged his men on.

Simms fired twice. A lascar toppled and fell. The Limey second mate clawed at his chest, screamed.

"On the bridge!" Haxton yelled. "We can't hold 'em here." He spun around as he spoke, slammed a wild blow at one of the Malays who had been forced to haul him. Then with the pack at their heels, the two men raced for the ladder.

On the bridge, Haxton leaped to the wheel-house, jerked down a rifle which was mounted on the inside wall. A cartridge belt hung below it.

They were safe for an instant. Simms crouched at the break of the bridge and fired at every head that mounted the ladder. Haxton edged carefully around the wheel-house, searching the well-deck for Ganler. He knew with grim clarity that it was only a question of time before it would be all over. Two against that rabid pack. The odds were too great.

Shots hammered into the deckhouses. Ganler evidently had lost no time in dealing out guns. A bullet splintered the glass by Haxton's head. Below, on the deck a figure moved into his vision. He fired deliberately, missed, fired again. The man fell.

SIMMS' warning shout whirled him about. Two lascars had climbed the port ladder. In front of them, lumbering toward him, face twisted in fury, came Ganler.

Haxton's rifle was ripped from his hands. Two iron fists pounded into his face. The skipper was fighting like an enraged tiger. Haxton, breathing hard, delivered blow after blow.

And then as he stood there swinging his arms, a hollow voice rang out over the water.

"*Morinda* ahoy! Stop firing. Stand by for boarding."

A heavy club came down on Haxton's head a split-second later. Ganler, the ship, whirled out in a circle of colored lights. He felt himself falling down—down into a pit of darkness.

There were two men in Haxton's cabin when he finally opened his eyes. One of those men was Simms, left arm swathed in bandages, a heavy welt over one eye. The other was unfamiliar, a short, heavy-set man in a white uniform with gold braid on his cap.

"How are you feeling?" Simms asked, smiling.

Haxton closed his eyes a moment, then fought to a sitting position. His head still throbbed dully.

"Feel elegant," he said sarcastically. "What happened? Who—?"

"Meet Captain Schaff of the ship, *Wilhelmina*. That's a Dutch patrol boat, in case you haven't heard. He came up here just in time, paid us a visit, much to Ganler's regret. Ganler's below in irons now."

Haxton swallowed hard. "But how come?" he asked slowly. "I don't understand—"

"*Mynheer* Simms talked with us by wireless last night," Captain Schaff answered. "He reported his suspicions of the *Morinda* and his position. These are Dutch waters, very valuable, and poaching is not tolerated. We've sighted Ganler here before, but he's always managed to slip through our fingers. You are to be congratulated—"

"Never mind that," Simms cut in. "Feel strong enough to go out on deck, Haxton? Then after we've had a good feed, we'll head this packet back to port."

And Haxton with a smile nodded his agreement.

DEAD MAN'S RIVER

The Malay Forest Holds a Death Trap for a Hunter of Priceless Orchids!

By
CARL JACOBI
Author of "Death Rides the Plateau," "Black Passage," etc.

Fletcher rocked backward—swung a rope high above him

T HE reward poster was fastened to the *nipa*-thatch wall of the rest hut by four bamboo splinters. The printed words were the same Hatfield had seen at Maraba'han, at Bandjermasin, and at Samarinda, damning words which had followed him relentlessly for more than a year.

WANTED FOR MURDER!
JAMES HATFIELD
Height: six feet. Hair: dark. Eyes: brown. Features: sharp. Known to speak Malay fluently. Reported to be living with Tabuyan tribes in upper Barito country.
For the arrest of this man, or information given at any military outpost leading to his arrest and conviction, the Borneo Government of the Royal Netherlands East Indies will pay a reward of 1,000 guilders.

Hatfield read the poster a second time while his lips tightened slowly. So they were looking for him even this far inland, were they? Still warning each resident official, each *controlleur* to sleep with one eye open and a pistol at his side. James Hatfield. From east to west coast his name had swept to spread a wave of fear and indignation. A white man gone native who used head-hunting Dyaks to fight law and order for his own profit.

His fists clenched. For a year he had stood it, a year of hypocrisy, of constant pursuit, of nerve grinding caution, always with the knowledge that he was a wanted man with a price on his head. They were persistent, these Dutchmen.

And now once again he stood on the brink of capture. The two men with whom he was to spend the night were bloodhounds on his trail. They were hunting him, yet—ironically—they didn't know he was the object of their search.

He rolled up the neck-protecting *puggree* cloth that hung down from his sun helmet and moved back to the fire. On three sides the jungle loomed, a black, impenetrable wall.

Mason, a young man with light blue eyes and sandy hair, was preparing the evening meal. Three feet away Gail Fletcher leaned against the bole of a Gaharu tree, idly smoking a whitish cheroot. He was big, bullet-headed, with a ragged mustache.

Hatfield had come upon the two of them an hour ago when, coming upriver in his dugout, he had decided to lay over at this, the last incountry rest hut. It was incidental, of course, that the rest hut had been taken over by a colony of elephant ants, forcing them to camp in the open.

"My name is Gage," Hatfield had lied cautiously. "I'm a trader."

The explanation had been accepted as it had been accepted before whenever he found it necessary to come into contact with white men. As for his physical appearance he had no fear about that. The printed description of him was brief, and a man changed a lot after a year in the bush.

He ate his food quietly. He was a lean man with a lean face and a powerful, determined jaw. High-topped, river-travel tennis shoes dressed his feet. Under his linen coat was a canvas holster and a light Webley revolver. A twist of the wrist, and that weapon could appear like magic—to split a five-grain quinine tin at twenty yards. More than once in the past Hatfield had lengthened his span of life by his shooting ability. But he could use his fists too, and it was fists he chose when his opponent was a human being.

Wary and tense, he watched the two men across the fire. Not until darkness closed in on them did Mason reveal the reason for his and Fletcher's presence. He got up then, walked to the reward poster and leveled a forefinger at it.

"I'm looking for that man," he said abruptly in a dry, bitter voice. "I'm going to comb all Borneo until I find him."

Hatfield started. He spilled tobacco from the pipe he was about to light, shot a swift glance upward.

"It may take two years," Mason continued, "but I'm going to find him. And when I do—" His teeth clicked together significantly.

Hatfield coughed. "Blood money, eh?" he said. "I imagine a lot of people would like to get their hands on that reward."

Mason shook his head. "I want this man, Hatfield, because of one crime he committed a year ago. In Bandjermasin, in the evil quarter, he killed a man. The man was John Mason—my brother."

SILENCE followed the statement. Fletcher refilled his tin cup from the coffee pot on the fire.

"Your brother?" repeated Hatfield slowly.

Mason nodded. "Hatfield killed him in cold blood," he said. "Then he fled into the jungle. I'm going to bring him back and make him pay."

For a long interval there was no sound save the queer *tok tok tok* of a distant Skipping-On-The-Ice bird. Off somewhere a *macaque* chattered loudly. Fletcher hooked his arms around one knee and smiled.

"We'll find him all right," he said. "Up to now no one's had the nerve to hunt him out. Even the native police are afraid."

The fire died. An hour snailed by. At length Fletcher unrolled his blanket, mumbled a terse good night and sprawled full length. A moment later Mason unlaced his mosquito boots and followed suit.

Alone by the darkening embers Hatfield sat scowling into space. Fate was ironic at times. The situation into which he had blundered was one that probably would not happen again in a hundred years. He, Hatfield, sharing camp with Clark Mason, brother of John Mason, the man who had been murdered.

His nails dug into his palms. For the first time in a year he wanted to tell again the whole story. He wanted to tell Mason that although his name was Hatfield, he was not a criminal. He wanted to explain that the murder of John Mason had been pinned on him whereas he was absolutely innocent. Kill John Mason? The man had been his friend.

BUT evidence was evidence, and without an alibi he had done the only thing possible. He had hacked his way out of the flimsy Bandjermasin jail and fled into the jungle. It sounded cowardly, but with all the cards stacked against him it was the only logical trail to take. Dutch law acts fast. Give the real murderer six weeks perhaps, and he might slip up and reveal himself.

The real murderer hadn't slipped. The six weeks dragged into two months, into a year. Hatfield fought his way from village to village, hoping to hear news that might filter that far inland. He heard news but not the kind he wanted.

Other crimes had been committed and blamed against him. His name now played an important part in military despatches, in mouth-to-mouth rumor. He was wanted for boarding and looting the old river scow, *Groningen*, assisted by savage Dyaks who supposedly followed his command; for running guns to and inciting a mutiny amongst the Siang tribes of the Upper Laung. And meanwhile the real murderer continued these operations, knowing he was safe in Hatfield's accepted guilt.

He looked across at the sleeping figure of Clark Mason and shook his head. No, it would do no good to tell all that. No one had believed him before. He couldn't expect them to believe now. He must go on hunting the man who stood between him and freedom. He smiled grimly. Quietly he lay back, closed his eyes and slept.

Morning, and the three headed up-river together.

The arrangement was inevitable, of course. White men, when they pass the last outpost, accept chance companionship without question. For Hatfield to suggest going alone would have aroused suspicion. Eyes hard, he paddled his dugout behind the *prahu* of Fletcher and Mason.

A blazing sun beat down upon them. The shores of the silt-heavy Barito were thick walls of poisonous green, out of which crept a sickly-sweet smell of decay and parasitical growth. Crocodiles drifted by.

All day with but two short stops they kept going. Nightfall found them at Mengkatib, a Maanyan *kampong*. Mason met the aged *kapala* at the log landing, spoke greetings and began to ask questions in Malay.

"We hunt a man named Hatfield. You know of whom I speak?"

The eyes of the Dyak chief glittered. "*Aiii, Tuan,*" he said. "It is an evil name. We have heard."

"Have you seen the man? Has he stopped at your village?"

"No, *Tuan*. The gods have been good. But—"

"Well?"

"But perhaps our brothers at Kampong Buntok three days upstream can tell you more."

They were given a hut at the far end of the clearing. Moving in, the three white men set about once again to prepare the evening meal. The meal over, Fletcher pulled a bottle of Irish whiskey from his knapsack, bit out the cork and began to drain its contents. Steadily he drank, while his voice grew thicker and a gleam entered his eyes. Abruptly he swung about to face Mason.

"You hired me as a guide," he said huskily, "because you were told I

know the country better than anyone else. But you didn't tell your
real reason for coming here."

Mason shrugged. "You're drunk,"
he said quietly.

A guttural l a u g h welled to
Fletcher's lips. "Of course," he
leered, "you're hunting the man who
killed your brother. That's what
you say. You fool, don't you think
I know there's another reason?"

Twisting around slowly, Mason
glared at him. "Just what do you
mean?"

"What do I mean? I mean John
Mason was knifed for a paper he carried in his pocket. A paper giving
the name and location of a big swamp
somewhere deep in the interior.
Mason was a—a—what do you call
it—an orchidologist—a flower-hunter.
He hired a string of natives to comb
the jungle with him and find rare
orchids. He shipped and sold those
orchids to the Botanical Gardens in
Batavia. Right, isn't it?"

MASON opened his mouth to
speak, snapped it shut again.
And Fletcher continued:

"I know that one of those natives
went farther than the others, came
back with an orchid that was different. Grey color, touching on black.
The Batavia people said it was a new
species of moth orchid and they'd
pay a thousand dollars for every one
like it they could get."

He lolled his head sideways. "That
is why Hatfield murdered your
brother," he drawled. "And that's
why you're here. You want to locate that swamp before anyone else
does. There's a fortune there for the
taking."

Frowning, Mason got up, stepped
across to the drunken man, seized
him by the shoulder. "I hired you as
a guide," he said. "I'll trouble you to
mind your own business."

After that Hatfield lit his pipe and
smoked. Rousing himself, he left his
two companions and strolled out into
the kampong clearing. He stood for
a moment watching a group of Dyaks
as they sat in a huddled group, drinking native tuak. Idly he surveyed
the hideous totem images before the

long-house. Then he paced on to the
river shore and stood scowling over
the black water.

The odds were piling up against
him. He hadn't thought anyone knew
about that paper. Now, he realized,
it was the motive behind the murder,
and possession of it added just another item to his apparent guilt. He
could throw it away, of course. But
John Mason had given it to him the
night before he was killed, given it
to him in a sealed envelope.

"I'm asking you to take care of
this for a day or so, old man," John
had said. "I've got an idea I'm being followed, and if anything should
happen to me, I want you to see
that this reaches my relatives."

Hatfield's jaw set hard. If the matter hadn't been so damned ironic, it
would be almost funny. He was
honor bound to deliver that envelope.
Yet if he did so, it would mean
writing his own jail ticket.

They continued upriver. At each
kampong the mockery was repeated.
Mason asked questions. The answers
he received were always the same.
The natives had seen no one.

Not until the mouth of the Lahei
River was reached was the monotony
broken. But here, like a festering
gunshot wound, the situation came
to a crisis.

Hatfield left camp to stalk a leopard whose spoor he discovered at the
water's edge. Returning after following a blind trail, he saw Fletcher advancing to meet him. Face twisted
in a grin of triumph, the guide
stopped short and extended his hand.
"This yours?" he asked.

Hatfield glanced at the open palm
and felt a cold ripple pass up his
spine. The hand held a worn money
wallet. *His* wallet which must have
dropped from his pocket. The top
flap was unfolded, and across the surface in faded lettering was the name:

JAMES HATFIELD

"Gage, eh?" Fletcher sneered. "And
you're a trader. Well, ain't that
nice."

Five feet away Clark Mason rose
to his feet slowly.

Hatfield gnawed his upper lip.

"Yes, I'm Hatfield," he said quietly. "But I had nothing to do with those crimes attributed to my name. I didn't kill Mason. He was my—"

With a quick movement Fletcher reached into his pocket, whipped out a three-foot length of rope.

"I'm takin' you back to Bandjermasin," he snarled. "Put out your hands."

Hatfield stood rigid. A muscle began to jerk perceptibly, low on his left c h e e k. Suddenly Fletcher reached forward, sent a clenched fist hard into the wanted man's jaw.

For an instant Hatfield made no return. Then, with the blind instinct of a man trapped, he swung into action. In quick succession he leveled a left, a right, and another right to the guide's chest. Fletcher rocked backward, belched profanity. Whipping the rope high above him, he slashed it downward.

The rope struck. A zigzag, blood-rimmed streak leaped across Hatfield's brow. As he swayed, a cruel kick lashed hard into his groin. He lowered his head and bored in, striking straight clean blows with machine-gun rapidity.

But it lasted only a moment. Fletcher heeled sideways, raised the rope a second time. Before he could bring it down, Hatfield slammed out his right fist with every ounce of strength he possessed. The guide's head jerked backward. He gave a hollow cry, went down and lay still.

And then as momentary quiet clamped down on the camp again, a voice from behind said slowly:

"Turn around and raise your hands."

Hatfield turned around. He raised his hands. Before him Clark Mason stood, gripping a revolver.

"If you move an inch," Mason said, "I'll kill you!"

Hot words swelled to Hatfield's throat, choking him. He licked his lips, swallowed hard. Then his shoulders fell in defeat, and he stood silent while Mason whipped out a pair of handcuffs and snapped them over his wrists.

Long after his two captors had gone to sleep that night Hatfield sat by the dying camp fire, brain in a turmoil. He was unbound. Only the manacles held him prisoner. But his Webley had been taken from him, and he knew that those steel bracelets were more effective than the strongest cage. A man couldn't escape into the jungle with those on. He would die before he could reach the next *kampong*, a victim of the first wild animal that blocked his path. As for the river, Fletcher had tied the mooring lines of the *prahu* and the dugout to his leg. The slightest move in that direction would awaken him.

Hatfield dug his tennis shoes into the matted *lalang* grass, smiled bitterly. After a year's fight he was back right where he had started. He would be returned to receive full penalty of the law. Mason would testify against him. And Fletcher—

He scowled as he thought about Fletcher. There was something queer about the man. After their struggle a few hours ago he had become silent and sullen. His every action was that of a man holding his guns, waiting for something before he chooses to act.

ACROSS the fire the guide stirred in his sleep and rolled. His dirty shirt was torn at the sleeve, and the movement exposed his left arm to the elbow. Hatfield glanced down absently, started, then stared with widening eyes.

The sweaty flesh gleamed dully in the half light. Four inches above the wrist was a bluish-black design—a tatooed likeness of a coiled cobra, with the head upraised as if about to strike.

Memory cut into Hatfield's brain like a knife thrust. An exclamation jerked to his lips. He silenced it, fought for control. Again he looked at that arm, and his teeth ground together savagely.

Two minutes later as calmness gradually returned, he drew from his pocket the envelope John Mason had entrusted in his care. For a moment he stared down at its blank, unaddressed surface. Then, careful not to injure the flap, he opened it and extracted two pieces of folded paper. The first sheet he saw at a glance was a technical description of the new orchid, details as how it could be differentiated from others. The second sheet contained the following:

Go up Barito River to Lahei tributary. Follow Lahei to headwaters. On right bank is my trail mark, a twenty foot bamboo mast stuck in river shore, to the top of which is fastened an old Dyak *prahu* paddle. Orchid swamp lies in a N.N.E. direction from here. Plan to arrive by middle of rainy season.

As Hatfield finished reading a frown crossed his lean face. Again he went over the message, mouthing each word carefully. At the end of a second reading he nodded and got to his feet, smiling grimly. John Mason, it was evident, had been a clever man.

Returning the papers to the envelope he resealed the flap and stored it back in his pocket. He glanced across the camp cautiously, stole slowly forward to Fletcher's side. He knelt there, staring down at the sleeping man. Then with a quick movement he reached in the guide's pocket, searched a moment, and drew out a small but accurate compass. He transferred the compass to his own pocket, returned to his place by the fire.

FOR another hour, he sat thinking. Morning, he knew, would bring the outburst. Even now Fletcher probably was dreaming of the cleverness that was his. But until morning there was nothing more that could be done. Hatfield had played his card.

Crimson sunlight filtered through the giant *taphangs* to light the camp in the glow of a new day. The call of a hornbill woke Hatfield, sent him stumbling to his feet. He looked around. By the blackened fire Mason still lay prone. At the river shore Fletcher was bending over the dugout. The guide turned.

"Finished your beauty sleep, eh?" he jeered. "Well, Mister Hatfield, I'm leaving now. Mason can take you back to Bandjermasin or any

place he damn well pleases. But before I go, I'll trouble you for something—that paper giving the location of the orchid swamp."

Feet planted wide apart, Hatfield sucked in his breath sharply. Mason had awakened, was staring upward with sleep-heavy eyes. With a jerk Fletcher got his revolver out of its holster, covered the two men.

"Hand it across!" he snarled.

"What makes you think there is such a paper?" Hatfield parried, stalling for time. "Even if John Mason did find a new orchid, wouldn't it be logical—"

"I'm not here to talk logic," Fletcher spat. "I know there is such a paper, and I know you've got it. You fool, do you think I went to the trouble of putting John Mason out of the way for nothing? Mason realized the information was too valuable to keep in his head. He didn't want those orchids to be lost for good in case anything happened to him. If he hadn't tricked me and passed the paper on to you, I'd have had it a year ago. I'll give you just five seconds to produce it."

It was Mason who acted then. Eyes wide, lips quivering, he leaped to his feet. With a hoarse yell he lunged forward.

"You!" he cried. "You killed my brother! You damned murdering swine—"

He crashed across the intervening space and clawed for Fletcher's throat. With an easy sweep of one arm the big renegade threw him off.

"Out of my way, Baby-face, or I'll drill you."

If Mason heard, the words brought no meaning to his enraged brain. He yanked his own revolver from his pocket, jerked it upward.

Leaping sideways, Fletcher threw himself out of range. He swiveled on his left foot, swept his fist forward. Then before the boy could retaliate he twisted his gun to aim and yanked the trigger.

A deafening report, and for a split second Mason stood there, lips parted, a look of surprise in his eyes. Slowly his hand came up to clench a darkening spot on his shoulder.

He gave a low sob, slumped forward and fell.

"All right," Fletcher whipped about to face Hatfield, "that paper. Quick, damn you."

Like a man in an opium stupor Hatfield seemed to hear the words from far off. He drew forth the envelope, handed it to Fletcher, stood in mute silence while the guide ripped it open with one hand and glanced at its contents.

"Fine!" Fletcher grinned triumphantly. "Now I'll just fix things so you won't be anxious to follow me."

He did his "fixing" with systematic thoroughness. Still covering Hatfield, he unfastened the moorings of the *prahu,* gave it a push, let it drift downstream. Into the remaining dugout—Hatfield's dugout—he dumped as much of the food and supplies as he could safely carry. The rest he tied loosely with a length of rope, weighted with a stone and sank into the river. As a final gesture he took Mason's revolver.

"That'll hold you for a while," he said, climbing into the dugout. "If you get hungry, you can walk to the coast. It's only a few hundred miles."

He dipped the paddle, and the dugout shot into the current. For twenty yards it followed the broad Barito. Then, turning, it nosed into the mouth of the Lahei tributary, moved rapidly up this smaller stream and presently was lost to sight.

Hatfield moved then. He bent down over the unconscious form of Clark Mason, lifted the younger man to a sitting position. He forced water from his canteen down Mason's throat, unbuttoned his shirt and gave the wound a quick survey.

A scowl came to h i s lips. Fletcher's bullet had struck well into the shoulder, close to the throat. A round hole was there from which blood was running freely.

Mason opened his eyes, tried to speak.

"Take it easy, son," Hatfield said. "You'll be all right."

His words failed to disguise his fears. It was a clean wound, but any wound was deceptive in the tropics. Food, supplies, both boats gone, and no weapons with which to obtain game. Nor could he expect help from the Dyaks. This was Tabuyan country, and he had been here before. There wasn't a native *kampong* within two days travel either direction.

"And I can't leave the kid while I get help," Hatfield muttered to himself. "The first cat that came along would make a meal out of him."

But his eyes failed to show defeat. A year he had spent in these jungles, evading one of the most efficient man-hunting organizations in the Eastern Circle—the Royal Netherlands Indies Army—evading them while he hunted the man he now knew to be Fletcher. He had learned to take care of himself in the bush, armed with only the raw materials Nature supplied.

FROM the medicine kit Fletcher had overlooked, Hatfield took out a bottle of iodine and a bottle of hydrogen peroxide. He applied both to the wound, bound it skillfully with clean bandages. Then, making Mason as comfortable as possible, he took out his belt ax and paced into the jungle.

He worked hard the rest of the day. Late afternoon saw a strange-looking craft floating before the camp at the river shore. Outwardly it resembled the *nipa* platforms upon which the Dyaks build their devil-devil houses. But actually it was of much stouter construction, a raft bound together with tough rattan, capable of supporting two men.

"All set, old man?" Hatfield turned to Mason. "This thing may not look exactly like a K.P.M. ship, but if it holds together, it's going to carry us on a little jaunt farther up the Barito."

He helped the younger man to his feet and carried him onto the raft.

"We're going upstream," Hatfield repeated. "We could head for the coast, of course. But I've got an appointment farther inland, and I always keep my appointments."

Paddling along steadily Fletcher

continued up the L a h e i River. The farther he penetrated incountry from the Barito, the narrower the tributary became. Now it was but a winding creek with the banks pressing close and the overbrush forming a tesselated ceiling through which the sun filtered in a shadowy half-glow.

The dense jungle shores teemed with animal life. Argus pheasants skuttled off as the dugout snaked past. Orang-utans leered down at him from the maze above. Once by a narrow margin and a quick twist of the paddle he escaped the coils of a giant python which depended vine-like from an overhanging branch.

* * * * *

The tributary wound back and forth. Long ago Fletcher had sought his compass and cursed violently when he found it was gone. Yet the loss seemed a minor one. He had only to keep to the Lahei, and so far the turbid stream had continued without fork or interruption.

He increased his pace. The monsoon wasn't far off, and he wanted to reach his destination and find the orchids before the rains set in. After that he could lay over somewhere, continue by easy stages to the coast.

And as the miles slid by he grinned triumphantly. It had been a clever move, his hiring out as guide for Mason. It had been clever too, the manner in which he had used Hatfield's name as a scapegoat for all his various enterprises. True, he had blundered once, when after waylaying John Mason he had discovered the man had already disposed of the orchid paper.

But luck was with him now. He began to watch the shores. A bamboo mast. That was Mason's trail mark. The thing should be near at hand now.

Two days and two nights had passed since he had left Hatfield and Clark Mason. To Fletcher the time had been an eternity of back-breaking labor, of nerve-racking impatience. He had seen orchids, hundreds of them, bizarre-looking plants on either shore. But he knew none of them was the kind he wanted.

The river turned to the east, turned to the west again.

And then abruptly at dawn of the third day he saw it. Out from the left bank a bamboo pole angled upward. Lashed horizontally to the top was a *prahu* paddle.

Fletcher gave a hoarse cry of satisfaction, headed for shore. The dugout nosed into soft ooze. He leaped out, ran forward.

Seizing the bamboo, he pulled it up and quickly examined the paddle. There was no mark on the blade's smooth wooden surface. Fletcher frowned, then nodded silently.

John Mason had been too clever to leave a clue here. But according to the paper the orchid swamp lay in a N.N.E. direction from this point.

He stood erect, looked upward. Dimly through the thick foliage he could see the sun rising in the east. North would be directly ahead then. And north-north-east a few points to the side. Even without his compass Fletcher knew he could find the swamp. The years he had spent in the jungle had taught him to follow a straight course.

He sighted a taller *seraya* tree and began to march toward it. He would continue in this manner, moving from tree to tree, watching the sun.

FIVE paces he advanced. Then something happened. His foot stepped into the waiting noose of a rope fastened to a bent-over tree. He tripped, stumbled forward. The noose jerked taut like a thing alive. Released, the tree sprang upright, whipping Fletcher off balance, jackknifing him backward.

A Dyak leopard trap!

As the ground came up to meet him Fletcher saw a lithe figure leap forward. Hatfield! The man shot forward in a flying tackle.

They struck like blocks of wood. With a mighty effort Fletcher twisted his body, kicked one knee up. He clawed out his revolver, pressed the trigger, fired twice in quick succession. Hatfield knocked the gun from his grasp, clamped his fingers about the man's throat.

They rolled over. Screaming curses

Fletcher pounded his fist into his assailant's jaw. He writhed, lunged, brought his heavy boot hard into Hatfield's spine.

Clawing fingers raked Hatfield's face. Infuriated fists gouged into his eyes. But he fought on grimly. He had kept his weight to a wiry one hundred and seventy pounds, and his muscles as he brought them into play were Toledo steel.

And then suddenly both men leaped erect. With a bellow Fletcher sucked in his breath, braced himself and charged. Like a maddened bull he leaped.

Hatfield ducked to the split second. Weaving in nimbly under the other man's guard he pounded his fist straight outward in a single triphammer blow.

The fist met Fletcher's jaw in full career. One instant he stood there swaying. With a moan he staggered backward and fell prone.

Hatfield stood over the fallen man, breathing hard.

"It's taken a year, Fletcher," he said quietly. "One long year. But I've got you, and you're going to tell the truth. When that's done, there'll be two accounts settled, mine and John Mason's."

DOWNSTREAM, down the Barito, a dugout bearing three white men floated. In the prow, hands manacled with the same handcuffs which had bound Hatfield a few short days before, Gail Fletcher sat in rigid silence. Midships Clark Mason half lay across an improvised center thwart. His face under the broad sun helmet was wan and pale. Bandages still swathed his shoulder. Hatfield paddled from the stern.

"I still don't understand," Mason said, shifting his arm carefully, "how you did it. How you knew—"

Hatfield rested his paddle and smiled. "It's a long story, son," he said, "but I'll skip the details. The most important fact is that I couldn't have caught Fletcher if it hadn't been for your brother, John Mason."

"My brother?"

Hatfield nodded. "Your brother wrote on a slip of paper the directions as how to find more of the orchids he had discovered. It was for that paper he was murdered by Fletcher a year ago. When Fletcher learned that John had previously given the paper to me—a man named Hatfield—he fixed the guilt for the crime on my shoulders, thus clearing himself. He assumed I'd escape from the Dutch police, and he figured he could catch up with me and obtain the paper later at his leisure.

"The odd part about it all is that Fletcher had never seen me, and I had never seen him. The only clue I had was one your brother gave me the night before he was killed—that the man following him had a cobra tattooed on his left arm."

Clark Mason looked perplexed. "But I still don't see," he said.

"Your brother John wrote in plain English on that paper the directions to the orchid swamp. Fletcher took them at face value, but he overlooked one sentence. That sentence was: 'Plan to arrive by middle of rainy season.' If Fletcher had thought more about that, things might have turned out differently."

The wounded man trailed one hand over the dugout, waited in silence.

"The Lahei River did the trick," Hatfield continued. "When the rainy season sets in, that tributary runs almost due north-east, penetrating far incountry. But in the dry season it's a different story. It branches from the Barito then, but it circles a short distance and heads right back in a half moon to where it started. Not a tributary at all, but simply a double arm in the main river."

"Then Fletcher—?"

"Went no place? Right. Without his compass he traveled in an arc, returning to the Barito. I had only to build a raft, pole upstream a few miles and wait for him at the second fork. You know the rest."

Clark Mason nodded. His eyes were shining. "Yes," he said, "I know the rest. And after this shoulder of mine heals up, after we've taken Fletcher to Bandjermasin, you and I are going to find that orchid swamp —together."

SUBMARINE I-26

by Carl Jacobi

Fighting its way through the dense East Indian jungle, an isolated outpost stumbles upon a Japanese submarine base.

IT was nightfall of the sixteenth day and they were bivouaced at the abandoned *kampong* of Pelaban. Hammond sat close to the fire, listening abstractedly to the ebb and flow of conversation about him. Beyond the fire crouched the jungle.

Thirty white men were camped in this native village tonight, but only ten sat by the fire. Five patrolled the river front, squatting behind machine guns in the darkness. Five more guarded the three jungle trails leading out from the clearing. The others had not yet returned from a foraging hunt.

Lieutenant Renburg leaned forward and asked for a match. Under cover of lighting his cigarette, he said softly,

"Do you know where the hell we are?"

Startled, Hammond nodded quickly. "You think we're lost, eh? Well, we're not. Five days up the Berau tributary. Two days down the Nimosi. That makes it Pelaban village without question. Tomorrow we swing into the Kayan, and then it's clear sailing to the coast."

The other met his gaze speculatively. Heavy-set with small opaque eyes and thick dark features, Renburg was comparatively new to the Netherlands Indies Army.

"And then . . ?"

Hammond turned back to the fire and shrugged. Yes, after reaching the Kayan River, what then? The nearer they approached the coast, the nearer they would come to the Japs.

The whole undertaking seemed futile. They couldn't win. Yet back there at Long Nawang, he had realized with the others there was no alternative.

On the official maps in the Colonial East Indies Office in The Hague, Long Nawang was a tiny button in the center of Dutch East Borneo. At Samarinda, before the Jap invasion and before the battle of Macassar Straits, the *controlleur* would have said that Long Nawang was the most remote interior outpost on the island, a watch garrison in the deep jungle country where thirty men, isolated from the world, served Holland's queen.

Hammond's teeth ground savagely on his pipe stem. The Jap invasion had cut Long Nawang off. He knew that with their racial cunning the Japs would make little attempt for the present to penetrate inland. Quite aware of the outpost's presence, they would sit like so many cats waiting for the mice to come out to them.

And now the mice were coming!

The thirty men had left the garrison and headed downriver in five *prahus*. But even if they did reach the coast, the shore waters would be teeming with Jap ships of war, the harbors filled with enemy troops.

A whistle sounded somewhere, and the challenging voice of one of the trail sentries sounded. A moment later the foraging party entered the clearing.

Hammond allowed them twenty minutes of rest, then abruptly gave orders to break camp.

A quarter of an hour later they were on the river again, paddling silently through the darkness. Hammond sat on the narrow stern thwart behind Arlot, the Belgian, and Channing, the Britisher. For two miles there was no sound save the muffled *chunk-swash* of the paddles.

Abruptly, splitting the silence, a rifle shot spanged from the opposite bank. Simultaneously a high-pitched voice shouted something in Japanese.

Even as he felt Arlot jerk convulsively and slump against his knees, Hammond gave a whispered command,

"Hold your fire! Double speed! Not a sound!"

Again the shouted command came from the opposite bank, and again a rifle spoke. Torches kindled into flame on shore. Their brassy glare outlined uniformed men knee deep in the shore ooze. More shots rattled like rain on the river, and an instant later there came the wheezy cough of a gasoline launch.

"They've got a launch," Hammond nodded, "which probably means it's a small advance patrol." He whispered again,

"Keep paddling. Not a sound."

The staccato reports of the gasoline launch dropped behind, but far ahead where the black river made a turn to the left an electric torch winked off and on three times.

They continued until almost abreast of the light.

"Inshore. Into the reeds."

They were not a moment too soon. Barely had the five *prahus* slid into the rip grass when the torch flashed on again, this time to spread a powerful revealing beam over the river. The men of Long Nawang sat motionless. There was no sound save

As the sailors swarmed onto the deck of the sub, Hammond and Bane were waiting for them. They quieted the Japs before they made an outcry.

their rapid breathing and the *pop
pop pop* of the oncoming launch.
The torch went out.

Three times in the next quarter
mile Hammond led his little flotilla
into the shore reeds. The last time
the Jap launch passed within twenty
yards of them, and he could see the
squat forms of Japanese soldiers
standing in the cockpit, rifles leveled
outward.

But at length the sounds were a
murmur in the distance and Channing spoke,

"We seem to have lost them, sir.
Do you think they'll come back?"

"No."

Hammond shook his head. "They'll
think we were a party of natives
and let it go at that."

He bent over Arlot, the Belgian
and fumbled for a pulse. His hand
touched something warm and sticky,
and the wrist hung limp. The expedition had had its first fatality.

Hammond had never quite realized what a cross section of humanity
the Royal Netherlands Indies Army
constituted until the party reached
the mouth of a nameless tributary
that branched into the Kayan. Here,
in the shade of a mighty Seraya tree,
he called a council of war.

There was Corporal Van Horn and
Sergeant Blommer; there was Lieutenant Channing and Sergeant Bane,
the last a lanky Australian who had
once been designing engineer for the
Queensland Submarine Works at
Brisbane. And there was Lieutenant
Renburg, a haughty brute of a man
with a savage temper, but an efficient soldier for all that.

Hammond was studying a Dutch
Ordnance Survey map. Lieutenant
Channing stood at his side.

"If we take this nameless tributary," Channing said, "we'll reach
the coast almost sixty miles south of
Tandjong Selor. I've been there before, sir, in '38. And here"—he
leveled a forefinger at the map—
here is a cove that might have been
made for us."

"What do you mean?" Hammond
demanded.

"I mean, sir, that the coast at that
point forms a pocket so naturally
concealed a battleship could be hidden there. The Dyaks call it 'lost
nowhere.' If we can get there, we'll
be safe."

Hammond rolled up the map and
got to his feet. "All right, Channing. I don't know what we're going to do when we reach the sea,
but at least that's our destination."

Tenseness gripped the men as they
took to the river again. The dark
poisonous green shores of the little
tributary pressed close, forming almost a tunnel above them. The heat
was oven-like.

Two days passed. It was at high
noon of the third day since leaving
the Kayan that Hammond suddenly
sighted far ahead a makeshift jetty
projecting out into the water. At
its far end a bamboo pole supported
a weather-scarred sign:

DUTCH EAST BORNEO TELEGRAPH
COMPANY
STATION NUMBER 5

Five minutes later the outpost officer jerked tensely upright. A lone

figure had appeared on the jetty, waving a white cloth. A girl!

A moment later Hammond was leaping to the planking.

"*Mynheer*. I'm so glad you're here. I thought at first you might be Japs."

A trick? You never could be sure these days. The girl appeared more American than Dutch, slim and tall, with chestnut hair hanging down from under the puggree cloth of her sun helmet.

"Who are you, Miss?" Hammond asked quietly.

"Terry Hollistan," she said. "I'm American. If . . if you'll come into the Station, I'll explain."

The men were tumbling out of the dugouts wearily, thankful of this rest after the long hours on the blazing river.

"Post double guards," Hammond ordered. "Lieutenant Renburg, two men and follow me."

For fifty yards the trail wound in and out through a grove of green bamboo. Abruptly it widened, and in the center of a clearing Hammond saw a shack on piles. He ordered Renburg and the two men to wait in the compound and followed the girl up the ladder. At the threshold he stopped short.

The room was a shambles. At the opposite wall the instrument table had been ripped from its brackets and smashed into kindling. Telegraph key, sounder, and relay lay in ruins on the floor.

"The monkey men were here," the girl said bitterly. "A Jap patrol came downriver. They killed Davis and Van Wickert, the two operators."

She continued. "I write for Consolidated News, an American newspaper syndicate. I was in Tandjong Selor when the Japs struck and barely had time to get out by plane. We ran into a storm and were forced back over the Borneo interior. Ran out of gas and had to make a forced landing. The pilot—a shudder passed through her—"was killed when we struck."

For a long moment Hammond studied her in silence. "Do you means to say you've been here alone all this time?"

"No. The pilot sighted this Station and tried to land on the river but overshot his mark. I've been here with the two operators until the Japs came."

She crossed to one of the remaining intact chairs and sank into it wearily.

"Davis and Van Wickert knew from last minute reports just how bad things were, but they preferred to stay on. As a matter of fact there wasn't much use in their attempting to escape anyway, what with all ports captured.

"A week ago"—the girl passed her hand over her eyes—"a week ago the Jap patrol came. Davis and Van Wickert insisted I hide in the jungle, and they sent their Malay servant, Sahar, with me for protection. Sahar kept me in the bush two days. When we finally returned we found . . . both operators murdered. I've been here ever since, hoping that some opportunity to escape might come."

As the girl concluded her story, a step sounded in the doorway, and a short brown man entered.

"This is Sahar," Terry Hollistan

said. "I owe my life to him."

From a worn tobacco pouch Hammond filled his bulldog pipe.

"The Jap patrol that raided here," he said, "must have been the same one my outfit blundered into farther upriver. What's important now, Miss Hollistan is that you're coming with us. I'll arrange accommodations for you and the Malay in my *prahu*."

On the river again, with the girl lounging easily on the thwart ahead of him, Hammond mused over the way his life had changed since this war began. Hammond was an American. He had entered the Royal Netherlands Indies Army for a number of reasons. There was his ancestry on his mother's side, good Dutch blood that went back to Peter Stuyvesant and New York. And there was the military influence passed on to him by a great grandfather who had fought at Appomatox.

Finally had come his Borneo commission and his assignment to the outpost of Long Nawang.

The tributary narrowed to a bare ten yards in width. Abruptly Channing maneuvered his dugout close to Hammonds'.

"This is it," he said quietly. "The cove I spoke of lies a few miles farther on."

Hammond nodded and gave orders. They made shore, pulled the *prahus* into the undergrowth and fought their way inland. With a pair of binoculars slung over his shoulder, Hammond climbed a tree and made a long and careful study of the surrounding country.

In camp, he announced his decision.

"Double guards. Renburg, you're in charge. I'm going ahead alone and look over the lay of the land."

He slid a long-bladed hunting knife in his belt and plunged into the bush. For an hour he moved onward when suddenly he became aware that he was being followed. He darted behind a tree and whipped out his service revolver. An instant later he lowered it with a sigh and stepped forth into the open.

"Miss Hollistan," he said coldly to the girl who had appeared before him, "I believe I gave strict orders no one was to leave camp."

"Captain," she said, "I flew over this district once, and I should know something about it."

Before Hammond could voice further protestations, she swung past him.

They crossed a *klubi* swamp. Beyond the swamp lay higher ground again. Suddenly Hammond halted, rigid.

Before them, beyond an intervening fringe of trees, lay a half-moon beach. Two promontories projected like twin breakwaters out to sea. Between them was a narrow lagoon.

There was more, and Hammond felt his pulse leap as he stared.

Moored in the center of the lagoon was a ship, a huge grey submarine. The streamlined vessel bore a painted rising sun on its conning tower. Underneath were the numerals, *I-26*.

Japs!

Terry Hollistan grasped Hammond's arm.

"A Jap sub! And look there!"

A hundred yards down the beach squatted three nipa thatch huts. Piles of equipment, stacked rifles, oil drums were scattered everywhere. Between them lounged a score or more of undersized Jap sailors.

"Do you realize what we've stumbled on?" the girl demanded breathlessly. "That's the I-26, one of Japan's newest and most powerful submarines. Captain Hammond, that sub is one of the reasons I'm here in Borneo. The Allies have suspected for a long time that the Japs were using these deserted shore waters as a base for undersea craft."

She fumbled in her pocket and drew out a leather notebook. Riffling its pages, she began to read in a hoarse whisper:

"I-26. Kawasaki type. Surface displacement estimated at 1,925 tons. Submerged, 2,480 tons. Over 350 feet long with a thirty foot beam. Her Diesels are 6,000 horsepower. Surface speed 17 knots. Submerged, 9. Two deck guns, two machine guns, six torpedo tubes."

She looked up, eyes wide. "Oh, if I could only get to a cable office."

Hammond made no reply, but his brain was working like a mill race. Suddenly an electric wave shot through him.

"Let's get out of here," he said to the girl. "I've—got an idea."

Five hours later Hammond stood once again on the lagoon shore. It was night now, the darkness broken only by the vague light of the stars. Behind him were his twenty-nine men, alert and ready, and at his side stood Bane.

In a few quick movements Hammond slipped out of his clothes. The Australian had already divested himself.

"All right," the Long Nawang officer whispered. "Give us sufficient time to reach the sub. Remember everything depends on complete surprise."

Only Renburg had been hesitant to accept Hammond's plan of attack. The Lieutenant stood there in the gloom now, frowning out at the black water.

"We've only twenty-nine men," he said slowly, shaking his head. "They must have two or three times that number. I still think we should head down the coast and take our chances of getting out on a raft."

Hammond bent down, picked up a half dozen six-inch sticks of Palapak wood and swiftly fastened them in a bundle to the back of his head. Then he gave a last warning.

"Keep Miss Hollistan out of the line of fire."

The two men waded out into the warm water and dived forward noiselessly. They swam rapidly, and presently the sub loomed up, a shapeless shadow before them. Hammond inched his way along the side of the steel hull until his groping hands touched a Jacob's ladder, hanging down from the deck. He waited until Bane had reached his side, then mounted silently to the deck.

He thought at first it was deserted, and that was his mistake. Groping forward, he stumbled against an inert body and fell headlong.

A startled gasp reached his ears, and a dark figure lurched upright.

In the uncertain starlight Hammond caught the glint of a revolver swept upward. He brought his hand snapping upward and heard the gun splash quietly in the water beyond the ship. The Jap opened his mouth to yell, and simultaneously Hammond struck with every ounce of strength he possessed. The figure collapsed against the rail.

Now Hammond began a feverish search for the engine room ventilator which on this type of Jap sub Bane had said opened off the deck. He found it, a large air intake vent and began ripping away its protective screening with his knife.

He selected one of the Palapak sticks from his bundle and began rubbing it until the soft wood grew spongy and aerated. Then he opened a metal tube and lit a match, cupping the flame so that its glow would not be detected on shore.

The Palapak wood ignited, but did not flare. Hammond lit more and shoved them down the shaft. Many times in deep jungle Dyak *kampongs* he had seen native witch-doctors stultify their superstitious tribesmen with this wood. In a few moments the sticks would give off a powerful overpowering vapor.

He tiptoed to the conning tower and peered down. An iron ladder led down into a dimly lit vault below. On shore all was strangely still. Only at intervals when the wind changed did it bring the murmur of voices in the three shore huts.

And then it happened! Below someone burst into a violent coughing spell. An instant later two squat figures began to climb the ladder.

Hammond tensed, and as a head and shoulders drew within range, bludgeoned his fist forward with calm precision. The two men fell in a heap.

More coughing below decks now, and twice more Hammond struck as the Japs drunkenly attempted to make their exit. Then apparently the effect of the Palapak sticks began to wear off, and other figures stumbled into view. Below a revolver exploded.

Bane had groped his way forward and taken control of the forward machine gun. As Hammond turned now and raced to his side, the Australian opened fire. On shore the voices in the huts broke off. The doors burst open, and startled commands echoed across the water.

Then in the jungle the men of Long Nawang opened up with their machine gun, and Hammond could hear Channing's voice give the order to advance. Jap sailors raced across the beach, firing wildly. On the sub white clad figures were staggering drunkenly out of the conning tower.

Flat on his stomach, protected by a low deck coaming, Hammond waited. A spurt of flame marked a Jap sailor rushing toward him. Hammond used his knife, moving like a well-oiled machine.

And now the Japs from below decks had taken positions behind the conning tower and were firing steadily at the two men on the forward deck. Bane started to swing the machine gun.

"Give it to the devils on shore," Hammond yelled. "I'll take care of those aft."

On shore a gasoline drum ignited, and a sheet of flame shot up. Under Bane's steady fire two dories loaded with Japs capsized, spilling uniformed men into the water. Utilizing the revolver he had taken from the Nipponese who had attacked him, Hammond triggered the weapon again and again.

Suddenly something hot and heavy slammed against his shoulder. The outpost officer's head swam and colored lights swirled up in his vision. The lights gave way to a curtain of blackness, and he knew no more.

When Hammond opened his eyes he was lying in a narrow bunk and a cold cloth was pressed against his temples. His right arm felt sore and numb. On the edge of the bunk, a basin of water on her knees, sat Terry Hollistan.

He propped himself up on his good arm and looked about him.

The girl smiled. "You're aboard the I-26," she said.

For a moment his brain spun as he sought to digest this information. Then a glow of satisfaction welled over him.

"Channing? Renburg?"

"All aboard and accounted for," Terry Hollistan told him. Her face sobered. "We lost seven men back there in the lagoon. Those Japs that weren't killed took to the bush. It was a terrible battle, but a glorious one."

Strength was returning to Hammond quickly now. He was in the officers' quarters, he saw, equipped with small folding bunks, a desk and a shelf filled with navigation books

and charts. In one corner was a duplicate repeater compass and depth gauges.

The outpost officer stood up groggily. "I want to take a look at this ship," he said.

In the crew's quarters he saw ten of his men quietly engaged in the task of patching up each other's wounds. They greeted him with broad smiles. In the control, grouped by the master compass, the officers of Long Nawang stood waiting to meet him.

Hammond smiled. "Good work, men." He turned to Lieutenant Renburg. "Where are we?"

Renburg scowled. "In dangerous waters, of course. I haven't been able to tell our exact position as yet. I can't read Japanese, and those charts mean nothing to me."

"We've got two lookouts topside," Lieutenant Channing said. "We didn't think it advisable to submerge until we were sure of our position."

Hammond nodded. "Keep her as she goes. I'll try and lay out a course directly." He turned and strode through the after battery compartment into the engine room.

Two huge Diesels pulsed there rhythmically like two gargantuan cats. Beside them were the motor generators, connected to the twin screw propellers with clutches.

"She's all ours," Terry Hollistan said. She had followed him and stood at his side. "The question is: where do we go from here?"

For a moment Hammond made no reply. Then he motioned the girl to follow and returned to the officers' quarters.

From the shelf over the convertible desk he took down the Jap charts and began to examine them. But as Renburg had said, they were in Japanese and meant nothing to him. The books next. He glanced at the last, a heavier volume, and a whistle came to his lips. It was a copy of the *British Pacific Islands Pilot Book*, volume V, East Indian waters.

"Look here," he began, and then broke off as Lieutenants Channing and Renburg entered the room.

"Beg pardon, sir," Channing said, "but I've been fiddling with that Nip wireless, and I found this on the instrument table. Can you make anything of it?"

Hammond took the slip of paper. The written words were in English:

To Professor J. Smith, Metropolitan Museum. Report research progressing satisfactorily in spite of war. 486 specimens found today. New flora on volcano. South shore has protection from monsoon, good anchorage. Details later.

Terry Hollistan frowned as she read the paper over Hammond's shoulder. "That's a strange message for a Jap submarine to be receiving."

"It's in code, of course," Channing said. "But why in English?"

Renburg ran a hand reflectively over his swarthy face. "Maybe the Jap operator was simply studying English and copied down the first thing that he pulled in out of the air."

Opening the desk drawer, Hammond began a thorough search of its contents. But at the end of five minutes he shook his head.

"No sign of a code book."

"How about the *Pacific Pilot?*" Terry Hollistan suggested.

Hammond stared at her blankly, then whipped around and picked up the British navigation volume again.

"Look, sir." Channing leaned forward. "The last two lines are separated from the first part of the message by a space. Might that not indicate that the Jap operator who took it down knew that they alone are the cypher and the first part of it is only a blind? And if it's a substitution cypher, as this seems to be, we need first of all a clue number."

Hammond read the message again, and his eyes fastened on the words: *486 specimens.* 486. But there were only 456 pages in the *Pilot.* Try 48 then. The 6 might refer to the line on the page.

Still he had no starting point, and he ran his long fingers through his hair in perplexity. If 48 were the clue number, it would mean that each cypher word would refer to a word in the *Pilot* 48 pages *before* or *after* the page where that word was found. The question was how was he to find that page?

Far back in Hammond's brain an idea began to grow.

"Look," he said. "It's a substitution cypher right enough. Assuming that only the last two sentences are the cypher, as Channing suggested, we have a total of fourteen words to decode. Now, if I know anything about cryptograms at all, it is rare that every word in a cypher sentence has a meaning. Let us say for argument's sake that in this case *every other* word is a part of the code. That would give us a total of seven words and would leave seven *in-between* words, which would probably be used to indicate the position of the code words in the *Pilot.*"

He paused and went on. "Take the first sentence: *New flora on volcano.*

In this case the words *flora* and *volcano* are logically the cypher words. The words *new* and *on* are position keys.

"Now the first letter of the word *new* is *N*, the fourteenth letter of the English alphabet. I'm going to take a long shot and say that here the key number is 14 plus 1; the 1 denoting the first word in the sentence. In other words, we have 141."

Terry Hollistan quickly fell in with his reasoning. "That would mean that the cypher word, *flora*, is found on page 141. And that to decode it, you would use the clue number and go back or forward 48 pages from page 141. Right?"

"Right." Hammond was already whipping through the pages of the *Pilot.* He gave a cry of triumph. "Here it is: *flora.* Now we go back 48 pages and take a word in a similar position on line 6, the last part of the clue number." Again he turned pages, and a moment later wrote down the word, *Meet.*

They stood in breathless silence watching him. Feverishly he counted off page numbers, scribbled down words. At the end of five minutes he leaned back, a strange expression on his face. He had written:

MEET FLEET TIGER ISLAND. PROCEED ATTACK DARWIN.

With a hoarse intake of breath the girl broke the silence. "Good God, that means . . !"

Hammond nodded. "It means that the Japs have, or will have, a fleet hidden at an island called Tiger and that they're planning an attack on Port Darwin on the northeast coast of Australia."

He seized the *Pilot* again:

Tiger Island: Latitude 1° 45' S.; longitude, 142° 52' E.

Hammond got to his feet. "Renburg, tell Bane to stand by for a change of course."

The days that followed were tense ones for the I-26. Past the coast of Halmahera they went. And south by east past the tip of Dutch New Guinea. The South Pacific continued blue and empty without sign of enemy ships or planes.

Once Hammond thought of transmitting a warning message with the radio of the I-26. But such an action would reveal the sub's position and would only hasten the Jap attack before adequate precautions could be taken.

It was at four bells of the afternoon watch that Lieutenant Channing suddenly called from the bridge, "Land Ho!"

A low smear was visible on the south horizon. Hammond stared at it a long moment through the glases, then nodded tensely to Terry Hollistan.

"That's it. Tiger Island." He turned to Channing. "Quarter speed. Down helm."

They advanced on the island slowly. The smear grew into a flat beach, backed by tall palms. To the east a slender peninsula extended at an oblique angle.

The I-26 advanced another quarter mile, then abruptly submerged. Hammond took a position before the periscope lens, began slowly turning the control handles. Through the glass he saw the eastern extremity of the island fall away. He saw a long ellipse of corral reef against which the sea pounded and fell away in frothing fury.

Channing stood before the depth gauge and diving rudder controls. At the speed indicator Lieutenant Renburg waited. There was no sound save the dull vibration of the electric motors.

On past the reefs the I-26 went, moving silently through the green depths. And then suddenly Hammond went rigid.

Before him, clearly focused in the scope were the ugly outlines of a huge grey battleship, her decks bristling guns, her mast-head flying the flag of the rising sun.

Heart pounding, Hammond watched the vessel grow in size.

Only one. There was no evidence of the Jap destroyers, cruisers, or subs he had expected. What was wrong? Had the message which he had decyphered been wrong?

It struck him suddenly. The fleet had not yet gathered. This was their meeting place, and this lone battleship must be the nerve center of the webb that was forming. Aboard her would be the Japanese admirals and officers who had schemed this attack.

The staggering significance of it all hit him squarely. Destroy this vessel, and he would destroy all.

"Forward torpedo room, stand by!" Hammond ordered.

Renburg had crossed to the far bulkhead and stood now facing the group. His head was thrown back in a strangely erect posture. His eyes were dilated, his thin grey lips parted. *In his hands was a revolver!*

"Hammond," he said, "you will countermand that order. You will direct your men to surface at once." His voice was brittle like bottles breaking under heat.

Hammond did not move. Renburg smiled sardonically.

"Not Lieutenant Renburg," he said, "but Lieutenant Hans Mueller, formerly of the German navy, at present representing Wilhelmstrasse. I've been away from the Fatherland a long time, Herr Hammond, but now it appears my services are to be of some value after all."

A piece of ice began to crawl up Hammond's spine as with a rush his brain began to piece details together.

Renburg swiveled his revolver to keep the men in the control room covered.

"You thought because I followed along with your plans that I was just another soldier of your miserable Colonial service. You didn't suspect that the Fuehrer had foreseen all these developments long ago.

"In my head"—he tapped his close-cropped skull—"is all the information which I have obtained as a Dutch trooper, information not only of the Borneo interior which will enable the Japanese to complete their conquest of that island, but also of the entire East Indies.

"You will never sink that battleship, Herr Hammond, and you will never escape alive. Within a few hours the fleet will gather here, another of your democracies will fall! —Australia."

He paced a step forward. "Give your orders to surface, Captain Hammond. Now, or I fire."

There was no sound in the control room save the hoarse breathing of the men. Hammond's eyes were fixed on Renburg, but out of the corner of them he was staring at a hair cross-line in the lens before him. And as he looked, mentally he was doing the necessary equations. Suddenly he spoke,

"Forward torpedo room. Tube 3. Fire!"

The revolver shot that exploded seemed to shatter the four walls of the submarine. Hammond felt a searing sword of agony jam into his left side. Then before Renburg could fire a second time, he threw himself low and catapulted across the intervening space to seize the German's legs in a flying tackle. The two men went down.

As he fought, Hammond heard his men press forward. "Keep away!" he panted. "This is my fight, and I'm going to finish it."

The gun was still in the German's hand, and twisting his arm frantically, he sought to fire point blank. The outpost officer grasped the weapon wrist, snapped it backward. There was a scream of pain, and the revolver clattered to the floor.

Uttering an animal-like snarl,

Renburg continued to pound out blows. Twice he sent his knee grinding upward into Hammond's groin. Then Hammond saw an opening. He drew his fist back and propelled it to the man's jaw with every ounce of strength he possessed. There was a dull thud and the German fell back.

Not until then was Hammond aware of the action of the submarine. It was rolling drunkenly from side to side. He sprang to the periscope, twisted the lens, fastening it once again on the battleship.

For an instant the scene appeared unchanged. Then, like a slow-motion picture, the huge vessel seemed to heel over slightly.

"Forward torpedo room. Tubes 1 and 2. Fire."

He could hear the thud of the breach doors and the vibration as the compressed air was expelled from its chambers.

This time the lens revealed a story of grim destruction. The Jap battleship buckled amidships as simultaneously a column of black smoke and debris vomited upward. A sheet of flame swept from bow to stern to form a raging holocaust. A moment later it was over. The vessel rolled over on her side, and the rising-sun flag sank beneath the green Pacific.

Half an hour later the I-26 was ploughing due east through a choppy sea. Astern a cloud of black smoke was dropping below the horizon.

"It's only one this time," Hammond said to Terry Hollistan as they stood on the little bridge, "but there will be more and more."

THE END.